CRIMINAL INVESTIGATION
An
Introduction

HARVEY BURSTEIN
Northeastern University

Prentice Hall, Upper Saddle River, New Jersey 07458

Library of Congress Cataloging-in-Publication Data

Burstein, Harvey.
    Criminal investigation : an introduction / Harvey Burstein.
        p.   cm.
    Includes bibliographical references and index.
    ISBN 0-13-575358-9
    1. Criminal investigation.   I. Title.
HV8073.B88   1999
363.25—DC21   97-48655
                                                     CIP

Acquisition Editor: Neil Marquardt
Editorial Assistant: Jean Auman
Managing Editor: Mary Carnis
Project Manager: Linda B. Pawelchak
Prepress and Manufacturing Buyer: Ed O'Dougherty
Cover Director: Jayne Conte
Cover Design: Miguel Ortiz
Cover Art: Theo Rudnak, The Stock Illustration Source
Electronic Art Creation: Asterisk Group, Inc.
Marketing Manager: Frank Mortimer Jr.

This book was set in 10.5/12 New Century Schoolbook
by The Clarinda Company and was printed and bound
by RR Donnelley & Sons Company.
The cover was printed by Phoenix Color Corp.

 © 1999 by Prentice-Hall, Inc.
Simon & Schuster / A Viacom Company
Upper Saddle River, New Jersey 07458

Printed in the United States of America
10   9   8   7   6   5   4   3   2   1

ISBN 0-13-575358-9

Prentice-Hall International (UK) Limited, *London*
Prentice-Hall of Australia Pty. Limited, *Sydney*
Prentice-Hall Canada Inc., *Toronto*
Prentice-Hall Hispanoamericana, S.A., *Mexico*
Prentice-Hall of India Private Limited, *New Delhi*
Prentice-Hall of Japan, Inc., *Tokyo*
Simon & Schuster Asia Pte. Ltd., *Singapore*
Editora Prentice-Hall do Brasil, Ltda., *Rio de Janeiro*

*To the men and women of the
Federal Bureau of Investigation,
past and present, who have made the FBI
one of the world's premier investigative agencies.*

CONTENTS

Chapter 13
The Laboratory   **154**

Chapter 14
Interrogating the Subject   **178**

PART III
PRINCIPAL TYPES OF INVESTIGATIONS

Chapter 15
Crimes of Violence   **190**

PREFACE

Criminal Investigation: An Introduction is based on my personal experiences as an investigator of both criminal and noncriminal cases, and as a teacher of an investigations course at Northeastern University's College of Criminal Justice. In the latter role, I have found that too often students' ideas about investigators and investigations, based largely on entertainment and news media portrayals, tend to be distorted. Consequently, I thought that a text for the uninitiated would serve a useful purpose.

The introductory form of this book will help criminal justice students get a better understanding of investigations before they elect to embark on law enforcement careers. It is not a substitute for the FBI's special agents' handbook, armed forces technical manuals on investigations, the formal training given to new federal investigators, or that given to newly appointed detectives by some police departments, where techniques are taught in detail.

In undertaking this project, I have drawn heavily upon my own training and work with the FBI and the U.S. Department of State, and as an attorney and corporate security director. My career has allowed me to witness numerous changes that have occurred in the field of investigations from which today's students, and investigators, benefit. For example, fingerprint searches by the FBI's Identification Division have progressed from time-consuming, tedious, manual searches using a reticle and the light of a gooseneck lamp to striking keys on a computer terminal. DNA is now another valid means of identification, and psychological profiling can be used to suggest leads that might otherwise be overlooked.

Many criminal justice students, this book's audience, hope to become police or federal investigators. Others may choose careers in either corporate security positions or the practice of law. They, too, may find this text useful because on occasion they will find it necessary to conduct, supervise, or evaluate investigations. In addition, almost all criminal justice students who ultimately find themselves doing investigative work, whether in any aspect of law enforcement, corporate security, or as practicing attorneys, will find themselves involved with non-criminal inquiries as well. Thus I would be remiss if I completely ignored such investigations in this book.

Over the years in which I have done investigative work, I have benefited greatly from what I learned and experienced as both a clerical employee and special agent of the FBI. Even as I write this I remain indebted to the late James S. Egan, who retired as the FBI's senior inspector in 1953, and to Gerard J. Engert, who was my special agent supervisor when I was assigned to the FBI's Identification Division's Technical Section in 1941, and who to this day is a close and cherished friend, for their having impressed upon me the need for and critical importance of objectivity and fairness in the conduct of all investigations, standards to which I have tried to adhere throughout my own career.

I especially want to thank Louis J. Freeh, the Director of the FBI, and Leslie Clemens, of the FBI's Office of Public and Congressional Affairs, for having provided me with so much invaluable material for use in illustrating the text, including several photographs that brought back memories. For their help with illustrations, I also want to thank Debbi Baer, Congressional and Public Affairs, U.S. Postal Inspection Service; Catherine H. Shaw and Rogene M. Waite, Drug Enforcement Agency; Alan M. Pollock, deputy director, National Transportation Safety Board; H. Terrence Samway, assistant director, Office of Government Liaison and Public Affairs, U.S. Secret Service; Don W. Walker, executive vice president, and Dereck Andrade, public affairs manager, Pinkerton Security and Investigative Services; and Howard Safir, Commissioner, New York City Police Department.

In a work such as this, one realizes that occasional errors may appear despite the best efforts of the author, editor, and production staff. Therefore, let me make it clear that all errors of omission or commission are mine and mine alone.

Last, but certainly not least, I must thank those at Prentice Hall with whom I have had the pleasure of working: Neil Marquardt, Rose Mary Florio, Jean Auman, and above all, Robin Baliszewski, who encouraged me to undertake this project. I hope that their faith in me has not been misplaced and that I have not disappointed them.

Harvey Burstein

ABOUT THE AUTHOR

Harvey Burstein, David B. Schulman Professor of Security at Northeastern University's College of Criminal Justice, is a graduate of the Creighton University School of Law. While an undergraduate, he entered on duty with the Federal Bureau of Investigation in 1941 as a clerical employee in the Identification Division, and he also was on assignment to the Translation Unit, a part of the FBI Laboratory. After wartime service in the U.S. Army, and while completing his legal studies, he returned to the FBI's Identification Division, where he received his first letter of commendation.

Following admission to the bar in 1948, Mr. Burstein served as a special agent of the FBI, during which time he received four additional letters of commendation. He conducted criminal and noncriminal investigations of matters under the FBI's jurisdiction, and he also continued on assignment to the Translation Unit as needed. Mr. Burstein was an approved FBI speaker and police training instructor. In 1953, he left the FBI to accept an appointment as Chief, Foreign and Domestic Investigations, Surveys, and Physical Security, U.S. Department of State.

Since leaving federal service, Mr. Burstein's career has consisted of practicing law, security management consulting for a variety of *Fortune* 500 companies, and employment as a corporate security director for major educational, lodging industry, financial, and manufacturing organizations. As an attorney, he has been retained by law firms to oversee investigations for the benefit of their clients. As a corporate security director, he has conducted or supervised various noncriminal investigations, and he has actively worked with a number of federal and local investigative agencies in corporate inquiries of a criminal nature.

Mr. Burstein joined the faculty of the College of Criminal Justice at Northeastern University in 1990 as a Visiting Professor. In 1992, he suggested adding a course on investigations to the curriculum, which he has been teaching since its approval.

The temper of detachment and scrutiny is not beguiling; men find it more often a cool jet than a stimulus, and it is a little curious that they ever can be brought to rate it highly. Yet, in the end, it has so obvious a place in any rational world that its value be forced upon their notice and they look behind to the disposition which produces it. If they do, they find it anything but cold or neutral, for the last acquisition of civilized man is forbearance in judgment and to it is necessary one of the highest efforts of the will.

Judge Learned Hand

PART I

INTRODUCTION

Part I does more than merely provide a historical background indicating how the field of criminal and allied investigations has evolved over the years. It introduces the reader to the subject of investigations in general, not merely to those necessarily undertaken in relation to crimes that have been committed.

Thereafter, attention focuses on who conducts investigations of the various types of cases covered in Part III of the text. It is helpful to know that some inquiries may be made by persons in the public sector who are not employed by law enforcement agencies, and that there also are those in the private sector who may have occasion to conduct investigations.

Being able to successfully conduct investigations and close cases depends on a number of factors. In some, especially criminal matters, good luck helps. However, in all, criminal or other, the investigator's personal characteristics are major contributors. Therefore, it is logical to do more than merely list those traits. The reader needs to appreciate how each contributes to making a good investigator.

Investigations are not undertaken on the basis of a personal whim; there must be a valid reason. Thus it is important for the reader to understand not only how inquiries are initiated, but also the important characteristics of those responsible for their conduct.

Chapter 1

Historical Background

Governments as far back as early biblical times have maintained armies and waged war. To say that armies were, and are, used only for defensive and never for offensive purposes would be to deny both ancient and modern history. However, to the extent that armies also maintain order, principally by means of exercising control over both friendly and unfriendly populations, they perform a duty normally associated with policing. Even today, armies in some countries also perform more traditional police duties, but for the most part, they do not serve as police agencies in the more accepted sense of that term.

EARLY POLICE AGENCIES

The history of policing, with which investigations tend to be associated, is not as deeply rooted. There are questions about when the first police agency to operate in a big city appeared on the scene. Some say there is evidence of policing in ancient Egypt and Mesopotamia; others believe that it was not until the time of the Roman Emperor Augustus (63 B.C.–A.D. 7).[1] Still others hold that it was not until sometime between A.D. 1000 and 1300 when anything resembling a structured law enforcement system appeared in England.

Regardless, evidence suggests that the position of shire reeve, from which the modern word *sheriff* is derived, existed before the Norman Conquest of England by William the Conqueror in 1066. Until then, the appointee was a shire's chief administrative and judicial officer, a shire being a geopolitical entity otherwise often called a "county." Afterwards, the shire reeve also served as a shire's chief law enforcement officer. As such, he generally was responsible for keeping the peace and executing court orders. Since so much of our law is based upon English law, a relationship undoubtedly exists between the shire reeve's role as a peacekeeper and the fact that statutes in the United States, dealing with police authority, often refer to sworn police personnel as "peace officers."

This primary peacekeeping function of early police agencies was accomplished largely through the visibility of and patrols by those employed for that purpose. However, during the Industrial Revolution, as England became increasingly industrialized and urbanized, criminal activity also increased. Although this developing problem prompted expansion of the police role to include crime prevention, the first sign of investigations being used for the detection and prosecution of criminals occurred following the 1748 appointment of Henry Fielding as London's chief magistrate.

Nevertheless, it was not until 1750 that Fielding, whose offices were on Bow Street, recruited a small group of plainclothes volunteers who would be sent to crime scenes to begin looking for the culprits. Since the recruiting process for these volunteers, who became known as the Bow Street Runners, was based in part on the theory that the best thief-catchers would be other thieves, it was not unusual for some of them to have been former thieves. To encourage them to make apprehensions, their only compensation consisted of a percentage of the fines collected from those who were successfully prosecuted. In 1752, Fielding began publishing *The Covent Garden Journal,* in which wanted persons' descriptions were set forth. After Henry Fielding died in 1754, his brother John continued the operation for another twenty-five years.[2] During this time, Bow Street became a clearing house for information on crime, and by 1785 at least four Bow Street Runners were on the government's payroll as detectives.[3]

The use of thieves to catch other thieves was not an exclusively British idea. During the early nineteenth century, a French thief-turned-informer, François Eugene Vidocq, noting the high crime rate in Paris, suggested that the Ministry of Police organize a plainclothes bureau. His suggestion was followed with the creation of the Brigade de la Surete, authorized to operate in all Paris police districts and to report directly to the Prefect of Police.

The next significant development occurred in 1822 when Sir Robert Peel was appointed Home Secretary. Peel, who is considered the father of modern policing and from whom London police officers derived the nickname "Bobby" (by which they still are known), was determined to make the police more efficient and effective. Thanks to his efforts, in

1829 Parliament passed the Metropolitan Police Act establishing a London police force. Interestingly enough, however, it was not until 1842 that Scotland Yard, as force headquarters became known, organized its first regular detective branch superseding Bow Street,[4] but limiting the number of investigators to a maximum of sixteen.[5]

The relationship between increasing urbanization and increasing crime was by no means limited to Europe. As "New World" cities developed and grew in size so did the concern for public safety. In 1783, New York City organized its first, though admittedly rudimentary, police force; in 1790, it became the first city in the United States with a paid daytime police force. Other cities used a variety of ways to keep the peace before they established police departments. It was not until well into the nineteenth century that the establishment of professional departments occurred. Among the cities that did so were Boston, 1837; New York, 1844; Chicago, 1851; New Orleans and Cincinnati, 1852; Philadelphia, 1854; Baltimore and Newark, 1857.

Other changes began to occur during this time. For example, early in 1845 the New York City Police Department had eight hundred plainclothes officers;[6] in 1857, it was authorized to designate twenty patrol officers as detectives.[7] This same year the New York City Police Department also began to develop its rogues' gallery.[8]

In 1846, two former St. Louis police officers, sensing a need for reliable investigators, formed the first recorded private detective agency in the United States. However, without doubt the most prominent nineteenth-century detective agency was established by Allan Pinkerton, who in 1849, two years before Chicago's Police Department was professionalized, was appointed as the city's first detective by the mayor.[9] In contrast, the Atlanta, Georgia, Police Department organized a Detective Bureau in 1885.[10]

On a broader scale, the need for and importance of investigations became more evident in 1865 when the U.S. Congress created the U.S. Secret Service, thus giving the Treasury Department an investigative unit to deal with counterfeiting problems. Other early federal investigative agencies were the U.S. Marshal's Service, Bureau of Customs, and Postal Inspection Service.

BUREAU OF INVESTIGATION

Interestingly enough, although the U.S. Department of Justice, headed by the attorney general as the federal government's chief law enforcement officer, was created by Congress in 1870, it did not have its own investigative organization. Instead, when investigations were needed, it had to rely on outsiders. Some of them worked part time, some were Pinkerton personnel or paid informants, and others were political hacks who were employed as a matter of patronage. Occasionally, the Department of Justice was able to use the on-loan services of the existing federal investigative agencies, a practice

Pinkerton's first office in Chicago, Illinois. (*Courtesy* Pinkerton Security and Investigative Services)

Allan Pinkerton. (*Courtesy* Pinkerton Security and Investigative Services)

The original Pinkerton logo. (*Courtesy* Pinkerton Security and Investigative Services)

U.S. Postal Inspectors in charge, 1903. (*Courtesy* U.S. Postal Inspection Service)

that continued until Theodore Roosevelt's presidency. Believing that the Department of Justice should have access to its own investigators, Roosevelt asked Congress to give the department a "force of permanent police."[11] Congressional refusal of his request out of pique due to the department's successful prosecution of both a senator and representative prompted Roosevelt to authorize his attorney general to establish a Bureau of Investigation that would report only to the attorney general.

Unfortunately, the bureau's creation was unaccompanied by mandated standards for employment; appointments were based on political connections rather than ability. The corruption and scandal that became the organization's trademarks reached their zenith during the presidency of Warren G. Harding, who died in office in 1923.

Harding was succeeded by Vice President Calvin Coolidge, who appointed Harlan Fiske Stone (later to become Chief Justice of the United States) attorney general. Stone, determined to clean up the Bureau of Investigation, offered the position of director to a young Department of Justice attorney, John Edgar Hoover, in 1924. Hoover accepted, but with conditions. He insisted that the Bureau of Investigation not come under civil service regulations, and that he alone would set the standards for appointments, promotions, and terminations. Furthermore, all applicants for appointment would have to have college degrees in either law or accounting and be subject to in-depth background investigations. Stone would not have it any other way and agreed.

Before 1924, there was no centralized repository in the United States for fingerprints. The two largest collections were on file at the federal penitentiary in Leavenworth, Kansas, and at the International Association of Chiefs of Police offices, where a National Bureau of Criminal Identification, consisting of sets of fingerprints sent in by various police departments, had been set up. However, with the new Bureau of Investigation's creation, it was believed that it now would be the logical place with which to file all fingerprints. As a result, in 1924, more than 800,000 sets of fingerprints were sent to the bureau. This nucleus eventually became the Federal Bureau of Investigation's Identification Division.

J. Edgar Hoover's belief that the forensic sciences could make a meaningful contribution to solving crimes prompted the Bureau of Investigation to develop a crime laboratory in 1932 to assist both its own investigators and police departments that needed forensic help, a practice that continues to this day. However, this was not the first police laboratory. In 1910, Edmond Locard organized the first one for the Lyon, France, police department. Other important advances also had been made before 1932

Seized counterfeit currency, 1995, Minneapolis, Minnesota.
(*Courtesy* U.S. Secret Service)

that ultimately would prove to be significant in examining certain types of evidence found at crime scenes. Two were particularly noteworthy. One consisted of Paul Uhlenhuth's 1901 discovery of a test that could make distinctions between human and animal blood. The other was the development in 1923 of a comparison microscope that could be used to help determine whether a bullet or cartridge found at the scene of a crime was fired by a particular gun.

Historically speaking, 1935 was an important year. The Bureau of Investigation's name was changed to Federal Bureau of Investigation (FBI); Congress for the first time authorized special agents to make arrests and be armed; and the FBI's National Police Academy, now known as the National Academy, was founded to offer specialized training and development opportunities for police personnel being groomed for leadership positions. In 1967, the FBI established the National Crime Information Center to offer police agencies more than just laboratory and identification help with their investigations.

OTHER FEDERAL INVESTIGATIVE AGENCIES

Today, there are federal investigative agencies other than the FBI, Secret Service, U.S. Marshal's Service, Bureau of Customs, and Postal Inspection Service. Under the Department of Justice, in addition to the FBI, are the Drug Enforcement Administration (formerly the Bureau of Narcotics and Dangerous Drugs), and Immigration and Naturalization Service. The Bureau of Alcohol, Tobacco and Firearms, and various units of the Internal Revenue Service, have joined the Secret Service as Treasury Department agencies. The Department of Defense has the Army's Criminal Investigation Command, the Navy's Naval Investigative Service, and the Air Force's Office of Special Investigations. There is the Office of Personnel Management, and the State Department has its Office of Security. Others also are found in the Labor, Health and Human Services, and Transportation Departments, Environmental Protection Agency, General Services Administration, Securities and Exchange Commission, the National Transportation Safety Board, and various Offices of Inspectors General.

A distinctive feature of all federal investigative agencies, unlike police agencies, is that their authority is determined by federal statutes that indicate which agency has jurisdiction over the violation of a particular federal law. For example, investigations involving the counterfeiting of U.S. currency are handled by the Secret Service, espionage cases by the FBI. In contrast, state and local police agencies investigate all state law or city ordinance violations that occur within their geographic boundaries. At the same time, one federal agency, the Office of Personnel Management (OPM), is responsible for conducting noncriminal investiga-

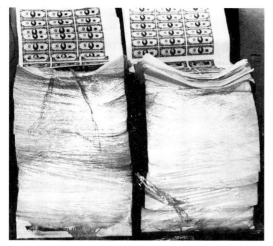
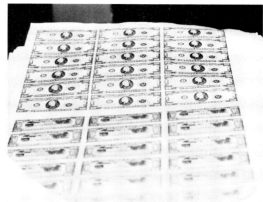

Ten million dollars seized counterfeit currency, 1991, New York City. (*Courtesy* U.S. Secret Service)

tions in the field of preemployment screening for many other U.S. government departments.

Sir Robert Peel's role and his influence on modern policing already have been mentioned, so have the roles of Hoover, Locard, and Uhlenhuth in the forensics field. However, it is also important to take note of Hans Gross (1847–1915), Alphonse Bertillon (1853–1914), Sir Francis Galton (1822–1911), and Edward Henry—especially as they relate to the subject of forensics. Each made a significant contribution to the criminal investigation field.

Gross, born in Graz, Austria, and the recipient of a legal education, was one of the earliest advocates of criminal investigation as a science. He developed his interest in the subject during his service as an examining magistrate and later as a criminology professor at the University of Vienna. His dissatisfaction with what he considered to be the absence of a scientific approach to investigations prompted him to write *System der Kriminalistik,* which, translated into English and published in 1906, remains a classic text on the subject.[12]

Bertillon, considered the father of criminal identification and a French anthropologist, developed the theory of anthropometry. According to Bertillon, all persons were unique in terms of their exact body measurements, and the sum of these measurements resulted in a characteristic formula for each one.[13] The Bertillon System, as it became known, was used in both Europe and the United States.

A 1903 incident at the U.S. penitentiary in Leavenworth, Kansas, served two purposes: it disproved the system's validity, and it proved the unique value of fingerprints as a means of identification. As Will West, a newly arrived prisoner, was being processed through the penitentiary's identification system, a staff member reported that his photograph and Bertillon measurements already were on file. However, when the records were examined, it was determined that Will West was almost identical in both appearance and Bertillon measurements with William West, a prisoner since 1901, whose data were on file, but the fingerprints of each prisoner were different.

At the time of the Will West–William West incident, the use of fingerprints for identification purposes was quite a new development. The idea that each person's fingerprints were distinct from everyone else's was based on the work of Sir Francis Galton, an English anthropologist, meteorologist, and writer, who also was a pioneer in the study of eugenics. His

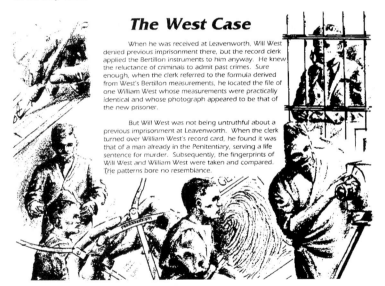

The West Case

When he was received at Leavenworth, Will West denied previous imprisonment there, but the record clerk applied the Bertillon instruments to him anyway. He knew the reluctance of criminals to admit past crimes. Sure enough, when the clerk referred to the formula derived from West's Bertillon measurements, he located the file of one William West whose measurements were practically identical and whose photograph appeared to be that of the new prisoner.

But Will West was not being untruthful about a previous imprisonment at Leavenworth. When the clerk turned over William West's record card, he found it was that of a man already in the Penitentiary, serving a life sentence for murder. Subsequently, the fingerprints of Will West and William West were taken and compared. The patterns bore no resemblance.

It would be hard to conceive a more nearly perfect case for refuting the claims of rival systems of identification. Although the two Wests denied being related, there was a facial resemblance like that of twin brothers. The formulas derived from their Bertillon measurements were nearly identical, allowing for slight discrepancies which might have been due to human variations in the measuring process. And, finally, there was the crowning coincidence of the similarity of names.

The fallibility of three systems of personal identification—names, photographs, and Bertillon measurements—were demonstrated by this one case. On the other hand, the value of fingerprints as a positive means of identifying people was dramatically shown.

William West

William West

Will West

Will West

FBI headquarters, U.S. Department of Justice building, Washington, D.C., prior to move to new building. (*Courtesy* FBI)

The current FBI headquarters, Washington, D.C. (*Courtesy* FBI)

Name search, Card Index Section, FBI Identification Division, Washington, D.C., circa 1940s. (*Courtesy* FBI)

Fingerprint classifying with a reticle, FBI Identification Division, Washington, D.C., circa 1940s. (*Courtesy* FBI)

Fingerprint classifiers searching prints, FBI Identification Division, Washington, D.C., circa 1940s. (*Courtesy* FBI)

Punch card searches for fingerprint patterns to narrow the scope of the search, FBI Identification Division, Washington, D.C., circa 1940s. (*Courtesy* FBI)

New FBI special agents searching for fingerprints and other clues, circa 1940s. (*Courtesy* FBI)

FBI special agents on one of the firing ranges, FBI Academy, Quantico, Virginia. (*Courtesy* FBI)

FBI special agents in training, 1936. (*Courtesy* FBI)

FBI special agents firing Thompson submachine guns for news-reel film, FBI Academy, Quantico, Virginia, October 16, 1936. (*Courtesy* FBI)

FBI special agents at physical training, U.S. Department of Justice Building, Washington, D.C., May 1, 1940. (*Courtesy* FBI)

FBI special agents learning to shoot from the rear of a moving automobile, February 1935. (*Courtesy* FBI)

FBI Training School entrance, Washington, D.C., circa 1940s.
(*Courtesy* FBI)

FBI officials who participated in apprehending Alvin Karpis,
New Orleans, Louisiana, May 1, 1936. Left to right, W. R.
Galvin, E. J. Connelley, Director J. Edgar Hoover, Clyde Tolson,
and Dwight Brantley. (*Courtesy* FBI)

book *Fingerprints,* published in 1892, set the stage for the identification of criminals based on fingerprint evidence found at crime scenes. However, the methodology needed to facilitate their organization into an orderly system for examination and comparison was the work of Edward Henry. While serving as inspector general of police in Nepal, he obtained a copy of Galton's book and ultimately developed what became known as the Henry System of Classification, a system adopted for use in England in 1900.

In 1904, Detective Sergeant Joseph Faurot of the New York City Police Department was sent to England for the express purpose of studying fingerprinting and training in the use of the Henry System of Classification. Unfortunately, while Faurot was in England, a new New York City police commissioner, who saw no value in fingerprint evidence, was appointed. When Faurot returned, he found himself assigned to walking a beat.[14] In 1906, while Faurot was on duty at the Waldorf-Astoria Hotel, he arrested a man leaving a suite who, wearing formal evening wear but no shoes,[15] aroused his suspicion. The man assured Faurot that he was a respectable person named "James Jones"; insisted that he be allowed to see the British Consul; and told Faurot that if his demand was refused, Faurot would suffer dire consequences.[16] Despite this threat, Faurot sent "Jones's" fingerprints to Scotland Yard;[17] he was identified as Daniel Nolan, a man who had twelve prior convictions for hotel theft and who was wanted for a home burglary in England.[18] Nolan, confronted with this information, admitted several thefts at the Waldorf-Astoria; he was sentenced to a prison term of seven years.

During the years that followed, the realization that each person's fingerprints are unique led to their increasing acceptance and use for identification purposes, and not only in criminal investigations. When deceased persons need to be positively identified, whatever the cause of death, the first step in the identification process usually will be to try to get a set of their fingerprints. Further, although it was and still is the practice of the FBI Laboratory to provide assistance to its own personnel, and upon request to police departments, during this time increasing numbers of state and big-city police agencies developed their own crime laboratories.

With respect to applying science to criminal investigations, of historical interest is the fact that deoxyribonucleic acid (DNA) was discovered in 1868. However, the scientific community was slow in appreciating its role in matters of heredity.[19] In fact, it was not until Alec Jeffreys and his associates at Leicester University, England, doing research into human gene structure in 1985, discovered that portions of the DNA structure of certain genes could be as unique to individuals as are their fingerprints.[20]

SUMMARY

To fully appreciate the historical evolution of criminal investigations, and the subsequent use of investigators for noncriminal matters, one must first look at the ways in which policing has developed. In the beginning, and certainly before democratic forms of government were developed, tribal chieftains, followed by emperors and kings, used their armies to maintain order, especially in conquered lands. Whether the first reported establishment of a big-city police force occurred in Egypt, Mesopotamia, or during the reign of the Roman Emperor Augustus, little seems to be known about the presence of even rudimentary police agencies until around 1066. It is at the time of William the Conquerer and the Norman Conquest of England that the office of shire reeve first appears.

Although there is evidence that shire reeves did perform some duties that even today are associated with policing, namely, serving court orders and keeping the peace, it does not appear that they engaged in any investigative activity. Thus, despite these early developments in the police field, as far as can be determined criminal investigators were unheard of until Henry Fielding organized the Bow Street Runners in the mideighteenth century.

The Industrial Revolution and the increasing urbanization of Great Britain brought about an increase in criminal activity and prompted the creation of police departments. A significant step in the field of policing was Sir Robert Peel's modernization of the Metropolitan London Police in 1829. Even so, it was another thirteen years before Scotland Yard had its first organized detective bureau.

Progress in employing detectives' services was equally slow in the United States. Police departments were created as cities grew, but investigators as such were not a part of those agencies during the early stages. Even when they were used, they had no special training; neither did they have to meet any particular standards of character or education prior to their appointments. Although a very limited number of federal investigators were employed during the nineteenth century, their roles were narrowly focused. Not until the Justice Department's Bureau of Investigation was created was there an expansion of and increased involvement with criminal investigations by U.S. government agencies. Changes within the Bureau of Investigation (the FBI) after J. Edgar Hoover's appointment as director—educational and character standards for employment, a crime laboratory, the Identification Division, and the forerunner of the National Academy—marked a radical departure from what had been the norm for federal investigations. In turn, they also contributed to important changes in the ways in which police investigations were handled.

However, credit for much of the progress made in the field of investigations must be given to such people as Gross, Bertillon, Galton, and

Henry, who, during the late nineteenth and early twentieth centuries, began to make their respective contributions. Although many of the early investigative aids are no less valuable now than when they were first discovered and used, new developments and methods that can be applied to criminal investigations, such as DNA testing, also have been discovered to help investigators solve crimes.

REVIEW QUESTIONS

1. How did the Industrial Revolution affect England's policing?
2. Who was Henry Fielding, and for what is he known?
3. Why is Sir Robert Peel often referred to as the father of modern policing?
4. What prompted Theodore Roosevelt to establish the Bureau of Investigation during his presidency?
5. What was the effect of the Will West case on the Bertillon System's use for identification purposes?
6. What two important changes to the Bureau of Investigation occurred in 1935?
7. Who was Hans Gross, and what is his importance to the field of criminal investigation?
8. Where and when was the first police crime laboratory established?
9. When and why did the Bureau of Investigation become the central repository for fingerprints in the United States? What formed the nucleus of the new Identification Division?
10. What did Alec Jeffreys and his Leicester University colleagues discover in 1985 that was important to modern criminal investigation?

NOTES

1. Martin A. Kelly, "The First Urban Policeman," *Journal of Police Science and Administration,* vol. 1, no. 1 (March 1973), p. 56.
2. T. A. Critchley, *A History of Police in England and Wales,* 2nd ed. (Montclair, NJ: Patterson Smith, 1972), p. 34.
3. Ibid.
4. Thomas A. Reppetto, *The Blue Parade* (New York: Free Press, 1978), p. 26.
5. Ibid., pp. 26–28.
6. Clive Ensley, *Policing and Its Context 1750–1870* (New York: Schocken Books, 1983), p. 106.
7. Augustine E. Costello, *Our Police Protectors* (Montclair, NJ: Patterson Smith, 1972 reprint of an 1885 edition), p. 402.
8. James F. Richardson, *The New York Police* (New York: Oxford, 1970), p. 122.

9. James D. Horan, *The Pinkertons* (New York: Bonanza Books, 1967), p. 25.

10. William J. Mathias and Stuart Anderson, *Horse to Helicopter* (Atlanta: Community Life Publications, Georgia State University, 1973), p. 22.

11. Don Whitehead, *The FBI Story* (New York: Random House, 1956), p. 19.

12. Hans G. A. Gross, *Criminal Investigation,* 5th ed., translated by John Adam and J. Collyer Adam, revised by R. L. Jackson (London: Sweet & Maxwell Ltd., 1962).

13. Jurgen Thorwald, *Crime and Science* (New York: Harcourt, Brace and World, 1967), p. 4.

14. Jursen Thorwald, *The Marks of Cain* (London: Thames & Hudson, 1965), p. 129.

15. Ibid.

16. Ibid.

17. Ibid., p. 139.

18. Ibid.

19. Richard Saferstein, *Criminalistics: An Introduction to Forensic Science,* 4th ed. (Englewood Cliffs, NJ: Prentice Hall, 1990), p. 334.

20. Ibid., p. 343.

Chapter 2

— ❖ —

What Is
an Investigation?

The word *investigation* is subject to different interpretations, depending upon who wants to define it. For instance, according to *Roget's International Thesaurus,* synonyms for the root word *investigate* are "discuss" and "explore"; for *investigation,* "discussion" and "research."[1] *Webster's New World Dictionary* defines *investigate* as "to search into; examine in detail; inquire into systematically"; and *investigation* as "careful search or examination; systematic inquiry." However, in trying to understand what an investigation is, it is worth considering the dictionary's synonyms for the word. The five listed are *investigation, probe, inquest, inquisition,* and *research.* Each has a different connotation, and each warrants a further look.

TYPES OF INVESTIGATIONS

Most people associate the word *investigation* with a formal, official inquiry conducted by some branch of government in an effort to uncover facts and determine the truth. In a sense, investigations of this sort most often are thought of as being related to some form of criminal activity; consequently, they are conducted by police departments or federal agencies.

Probe also is considered an extensive, searching inquiry by government. However, people tend to associate probes with committees, usually in the form of legislative inquiries.

Inquests are usually thought of as attempts to get to the underlying cause of occurrences. Today, the word is used to refer to a form of judicial inquiry, frequently associated with investigations conducted by coroners or medical examiners to determine the cause of death when it is not readily apparent.

The word *inquisition* has more historical than current usage. Strictly speaking, it simply refers to any penetrating investigation. However, as a result of its ruthless application to ecclesiastical inquiries to suppress suspected heretics, particularly in Spain during the fifteenth century, the word is regarded as distasteful and therefore seldom used.

Research is most often employed in referring to the careful, patient investigations by scientists or scholars in their efforts to identify original sources of data or causes of problems. This, in turn, helps them develop additional information in order to try to clarify previously unclear facts, or lead to the solution of medical or scientific problems.

Another type of investigation is a relatively recent phenomenon, namely, investigative reporting. This avenue is one pursued by the news media on their own initiative. Investigative reporting, unlike most other types of investigations, is designed to serve a dual purpose. Primarily, if done by hardcopy media, it is intended to attract readers; if by radio or television reporters, to attract listeners or viewers. Regardless of the form, it is their hope that this kind of reporting will increase revenues. The importance of getting to the root of a problem often seems almost secondary.

Since our focus is on investigations conducted by law enforcement personnel (whether at city, county, state, or federal level), by security management representatives or by attorneys or those working in their behalf, two questions need to be addressed. First, what, if anything, distinguishes investigations of this sort from those conducted by the various aforementioned investigators? Second, if there are distinguishing characteristics, is more than merely searching for dictionary definitions or synonyms warranted?

In answer to the first question, yes, there are distinctions. One of the most noticeable is that time is a factor. Victims and witnesses must be identified and, where possible, interviewed as soon as possible, and although we discuss the collection and preservation of evidence in detail in Chapter 12, unless investigators move quickly to collect and preserve evidence, they risk its loss. It is immaterial whether the incident being investigated involves a crime, a tort, a breach of contract, or a violation of a corporation's or institution's policy; unless these steps are taken, there cannot be a meaningful resolution. The other types of investigations previously mentioned, with the possible exception of those conducted under the guise of probes or by medical examiners, rarely are faced with evidentiary concerns.

Another distinguishing feature, also related to time and particularly to criminal investigators, is pressure—pressure to quickly identify and arrest those persons suspected of involvement. It can be unrelenting, especially if the crime is particularly heinous or unusual or involves high-profile victims. Cases of this sort understandably attract the news media. Unfortunately, and not infrequently, the way in which a story is reported puts pressure on both the head of the political subdivision in which the offense occurred and the police chief, leading to even more pressure on the investigators.

For example, it is not unusual to watch a news telecast or listen to a radio newscast reporting a homicide or a robbery that occurred only shortly before airtime yet hear a statement to the effect that "The police have not yet made any arrests or identified any suspects." Unlike entertainment industry–created investigations, those conducted in real life rarely are completed in sixty to ninety minutes, less time out for commercials. Thus it is evident that some very clear distinctions exist between the types of investigations on which we are focusing and the others.

This, in turn, suggests a need to further clarify and distinguish the investigations conducted by those employed in law enforcement, in corporate security functions, or as private investigators. A logical starting point for this phase will be found in Chapter 4. There we consider the requisite characteristics of good investigators, and while noting their combined value, we underscore the importance of integrity and objectivity.

Among the reasons for this is investigators' unassailable relationship to our ideas about justice in general, not only in our criminal justice system. The impact of prejudiced investigators on criminals and noncriminals alike can lead to injustice. One would hope that these same traits would be equally important to legislators and the news media, yet their enjoyment of certain immunities and privileges does not always prompt them to exercise the same high standard of care that is considered essential for other investigators. Insofar as the scientific and academic communities are concerned, integrity and objectivity are important, but justice is not an issue.

Realistically, what is lawful may not always be just, yet in contrast to legislators and the news media, justice is very much an issue for those who are or hope to become involved with careers in law enforcement, corporate security, the practice of law, or as private investigators employed in connection with legal matters. The importance of justice is by no means a new idea. In 163 B.C., Terence, a Roman writer, observed that "Rigorous law is often rigorous injustice."[2] Robert F. Kennedy, a former attorney general of the United States, remarked that "Justice delayed is democracy denied."[3] Courts, not investigators, are the arbiters of the law, yet the kinds of investigators with whom we are concerned are mindful of the fact that how courts and juries render justice often depends on how they conduct their inquiries.

What, then, is an investigation, and what is the relationship between justice in the word's broadest sense and the subject of investigations? In 1948, Hugh Clegg, assistant director in charge of the FBI's Training and Inspection Division, welcomed a class of newly appointed special agents. Included in his address to them was a definition of investigations from the FBI's perspective. He said an investigation was a fact-finding function. In other words, investigators are fact-finders, not prosecutors, judges, or juries.

Clegg's accurate definition also, in some ways, is a statement of an investigation's purpose. Consequently, in an effort to more clearly describe an investigation, one might think of it as a monstrous jigsaw puzzle comprising many irregular pieces (the facts), which, when correctly fitted together, form a picture. Examples of this will be found among the specific cases cited in later chapters.

Nevertheless, because of the context in which varied criminal and noncriminal incidents are used, they may not by themselves give the uninitiated any idea of why investigations are comparable to puzzles. However, in this comparison we also need to explore the investigations–justice relationship, and especially the meaning of the word *justice*. Although *Webster's New World Dictionary* defines *justice* in several ways, the definitions that seem to be most closely allied to investigations read: "sound reason; rightfulness; validity," and "the use of authority and power to uphold what is right, just, or lawful."

❖ Case 2-1

The Incident.   In the summer of 1956, a large textile manufacturer, with a mill in one city and a finished goods warehouse in another some forty miles away, learned from an independent auditor of a $180,000 piece-goods shortage at the warehouse.

The Victim.   The victim's perception of justice required that the investigation do more than identify, arrest, prosecute, and punish whoever was responsible. It had to determine how the loss occurred, why the burglar alarm did not function, if there was a buyer for the goods, who that buyer was, and whether or not it might recover the goods or their value from that buyer.

The Investigation.   Among the questions for which the investigators wanted answers were the following:

How did the thief or thieves gain access to the warehouse?

If there was evidence of a forced entry, what tool or tools were used?

Had the central station burglar alarm gone off? If not, was there any evidence that it had been bypassed?

There were no signs of a forced entry. There was neither a report of the burglar alarm's activation nor any indication that it had been bypassed. This made it likely that one or more employees were involved. No employee was assigned to the warehouse on a full-time basis, but there was one particular employee who always accompanied the company truck driver whenever finished goods were either to go from the mill into the warehouse's inventory or to be picked up for delivery to customers or shippers.

Mill management personnel interviews indicated that both employees had access to the warehouse keys, knew where they were kept when not in use, and knew the password used for clearing the alarm with the central station. It also was learned that the mill owners, Orthodox Jews, closed all of their facilities on all religious holidays, and from sundown on Friday because of the Sabbath. Review of the central station alarm company's records showed that the warehouse had been entered on three successive Saturdays. In addition, the company's truck records reflected mileage discrepancies on the truck's trip tickets and gasoline purchases for those Saturdays.

Both employees who had access to the keys and knew the password were interviewed. The one who always accompanied the driver had an alibi that investigators confirmed; the driver did not. This prompted a check of the driver's criminal, credit, and court records. He had no criminal record; however, court records reflected a recent divorce with alimony and child support payments. His credit record was poor. The driver was taken into custody, interrogated, confessed, and admitted selling the goods but refused to name the buyer. He was tried and found guilty.

Based on what they now knew, the investigators figured that the buyer or buyers probably were in business fairly close to the warehouse. From a reliable confidential informant, they learned of two small piece-goods outlets in an adjoining city, less than seven miles from the warehouse. They contacted the local police and were told that though the owners had never been arrested, they reputedly bought whatever was offered to them, no questions asked.

With a description of the stolen goods, and having learned from the mill owner that the particular weave of its materials was unique and thus identifiable, one investigator, posing as a buyer, visited both stores. Only one had material that fit the goods' description; he bought several pieces. Based on their weave patterns, they were identified as part of the stolen piece goods. The store owner was taken into custody. As part of a plea bargain, based in part on his anxiety and the district attorney's willingness to avoid further embarrassment to the store owner's prominent family, it was agreed that he would plead guilty and compensate the mill owner for the cost of the goods.

❖ **Case 2-2**

The Incident. A vice president for a high-technology company received an anonymous, handwritten note alleging that a section manager, on his own, had awarded several contracts for some rather sophisticated work to some small businesses, resulting in kickbacks for the manager. The author also alleged that the work could have been done better and for less money in-house.

The Victim. In this case, the question of justice required the investigators to consider two equally important factors: justice to the employer if the allegations were true, and justice to the section manager if they were not.

The Investigation. As with Case 2-1, there were questions for which there had to be answers:

Was there anything in the manager's employment history to suggest that he might do something like this?

Was there anything about his lifestyle in relation to his salary that seemed unusual and that might warrant further inquiry?

Were any of his subordinates dissatisfied with him? If so, who were they, and why were they dissatisfied?

Of those who might be unhappy, was there anything in handwriting in their personnel files that resembled or matched that of the anonymous note?

Did the way in which these contracts were awarded violate the employer's purchasing policies?

What was the dollar amount of each of the cited contracts?

Technically speaking, was the quality of the work done by the contractors at least as good as it would have been if done in-house?

If it was at least as good, did it cost less than, as much as, or more than if it had been done in-house?

Could the work have, in fact, been done in-house?

The investigation would move forward on three fronts. One, the manager's personnel file and those of his subordinates would be reviewed. Two, help would be needed in terms of objectively evaluating the technical aspects of the allegations. Three, the contracts themselves would be examined from a cost standpoint and to determine whether, under the circumstances, purchasing policies had been violated.

Since none of the contracts exceeded $500 in value, the way in which they were awarded did not violate policy. Technically, the quality of the contracted work was described as at least as good as if it had been done in-house, and also as having been done for less money.

Nothing in the manager's personnel file raised questions about his employment history. Neither was there anything suspicious about his lifestyle.

Examination of his subordinates' files reflected that one person had not gotten any salary increase during his two most recent performance reviews. That person's file also contained several handwritten items that appeared to be similar to the handwriting on the anonymous letter.

The manager and all of his subordinates, except the one whose handwriting appeared to match that of the anonymous letter, were interviewed separately. The manager knew of no reason why anyone would make the allegations that were being investigated. Neither did any of the others interviewed although several described one of the unit's members as a chronic complainer, naming the employee who had not received raises.

Based on the file reviews and interviews, the writing specimens in the one employee's file and the anonymous letter were subjected to a forensic examination. The results were conclusive; that employee was the anonymous letter's author.

He was interviewed and admitted his guilt. He said the letter was prompted by his having gotten two successive zero performance reviews and his wanting to get back at his manager. Copies of the investigative report were made available to the company's general counsel, human resources director, and the errant employee's divisional vice president for whatever action they deemed appropriate.

In both of these investigations, one by public-sector investigators, the other by corporate security, a contribution to justice was made. In the first, the thief and the buyer of stolen goods were identified, apprehended, and punished; the victim was compensated for its loss. In the second, an employee's job and, even more important, his reputation were saved. Both cases illustrate the extent to which good investigators must go in solving cases. All the bits and pieces that make up the whole must be carefully and objectively examined. Facts, not the personal opinions of investigators, the heart and soul of every investigation, must be allowed to speak for themselves.

Regrettably, these precepts are not always followed. A lingering question that may never be answered is whether O. J. Simpson's acquittal in his trial for murder was due to the way in which the investigation was conducted or the way in which the case was presented to the jury. Also, new criminal trials may become necessary because a few New York State troopers were found to have planted fingerprint evidence at some crime scenes.[4] British police investigators have been criticized for hurried investigations—having overlooked evidence, having used negligent investigative techniques, and having been swayed by media pressure—prompting the High Court to release convicted persons from jail in four cases since 1991.[5]

SUMMARY

Although most people associate the word *investigation* with the work done by detectives or other law enforcement personnel, others, such as government bodies, private-sector organizations, or individual people, also conduct investigations. For example, corporate security personnel, private investigators, attorneys, legislative committees (whether federal or state), medical examiners or coroners, scientists, scholars, and news media representatives also investigate.

However, although the underlying objective of all investigations presumably is a search for facts to prove a proposition or theory, there are motivational differences between those conducted by criminal justice agencies, and to a degree by corporate security representatives, and those engaged in by others. Police department and federal agency investigators have no profit motive; their motivation comes from the need to bring their inquiries to a logical conclusion. This is true even when investigating noncriminal matters. In many respects, this same need, and the importance of protecting an employer's assets, is the principal motivator for corporate security investigators. Medical examiners or coroners are motivated by a challenge to their professional skill in determining what caused a seemingly healthy person's death. Although profit may not be the direct motive for investigations by members of the scientific or academic communities, it would be naive to deny that it plays a role with varying degrees of importance. And despite possible denials, profit does motivate news media investigations.

Motives aside, another feature that distinguishes investigations conducted by law enforcement personnel is that every inquiry undertaken by them, criminal or other, is governed by law and rules of evidence, matters discussed more fully throughout the text. For the most part, their work is reactive; there must be a valid reason for opening and conducting any investigation. They can do only what the law permits, and they are prohibited from engaging in activities that the law does not permit. Failure to adhere to the rules of law and evidence may cause all of their efforts to go for naught in terms of their contribution to the cause of justice.

Other types of investigations are not similarly bound. Private-sector investigations in which subjects have not been given a Miranda warning do not vitiate their admissions of guilt. Scientists or scholars who plagiarize will lose their colleagues' respect, and they even may be sued civilly, without an impact on someone's life and liberty. On the other hand, news media investigations may affect a person's life without giving any thought to the question of justice.

In a democratic society, a burden is imposed on all classes of government investigations and investigators. For them, there can be no separation between the investigative process, facts, the rules of law and evidence, and justice, even in noncriminal inquiries. Equally important, in a democracy, even such private-sector investigations as those conducted by security personnel, as illustrated by Case 2-2 in this chapter, cannot deny that a relationship exists between the way in which an investigation is pursued and justice for its subject.

REVIEW QUESTIONS

1. Which dictionary synonym for the word *investigation* best suits police inquiries?
2. With what type of activity is the word *investigation* most closely associated?
3. Distinguish between an investigation and a probe.
4. Why is the word *inquisition* in disfavor?
5. Describe the two features that most distinguish investigations conducted by law enforcement personnel from those done by others.
6. What private-sector investigations most closely resemble those conducted by public-sector investigators?
7. How can the pressure of time affect a criminal investigation?
8. What is the most basic definition of an investigation?
9. Why is an investigation comparable to a jigsaw puzzle?
10. On what is the investigations–justice relationship based?

NOTES

1. *Roget's International Thesaurus, 3rd ed.* (New York: Thomas Y. Crowell Company, 1962), p. 943.
2. Terence, *The Self-Tormenter* (163 B.C.) 4.5.48, translated by Henry Thomas Riley. *The International Thesaurus of Quotations* (New York: Thomas Y. Crowell Company, 1970).
3. "To Secure These Rights," *The Pursuit of Justice* (1964).
4. "Two Troopers in Inquiry Get Warning, Then Quit," *New York Times,* January 9, 1997, p. B6.
5. "Again, Britain Must Free Men Who Were Wrongly Convicted," *New York Times,* February 22, 1997, p. NE7.

Chapter 3

❖

Who Conducts Investigations?

It probably is safe to say that relatively few people have any personal or even indirect contact with either investigations or investigators. Consequently, they tend to rely on what they hear, see, or read about the subject. For many, if not most, the very word *investigations* brings to mind the image of the intrepid detective, whether in public or private service, who devotes his or her time and energy to solving crimes. In truth, since so much of the public's perception of investigations and investigators comes from literature or entertainment (whether stage, screen, or television) and the news media, many people have a rather limited understanding and somewhat distorted portrait, rather than a reasonably true one, of the different types and classes of people who actually do conduct investigations.

FICTITIOUS INVESTIGATORS

Undoubtedly, one of the oldest and best known investigators comes from literature in the person of Sherlock Holmes, a private investigator who was assisted by his friend Dr. Watson. Holmes, famous for his powers of deduction, and Watson were the creation of Sir Arthur Conan Doyle (1859–1930), an English physician and novelist who wrote a series of stories with Holmes and Watson as the centerpiece.

More contemporary literature has offered the general public a host of other well-known private investigators, among them such supersleuths as Miss Marple, Ellery Queen, and Hercule Poirot. Today, they, as well as Holmes and Watson, are found not only in literature, but also as characters in the entertainment field. Among other well-known private investigators, who also first appeared in books before they were seen in motion pictures or television programs, are Mike Hammer and Sam Spade. A fictitious character in public service is Inspector Maigret of the Sûreté. Perry Mason, a fictitious lawyer famous for defending clients charged with serious crimes, usually homicides, has on retainer a private investigator who does Mason's legwork and invariably helps him prove his clients' innocence.

Still others, largely in the public-service sector, owe their fame to motion pictures or made-for-television movies. Among them are Inspector "Dirty Harry" Callahan, San Francisco Police Department; Sergeant Joe Friday, and later Lt. Columbo, both of the Los Angeles Police Department; Cagney and Lacey, two women detectives in New York City's Police Department; Inspector Erskine of the FBI; and the various "detectives" who appear in programs such as *NYPD Blue* and *Law and Order*.

Occasionally, the motion picture and television industries also have offered programs based on the work of actual investigators. Notable examples are a movie and television series called *The Untouchables*. Both were based on the work of Eliot Ness, a federal agent whose investigation of Al Capone brought about Capone's downfall and resulted in his receiving a ten-year sentence in 1932 for tax evasion. There also have been movies about John Dillinger's death at the hands of the FBI, outside the Biograph Theatre, under the direction of Melvin Purvis, then special agent in charge of the FBI's Chicago Field Office. Even so, in these and other fictionalized accounts of actual incidents, liberties often have been and are taken in portraying the real-life characters, both good and bad. They are glamourized, or dramatic elements that never actually happened are added in order to stimulate favorable reviews, public interest, and sales.

In any event, whether in literature or entertainment, or even entertainment under the guise of real life, the investigations portrayed almost invariably involve major crimes; it is immaterial whether the investigators happen to be in public or private service. Thus the portrayal of investigations, and of those who conduct them, can be misleading. Although criminal investigations and criminal investigators are critical in today's society, one also must be made aware that not all investigations involve crime; neither are all investigators, whether public or private, necessarily involved with the criminal justice system.

With this thought in mind, and recognizing the importance of both criminal investigations and investigators in the more commonly accepted sense of the terms, the question of who conducts investigations needs to be explored. The answer may come as a surprise to the uninitiated.

**IDENTIFICATION
ORDER NO.** 1217
March 12, 1934.

DIVISION OF INVESTIGATION
U. S. DEPARTMENT OF JUSTICE
WASHINGTON, D. C.

Fingerprint Classification

12 9 R 0
----
14 U 00 9

WANTED

JOHN DILLINGER, with alias,

FRANK SULLIVAN

NATIONAL MOTOR VEHICLE THEFT ACT

DESCRIPTION

Age, 31 years
Height, 5 feet 7-1/8 inches
Weight, 153 pounds
Build, medium
Hair, medium chestnut
Eyes, grey
Complexion, medium
Occupation, machinist
Marks and scars, 1/2 inch scar
  back left hand; scar middle
  upper lip; brown mole between
  eyebrows
Mustache

Photograph taken January 25, 1934

John Dillinger

CRIMINAL RECORD

As John Dillinger, #14395, received
State Reformatory, Pendleton, Indiana,
September 16, 1924; crime, assault and
battery with intent to rob and conspiracy to commit a felony; sentences,
2 to 14 years and 10 to 20 years respectively;

As John Dillinger, #13225, received
State Prison, Michigan City, Indiana,
July 16, 1929; transferred from Indiana
State Reformatory; paroled under Reformatory jurisdiction, May 10, 1933;
parole revoked by Governor – considered
as delinquent parolee;

As John Dillinger, #10587, arrested
Police Department, Dayton, Ohio, September 22, 1933; charge, fugitive;
turned over to Allen County, Ohio,
authorities;

As John Dillinger, received County

Jail, Lima, Ohio, September 28, 1933; charge, bank robbery; escaped October 12, 1933;
    As Frank Sullivan, arrested Police Department, Tucson, Arizona, January 25, 1934; charge, fugitive; turned
over to Lake County, Indiana, authorities;
    As John Dillinger, #14487, arrested Sheriff's Office, Crown Point, Indiana, January 30, 1934; charge,
murder - bank robbery; escaped March 3, 1934.

    The United States Marshal, Chicago, Illinois, holds warrant of arrest charging John Dillinger with feloniously and knowingly
transporting Ford V-8 four door sedan, motor number 256447, property of Lillian Holley, Sheriff, Lake County, Indiana, from Crown
Point, Indiana to Chicago, Illinois, on or about March 3, 1934.
    Law enforcement agencies kindly transmit any additional information or criminal record to the nearest office of the Division
of Investigation, U. S. Department of Justice.
    If apprehended, please notify the Director, Division of Investigation, U. S. Department of Justice, Washington, D. C., or the
Special Agent in Charge of the Office of the Division of Investigation listed on the back hereof which is nearest your city.
                                        (over)   Issued by: J. EDGAR HOOVER, DIRECTOR.

March 12, 1934, Identification Order on John Dillinger. (*Courtesy* FBI)

POLICE INVESTIGATORS

Despite the entertainment industry's portrayals of public and private investigators, the general public is inclined to associate investigations and investigators with police work. When people think of private investigators, they seem to do so in a much more limited way. Therefore, in considering just who does conduct investigations, it may be best to first examine not only those in some form of policing, but also those who focus on criminal investigations.

The vast majority of federal agencies are distinguishable from the police in that they *are* primarily investigative. Therefore, a look at police departments, sheriffs' departments (in those jurisdictions where they do more than merely operate the county jail and serve legal papers), and state police departments is a logical starting point.

First, remember that most police personnel are not investigators. Traditionally, the high visibility of uniformed police officers has been accepted as one of the three elements needed to prevent crime; the other two are the early apprehension of criminals and speedy trials resulting in punishment. In other words, the primary role of uniformed officers, whether walking beats or patrolling in marked cars, has been and continues to be one of deterring crime and responding to those committed. The secondary mission, to be of service to the community, is one that is changing as an ever-increasing number of departments are adopting a community policing approach. Nevertheless, although neither role focuses on investigations, there are occasions when patrol personnel are involved with some investigative work, even if only in a limited way.

An incident occurs. Perhaps a crime has been committed or there has been an accident. A victim or a witness believes that it is a police matter and reports it to an appropriate agency. Or maybe a person who is neither a victim nor a witness knows of the incident, but not if the police have been informed. Believing that they should be, he or she calls. Regardless of who makes the call, patrol officers are invariably the first to respond to the scene. They are expected to perform several acts almost simultaneously, only one of which is to initiate an investigation, even though a limited one.

For instance, the very nature of the report received by the police dispatcher may evidence a need for detectives to proceed to the crime scene, such as a reported bank robbery or homicide. The reality is that some of the first responders' work is investigative, that they are patrol officers is immaterial. This may be even truer when nothing about a reported incident, as might be the case of an accident, initially seems to require detectives' involvement.

Obviously, whether responding to a crime or an accident that already has occurred, the deterrent value of patrol officers is of no consequence, yet the importance of their service role may be heightened. Thus upon arrival at the scene, they must quickly evaluate what they see and take appropriate action. Among the items that need their attention are the following:

1. Whether a crime or an accident occurred, if anyone was injured or appears to need medical attention, they must arrange for his or her care. This humanitarian service is a first responder's responsibility. It is not an investigative function, yet showing concern may help make the investigators' work easier once they arrive.

2. Whether a crime has been committed or an accident has occurred, the patrol officers must preserve the integrity of the scene for the benefit of the investigators when they arrive. This is crucial to the investigators since any compromise of the scene lessens its investigative value.

3. The role of patrol personnel as investigators begins with their obligation to make every effort to get information that not only will help identify the perpetrator(s), but also will help them determine whether he, she, or they still are at the scene so that an arrest can be made.

4. If the perpetrator(s) have fled the scene, the patrol officers must obtain all pertinent information about the crime and suspects for broadcast to other patrol personnel in an effort to effect an early apprehension. Gathering this information is an investigative function.

5. Another investigative activity consists of their identifying all witnesses and getting statements from them while what happened is fresh in their minds. They also must get the witnesses' names, addresses, and telephone numbers at both home and at work, for the benefit of the investigators to whom the case already has been or will be assigned. In this connection, the patrol officers also must see to it that the witnesses are interviewed separately to ensure the integrity of their respective versions. If this is not done, the contents of one or more witness statements may be influenced by what another witness reports.

6. If the incident is one that results in investigators being sent to the scene, patrol personnel must assist in every way possible. This may involve additional investigative work, such as going door-to-door to try to locate and identify other witnesses who were not necessarily physically present at the scene, or possibly even as part of a search for the perpetrators. They also may be called upon to direct traffic or help with interviews or processing the scene.

The foregoing list serves to highlight two things. First is the obviously important role played by patrol personnel during a preliminary investigation. Second, the multiple tasks to be performed by them, whether working in pairs or alone, make it evident that upon their arrival, particularly at a crime scene, they must call for backup unless additional patrol officers already are enroute. An insufficient number of officers could result in

A delay in getting medical attention for anyone who has been injured

A contaminated crime or accident scene and the loss of physical evidence

A possible loss of witnesses and the information they might be able to provide

The possible escape of the perpetrator(s)

A disastrous effect on the ultimate outcome of the investigation

The ultimate responsibility for the success or failure of a criminal case rests with the way in which the investigation was conducted and the evidence was presented by the prosecutor. Nevertheless, if a case is lost because patrol officers failed to call for the help they needed to handle the many tasks required of them, they will not endear themselves to either the investigators to whom the case is assigned or the prosecutor.

In terms of who conducts investigations, patrol personnel also may be used as investigators for more than preliminaries. Some departments have been moving toward letting them handle entire investigations of matters not considered so time consuming or complex as to warrant assignment to detectives. In small departments that do not have detectives, all investigative work is done by patrol officers.

Then, too, some departments have and use plainclothes officers, whose role is different. In some situations, they are used as a deterrent to certain types of crimes. However, in some departments either budgetary or policy limitations limiting the number of detectives available may prompt their use as investigators. The types of cases to which they may be assigned depend largely on a department's managers and the extent to which they are influenced by the investigative workload.

Who conducts investigations for sheriffs' departments depends on each department's law enforcement role. Although statutes refer to sheriffs and their deputies as "peace officers," as we noted earlier, some sheriffs' departments nevertheless do nothing more than manage their county jails and serve legal papers. In those sheriffs' departments that perform all the duties normally associated with municipal police agencies, the investigative work associated with uniformed patrol officers may be done by deputies. These departments also have their own detective bureaus.

The investigative roles of state police agencies may be either limited or unlimited. By law, some states limit them to highway patrol work, including related crimes and accidents. In others, they perform a full range of police work. In the latter case, the only real difference between their operations and those of local police departments is one of jurisdiction. Although the authority of state police is statewide, unless there are unusual circumstances, their limited numbers and the state's size usually combine to keep them out of cities and towns. But in terms of operating principles applicable to investigative work, their patrol personnel and detectives function much the same as those employed by municipal police departments. Although criminal investigations obviously are a primary concern of all the foregoing agencies, from time to time all of them may be called upon to conduct noncriminal investigations.

FEDERAL INVESTIGATORS

Answering the question of who conducts investigations is not quite as clear-cut at the federal level. True, as pointed out in discussing the historical background of criminal investigations in Chapter 1, the many federal government agencies are distinguishable from local, county, and state police departments in that they are primarily investigative. Nevertheless, there are some exceptions. The U.S. Park Police is in many respects organized much the same as a police department with both uniformed personnel and investigators. The Secret Service has a uniformed branch that largely performs a police function, less a broad range of investigative work, in protecting the White House. Other uniformed officers, such as those employed by the General Services Administration and responsible for the security of federal buildings, serve primarily in a police role, yet crimes committed on U.S. government property are investigated by other agencies, principally the FBI.

The investigative jurisdiction of the many different federal agencies is prescribed mainly by the statutes that create specific federal crimes, although on occasion the work of some may overlap with that of others. To illustrate, both the Drug Enforcement Agency (DEA) and the FBI conduct drug investigations; an explosive sent through the U.S. mail to a federal judge might find the Postal Inspection Service, Bureau of Alcohol, Tobacco and Firearms (ATF), and the FBI working together as a task force. However, it is safe to say that of all the federal agencies, the FBI is the one best described as having general rather than special or limited investigative responsibilities when matters of federal jurisdiction are involved. Of course, these limitations do not prevent federal agencies from rendering assistance to local or state agencies when asked to do so.

Thus, there are distinctions in terms of who conducts investigations even within the ranks of the federal agencies. As with police departments, the federal uniformed law enforcement services tend to focus on crime prevention and the protection of U.S. government property; nonuniformed personnel concentrate on criminal investigations. Of course, the federal investigative agencies also may conduct noncriminal investigations. As an example, the FBI conducts its own background investigations on applicants seeking employment with that agency. As noted in Chapter 1, applicant background investigations for many of the other federal departments and agencies are made by the OPM.

Both in Chapter 1 and this chapter we noted that the specific jurisdictional responsibilities of each of the various federal agencies are prescribed by statute. However, among the most restricted of federal investigators are those employed in the different Offices of Inspectors General. Before the U.S. Congress passed the Inspector General Act of 1978,[1] inspectors general at the federal level were found only in the armed services, not in civilian departments or agencies. When passed, the act created the Office of Inspector General and Auditor General in seven executive departments and six executive agencies so as to deal with "fraud, abuse, waste and mismanagement in the programs and operations" of those departments and agencies. Furthermore, when the act was amended in 1988,[2] one of the specifically assigned charges addressed to all was to prevent and *detect* fraud and abuse. Thus in order to protect the integrity of their respective organizations' programs and operations, they have been given criminal investigative responsibilities.

PRIVATE INVESTIGATORS

Chapter 1 also took note of the historical role of private persons in the field of investigations. Even though most criminal investigations today are conducted by various government agencies, any discussion of investigations would be incomplete if it failed to take into account those that may be done by private persons, which may involve both criminal and noncriminal matters. For instance, people engaged in research really are investigators, but their work has no relationship to the criminal justice system, or even to the legal system in general. Today, all facets of the news media employ investigative reporters. However, for the purposes of this chapter, we focus only on those who either conduct criminal investigations or need to be aware of how they are conducted. Among these people are licensed private investigators, private security management personnel, and attorneys.

Private persons who can satisfy the requirements of the states in which they intend to do business may be licensed as private investigators. The requirements may vary from state to state, but they generally call for applicants to be not less than a certain age, have no criminal record, be able to be bonded, and possibly to have at least some investigative experience. Not infrequently, these same statutes will authorize them to engage in related activities such as offering contract security services.

Licensed private investigators may conduct a wide range of investigations. Occasionally, if funds to pay them are available, they are hired by defense counsel in criminal cases to help prove a defendant's innocence. They also may be employed by both plaintiffs' and defendants' lawyers in a variety of civil cases, including those based on, but not necessarily limited to, tort and domestic relations matters, environmental protection issues, and insurance claims.

In addition, there may be times when businesses and institutions, whether with or without their own security departments, have reason to suspect that some employees are engaged in questionable activities, most often stealing, or possibly using or selling illegal drugs at work. This may prompt hiring private investigators, who also offer security-related services, for the purpose of placing undercover operatives in the workplace. When this is done, the objective is to identify the employees and collect sufficient evidence to justify their being disciplined or terminated, and not infrequently so that the matter can be referred to the authorities for prosecution.

Proprietary security personnel, who are on an entity's payroll rather than a contractor's, and who do not necessarily have to be licensed, also conduct a variety of investigations for their employers. Normally, they would investigate all matters related to questionable employee activities, both criminal, such as those mentioned in the preceding paragraph, and noncriminal, such as policy violations. Not surprisingly, many insurance companies employ their own investigators to look into the filing of suspected fraudulent claims. Bank investigators work on credit card fraud and counterfeiting cases, and those who work for public utility companies conduct investigations when services are stolen.

Attorneys, especially litigators, whether in a civil practice or practitioners in the criminal justice system, dare not go into court unprepared. In fact, they cannot even think about entering into negotiations with a view to an out-of-court settlement or a plea bargain unless they know both the strengths and weaknesses of their client's position. Winning a lawsuit in either a criminal or civil case requires proof. Proof depends on the quality and quantity of evidence, and evidence is collected by investigators.

Thus attorneys, whether employed by the government or engaged in private practice, also are among those who conduct investigations. True, some may be fortunate enough to have access to investigators, but since they are the ones who ultimately must evaluate the quality and quantity of the evidence presented to them by their investigators, it is to their advantage to understand what investigations are all about. Certainly, this is best illustrated by the close working relationship that must exist between prosecutors and police or federal investigators if the government's position is to prevail. This is equally true in the case of some large law firms that employ their own full-time investigators. For lawyers who do not have access to their own investigators, the responsibility for and task of collecting evidence, which is the essence of a trial practice, is theirs.

SUMMARY

For most people to whom the question "Who conducts investigations?" would be posed, the answer would be relatively easy: the police. However, that answer would be an oversimplification.

Even when the police are involved, there are different levels of participation in the investigative process. We have seen that as a general rule patrol personnel, whether in local or state police agencies or sheriffs' departments, play a limited role in investigations. Their primary involvement consists of a preliminary investigation conducted upon their arrival at the scene and providing whatever help the investigators may ask of them. Of course, this may vary depending on any given department's size and needs. This is also true of the role of uniformed federal police officers.

As a rule, investigations based on violations of state law are conducted by detectives in local and state police agencies and sheriffs' departments. Whatever limitations are imposed upon them are based on territorial issues, not on questions of substantive law. In contrast, investigations of violations of federal law are limited to the specific agency or agencies to which particular offenses, or particularized investigations such as those handled by the OPM, are or may be assigned.

However, to assume that only government employees conduct investigations would be wrong. Private persons conducted investigations, including those of a criminal nature, long before such matters were considered to be a proper government function. Today, private investigators continue to provide investigative services for individual clients, businesses and institutions, and attorneys.

The explosion of corporate security departments, particularly since the end of World War II, has been accompanied by the noticeable role of proprietary security personnel in the field of investigations. Although much of their work involves noncriminal matters, they also conduct criminal investigations to determine whether there is sufficient evidence to warrant a referral to the authorities, or if there merely is enough to justify administrative action by the employer.

Both government and private attorneys, especially those who litigate and know that they must have evidence to prove their cases, also conduct investigations either directly or indirectly. Some must do their own investigations. However, even those with access to investigators are involved. Realistically, their ability to properly evaluate the evidence collected by their investigators means that they are indirectly involved in an investigation.

REVIEW QUESTIONS

1. Who was Sir Arthur Conan Doyle, and for what is he best known?
2. Were Eliot Ness and Melvin Purvis fictional or real characters? For what are they remembered?
3. Although local and state police agencies have investigators, sheriffs' departments may not. Under what circumstances would a sheriff's department not have its own investigators?
4. Are all government investigations criminal in nature? If not, what other types of investigations are conducted?
5. Explain the difference between police and federal investigative agencies in terms of the laws enforced.
6. Who conducts most applicant background investigations for agencies of the U.S. government?

7. Of all the federal investigative agencies, which one is best described as being responsible for the broadest range of investigations?

8. What is the legal basis for inspectors general in the various executive departments and agencies to conduct investigations?

9. Do private investigators and corporate security personnel conduct investigations in the normally accepted sense of the word?

10. In what ways do attorneys, particularly litigators, function as investigators?

NOTES

1. Pub. L. No. 95-452.
2. Inspector General Act of 1978 as amended by Inspector General Act Amendments of 1988, Pub. L. 100-504; 102 Stat. 2515.

Chapter 4

— ❖ —

Characteristics
of a Good Investigator

Reportedly, someone once said that heroes were made, not born. One is tempted to ask whether or not this is equally true of good investigators—can they be made or do they have to be born? Certainly, those who work for the various investigative agencies of the federal government, and for larger police departments, have the benefit of training. Today, even police personnel in smaller law enforcement agencies are trained, and if their investigators have not been given specialized training in the field of investigations before being assigned to such duties, they at least have learned the fundamentals from the experience that they gained as patrol officers conducting preliminary investigations. But this raises yet another question: is training alone enough to make them *good* investigators?

According to the National Institute of Justice, the eleven most commonly desired traits for investigators are as follows:

Motivation	Street knowledge	Dedication
Intuition	Teamwork	Integrity
Stability	Persistence	Reliability
Judgment	Intelligence	

Without disputing the desirability or necessity of these traits, a good investigator also needs to have a retentive memory, patience, and good powers of observation. He or she also must pay attention to detail.

A look at what each of these attributes really means in terms of their application to investigators suggests that though the importance of street knowledge and teamwork can be learned from experience, realistically none of the other qualities can be taught in a classroom setting or learned by doing; they are ingrained. Another important characteristic is complete objectivity in all matters investigated, criminal or other. Consequently, in examining these various traits, a logical starting point is the need for objectivity and integrity.

INTEGRITY AND OBJECTIVITY

Understanding and fully appreciating an investigator's impact on the persons or organizations under investigation is imperative. In criminal cases, prosecutors guide and direct the investigators. Nevertheless, they also must depend on them for the collection and preservation of the evidence needed for a successful prosecution. Consequently, criminal investigators who are not objective, or who lack integrity, conceivably can be responsible for a guilty person's acquittal, an innocent person's imprisonment, fine, or possibly even death, or the ruination of an organization's reputation. In civil matters, they may be responsible for an unfair judgment, and in noncriminal cases, such as applicant investigations, they unfairly may cost an otherwise qualified person a chance to be gainfully employed.

The importance of integrity and objectivity has been and continues to be commented upon. For instance, many years ago Scotland Yard showed its concern with the adoption of the precept "Above all, it is far better to let ten guilty persons escape than that one innocent person should be falsely accused."[1] While speaking at the Harvard Law School in November 1995, William Bratton, then New York City's police commissioner, said, "I know that the price of total integrity may be that we lose a few more cases. . . . Maybe we'll lose a lot more. And when we lose a case or two I won't mind hearing a judge say 'But officer, I would like to compliment you on your honesty.'"[2] And the *New York Times* quoted Richard A. Brown, district attorney for Queens County, who said, "You've got to impress upon the police officers that they are going to lose cases if the perception exists that they are bending the truth."[3]

Contrast the foregoing attitudes about integrity and objectivity with information reported in a November 30, 1995, item in *The Boston Globe* concerning Jean Lewis, a federal investigator whose work on the Madison Guaranty Savings and Loan case included allegations of a diversion of depositor funds to the Whitewater land venture and gubernatorial campaign of the then Governor Bill Clinton. In testimony before the Senate Whitewater Committee, she acknowledged not only that she was a conservative Republican, but also that in 1992, a month before starting the investigation, she had written a letter to a friend in which she referred to

Clinton as a "lying bastard." The same newspaper article said that the August 31, 1992, handwritten notes of FBI special agent Steve Irons, assigned to Little Rock, Arkansas, contained a reference to Lewis's having told him that her work on the Madison case "could alter history."[4] Certainly, this information at the very least suggests a lack of objectivity on Lewis's part as an investigator in this particular case.

By no means are these failings necessarily confined to criminal or even governmental investigations. They also are, or should be, matters of concern in a corporate environment when security personnel undertake inquiries involving employees. This, too, warrants illustration. An audit manager for a multinational corporation, returning from an internal audit of a country headquarters office, reported that he had uncovered information that caused him to believe that a senior manager was engaged in activities detrimental to the employer and profitable to himself. The nature of the allegations obliged the corporate security director to personally conduct the investigation.

When interviewed, the audit manager repeatedly stated that the suspect manager was as "guilty as hell." He repeated this whenever he asked the security director about the investigation's progress. He was visibly annoyed when told not only that it was too early in the investigation to come to any conclusion, but also that the final outcome would be based solely on the facts and evidence. The completed investigation showed only that the suspect was guilty of extremely poor judgment in terms of his relationships with certain people and suppliers; there was no evidence either of a crime or of his having personally benefited from his activities.

MOTIVATION

Important in most types of work, motivation often is thought of as a supervisory or managerial function—a need to motivate one's subordinates to do a good job. Although superiors in police or investigative agencies can help motivate investigators, much of their motivation is self-generated. Good investigators are motivated by more than the efforts of their superiors or the prestige normally associated with the job. True, identification as a federal agent or having the "gold shield," increased earnings, and not having to wear a uniform are satisfying, but investigators' primary motivation comes from knowing that their skills will enable them to be assigned to the more challenging, complex, seemingly insoluble, and interminable cases. For truly good investigators, the more difficult an investigation, the greater the motivation to solve it. Furthermore, consciously or subconsciously, they also are motivated by knowing that once their ability has been recognized, they will continue being assigned to high-profile investigations.

STREET KNOWLEDGE

Street knowledge refers to "being wise in the ways of the world." Applicable to all good investigators, it is particularly important to those assigned to criminal investigations. Investigators who lack this characteristic often find it hard to relate to and communicate with many of the people with whom they must deal in the course of their work, whether they are sources of information, witnesses, confidential informants, or suspects. Street knowledge also helps explain why, for police as distinguished from federal agency investigators, promotions to detective usually are made from the ranks of uniformed or plainclothes officers as rewards for good police work rather than on the basis of examinations. Their exposure to people whose backgrounds and life experiences are far different from their own has given them an invaluable perspective that makes it easier for them to work more effectively.

Perhaps this trait's importance can be illustrated by the experience of an FBI special agent who happened to have certain skills in a language with which no other agent was familiar. Knowing this particular language, its idiomatic expressions and dialects, and the customs and holidays of the people who spoke it, not only helped him greatly with many of his cases, but it also allowed him to help other agents whose work involved contact with members of this particular ethnic group.

INTELLIGENCE

Three particular definitions of *intelligence* are applicable in relation to the characteristics of good investigators. One is the ability to acquire and retain knowledge; another is the ability to respond quickly and successfully to new situations; the third is the use of the faculty of reason in solving problems. One might also add a quotation from René Descartes (1596–1650), the French philosopher and mathematician: "It is not enough to have a good mind; the main thing is to use it well."[5]

Investigations within both the public and private sectors, criminal and noncriminal, are based on problems for which solutions are being sought. In some cases, they may be relatively easy to obtain and pose but a minimal challenge to the investigator. In others, they may be so difficult as to seem insoluble; in still others, they actually may be insoluble. However, change is something good investigators must be ever mindful of, and being able to compensate for change can tax their intelligence.

For instance, the elements of larceny or fraud may be no different today than they have been for years, yet some of the methods used to commit these crimes may have been radically altered as a result of computer technology. Investigators also must deal with new offenses, some of which are linked to the evolution of people and machines. Investigators must be able to use their minds to adjust to these changes.

To be able to think logically, whether using inductive or deductive reasoning, is critical for investigators, but if their thought processes are stymied by newness their ability to solve cases and their value as investigators decrease. When they can adjust, the opposite is true. To illustrate, child pornography is a matter of increasing concern to both parents and the government. The situation's gravity has been heightened by the illicit use by a few online subscribers of one of the nation's largest computer networks to peddle such material. In pursuing its investigation, a decision was made by the FBI to go undercover,[6] something that obviously could not be done without intelligent personnel who understood how both computers and networks function.

Today, computers also play a major role in fraud cases. Investigators assigned to such cases must have the intelligence to understand precisely how computers are used to perpetrate the fraud. Still another example of how investigators' intelligence, in the broadest sense, can be used to benefit law enforcement and the general public is the assistance rendered to police agencies by the special agents assigned to the FBI's Behavioral Science Unit or the work of police personnel and federal agents who serve as hostage negotiators in extremely sensitive situations.

Good investigators who use their intelligence serve as good role models for persons interested in getting jobs in the field of investigations. However, when law enforcement personnel fail to use their intelligence, they also can make the work of investigators much harder and time consuming. When this happens, they may be guilty of adding an element of risk for certain members of the community.

Here is a good example. Several hours before his arrest, a friend of a California reserve deputy sheriff told her he had been involved in the death of a model, a matter then under investigation by detectives. The deputy later tried to explain her not having told the detectives by saying she did not believe her friend because he had a reputation as a practical joker.[7] One cannot ignore what this failure could have meant in terms of both additional investigative time and risk to the general public if the friend had fled the state in the time between his admitted involvement and his arrest.

INTUITION

One definition of *intuition* in *Webster's New World Dictionary* is "the immediate knowing or learning of something without the conscious use of reasoning; instantaneous apprehension." Two synonyms for the word are "hunch" and "sixth sense." Intuition can be an invaluable ally of good investigators.

Although the value of intuition can be illustrated in various ways, we offer two examples. In one, investigators working on a series of jewelry store robberies have detected a certain commonality among the victims with respect to the type of jewelry sold, neighborhoods in which the stores were located, and time of day when the robberies took place. On the basis of what the investigators know, intuition tells them which jewelry store most likely will be the next target. They put that particular store under physical surveillance and succeeded in arresting the perpetrators.

The other example also involves surveillance, but under a different set of circumstances. The case involves espionage against the United States; the subject of the investigation—a foreign diplomat—is known to the investigators; his diplomatic status adds to the investigation's delicacy. This makes it necessary for those conducting the surveillance to exercise caution to avoid alerting him to the fact that he is being watched. Nevertheless, he must be kept under surveillance as he moves about the city in order to learn with whom he meets so that these people can be identified and investigated as his possible sources of information. To minimize the risk of detection, and possible compromise of the investigation, the investigators have become so familiar with the subject that, on occasion, they will discontinue the surveillance and rely on their intuition in terms of where and when it can be easily resumed.

TEAMWORK

John Donne (1573–1631), an English poet and clergyman, wrote that "No man is an island, entire of itself; every man is a piece of the continent."[8] This quotation's sentiment has application to all good investigators; they cannot hope to do their jobs, and especially to do them well, if they prefer to work alone. This truth persists regardless of the types of investigative agencies for which they work or the differences in their operating procedures.

The importance of teamwork cannot be overemphasized in those situations in which offenses subject to a city police or sheriff's department or state police agency's jurisdiction have been committed and the first response is by uniformed patrol personnel. If the crime is to be solved—that is, the perpetrator is identified, apprehended, prosecuted, and punished—there must be effective teamwork from the inception of the preliminary investigation through sentencing. This requires the fullest cooperation among the first responders to the crime scene who conduct the preliminary investigation, the detectives to whom the case is assigned for investigation, and the assistant district attorney or prosecutor who will present the state's case in court. If there is physical evidence, the crime laboratory's participation and cooperation are mandatory; the same is true with regard to the medical examiner when a cause of death is questionable.

Teamwork is equally important in federal agencies' investigations. Not only do the investigators need the cooperation of all pertinent personnel within their own offices, such as technical, clerical, and secretarial personnel, but they often may need some help from other field offices. As an example, the FBI sets time frames within which investigative reports must be submitted; agents who do not adhere to those deadlines are considered delinquent. Consequently, an agent has set out investigative leads for coverage by another field office, he or she must rely on teamwork from the other office's agent to whom the case was assigned if the report is to be submitted on time. It is not uncommon for federal agencies to seek help from police agencies in the area in certain types of investigations, or vice versa. In other words, teamwork is essential at all levels of investigations. Investigators who are not team players will find that success does not come easily.

DEDICATION

Good investigators are singularly dedicated to their work and are in some respects comparable to members of the clergy insofar as their devotion to the job is concerned. Generally highly regarded and respected, ministers, rabbis, and priests rarely place limits on what they are prepared and willing to do for their churches or synagogues and congregants, or on when they are available to serve them. Highly focused, good investigators, frequently will make personal sacrifices when necessary.

Good investigators are not "clock-watchers." Coming to work earlier or staying later than prescribed hours is common, as is taking less than the time allowed for lunch or, when necessary, foregoing it altogether. Overtime pay is not the predominant factor that prompts investigators to devote so much of their time and energy to solving cases. Dedication to their work frequently finds them making adjustments to their private lives, and willingness to put what they see as the job's needs ahead of their families' needs sometimes wreaks havoc with their personal lives.

Perhaps an example or two can better illustrate what dedication means. Probably no better examples of dedicated investigators can be found than among FBI special agents, particularly during the Hoover years when agents were not paid overtime. At a time when there were far fewer resident agencies (a field division's branch offices) than there are today, road work had to be assigned to some agents. This was especially true of those field divisions whose headquarters were located in some of the midwestern or western states where the population did not justify having even a resident agency let alone a field office. Agents assigned road work handled bureau investigations when their field divisions were the office of origin, they covered leads from other divisions, and they were expected to establish and maintain contact with local police departments and sheriffs' offices. In many cases, the distances involved and number of cases assigned to any one agent meant relatively long absences from home.

FBI agents working in large cities also exemplified dedication. For instance, it was not unusual for those assigned espionage and foreign intelligence or internal security cases to work their regular hours, and as the workday's end approached, to learn of an unexpected development that would require an evening or possibly an overnight surveillance. This meant that those agents worked ten-hour, twelve-hour, or longer days, causing changes in personal and family plans. They did so because the work had to be done, and they were dedicated to that end.

Today, working conditions are much improved in the FBI as well as in other investigative and law enforcement agencies. Still, there is no substitute for dedication on the part of investigators if crimes are to be solved, perpetrators successfully prosecuted, noncriminal cases closed, and the public's confidence in the process sustained.

STABILITY AND RELIABILITY

Roget's International Thesaurus cites five synonyms for *stability:* "substantiality, permanence, firmness, strength, and reliability." Each represents important traits for law enforcement personnel generally. However, for investigators, stability means not only that everyone working on a case can be counted on to do his or her part, but also that investigators are emotionally stable considering the stress under which they may have to work.

It is immaterial whether it is a patrol officer conducting a preliminary investigation, a crime scene technician, a detective or other investigator, or an evidence examiner in a forensic laboratory. If that person cannot be relied upon to handle his or her part of the investigation in a thorough and meticulous way, the final outcome may be jeopardized.

Stability, or reliability, also means that good investigators must be able to control their emotions even under the most trying conditions. For instance, homicide investigations can be emotionally trying even for seasoned investigators. Crime scenes where children are victims or adult deaths are particularly heinous, or being present at autopsies, which investigators attend in order to benefit from a medical examiner's observations, can be both unpleasant and highly charged emotionally. Yet good investigators cannot permit themselves to be swayed or influenced by what they have seen. If they are, and they subsequently identify and arrest the perpetrators and the case goes to trial, they can be certain that their reliability will be challenged by defense counsel in an effort to discredit the prosecution's case.

PERSISTENCE AND PATIENCE

Persistence and patience have a common meaning: perseverance. Edmund Burke (1729–1797), an English statesman, said, in reflecting on the French Revolution, "Our patience will achieve more than our force."[9] Euripides (fifth century B.C.), a Greek tragic dramatist, wrote, "To persevere, trusting in what hopes he has, is courage in a man. The coward despairs."[10]

Unfortunately, many who are uninitiated but interested in investigations do not understand the importance of persistence and patience as necessary attributes of good investigators. No doubt this is largely due to their exposure to the entertainment industry's portrayals of investigations and investigators. In motion pictures, police, private detectives, or government agents usually solve even the most complex cases in ninety or so minutes. In those made-for-television programs, crimes are solved, arrests made, and trials completed all within sixty to ninety minutes, minus time out for commercials. Realistically, many investigations are not completed in a matter of days, let alone hours. In fact, some never are solved.

It is essential for aspiring investigators to understand the importance and application of persistence and patience, along with all the other characteristics, and to be able to distinguish real from fictional situations. The following cases are worth noting because they illustrate what real-life investigators may confront.

❖ Case 4-1

The *New York Times* for February 18, 1996, noted that although Swedish investigators working on the murder of Olaf Palme, the prime minister of Sweden, and the shooting of his wife on February 8, 1986, have followed up on 18,000 leads, they had not yet found the murder weapon. Despite the assignment of more than 300 detectives at the height of the investigation, 14 continue to work on the case.[11]

❖ Case 4-2

Despite its resources, it took the FBI more than seventeen years before it succeeded in taking into custody a man believed to be the "Unabomber." Over that period, his activities resulted in the explosion of sixteen bombs, the deaths of three people, and injuries to twenty-three others.

❖ Case 4-3

A lead paragraph in a newspaper article reads: "Almost three decades after a 7-year-old girl was stabbed to death in downtown Elizabeth, New

Jersey, eight witnesses have resurfaced and are trying to help detectives crack one of New Jersey's most puzzling homicides." It goes on to say that since late October 1995, the witnesses, whose homes now are scattered around the eastern United States, have been visited by detectives and shown photographs of a man who was not among the many people interviewed in the investigation's early years.[12]

❖ Case 4-4

About 8:45 P.M., November 2, 1981, three men shot and killed a surgical resident from New York's Columbia-Presbyterian Medical Center while attempting to rob him. All leads had been exhausted, yet the detective who had worked the case continued to speak with friends and associates of a suspect whom he had interviewed early in 1982 relative to another killing. When he learned from another detective that a man had threatened a group of people with a 9-millimeter pistol, and reportedly made a statement (not a confession) about the 1981 killing, that the police believed only the killer or killers would know, he arrested the subject for the 1981 incident.[13]

❖ Case 4-5

The body of a female jogger, presumably killed sometime the night of September 16, 1995, was found in New York City's Central Park the next morning. Within two days, detectives assigned to the investigation had interviewed scores of joggers, bicyclists, and skaters searching for leads; they also responded to about sixty calls placed to the police department's anonymous tip line. After thirty-five days of exhaustive investigation, and interviewing more than a hundred homeless people in a search for witnesses, the fifty detectives working the case had little to go on and hoped for a break.[14]

❖ Case 4-6

L. Richard Rosenberg, a builder and developer, was killed sometime after 5:30 P.M., November 9, 1995. He was described as having enemies in many places, a frequent opponent of unions and tenants' groups, and a plaintiff or defendant in more than eighty cases. New York State Police investigators assigned to the case would interview all of Rosenberg's former and current business associates, as well as every resident of his 834-unit apartment complex, in their effort to identify and apprehend his killer.[15]

❖ Case 4-7

Around 1992, the U.S. Customs Service Miami office received a complaint alleging that a Korean organized crime ring was manufacturing clothing, handbags, and sporting goods overseas and importing the goods into the United States under counterfeit labels as part of a $300 billion illegal business. After a two-and-a-half-year investigation that tracked the flow of goods from manufacturers to distributors to sales outlets, Customs officials, in late September 1995, raided factories, warehouses, and shops in New York City.[16]

❖ Case 4-8

In 1952, a document classified "Top Secret," found on a Washington, D.C., street corner, was turned over to the FBI; it also was identified as a NATO (North American Treaty Organization) document. As a first step, the case agent, hoping to learn who might have had access to the document, interviewed a member of the NATO general staff. He asked how many people legitimately might have had access; the reply was in the neighborhood of five hundred people in the Washington area alone.

These eight cases help illustrate that unlike the entertainment industry's versions, most real-life investigations are not quickly solved. They also show that patience and perseverance are virtues for good investigators.

JUDGMENT

The need for good judgment is inherent throughout the investigative process. Investigators have to make decisions, and those decisions have to be correct. For example, it would be rare to find an agency, particularly a large one, whether at city or federal level, with so few matters requiring attention that its investigators would be assigned to only one case at a time. However, since not all the cases assigned to an individual investigator are of equal importance, each investigator must set his or her priorities with respect to the total caseload as well as to the work to be done regarding each individual investigation.

Of course, setting priorities is not the only task that requires good judgment. Some examples of the investigative process where good judgment is required include the following:

What should be the order in which witnesses are interviewed?

In considering the resources needed for physical or electronic surveillances, would either or both be productive?

Would a court be receptive to authorizing electronic surveillance?

How much detail about an investigation should be made available to the news media?

If it appears that a confidential informant might be in a position to provide some information, is the informant sufficiently reliable?

When two or more suspects appear to be involved, is there a possibility that one can be turned into an informant?

Once there appears to be a logical suspect, at what point should he or she be brought in for interview or interrogation?

Failing to exercise good judgment with respect to any of these examples, or in the many other aspects of the investigative process, might well jeopardize an investigation and could put a prosecution at risk. Imagine the consequences if an application for a search warrant was based on information from a confidential informant whose reliability was questionable, or if a logical suspect were to be interviewed prematurely. It is unlikely that police departments or other investigative agencies, whether public or private, will retain investigators whose good judgment is in doubt.

Exercising good judgment with respect to the investigative process and the handling of victims, witnesses, subjects, and the news media is important; it also must be exercised in maintaining the confidentiality and confidence of sources of information and informants. Good judgment also helps lessen the risk of questions being raised about investigators' ethics and the way in which they work their cases.

At the outset of this chapter, we added characteristics other than those cited by the National Institute of Justice to the list of traits needed by good investigators. Among them were a retentive memory, good powers of observation, and attention to detail. As with the others, their value is best illustrated by examples.

In discussing persistence and patience, we cited several actual cases. Among them was Case 4-4, a July 1994 arrest for a November 1981 homicide. A subject was brought in for booking on a completely different matter in the precinct to which a detective, who in 1981 was on the Manhattan homicide squad, now worked. When the detective learned about the circumstances of the suspect's current arrest, it was his memory and his noting similarities between the latest offense and the earlier murder that resulted in the subject's homicide arrest.

The first order of business for an FBI agent assigned a four-year-old espionage case was a complete review of the eighteen-volume case file. The recipients of information were known; the identity of the person who made it available was not. Identifying the unknown subject (UNSUB) was critical. Some months after the initial file review, the agent received a report from another field office covering leads that had been sent to it. Reading that report, he recalled information that he had seen in the eighteen volumes relating to a person whose name now appeared in the report. His retentive memory made it possible to positively identify the UNSUB in relatively short order.

Other significant assets include being observant, alert, and attentive to detail. Examples help illustrate their importance.

❖ Case 4-9

About 1:32 P.M., December 21, 1994, a burst of flames in a New York City subway car injured forty-one people. At 2:10 P.M., two police officers saw a man at another subway station wearing blue jeans, the legs of which were singed and shredded. His legs were bloodied below the knees, his arms were burned, his facial skin was peeling away, and through his tattered gloves, they noticed severe burn marks on his knuckles. They called an ambulance.[17] Enroute to the hospital, they heard a description of a suspect in a subway explosion; it matched that of the man in the ambulance. As a result of their being observant and alert, less than an hour after the subway explosion and fire, the police had a likely suspect for this investigation and a similar incident that had occurred a week before.

❖ Case 4-10

On a February morning, a nightgown-clad woman was found impaled on three spikes of a metal fence five floors below her apartment. Since there were no signs of a struggle and everything seemed to be in order, it had the appearance of a suicide. However, the detectives were puzzled by two things that made them refuse to call this a suicide: a 1/2-inch screw on the victim's bedsheet, and the fact that she had landed differently from others who committed suicide by jumping out windows or off ledges. The screw was inconsistent with her meticulously clean apartment, and if she intended to commit suicide, she would have jumped from the ledge head first, away from the building. The crime scene suggested she had intended to land feet first. Because of their observations, attention to detail, and sound judgment, after a four-month investigation, detectives determined that the victim had jumped while trying to escape from robbers. The two perpetrators were arrested.[18]

❖ Case 4-11

At about 1:40 A.M., February 17, 1995, a prostitute and her customer checked into a hotel in New York City's East Village for a short stay. However, not until almost four hours later was she found in the room, nude, face down on the bed. The night of June 29 another prostitute and her customer checked into a hotel; at 1:15 P.M., June 30, her partially nude body was found in the room, face down on the bed, her hands tied. Sometime between 12:30 and 1:40 A.M., September 21, a third prostitute was raped and sodomized in Chinatown by a man who had stalked her, followed her into her apartment building where he displayed a gun, forced her to the roof, and tried to strangle her. There had been intercourse with the first two victims, but not with the third.[19] The detectives, attentive to such details as the victims' lifestyle, similarities in the nature of the crimes, and the ways and neighborhood in which they were committed, concluded that a single perpetrator committed all three.

Even though arrests were not made in all the cases cited, they illustrate the importance of good powers of observation, alertness, and attention to detail. In Case 4-10, these traits caused the investigators to treat the victim's death as a homicide instead of a suicide. In Case 4-11, these characteristics helped the detectives connect the three homicides and attribute them to one person.

SUMMARY

It is unlikely that any empirical research will ever be done to determine whether or not good investigators can learn these commonly desired characteristics, or if they are inborn. In any event, unless they either have or can acquire these traits, acceptable solutions to, and the ability to close, cases becomes exceedingly difficult.

Each characteristic discussed may have some rather distinct features of its own, but all of them must come together for optimum success in solving and closing cases. It is difficult to say which of the characteristics is of most value to an investigator since each, in its own way, can make a significant contribution.

Since investigations require a cooperative effort, teamwork is essential, but a team whose members are not motivated or dedicated to the task ahead, or who lack stability or are considered unreliable, risk failure or being slow in achieving success. Unless street knowledge and intuition are accompanied by sound judgment, there is no guarantee of success. Examples have been given to illustrate the value of persistence, patience, a retentive memory, attention to detail, and the power of observation.

Good investigators most likely would say integrity and objectivity are the traits of most importance because of the impact that they can have not only on their investigations, but also on the agencies that they represent, on the subjects of investigations in criminal cases, and on the criminal justice system itself. Scotland Yard's precept and the remarks of New York City's police commissioner about honesty, quoted earlier in this chapter, must be the cornerstone of the investigative process. For persons to be investigated and convicted of crimes they did not commit because an investigator lacks integrity or objectivity is an injustice. No less is it an injustice if a person is denied employment, or a recovery for an injury in a civil lawsuit, because of an investigator's prejudices or personal dislikes.

REVIEW QUESTIONS

1. Name the National Institute of Justice's eleven most desirable traits for investigators.
2. What other traits are equally desirable?
3. Are good investigators more likely to be born with or to acquire the needed characteristics? Why?
4. Why are integrity and objectivity important traits for all investigators regardless of the types of cases handled?
5. What is the Scotland Yard precept?
6. Give an example of an investigator's prejudice.
7. What motivational characteristics distinguish investigators from other people?
8. What is meant by "street knowledge"? Why is it an important characteristic?
9. Give an example of how good investigators use their intelligence.
10. Illustrate how attention to detail can influence the course of an investigation.

NOTES

1. George Dilnot, *Great Detectives and Their Methods* (Boston: Houghton Mifflin, 1928), pp. 4, 7, 9, 120.
2. "Bratton Announces Plan to Train Officers to Testify," *New York Times,* November 15, 1995, p. B3.
3. Ibid.
4. "Whitewater Investigator Challenged as GOP Conservative," *The Boston Globe,* November 30, 1995, p. 8.
5. René Descartes, *Discourse on Method* (1639), p. 1.
6. "As Pornography Arrests Grow, So Do Plans for Computer Stings," *New York Times,* September 16, 1995, pp. 1, 8.
7. "Man Charged in Murder Is Linked to 24 Killings," *The Boston Globe,* November 30, 1995, p. 66.
8. John Donne, *Devotions* (1624), p. 17.
9. Edmund Burke, *Reflections on the Revolution in France* (1790).
10. Euripides, *Heracles* (c. 422 B.C.), translated by William Arrowsmith.
11. "Swedes Haunted by Palme's Killing, Unsolved After 10 Years," *New York Times,* February 18, 1996, p. 13.
12. "After 30 Years New Clue Pursued in Unsolved Killing," *New York Times,* November 30, 1995, p. B11.
13. "After 13 Years, an Arrest in a Manhattan Doctor's Slaying," *New York Times,* July 31, 1994, pp. 33, 35.
14. "Possible Witnesses and Tips Are Focus of Jogger Murder Investigation"; "Evidence Is Elusive in Central Park Jogger Killing," *New York Times,* September 20, 1995, p. B4; October 23, 1995, p. B3.

15. "The Late Mr. Rosenberg Left a Mystery Behind," *New York Times,* November 21, 1995, p. B4.

16. "Agents Raid Counterfeiters of Apparel," *New York Times,* September 28, 1995, pp. B1, B3.

17. "Suddenly, Injured Man Is Target of Inquiry," *New York Times,* December 22, 1994, pp. A1, B6.

18. "Tiny Clue Prevents a Slaying from Being Listed as a Suicide," *New York Times,* August 27, 1995, p. 34.

19. "Serial Killer May Be at Large, Police Say," *New York Times,* September 28, 1995, p. B3.

Chapter 5

How Investigations Are Initiated

Investigations are initiated in different ways; the differences depend largely upon who conducts them. For instance, one would like to believe that legislative bodies begin their probes solely for the betterment of government and the benefit of the people whom they represent. However, it would be naive to ignore the partisan political agenda of many such inquiries, or the opportunities afforded to legislators for much sought-after publicity. Scientists and scholars frequently are attracted by unexplored areas. Scientists see a chance to make a meaningful contribution to humankind. For scholars, it is an opportunity to add new knowledge on a subject, although some, and then only on rare occasions, undertake investigations for the express purpose of revising history to conform with their own points of view. Investigative reporters often start inquiries about someone or something because they have heard rumors or gotten tips that they believe are newsworthy. As a result, these types of investigations are initiated principally by those who will do the investigating, and many tend to be proactive rather than reactive.

The tendency to be proactive rather than reactive contrasts sharply with the way most investigations are undertaken by police departments or federal agencies, as well as most corporate security departments. True, under certain controlled conditions, the police or federal authorities may undertake investigations on their own initiative, possibly in connection with drug cases or for strategic intelligence purposes. However, the majority of cases, both criminal and noncriminal, assigned to detectives or federal investigators are in response to complaints filed with the agency or requests from authorized sources. This procedure also is followed by ethical and professionally managed security departments. That law enforcement agencies and security departments follow these practices for initiating the majority of their investigations is a characteristic of how inquiries are undertaken in a democratic society.

Despite the differences between how law enforcement and security begin their investigations, and the ways that others are begun, this is not to suggest that there necessarily is uniformity in terms of how the former are initiated. As an example, one finds that the procedures for police departments to open inquiries are not the same as those employed by federal agencies.

FEDERAL AGENCIES AND CORPORATE SECURITY DEPARTMENTS

For illustrative purposes only, since the differences in noncriminal investigations are fewer, we look first at the way in which noncriminal inquiries are begun by law enforcement agencies and corporate security departments. Most police noncriminal inquiries involve applicants for appointment to an agency, such as a city or state police department or a sheriff's department. At some point in the hiring process, if the department personnel believe an individual is a viable candidate for appointment, the applicant's file will be forwarded to the departmental unit responsible for background investigations. The investigation then is assigned to an investigator, and only then does he or she begin an inquiry.

Although the same in principle, applicant investigations for federal employment are handled somewhat differently. Some federal agencies, such as the FBI, DEA, and Secret Service, among others, conduct their own background investigations. The Office of Personnel Management conducts most of the other inquiries.

To better understand how such investigations are initiated, a look at the FBI's applicant procedure may be instructive. Once an applicant has satisfactorily completed all the preliminary stages of the hiring process and becomes a serious candidate for appointment, the office through which the application has been made, called the "office of origin," will undertake a detailed background investigation. The task is assigned to a special agent on the applicant squad. If all the investigative leads are within the office of origin's territory, the case agent does the entire investigation. However, if the applicant has lived, worked, or gone to school outside this geographic area, the case agent will direct investigative leads to other offices for coverage. No investigation will be undertaken by any office until it is appropriate as part of the appointment process.

Regarding applicants for private-sector employment, it is unlikely that background investigations, in the sense that the word is used here, will be conducted. However, in-depth inquiries may be considered both necessary and advisable for certain positions. Should this be the case, the investigation may be done by corporate security personnel (if such a department exists), by a private investigator, or by both of them. Regardless of who will conduct the investigation, no inquiry should be initiated until the prospective employer authorizes it.

An exception to the rule for initiating noncriminal investigations is the work of the National Transportation Safety Board (NTSB), a federal government agency. When accidents involving some form of transportation occur, other than those related to automobiles, the NTSB responds and begins an inquiry, retaining investigative responsibility unless evidence suggests the disaster was caused by some form of criminal activity. In that case, it assumes a support role.

Thus it is evident that neither law enforcement nor private security departments or agencies initiate even noncriminal investigations without a specific need for them. A more detailed discussion of the actual applicant investigation process appears in Chapter 18.

Applicant investigations aside, corporate security personnel also are called upon to investigate legitimate business concerns, such as conflicts of interest and other violations of company policy. Although this is a proper security function, there should not be any inquiry until the department head has received either allegations of misconduct or a specific request for an investigation from an authorized corporate officer. For a security director to initiate an inquiry on his or her own initiative would be improper; there must be a good reason for doing so. The characteristics of good investigators, discussed in Chapter 4, particularly integrity and objectivity, are as important for private-sector investigators as they are for those employed by police or federal agencies.

POLICE AND SHERIFFS' DEPARTMENTS

In initiating criminal investigations, the process for police and sheriffs' departments is different from that of federal agencies and corporate security. Although we examine law enforcement jurisdictional issues in detail in Chapter 7, the concept of jurisdiction cannot be ignored in considering how investigations are initiated. In doing so we note that in many ways the question of jurisdiction is considerably less complex for police departments than it is for federal agencies.

This is largely due to two factors. First, a number of crimes may be violations of both state and federal laws. For instance, most bank robberies are both a state and federal offense. Consequently, a local police department has as much justification for opening a bank robbery investigation as does the FBI. Second, as we pointed out in Chapters 1 and 3, even when a federal law is violated, the investigative jurisdiction of the various federal agencies is prescribed by statute. As an example, the FBI investigates espionage against the U.S. government in both the United States and its possessions. Thus even though the FBI may have the largest role to play in terms of statutes under its investigative jurisdiction, no single federal agency is responsible for investigating all violations of federal laws.

Let us turn then to the question of how local and state police agencies, and sheriffs' departments that engage in a full range of police services, initiate criminal investigations for which they are responsible. As stated before, in the majority of cases, they receive a complaint or they respond to an incident; then arriving at the scene, they find evidence that a crime appears to have been committed. An illustration would be a response to what initially seems to be a suicide by a handgun, but upon closer examination of the deceased, the entry wound suggests that it is a homicide.

Regardless of what prompts a police response, it is safe to say that most complaints are received in the form of telephone calls, most likely 911 calls. Other complaints may come in the form of someone speaking with a uniformed officer walking a beat or in a patrol car. On rare occasions, someone might go to a precinct house or district headquarters, or there might be a written complaint, most likely from a person who wants to remain anonymous.

Telephone complaints normally are referred to radio patrol or beat officers for a preliminary inquiry to determine if, in fact, an offense has been committed, or if there is at least probable cause to suspect that there has been a crime. The circumstances surrounding the complaint, and the responding officers' evaluation, usually will dictate whether the matter should be referred to detectives for a full-scale investigation. Patrol personnel to whom complaints are made directly will generally conduct a preliminary investigation. If they believe the matter is beyond their immediate capabilities, they will refer it for an in-depth investigation.

Complainants who appear in person are interviewed, either by desk personnel or by detectives, in an effort to find out whether there appears to be enough information to warrant at least a closer examination of the allegation that a crime has occurred, and a possible visit to the crime scene. The written, anonymous complaint is the most difficult to evaluate in terms of whether or not to undertake an investigation. This type of complaint may be referred to detectives, who may have to rely largely on their experience and intuition in evaluating it since they have no way of knowing the complainant's motive or veracity. Therefore, a constant in dealing with all complaints is that they must be considered carefully before they are referred for investigation to ensure that there is a good reason for starting an inquiry.

This same principle applies to the opening of investigations by federal agencies even though the way in which they receive complaints is different. In some cases, a person suspecting a violation of federal law might call a federal agency's office. If so, the complaint may be taken over the telephone, or the caller may ask to see an investigator. If it appears that a federal crime may have been committed, a case file will be opened and assigned to an agent for investigation. There also will be times when persons who have reason to believe that there has been or is about to be a violation of the criminal law will visit a federal agency's office where they will be interviewed by an agent on complaint duty. Again, if it seems likely that an incident has occurred or that there may be a conspiracy to commit a crime, a case will be opened and assigned for investigation. In all these situations, the federal agency receiving a complaint must determine both whether an investigation is warranted and whether the matter to be investigated falls under that particular agency's jurisdiction.

If the matter being complained of to a federal agency is not within its investigative jurisdiction, the agent taking the complaint usually will follow one of two courses of action. He or she may inform the complainant that this is a matter for another agency and suggest that the information be made available to it, or the agent will take the information and refer it to the appropriate federal agency or police or sheriff's department.

Consequently, referrals are another way in which federal agencies may get complaints that justify initiating an investigation. To illustrate, someone might complain to the Secret Service about suspected espionage, in which case the matter would be referred to the FBI, or the bureau might refer a complaint about counterfeit U.S. currency to the Secret Service.

There also may be times when circumstances suggest the commission of a series of crimes that violate both federal and state laws. For instance, a community may be confronted with a rash of bank robberies. If that occurs, the duality of jurisdiction is such that instead of both the local police department and the FBI undertaking separate investigations, it would not be at all unusual for them to work the case as a joint task force.

The circumstances surrounding the initiation of investigations by government agencies are subject to legal controls in the interest of safeguarding the public. However, private investigators, including corporate security personnel, who on occasion conduct criminal investigations, may not necessarily work under such limitations. As a result, one can only hope that they will adhere to the highest ethical standards.

Private investigators may initiate investigations if they have been retained by defense counsel. The likelihood of this happening is greatest in high-profile criminal cases, particularly if the defendant is something of a celebrity and can afford such services. In such cases, the investigation is undertaken in an effort to develop evidence that will either exonerate the defendant or suggest the existence of mitigating circumstances in the hope of getting sentencing consideration for the client. There also are times when private investigators will initiate inquiries at the request of businesses or institutions that want an undercover investigation to determine whether employees are engaging in unlawful activities.

Although criminal investigations also are initiated by corporate security departments, the ethical and normal procedure for doing so is in response to a complaint. They do not simply decide to investigate someone. Many of their criminal investigations are undertaken with one of two objectives in mind: (1) to determine if there is any evidence of criminal activity that should be referred to a law enforcement agency for further inquiry, and (2) depending on the results of the preliminary investigation and employer's practices, to decide if the incident is best treated as a policy violation and disposed of administratively.

SUMMARY

Integrity and objectivity must be kept in mind in terms of how investigations are initiated and conducted since the results of any inquiry can have a significant effect on the person or persons involved. In some cases, imprisonment, or possibly even death, may be at stake; in others, it may be access to or a denial of employment opportunities. Decisions relative to civil litigation may be influenced by investigations.

History is replete with illustrations of investigations that have been initiated without real justification. Inquiries have been undertaken primarily to satisfy the political or religious beliefs of those in positions of power, or by people who consider themselves above the law. To deny that in the United States questionable motives have prompted investigations, and occasionally still do, would be naive.

Because of this potential for harm, it is imperative in a democratic society such as ours that no investigations be initiated without a recognizable need for an inquiry and that all investigations be conducted in conformity with the highest ethical standards. In noncriminal matters, that need might be to determine the character and fitness of an applicant for a certain position, or to find out what was the actual cause of an accident. These standards should be adhered to whether the investigation is being done for the benefit of the government or the private sector.

A safeguard relative to criminal investigations conducted by the police or federal agents lies in the fact that for the most part they are begun only on the basis of a complaint, or because something questionable has happened and comes to their attention. Similarly, ethical and professionally managed corporate security departments and private investigation firms that occasionally may be called upon to conduct a criminal investigation should do so only in response to a justifiable need.

REVIEW QUESTIONS

1. Are most investigations reactive or proactive?
2. Give two examples of proactive investigations.
3. Do police and federal agencies initiate their investigations the same way?
4. What is the procedure for beginning an applicant investigation?
5. How do federal applicant investigations differ from those of police departments?
6. Under what circumstances are National Transportation Safety Board investigations initiated?
7. On what basis are most police department criminal investigations initiated?
8. What two things do federal agencies consider before opening a criminal investigation?
9. How do federal agencies and police departments often respond in investigating offenses that violate both federal and state laws?
10. What is your opinion of corporate security personnel or other private-sector investigators who simply initiate criminal inquiries on their own?

PART II

ELEMENTS OF AN INVESTIGATION

In Part I, we provide a background of how investigations have evolved, what they are, who conducts them, the traits of good investigators, and how inquiries are initiated. In Part III, we examine principal types of investigations. However, since many investigations, whether of crimes or accidents, have a number of things in common, it helps to know what these elements are before beginning a discussion of specific types of incidents.

Preliminary investigations and searches of incident scenes are universally applicable, but who conducts them is a matter of jurisdiction. Using sources of information and, where appropriate, confidential informants can be helpful. The role of surveillance and intelligence in criminal cases has to be understood. Locating and interviewing witnesses, and collecting and preserving evidence, are critical.

Evidence collection is meaningless unless it can be connected to particular incidents and persons. Therefore, the many contributions that can be made by laboratories need to be understood.

Since so many criminal prosecutions are based on circumstantial evidence, admissible subjects' confessions are highly desirable. Thus subject interrogations must be conducted with the utmost care to be admitted at trial.

Chapter 6

— ❖ —

The Preliminary Investigation

To convict a person for the commission of a crime, investigators and prosecutors must first know what the elements or distinctive parts of the offense are. They then must collect evidence to prove the fact that not only was the particular crime committed, but also that it was committed by the defendant. Thus in many respects, the elements are guidelines used by investigators when conducting criminal investigations.

ELEMENTS OF AN INVESTIGATION

Just as there are elements of a crime, so too are there elements of an investigation. In other words, a number of distinctive parts have to come together for the conduct of a good investigation. Rarely, if ever, does a single step in an inquiry represent the entire investigative process from the time a case is opened until it is closed. The preliminary investigation is the first logical step in the process.

As for police and sheriffs' departments, whether investigations are initiated on the basis of telephone calls or personal contact with beat or motor patrol officers, the first responders to crime scenes generally are patrol officers. Because of the speed with which they normally are able to respond, and the urgency of the situation, they conduct the first phase of the investigation as set forth in Chapter 2. Because of the number of critical matters that require the first responders' attention, the number of patrol officers responding must be adequate for what needs to be done.

Upon arriving at the scene, uniformed personnel must quickly evaluate what they see. Having done this, they then must take whatever action is necessary. It is largely because several things have to be done almost simultaneously that the number of patrol officers responding is so important. For instance, of primary concern is the victim's identification and well-being, especially if there has been either physical or emotional injury. Although not considered part of the investigation, performing this humanitarian service is the first priority; it also may prove helpful in making the later work of the investigators easier. Next, the patrol officers must try to learn all that they possibly can about the perpetrators and broadcast their descriptions to radio units. On the chance that the perpetrators still might be in the area, the patrol officers have to consider the possibility of making an arrest themselves. Since even an immediate apprehension does not vitiate the need for evidence, patrol personnel also must protect the crime scene.

No matter how quickly the investigation may be assigned to detectives, or how soon they arrive, the patrol officers who first respond cannot allow anyone to enter the crime scene area whether it is indoors or outdoors. It is their responsibility to preserve the scene's integrity for the investigators' benefit.

There is no disputing the fact that uniformed personnel, responsible for getting as much information as they possibly can about victims, perpetrators, and incidents, are performing an investigative function. These first steps are of invaluable help to the detectives to whom the investigation is assigned.

Since in most cases the perpetrator(s) will have fled the scene, patrol personnel or investigators, once they arrive, will broadcast all pertinent information about the crime and the suspects to other patrol personnel in the hope of realizing an early arrest. However, to do this effectively, they need to have more than physical descriptions and possibly names. To protect the general public and other officers, they also must try to find out whether the perpetrators are armed and, if so, how. They also need to discover the perpetrators' means of transportation, vehicle identification and registration included.

Regardless of the state in which victims are found, or the information that they can provide to patrol personnel, a good deal of the help gotten during preliminary investigations conducted by first responders will come from witnesses. Their names, addresses, and home and work telephone numbers must be obtained, and statements must be gotten from each of them while details about what happened are fresh in their minds. All these preliminary investigative steps are taken for the ultimate benefit of the investigators to whom the case is or will be assigned. In interviewing witnesses, patrol officers must ensure that they are separated to prevent their versions from being influenced by the statements of others. If the integrity of witness statements is jeopardized, the resulting investigation will be less than satisfactory.

Once the primary investigators arrive and take charge of the case, they may ask patrol personnel for additional help, and they should be able to rely on them in every way. For example, despite the efforts, and possible success, of patrol officers to get witness statements, it would not be at all unusual for the investigators to have them canvass the neighborhood looking for still others who might have useful information. This phase of the preliminary investigation might well mean going door to door and asking questions, a task that needs to be done although it often is a thankless and tedious one.

IDENTIFYING AND PROTECTING CRIME SCENES

An essential part of any preliminary investigation in criminal cases is identifying and protecting crime scenes. Crime scenes and the collection and preservation of evidence are discussed in detail in Chapters 8 and 13, but one cannot overemphasize the importance of ensuring that those who first arrive at any crime scene determine the geographic extent of the actual area in which the incident appears to have taken place and then take action to protect it against even the slightest intrusion by unauthorized persons, or possible deterioration due to weather conditions. At this stage of the preliminary investigation, it is immaterial whether actual crime scenes will be scoured for evidence by detectives to whom the cases are assigned or, following a relatively recent trend, by specially trained crime scene technicians. Altered crime scenes or lost evidence make the principal investigators' work infinitely more difficult and can have a major and adverse effect on the outcome of a case.

In Chapter 4, the Rosenberg case (Case 4-6) and the one linking a single attacker to the strangulation of two prostitutes and assault on a third (Case 4-11) help illustrate some of the information that can be developed during preliminary investigations. However, it also is possible that occasionally, under the right circumstances, what may begin as a preliminary investigation will end with patrol officers making an arrest.

Such a situation occurred about 8:10 A.M., January 1, 1995, in New York City. Two patrol officers responded to a 911 call from a woman who said she had been raped in the back of a scruffy black van, then thrown back onto the street. While waiting for an ambulance to take the victim to a hospital for examination and treatment, the officers began a preliminary investigation by asking questions about what had happened, and also about both the van and the perpetrator. The victim provided descriptions of both. Around 10:15 A.M., having resumed patrol of their sector, they saw a van and driver, both of which fit the victim's description, about six blocks from the crime scene. They took the perpetrator, who later was identified by the victim, into custody.[1] Information gotten from the victim during the preliminary investigation allowed the officers to make the arrest.

These few examples illustrate the importance of both preliminary investigations and the role played therein by patrol personnel. It is undeniable that if those involved with the first phase of a criminal inquiry, whether in or out of uniform, fail to protect crime scenes against contamination or the possible loss of physical evidence, or if they fail to get the names, addresses, and telephone numbers of likely witnesses as well as at least some idea about what information they may be able to provide, the work of those ultimately responsible for the major part of the investigation will be much more difficult or may even be jeopardized.

The procedures cited thus far normally would also apply to federal police agencies such as the U.S. Capital Police and the U.S. Park Police. The initial response and preliminary investigation would be handled by uniformed personnel; their respective plainclothes investigators would then assume the responsibility for the second phase. The Vincent Foster case illustrates this point. Mr. Foster, who had been a member of the White House staff, was found in his automobile dead from a bullet wound. Since the vehicle was found in a U.S. government park, both the preliminary and secondary phases of the investigation were handled by the U.S. Park Police.

Under different circumstances, there might have been evidence to warrant referring the matter to another federal investigative agency. An example would be a case in which the U.S. Capital Police received a complaint about the suspected theft of mail sent to members of Congress. They might well conduct a preliminary investigation for the express purpose of determining if the complaint had any validity. If it did, they would refer the investigation to the Postal Inspection Service.

Another illustration of one federal agency's referral to another might involve an incident that, when first reported, does not seem to have any criminal overtones. As a result, the preliminary investigation would be undertaken by an appropriate investigative agency. However, if, as the preliminary investigation proceeds, the incident appears to indicate criminal activity, the matter then would be referred to another agency with the first one lending its expertise and support to the second. For instance, if there has been a train wreck or an airplane crash, the first response is by investigators from the National Transportation Safety Board. But if its preliminary investigation indicates that the wreck or crash was caused by a criminal act, the NTSB would turn the inquiry over to the FBI and assist the bureau in a supporting role.

Unlike preliminary and secondary investigations conducted by local and state police and sheriffs' departments, and possibly by federal police agencies, there is little if any real distinction between the two phases in most cases involving federal matters even though there may be some exceptions other than those cited. Although we examine jurisdictional issues in Chapter 7, an illustration of such an exception would be a reported bank robbery in violation of both state and federal law. The first notification most likely would be to the police department, and the initial response would be by patrol officers. In this situation, the preliminary investigation would be conducted by the first responders; thereafter, detectives and FBI special agents would work the case together.

Nevertheless, as a general rule, the nature of the work of the various federal investigative agencies is such that all aspects of an investigation come together and are handled by the agent to whom the case is assigned. This does not mean that those agents are expected to do everything that first responding patrol personnel do as part of a preliminary investigation by themselves; they can be and are helped by others, depending on the nature of the investigation. For example, in a kidnapping case, one would not find the case agent doing the initial interviews, protecting the crime scene and searching it, and looking for possible witnesses alone. However, because of the way federal agencies' investigations are initiated, as distinguished from those of others, the agent to whom the kidnapping case is assigned is personally responsible for either doing or overseeing everything related to his or her case.

Preliminary investigations in most federal cases involve interviewing victims or complainants. This helps make several determinations. First, has an offense warranting investigation been committed? Next, does the agency contacted by the victim, or with which the complaint is being filed, have jurisdiction? If both answers are yes, the initial interview now offers the opportunity to start developing investigative leads and to consider what evidence to look for. For instance, suppose a mail bomb has been received. Who are the persons in the recipient's organization with whom there might have been some disagreement or problem so that researching their backgrounds can begin? Where did the parcel enter the postal system, how was the packaging prepared, what was the nature of the explosive used, how accessible is it to the general public, and what types of persons might know how to use it? As aspects of this phase are completed, the investigator simply moves into the second phase. Unlike a police inquiry, there is no break in terms of who does what.

Corporate security investigations are very much like those of the federal agencies. An allegation is made or a complaint is filed with the security department. The information must be evaluated in terms of the likelihood that the incident complained of did in fact occur. If it did, was the act a crime or merely a violation of the employer's policies? Determining the nature of the offense will have a bearing on the next step in the preliminary investigation. Whether there has been a crime or a violation of company policy, and even though there may not be a crime scene in the more accepted sense of the term, it is no less important here than in any preliminary investigation to take all steps necessary to identify and secure everything that may have evidentiary value.

If it appears that a crime was committed, its magnitude and the employer's human resources policies may influence the decision about a referral to a law enforcement agency. Even in organizations where, as a rule, minor crimes are investigated and disposed of internally, the security department head must first consider the need for evidence and whether the department has the resources needed to successfully complete the inquiry. If it does not, there may be no choice but to refer the matter to an appropriate agency. On the other hand, if there is no question but that the nature of the crime warrants investigation by a government agency, the security department's preliminary investigation should be a factor in deciding the agency to which the referral should be made. In other words, is this a case for the local police or sheriff's department, or is it one for a federal agency? If the latter, which one?

If policy violations are reported, as with alleged crimes, the basis for such suspicion must be evaluated at the outset. If further investigation then appears justified, the preliminary inquiry must determine what evidence needs to be collected and protected, and steps must be taken to do just that. It also has to identify those persons to be interviewed for what help they can provide in disposing of the matter.

SUMMARY

There must be a beginning to everything, investigations included. Chapter 5 discussed how investigations are initiated, but once a complaint is filed or allegations are made, the preliminary investigation becomes a matter of utmost importance. According to an unattributed old English proverb, "A good beginning makes a good ending." Conversely, Euripides (fifth century B.C.), a Greek tragic dramatist, said "A bad beginning makes a bad ending."[2]

Whether one prefers the proverb's optimism or Euripides' pessimism, the way in which preliminary investigations are conducted can significantly impact the outcome of any case. That there may be differences between the way in which police and sheriffs' departments and federal agencies approach preliminary investigations is immaterial. A well-done preliminary investigation should do more than protect crime scenes and the evidence found there. It should also help identify and locate possible witnesses, as well as help bring matters into focus for the second stage of the inquiry.

Even though as a rule investigations are not completed in a matter of minutes, or even a few hours, the importance of time cannot be underestimated in every inquiry, criminal or not, where the nature and reliability of evidence can be crucial to the outcome. Consequently, although good investigators take nothing for granted and consider no detail too small, preliminary investigations can help expedite the separation of the important from the unimportant. This, in turn, allows those to whom cases are assigned to concentrate on matters that offer the best chance of bringing investigations to successful conclusions.

REVIEW QUESTIONS

1. In what way are the elements of investigations similar to those of crimes?
2. What is meant by the elements of an investigation?
3. Who normally conducts preliminary investigations in police and sheriffs' departments?
4. What are the matters to be covered during preliminary investigations?
5. Why is rendering care to injured victims important?
6. Who has primary responsibility for identifying and protecting crime scenes in most cases?
7. Why should potential witnesses be interviewed separately?
8. How do federal agencies' preliminary investigations differ from those of police and sheriffs' departments?
9. Is it possible for a preliminary investigation by patrol officers to lead to an early arrest by them?
10. What is the purpose of preliminary investigations conducted by corporate security departments?

NOTES

1. "A Good Description and Good Police Work Lead to the Capture of a Rape Suspect," *New York Times,* January 2, 1995, p. 27.
2. *Aeolus* (c. 423 B.C.), 32, translated by M. H. Morgan.

Chapter 7

———— ❖ ————

Jurisdictional Issues

This Constitution, and the laws of the United States which shall be made in pursuance thereof; and all treaties made, or which shall be made, under the authority of the United States, shall be supreme law of the land; and the Judges in every State shall be bound thereby, any thing in the Constitution or laws of any State to the contrary notwithstanding.

Constitution of the United States, Article VI, Section 2

Jurisdictional matters cannot be fully understood, or even discussed in a meaningful way, without first considering Article VI of the Constitution of the United States and other relevant constitutional provisions, especially Article IV and Amendment X.

Article IV, Section 1, generally referred to as the "full faith and credit clause," requires each state to honor the public acts, records, and judicial proceedings of every other state. Section 2 provides that any person charged in any state with a crime, who flees from justice and is found in another state, should, on the demand of the executive authority of the state from which that person fled, be delivered up to be removed to the state having jurisdiction of the crime. Amendment X states: "The powers not delegated to the United States by the Constitution, nor prohibited by it to the States, are reserved to the States respectively, or to the people."

Thus although the Constitution of the United States is the supreme law of the land, to be adhered to by the several states (and U.S. territories), it recognizes that each state has its own constitution. Furthermore, though the states must conform with the federal Constitution's provisions, it does not mean that each state constitution has to be a mirror image of the U.S. Constitution. In fact, although state constitutions cannot be more restrictive than the U.S. Constitution, they can be more liberal.

Since neither the federal nor state constitutions are easily amended, the appropriate legislative bodies enact statutes to deal with the day-to-day activities of their respective governments. For the federal government, Congress passes, amends, and repeals laws, some of which, depending on their nature, also may affect the several states. As for the individual states, their legislatures pass, amend, and repeal laws for the governance of their own inhabitants provided they do not contravene any applicable federal statutes. In matters of criminal law, it also is possible to find any number of federal and state statutes that deal with the same offense. Examples would be bank robbery and kidnapping, subject to satisfying the criteria for federal involvement. Furthermore, counties within states may have legislative bodies, and most cities and towns have councils that pass, amend, and repeal local ordinances to govern their communities' activities.

Most laws when violated are classified as either offenses against the state or offenses against persons; some can be offenses against both a state and a person. Offenses against the state are crimes; those against persons are torts. Assault and battery is an example of both a crime and a tort.

That crimes must be investigated when committed and reported is undisputable. Although a large segment of the general public may understand the kinds of activities that constitute a crime, they do not necessarily know to whom such incidents should be reported. It is not unusual for a person to report what actually is a federal offense to a local police department, but neither is it unusual for someone to complain to the FBI about an offense that is under another federal agency's jurisdiction, or possibly that of a local police department. As a result, in any given case, questions may arise with regard to which department or agency has jurisdiction. What, then, is "jurisdiction"? It is the legal authority to undertake an investigation.

INVESTIGATIVE JURISDICTION

Investigative jurisdiction does not automatically reside in the agency or department with which a complaint has been filed. It is a mistake to assume that all federal agencies share jurisdiction in all federal matters, or that because a state's laws apply to all parts of that state, all police and sheriffs' departments have statewide authority. Equally true is the fact that in some instances the legal authority to undertake an investigation may be a responsibility shared between or among two or more departments or agencies. To make any of these assumptions is to oversimplify the ways in which governments function.

Consequently, once a complaint has been received, the question of jurisdiction is one of the first issues to be resolved. The nature of any given offense helps determine whether investigative authority rests with one particular department or agency, if it might be a shared responsibility, or if it rests with a single organization but the cooperation of others will be needed. If responsibility is shared, then between or among what departments or agencies—city, county, state, federal—or does it possibly involve two or more federal agencies?

If jurisdiction is divided, it is important to remember that for the investigation to be efficiently and effectively conducted sharing must be confined to the "legwork" aspects of the case. Responsibility for the overall direction must be assumed by one particular organization. The question is which department or agency will have the supervisory role.

In the majority of cases in which jurisdiction is divided between a federal agency and a state or local police or sheriff's department, the federal agency will have the primary role. This is because if the investigation is predicated on a violation of both federal and state law, the federal agency's primacy is based on the supremacy of the Constitution and laws of the United States.

The need for cooperation, discussed more fully later in this chapter, is easy to understand. It generally is forthcoming, though grudgingly on occasion. The matter of jurisdiction is more complicated, and occasionally, it can cause friction between or among departments or agencies. Law enforcement agencies, not unlike people, jealously guard their respective areas of operation and spheres of influence. Showing high levels of activity and the ability to successfully solve cases assumes a good deal of importance to agency supervisors and directors. This is partially due to agency heads' reliance on statistical data to show that their departments or agencies are doing a good job. It helps justify budget increases for new and modern equipment as well as for additional personnel.

Thus if jurisdictional disputes arise, the result may well be a feeling of mistrust. This, in turn, can make the participants reluctant to share information and work together. Under such circumstances, the agencies involved suffer, and inevitably, the investigation itself also suffers. Therefore, once an offense is reported, it is in the best interest of the organization receiving the complaint to make certain that it has jurisdiction, whether wholly or partially, before it assigns the matter for investigation. Occasionally, jurisdiction is so clear-cut that cases can be assigned or referred to another department or agency quickly and easily. On other occasions, careful analysis may be needed in order to determine if the offense involves joint jurisdiction. If so, does the department or agency to which the report was made have primary jurisdiction, or does that responsibility more properly rest with the other organization?

Parenthetically, deciding on investigative jurisdiction should not be confused with the issue of jurisdiction for purposes of prosecution, especially in matters that fall under both federal and state jurisdiction. Investigation and prosecution are distinct issues. For instance, it does not necessarily follow that when the legal authority for an investigation results in a shared inquiry, the prosecutor who normally works with the organization having the primary role will handle the subsequent prosecution. Who prosecutes an offense often will be determined by agreement between the prosecutors and most likely will be based on which of the two jurisdictions provides for the more severe punishment upon conviction.

As an example, under federal law there are relatively few capital cases, but a number of states provide for capital punishment for certain offenses. Suppose an offense is both a federal and a state crime, and both the local police department and the FBI are working the case together. Suppose further that the federal penalty upon conviction would result in life imprisonment; under state law, it could mean death. Here the U.S. Attorney and the district attorney might agree to have the matter prosecuted under state law. To further illustrate this point, but from a different perspective, assume a person in police custody died under questionable circumstances; the officers involved are tried and acquitted under the state's manslaughter statute. The district attorney now might ask the U.S. Attorney to prosecute the case in federal court as a violation of the deceased's civil rights. Since each prosecution is based on a violation of a completely different statute (one for manslaughter and the other for a deprivation of civil rights), double jeopardy is not an issue.

We already have pointed out that a federal agency's authority to investigate violations of federal law is determined by the particular statute that establishes the offense. To illustrate, violations of laws that involve currency, such as counterfeiting, are assigned to the Secret Service; thefts from the U.S. mail, to the Postal Inspection Service; tax law violations are under the jurisdiction of the Internal Revenue Service; federal safety standards' violations are investigated by the Department of Labor; and violations of federal firearms laws are handled by the Bureau of Alcohol, Tobacco and Firearms, a Treasury Department agency.

The federal agency with the broadest general investigative jurisdiction is the FBI, whose responsibility has grown over the years. For instance, in the late 1940s, it had investigative jurisdiction over approximately 125 federal laws; today, that number exceeds 250. Just a few examples to illustrate the wide variety of investigations conducted by the bureau would include espionage and counterintelligence cases, bank robbery and kidnapping (once the criteria for federal intervention have been satisfied), the interstate transportation of stolen property, internal security matters, antitrust and civil rights cases, and terrorism. The FBI also conducts background investigations on presidential appointees, including persons nominated for appointment to the U.S. Supreme Court.

True, Congress has given exclusive investigative jurisdiction to specific federal agencies when federal laws have been violated. Nevertheless, there are some matters in which jurisdiction may be concurrent, for example, cases involving the importation, sale, and distribution of controlled substances. Here, both the DEA and the FBI are authorized to conduct investigations. On the other hand, there also are numerous instances when a particular offense is a violation of a state's criminal laws. For instance, cases of espionage against the U.S. government are strictly federal violations handled by the FBI, but under certain conditions, a kidnapping can violate both federal and state laws.

When specific federal and state laws are violated with a degree of frequency, it is not unusual for the appropriate agencies at both levels of government to form a task force to combat the problem. A good example has been the formation of FBI and local police department task forces to investigate continuing problems of bank robberies since most, but by no means all banks, have a federal relationship that gives the bureau jurisdiction. Task forces also can be set up to investigate other types of crimes, even if only for a single case, if they are of a magnitude that will overly tax the resources of a single department or agency. This approach is not necessarily limited to investigations involving federal and local agencies and departments; it also can be used to pool the resources of local and county or state departments when deemed advisable.

Despite the breadth of the federal criminal laws, there are any number of offenses that, if committed, violate only state laws. That this is true does not lessen the need to consider jurisdiction before beginning an investigation. As noted, the investigative jurisdiction of federal agencies is prescribed by Congress. State legislatures do not follow a similar practice in granting legal authority to investigate to state departments and agencies, or to any of the counties or municipalities. Their investigative jurisdiction is determined by geography; departmental jurisdiction depends on the political subdivision in which a department or agency works.

As a result, at the state level, the question of jurisdiction may be only somewhat less complex than it is when it involves a possible violation of federal and state law. Jurisdictional complexity can be illustrated by noting the condition that existed in New York City before the consolidation of what had been three separate police departments within the city's geographic boundaries. Until their 1995 merger into the New York City Police Department, New York City had the New York City Police, New York Transit Authority Police, and New York City Housing Authority Police Departments, each with its own command structure, training, and detective bureau. Although they cooperated with one another, if prior to the consolidation a homicide occurred during a subway robbery or in a public housing development, and the perpetrator fled the scene, the question of which department would have primary investigative jurisdiction—the Transit Authority Police, the Housing Authority Police, or the New York City Police Department—often arose. This no longer is an issue.

Another illustration occurs when there is a city police department within a county that has a sheriff's department that is a full-service police agency. For instance, the City of Los Angeles, in Los Angeles County, has its own police department, but the Los Angeles County Sheriff's Department also is a full-service police agency. If a state crime is committed on a boundary separating the city from the rest of the county, which department has jurisdiction?

By way of contrast with Los Angeles and Los Angeles County, there also are some places where similar problems existed, and legislative action was taken to overcome them. An example is Miami, Florida. Miami, which had its own police department, is situated in Dade County. Dade County had a full-service police agency in its sheriff's department. Today, the Metro Dade County Police Department services both Miami and Dade County.

COOPERATION AMONG AGENCIES

Of course, consolidation may not always be possible, or even advisable, but even when city and county or other political subdivisions are maintained, this should not preclude cooperation between and among law enforcement agencies, an invaluable investigative tool that can surmount purely jurisdictional issues.

Suppose a local police department is investigating a home invasion, robbery, and assault. The victims, recent arrivals from China, neither understand nor speak English; they also fear government authority, especially the police. The police department has no Chinese-speaking or even Asian American officers. However, the chief knows that there is a Chinese-speaking state police officer. He asks for and gets his help not only in interviewing the victims, but also in assisting the investigators with other aspects of the case. Perhaps other examples, based on actual cases, will be even more instructive.

In one, involving paramilitary-style operations used in robbing businesses that needed large quantities of computer chips, there were more than 400 victims. One firm alone lost some $9.9 million in computer parts. This led to an eighteen-month undercover operation conducted jointly by the FBI and the San Jose, California, Police Department. Working together, they developed enough evidence to justify conducting a raid in which more than 500 police officers and FBI special agents participated, and more than 120 persons were arrested.[1]

In the New York City area, eight persons, with contacts in the United States, Europe, and Asia, were indicted in connection with a four-year multimillion-dollar credit card fraud scheme. This resulted from the close cooperation and joint efforts of city, state, and federal investigators over a period of five months.[2]

A double homicide that occurred in Brookline, Massachusetts, the morning of December 30, 1994, is another example of both jurisdictional issues and cooperation. Initially, the Brookline Police Department had nothing to go on but the shooter's physical description and evidence recovered at the second of the two crime scenes. Nevertheless, they got a name, and the perpetrator was apprehended in Norfolk, Virginia, the following day. The success was due to the combined efforts of the Brookline Police Department, Massachusetts State Police, FBI, New Hampshire and Massachusetts Registries of Motor Vehicles, Rhode Island State Police, and the Norfolk Fire and Police Departments.[3]

The night of May 10, 1976, a woman was fatally shot in a New York City drive-by shooting. A suspect, identified by witnesses at the scene, managed to flee. He settled in South Carolina, changed his name, married, and became the father of two. Shortly before being taken into custody on August 8, 1995, by New York City detectives and the FBI, he was fingerprinted so that he could access his employer's bank account. His prints were sent to the FBI's Identification Division for a search, his flight to avoid prosecution was noted, and the New York City Police Department was advised that he had been located.[4]

Cooperation is not necessarily confined to purely domestic investigations. It also can help fight crimes that have international ramifications. An example of such a situation was the February 1996 arrest of three Russian immigrants after a two-year investigation in which the Russian Ministry of Internal Affairs made information available to the FBI and the two organizations worked together.[5]

There are countless other examples of the involvement of several agencies or departments with cases in which one has primary jurisdiction yet needs the cooperation of others to bring the investigation to a successful conclusion. There can be no better illustration of this point than the New York City World Trade Center bombing on February 26, 1993. Although the FBI had the lead in the investigation because of the terrorist nature of the event, it had help from three other agencies. The use of explosives warranted ATF's involvement, and since the crime was committed in New York City, the New York City Police Department had a vested interest in the case. As the investigation progressed, and it appeared that a foreign element might be involved, Immigration and Naturalization Service records were checked and proved helpful to the FBI.

Although investigations of that magnitude are relatively rare, there are other, and more frequently used, forms of cooperation. Some are attributable to clear-cut jurisdictional issues; others are based on overlapping jurisdictions.

For instance, suppose a state criminal law has been violated. The subject is known to the detectives and prosecutors but leaves the state to avoid arrest or prosecution. The local authorities have the right to continue their investigation even if they have reason to believe the person has fled the state, but they have no investigative jurisdiction beyond their state. However, a logical extension of the provisions of Article IV of the Constitution of the United States, cited earlier in this chapter, and particularly Section 2, enables the FBI to enter the case under the federal government's so-called unlawful flight statutes since a state line has or may have been crossed. Here the local authorities refer the investigation to the bureau, it conducts whatever investigation is necessary to find the subject, and upon apprehension the case reverts to the state for prosecution.

Other examples of cooperation based on overlapping jurisdiction might be an investigation of an explosion with state or local police and the ATF working together. Or it might be a case of the importation and distribution by mail of controlled substances, with the DEA, U.S. postal inspectors, and Internal Revenue Service cooperating. The DEA's jurisdiction, based on the illegal drugs, would be shared at least in part with postal inspectors because the U.S. mail had been used. Since this type of activity tends to generate large profits for the participants, the Internal Revenue Service would be interested in finding out whether taxes on those profits had been reported and paid. Thus it is clear that despite possible jurisdictional questions, law enforcement agencies generally cooperate with one another in the interest of successful crime solving.

SUMMARY

Law enforcement agencies in the United States are created by law, and their activities are governed by law. The U.S. Constitution, although the supreme law of the land, recognizes the rights of the several states and limits the extent to which the federal government can regulate or become involved in matters reserved to the states and the people. The states have done much the same with regard to their own political subdivisions. This chapter shows how, despite these restrictions, various agencies can and do cooperate in fighting crime.

The legal authority of federal agencies to conduct investigations on behalf of the U.S. government is not all inclusive. Each agency's authority is based on the specific statutes that define federal crimes. State law enforcement agencies' investigative jurisdiction largely depends on geographic considerations.

Some crimes are clearly defined; there is no question about which agency or department has jurisdiction. In other crimes, the line is blurred, and a decision has to be made before an investigation can be started. This blurring is not necessarily confined to whether a federal agency or a city or state police department has jurisdiction; it also can occur between or among federal and other organizations.

When jurisdiction overlaps and an investigation will be conducted jointly, one agency or department must have primary responsibility for the case's management. Occasionally, dual jurisdiction may result in forming task forces, but the principle of primary responsibility for managing the investigation is unchanged. As a rule, where dual federal–state or federal–local jurisdiction is at issue, the federal agency takes the lead role. Similarly, if the question is state–county or state–local jurisdiction, the state organization has primary responsibility.

There also are times when jurisdiction per se is not an issue, but the agency or department conducting an investigation simply lacks some of the resources needed to properly pursue the matter. At times like this, good relationships with other organizations can ensure getting their cooperation and what help they may be able to provide in solving a particular crime.

REVIEW QUESTIONS

1. What makes federal law supreme?
2. On what is FBI jurisdiction in unlawful flight cases based?
3. Can state constitutions be more restrictive than the U.S. Constitution?
4. What are the two principal categories of crimes?
5. Do people always report crimes to the proper agency?
6. Do all federal agencies have the same jurisdiction?
7. Does the FBI have jurisdiction in all bank robbery cases?
8. Distinguish between the way in which federal and state investigative jurisdiction is determined.
9. When might a task force be set up to conduct investigations?
10. Why is cooperation important even when jurisdiction is not an issue?

NOTES

1. "Chip Thieves Are Arrested After a Sting in California," *New York Times,* March 1, 1996, p. A10.
2. "Authorities Break Credit-Card Fraud Ring," *New York Times,* February 8, 1996, p. B5.
3. "Though Hunt for Suspect Was Vast, Chance Proved Crucial for Capture," *New York Times,* January 2, 1995, p. 10.
4. "Fingerprints Reveal Suspect on the Run from '76 Killing," *New York Times,* August 19, 1995, pp. 1, 22.
5. "F.B.I. and Russian Police Cooperate to Bring Fraud Charges," *New York Times,* March 1, 1996, p. B5.

Chapter 8

❖

Crime Scenes

Since most people associate investigations with crimes, it is not surprising that we tend to think of the place where the incident occurred as the "crime scene." However, it might be just as appropriate to think of that particular locus as an incident scene because the need to collect and preserve evidence is no less important in certain types of noncriminal cases, and the first requirement for the collection and preservation of evidence is protection of the involved site.

Unless an airplane crash or a train derailment is caused by a criminal act, National Transportation Safety Board investigators have as much need to search the accident scene as detectives have to carefully examine the scene of a homicide. The NTSB investigators must collect and preserve evidence in order to determine the accident's cause; the detectives need to scour the crime scene for clues to help solve a possible murder. Similarly, should an employee be suspected of involvement in a conflict of interest, which is not a criminal act, corporate security investigators nevertheless have to search the employee's work and related areas for evidence to support whatever subsequent action the employer may choose to take against that person.

PROTECTING THE CRIME SCENE

Regardless of the type of investigation, if a search for evidence of an offense or incident is material, it is imperative that the location or locations that have any bearing on what happened be carefully protected and thoroughly examined. Nowhere is there a greater need for being alert and paying close attention to detail than there is when dealing with crime or incident scenes. Remember, being alert and paying attention to detail are among the several characteristics needed to be a good investigator.

In addition to protecting the scene upon arrival, it is important to make no assumptions. This is well illustrated by John Douglas, who was supervising the Investigative Support Unit at the time of his retirement from the FBI. In his book *Mindhunter,* Douglas states that when he assisted police officers or detectives in solving what could be the work of a serial killer or a high-profile homicide, he would be told that nothing had been removed from the crime scene. This would prompt him to ask, "How do you know?" Douglas would point out that something as subtle as a lock of hair or a barrette, something difficult to trace, could be missing. He wrote that "The mere fact that nothing appeared to be missing was never a definitive finding in my mind."[1] All good investigators should approach incident scenes with that same thought in mind.

Just as it is unwise to assume that the scene has not been disturbed, it is unwise to assume that there is but one scene, especially in criminal investigations. Not only is it possible that a crime scene's boundaries may be either well defined or in dispute, it also is possible that more than one location is involved.

For purposes of examination, crime scenes should include every area or location over which the victim, the person who committed the offense, and witnesses may have moved while the crime was being committed. For example, if a business executive was kidnapped near his home, transported by automobile to a cemetery, and buried alive while the perpetrators waited for payment of their ransom demands, the place where the abduction took place, the vehicle used to transport the victim, and the cemetery, particularly the site where he was held, are all part of the crime scene.

Therefore, it is obvious that crime scenes must be defined before they can be secured and the search for physical evidence can begin. This is true even if that definition is not precise. However, once definition is complete, the crime scene(s) must be secured. Failure to do so can adversely affect the entire investigation. It certainly will have a decidedly negative impact on both the discovery and collection of physical evidence and the investigator's ability to reconstruct the crime. Everything possible must be done to preserve the crime scene in order to minimize the risk of losing or contaminating what may be valuable physical evidence.

MAKING FIELD NOTES

Of course, important as it is to define and secure a crime scene, these steps are but the beginning of the process for the investigators. Next, they need to make detailed field notes that, among other things, include the

Crime scene training photographs, FBI Academy, Quantico, VA.
(*Courtesy* FBI)

dates, times, and locations of everything observed at the scene. The crime scene also should be photographed and sketched. Merely taking photographs and noting dates, times, and locations is not enough; the combination of sketches and photographs lends perspective to the scene for the benefit of investigators, prosecutors, and jurors. Each individual photograph should include information about the camera's make and type, the shutter speed and F-stop used, the distances and directions related to each one, and the weather conditions at the time.

Most investigators use one of three primary methods of sketching: coordinate, triangulation, and cross-projection. The coordinate method involves focusing on two fixed points, then measuring the distance of the object of interest from those points. This also can be done by drawing a baseline between two known points.

When it comes to sketching outdoor crime scenes, some investigators believe triangulation is the most useful method because on those occasions it may be hard to establish a baseline from which measurements can be made. Therefore, they locate the objects of interest by measuring in a straight line from two or possibly more points of reference that are widely separated.

The cross-projection method often is used when the items in which the investigators are interested are found on or in walls or in enclosed spaces. Use of this method involves drawing doors, walls, and windows as if they were folded open and flat on the floor. The sketches then show the measurements from a given point on the floor to the object on or in the wall.

In sketching crime scenes, remember that though the measurements must be accurate, the sketches themselves, drawn at the scene, do not have to be made to scale. When scenes are to be reproduced for the benefit of jurors at time of trial, the best practice is to have models made to scale rather than rely on the investigator's artistic ability. However, it is permissible to draw rough sketches at the scene in pencil, and then to define them more clearly and finish them in ink upon returning to the office.

Different types of incidents will prompt investigators to focus on different objects found at the scene. For instance, once the scene in a criminal homicide is defined and secured, the concentration will be on the victim, his or her identification, the weapon or weapons used, the location and identification of witnesses (which possibly may include the perpetrator), the scene in general whether it is indoors or out, and everything else that may represent an item of physical evidence. Among other things, this could include imprints of any sort, such as foot, heel, tire, or tool marks; hairs and fibers (sometimes referred to as transfer evidence); objects on which there might be fingerprints; and blood stains or splashes. Collecting and preserving evidence are discussed in detail in Chapter 12, but it is important to remember that in homicides, although the body is not moved until the investigator is done with it, it is the medical examiner or coroner, not the investigator, who authorizes the removal.

At a burglary scene, investigators focus on many of the same things as in a homicide, but with particular attention to any instruments that might have made tool marks. The focus on the victim includes getting complete information, including descriptive data of what was stolen. Blood becomes a factor only if evidence suggests that the burglar may have cut himself or herself either while on or when entering or leaving the premises. Every effort would be made to locate witnesses, but in all likelihood their contribution would be limited to what they may have seen or heard that aroused their suspicion or at least peaked their curiosity.

The same scene search principles apply in noncriminal incident investigations such as airplane crashes, or even certain corporate security cases. In the former, investigators comb the crash site and surrounding area looking for even the most minute parts of the aircraft with a view to reassembling it in the hope that doing so will help determine the cause of the crash. Investigating an accident that resulted in a corporate employee or visitor being injured requires security personnel to examine the scene in order to find out just what conditions contributed to the incident.

Because evidence collection and preservation are critical in criminal investigations, as well as in certain noncriminal matters, definition of the incident scene should be accompanied by sealing off the area in order to deny access to unauthorized persons. The slightest suggestion that evidence, or even the scene itself, has been exposed to alteration or contamination can have a major impact on the investigation and the case's ultimate disposition. In criminal matters, it could raise serious questions in the minds of jurors, assuming that the defense counsel's motion to suppress the evidence was denied; and in noncriminal incidents, it might undermine any effort to determine cause.

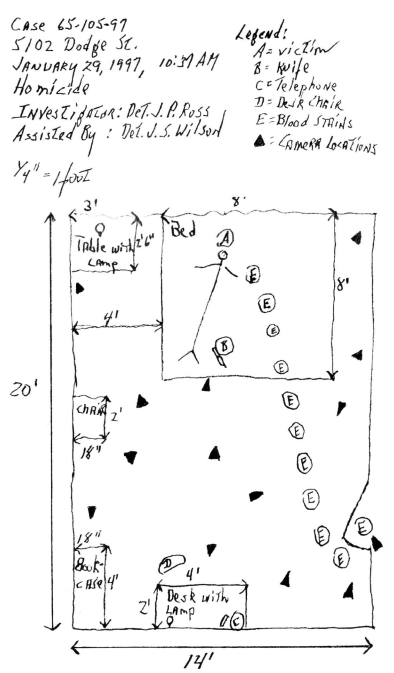

Rough sketch of homicide crime scene.

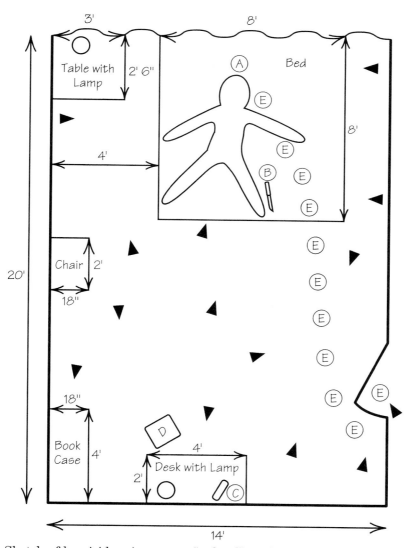

Case 65-105-97
5102 Dodge St.
January 29, 1997, 10:37 AM
Homicide
Investigator: Det. J. P. Ross
Assisted By: Det. J. S. Wilson

1/4" = 1 Foot

Legend:
A = Victim
B = Knife
C = Telephone
D = Desk Chair
E = Blood Stains
▲ = Camera Locations

Sketch of homicide crime scene "refined" in the office.

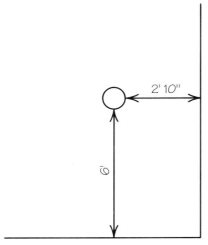

Coordinate method for locating an object.

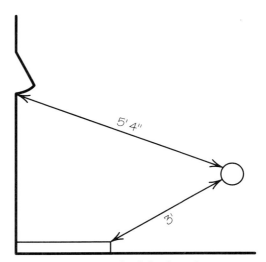

Triangulation method for locating an object.

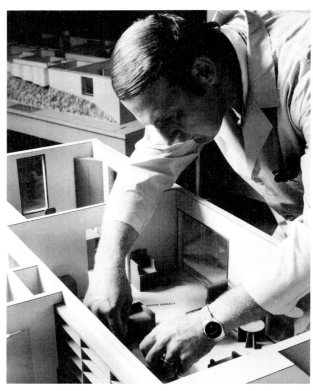

Scale model for use as courtroom exhibit. *(Courtesy* FBI)

We have mentioned the importance of good note-taking. In addition to recording all the incident scene details, the investigator's notes must indicate precisely how every item of evidence was handled and by whom. Although we discuss collecting and preserving evidence in Chapter 12, investigators dare not forget how failure to maintain the chain of custody of evidence can affect the prosecution of a criminal case, and it is at the crime scene itself that establishing that chain begins.

It often is during examination of the scene of an incident that investigators start to develop their theories about how and why a crime or accident occurred. The objectivity that good investigators maintain throughout their work applies to questions of guilt and innocence, but this does not preclude developing an opinion on all facets of the incident. This is when investigators begin to consider not only the standard what, when, where, how, and why, but also who had the motive and the opportunity. In other words, as a practical matter, an incident scene represents the third stage in the investigative process. The first stage is the incident's occurrence. The second stage is its being reported and an investigation being initiated. The third stage is defining with the greatest possible precision where the incident happened, starting the search for evidence, and developing a theory as a basis on which the investigation will proceed.

In earlier chapters we referred to the role played by patrol personnel at a crime scene, particularly with respect to its preservation and in the early stages of evidence collection. Nowhere is the significance of crime scenes better expressed than in those cases in which teams of crime scene specialists have been established to handle crime scenes and the collection and preservation of evidence found there. The work of these investigative specialists has proved to be of such value that among the departments and agencies that have used them are the New York City Police Department and the FBI. For example, New York's Crime Scene Unit—a part of the detective bureau that consists of 78 detectives and supervisors who also have been trained as serologists, entomologists, embalmers, architects, and engineers—answered more than 3,000 calls for help during 1995.[2]

The preceding discussion illustrates the importance and value of crime scenes. However, briefly citing some of the kinds of evidence actually found at crime scenes during investigations may prove helpful. We discuss how they were found and handled, and their evidentiary value, in Chapters 13 and 14.

❖ Case 8-1

When the Rochester, New York, Brink's depot was robbed on January 5, 1993, minivan tire tracks at the scene helped connect one of the suspects to the crime.[3]

❖ Case 8-2

The decomposed body of a woman was found in a tractor-trailer on September 20, 1994. She appeared to be a jogger in good physical condition, who had maintained a healthy diet; her fingernails were neatly manicured; and her teeth were in good condition. Among items found at the scene were her expensive running shoes and a modestly priced jogging outfit.[4]

❖ Case 8-3

The hunting knife used by the killer of a 7-year-old girl, stabbed to death March 8, 1966, was found at the scene.[5]

❖ Case 8-4

On December 30, 1994, two women were killed and several others wounded by gunfire in separate incidents that took place within a short time; a lone gunman was responsible. Aside from the victims and spent shell casings found at both scenes, at the second, investigators also found a duffle bag containing a .22 caliber handgun, a receipt from a gun shop, and ammunition clips that had been left behind by the perpetrator.[6]

❖ Case 8-5

Finding a 1/2-inch screw at the crime scene, on a bedsheet in an otherwise meticulously kept apartment, coupled with the deceased's position, led to the conclusion that this was a homicide rather than a suicide.[7]

❖ Case 8-6

A female jogger was attacked and killed in a park in the early morning of September 17, 1995. From examining the crime scene, it was possible to conclude that the initial attack occurred about 20 feet from where the victim was found, and that she had been dragged to the spot under a footbridge.[8]

❖ Case 8-7

The crime scene from which a multimillion-dollar credit card fraud ring had operated yielded stolen invoices; stolen and counterfeit Visa, MasterCard, American Express, and Discover credit cards; and equipment such as holograms, magnetic tape, and embossing and encoding machines needed to make the cards.[9]

❖ **Case 8-8**

A piece of a "cosmos black" automobile grille found at the scene of a hit-and-run homicide led to the driver's arrest.[10]

SUMMARY

In investigations, recognizing the invaluable contribution that properly handled crime and accident scenes can make to solving cases is best illustrated by the fact that a number of local and federal investigative agencies, whether involved with crimes or accidents, now have special teams whose job it is to define and search incident scenes for evidence. Of course, in those organizations that do not have the benefit of specialists, investigators remain responsible for such searches and evidence collection.

Regardless of who does the work, the first thing that must be done upon arrival is to define and secure the scene. Defining it ensures that the scene is all-inclusive; securing it prevents the contamination or removal of even the most minute particle of evidence. Whether done by specialists or case investigators, the next step is to photograph and sketch the scene before the search for and collection of evidence is started.

Throughout the entire process, those working the scene must make detailed, accurate notes. Photographs and sketches, and everything that appears therein or thereon, must be fully documented. This is important for investigators not only in terms of the investigation itself, but also because all these details eventually will have to be incorporated in a written report. Furthermore, this is critical, especially in criminal cases, if models or other materials are to be made or developed to help jurors understand what happened at the time of trial. Investigative leads are the product of what is observed and of evidence collected at incident scenes.

REVIEW QUESTIONS

1. Why do we refer to *incident* instead of *crime* scenes?
2. Give an example of a scene in an investigation where no apparent criminal activity is involved.
3. Why is it important to pay close attention to detail at any incident scene?
4. Is it really possible for an investigator at a crime scene to know with certainty whether something has been removed?
5. How might there be multiple crime scenes within a single investigation?

6. What must be covered in examining any crime scene?
7. What are the first two things to be done upon arrival at an incident scene?
8. Why are an investigator's field notes important?
9. Name the three most common methods used to sketch crime scenes.
10. On what should investigators focus when they arrive at the scene of a criminal homicide?

NOTES

1. John Douglas and Mark Olshaker, *Mindhunter* (New York: Scribner, 1995), pp. 171–172.
2. "Anatomy of a Murder Scene," *New York Times Magazine,* January 28, 1996, pp. 42–45.
3. "U.S. Details Evidence in Brink's Robbery Arrests," *New York Times,* November 14, 1993, pp. 1, 40.
4. "After a Slaying a Question Is Asked: Who Was She?," *New York Times,* September 25, 1994, pp. 39, 45.
5. "After 30 Years, New Clue Pursued in Unsolved Killing," *New York Times,* November 30, 1995, p. B11.
6. "Though Hunt for Suspect Was Vast, Chance Proved Crucial for Capture," *New York Times,* January 2, 1995, p. 10.
7. "Tiny Clue Prevents a Slaying From Being Listed as a Suicide," *New York Times,* August 27, 1995, p. 34.
8. "Evidence Is Elusive in Central Park Jogger Killing," *New York Times,* October 23, 1995, p. B3.
9. "Authorities Break Credit-Card Fraud Ring," *New York Times,* February 8, 1996, p. B5.
10. "Scion of Rich Family in Colo. Is a Suicide," *The Boston Globe,* March 21, 1996, p. 3.

Chapter 9

❖

Sources of Information and Confidential Informants

Both sources of information and confidential informants can be of inestimable value to investigators. There are those who distinguish between sources of information and informants by placing all persons who provide information in the latter category. Others consider some classes of persons as sources of information rather than as informants. To them, persons whose identities need not be kept confidential, but who are in the unique position of being able to either provide or validate information that otherwise might not be readily available to investigators, are sources of information. Deciding whether to consider some persons as sources or all persons as informants is a matter of choice, but examples may help clarify the difference.

During the early stages of the war between North and South Korea, when the former's principal ally was the People's Republic of China, the United States was concerned about members of large ethnic Chinese communities possibly being pressured to send money to China. If true, those efforts might have their greatest success among families who still had relatives there and feared for their safety. This prompted the FBI to undertake a survey of the larger Chinese communities to try to determine if in fact such pressure was being applied.

Since each community had its own "mayor," a logical starting point was to meet with him, explain the project's purpose, and ask about that community's size in order to get some idea of the magnitude of the undertaking should there be evidence of pressure. According to Chicago's "mayor," with whom the field office had had no prior contact, there were about 3,000 people "in my Chinatown." Wanting to confirm this figure, a highly respected member of that same community who previously and willingly had helped with various matters related to Chinese American affairs was contacted. He reported that his family association alone had a larger membership. This information was not confidential; neither was there a need to protect his identity. He was a source of information available to all Chicago Field Office agents in matters pertaining to the city's Chinese community. Without access to him, validating the "mayor's" numbers would have been virtually impossible.

In contrast, the very nature of much of the information provided by confidential informants mandates keeping their identities confidential both to avoid compromising the investigation and for their own protection. Although persons as sources of information and confidential informants are developed individually by investigators, source contacts are open to all investigative personnel, whereas contacts between investigators and confidential informants are restricted to the particular investigator who developed the informant, and possibly one other person with whom he or she closely works. This is true even though the informant may at times be in a position to provide useful information to other investigators.

SOURCES OF INFORMATION

Sources of information actually fall into two principal categories. One consists of various types of records and allied documentation; from our example, the other obviously consists of people. The question is, what people? Relatives of victims, especially parents, a spouse, and children, are among the best sources, but others also may be able to provide useful information. Close friends and acquaintances, coworkers, business associates and competitors, members of the clergy with whom victims may have associated, former and possibly current teachers and classmates, and neighbors are possible sources. Others who possibly can help include community leaders or those of religious or ethnic organizations or labor unions, and neighborhood merchants. Even newspaper delivery persons, mail carriers, and garbage collectors are among those who might be able to offer useful information. Remember that there may be any number of people who, unless contacted by investigators, will hesitate to volunteer information. Either they do not want to become involved or they doubt that what they have to say would be useful. However, to the person whose case it is, what those persons might contribute, if asked, could prove to be valuable in the context of the overall investigation.

Although most investigations are reactive, in other words, they are in response to an incident that has occurred, we also noted in earlier chapters that some, however few, are proactive. One of the proactive kinds is designed to help interested agencies and departments collect intelligence information with regard to terrorist activities. Since the very nature of these investigations falls principally under federal jurisdiction, the involved federal agencies rely on their more traditional approaches to intelligence gathering, but they also avail themselves of the considerable resources of private human rights organizations that have spent years keeping track of the "fringe right."[1] This, too, is illustrative of persons (as well as data) being used as sources of information.

Good investigators also find innumerable, and helpful, sources of information in the form of various types of data. Of course, though virtually all these are available to law enforcement personnel, on either a voluntary basis or through the use of court orders, many are unavailable to private persons such as corporate security personnel and other private investigators.

For instance, government investigators have access to criminal histories, including offense and arrest records even when individuals have not been convicted, modus operandi files, fingerprint records, Internal Revenue and Social Security information, law enforcement investigative and missing persons' reports, and prison records. They also can obtain gun and motor vehicle registration data. Corporate or other private investigators obviously have access to their own prior investigative and incident reports, but as a rule, not to those of government police or investigative agencies. They may or may not be able to get data on gun or motor vehicle registrations, and their access to criminal history information, if at all allowed, is tightly controlled by state law.

It is not surprising that the foregoing, representing a variety of government agencies or departments, are sources of information readily available to police and federal investigators. Nevertheless, there are numerous nongovernment activities from which useful information can be gotten by sworn law enforcement personnel, and possibly even by private sector investigators. From the government investigator's perspective in some cases, such sources willingly cooperate because they have a vested interest in the investigation's outcome; in others, they do so as an act of good citizenship. In still others, it may be necessary to obtain and serve a subpoena in order to gain access to information that may or may not eventually be used as evidence.

Examples of nongovernment sources that offer cooperation because of a vested interest would be banks in credit card fraud cases, or insurance companies in arson or stolen motor vehicle investigations. Hotels and motels or public utilities may provide information as acts of good citizenship. Hospitals and clinics, because of the patient–doctor privilege, and employers concerned with privacy issues, may require a court order before their data can be used as sources, and even then there may be restrictions.

In addition to these possibilities, public libraries, available to both public and private sector investigators, are excellent sources for some types of information. As a rule, they will have telephone, city, and street cross directories. Such business directories as Moody's and Dun & Bradstreet generally can be found there, along with the various editions of publications like *Who's Who in America, Who's Who in Commerce and Industry,* and *Who's Who in Law.*

Many other sources of information are also available, some to all investigators and others principally to law enforcement personnel. Included among them are school, unemployment, credit card, telephone, gas and electric, airline, military, business, car rental, oil company, loan and credit, delivery service, newspaper delivery and "morgue," pawnbroker, moving and storage company, and taxi company records.

Government records that are open to the general public also can be helpful. Among them are records in court clerks' offices that contain information about divorces and the probate of wills, criminal trials, and bankruptcies. Registrars of Deeds offices have data on real estate transactions; information about corporate matters and dates of birth can be found in the offices of secretaries of state. A city clerk's office also may have birth date information, as well as data on death certificates and marriage licenses.

Although the nature of an investigation will dictate to which of the available human sources of information one should turn, which of the many other sources may not be as obvious. It is here that investigators need to be both imaginative and resourceful. The following examples of actual cases illustrate how various sources of information can be helpful to investigators:

❖ Case 9-1

The ringleader of a gang with New York origins was wanted by six county, state, and federal agencies. Investigators learned that he was using an alias. Credit card records based on the alias were checked and led to his arrest in Los Angeles in September 1995.[2]

❖ Case 9-2

Telephone records, airline manifests, and a work permit application filled out at an Immigration and Naturalization Service (INS) office in Kansas City by a suspect in the World Trade Center bombing were factors that led to his arrest in Jordan after a two-and-a-half-year search by the FBI and the INS.[3]

❖ Case 9-3

Records of the use of a single telephone credit card helped link extortion victims in Brooklyn, New York, Seattle, Washington, and the People's

Republic of China. The result: the arrest of two men in Seattle and one in New York.[4]

❖ Case 9-4

The victim in a November 1995 murder investigation was described as having enemies in many places. Looking for leads, investigators checked records in the county clerk's office for Dutchess County, New York. The records revealed that between 1987 and the date of the victim's death, he had filed lawsuits in more than sixty cases, had been named as a defendant in another twenty-two, and was a plaintiff in several others where the action was brought under one of his corporate names.[5]

❖ Case 9-5

During the course of the investigation of the November 1993 robbery of the Rochester, New York, Brink's depot, the FBI examined the bank records of three suspects. The information proved very useful and helped bring about their arrest.[6]

❖ Case 9-6

The records of a gun shop and the motor vehicle departments of both New Hampshire and Massachusetts played a role in identifying and apprehending the assailant in the case of two Brookline, Massachusetts, abortion clinic killings in December 1994.[7]

❖ Case 9-7

Among the sources of information used to help locate three members of a smuggling gang wanted in connection with the killing of an immigrant in Brooklyn, New York, were public utility records in the name of one of them for a safe house that they had rented in Brooklyn. The records helped track them to Milpitas, California, where they were apprehended.[8]

❖ Case 9-8

The morning of July 29, 1992, the unidentified body of a teenage girl was found in the Chelsea section of New York City. An examination of missing persons' reports helped identify the victim, an essential first step in the investigation that led to an arrest on August 6.[9]

❖ Case 9-9

Almost thirty years after a 7-year-old girl was stabbed to death in downtown Elizabeth, New Jersey, on March 8, 1966, a woman, though not a witness, provided the police with a tip that prompted them to reopen the investigation.[10]

❖ Case 9-10

In the FBI's investigation of Theodore John Kaczynski, suspected of being the Unabomber, records of a Sacramento, California, hotel reportedly showed Kaczynski as having been a registered guest on the same days that some of the bombs were mailed to victims from Sacramento.[11]

As these cases show, sources of information, in the form of both people and assorted records, can be invaluable investigative tools. However, it is incumbent upon investigators to remember that even though such sources may be used to confirm data or to provide additional leads, they also must make certain that information obtained from sources is accurate before its inclusion in any affidavits or reports that may be used as a basis for further action. This means going back to original sources whenever there is even the slightest doubt about the accuracy of any information.

The importance of reverting to original sources is well illustrated by a 1995 incident when an FBI affidavit submitted to a U.S. District Court erroneously referred to the head of one of the largest casinos in the United States as an associate of an organized crime family. Subsequently, the FBI admitted that errors can occur in interpreting files or taking information directly from a data bank without reviewing the files on which the data are based. As John McGinley, the Special Agent in Charge of the FBI's Newark, New Jersey, Field Division from 1985 to 1989 said, "if you don't go back to the original sources, you stand that chance of mis-interpreting things."[12]

CONFIDENTIAL INFORMANTS

The tendency is to think of confidential informants only in terms of people, yet for report-writing purposes, information derived from certain types of surveillances may be referred to as confidential informants. This is largely because police and federal investigative agencies—concerned about protecting the very nature of physical or electronic surveillances, telephone taps, mail covers, or pen registers—prefer to cite information from these sources in reports as coming from confidential informants. We expand on the various forms of surveillance in Chapter 12.

Of course, a major concern of all investigators who use confidential informants is their reliability. In other words, how trustworthy are the informants, and to what extent can the information provided by them be relied upon? Since physical or electronic surveillances, or telephone taps conducted or monitored by investigative personnel, are accompanied by appropriate logs and possibly recordings, the sources are deemed reliable, but that does not necessarily mean the information is. Since mail covers and pen registers, when requested by investigators, are handled by the postal authorities and telephone company personnel, respectively, the information gotten also is considered reliable.

By way of contrast, the same standards of reliability are not as easily determined when the confidential informants are people. Here, of course, a distinction has to be made between those select law enforcement personnel who go undercover in order to gather information about illegal activities and those persons whose connections to police or federal investigative agencies may be limited to their contributions as informants. In those cases where investigators go undercover in order to collect information as well as evidence, reliability is assumed. Nevertheless, considering the nature of such work, and the pressures and temptations with which the investigators may be confronted, their activities need to be closely supervised and monitored to ensure continued reliability and to maintain the investigation's integrity.

Private organizations occasionally will use the services of private investigators for undercover work when they suspect wrongdoing in the workplace. This usually is done at the behest or suggestion of security directors. However, this alone does not guarantee the reliability of those assigned to undercover work by their employers. It would be naive to think that all companies providing services of this kind screen their applicants and supervise their employees as closely and carefully as do most police departments and federal investigative agencies.

Turning then to other persons who become confidential informants (unlike people who may be used as sources of information), the inherent nature of the information they provide is such that neither is it readily available to investigators nor does it always lend itself to easy verification. This heightens the importance of reliability. It also means that the confidential informant's identity must be safeguarded if he or she is to be of value.

Because of the methods employed to get meaningful information for investigators, each informant's degree of reliability is a matter of almost constant concern, evaluation, and reevaluation by the investigator responsible for that individual's development and use. Therefore, a first step is to consider a person's motivation for becoming a confidential informant. This is especially true when one considers the fact that informants—often referred to as "snitches," "tattlers," "squealers," "stool pigeons," "stoolies," and "finks"—are unwelcome and unpopular among criminals, and even so-called good citizens often find them distasteful. Nevertheless, they can serve a useful purpose. As Judge Learned Hand has written, "Courts have countenanced informers from time immemorial."[13]

Although on occasion a person will provide useful information anonymously, more times than not confidential informants will fall into one of two classes. This is true whether they are functioning as such for a single investigation or on a much broader scale.

One group consists of those motivated by good intentions and a genuine desire to help fight crime. They volunteer their services. However, in developing confidential informants from among such volunteers, investigators should be wary of persons who, despite their good intentions, may have an additional, undisclosed motive—a desire to play "cops and robbers."

Another group comprises people whose own involvement with criminal activities, whether direct or indirect, positions them to be helpful to law enforcement. Persons in this category may or may not willingly or voluntarily agree to become informants. If they can be developed, they will want to be compensated. Some will want cash payments for their information. Others will want to get a "deal" from prosecutors with regard to crimes for which they stand to be tried. Then, too, some active criminals may be motivated to become informants not only for cash or a deal, but also for revenge.

By and large, confidential informants, including those highly motivated as good citizens, do not simply walk into law enforcement agencies' offices and offer to assume roles that may entail more than a little personal risk. Consequently, most have to be developed by investigators, a process that involves a good deal of analysis on their part if those who become confidential informants are to be truly effective.

Because of the impact that the use of human informants can have on the ultimate outcome of a criminal investigation, investigators need to ask themselves a number of questions. An obvious first question is whether the information needed could be obtained in a timely and effective way by some means other than the use of an informant. If not, what is the nature of the investigation, and just how important is the information that an informant can provide? Does the investigator have a prospective informant in mind? If so, what would motivate that person to become an informant? How great is the risk of this aspect of the investigation being compromised? And of critical importance are questions about the prospective informant's reliability and truthfulness, and difficulties that might be encountered in monitoring the informant's activities. Good investigators make every effort to avoid developing and using informants whose lack of credibility, more than anything else, ultimately invalidates the investigator's work by becoming such an embarrassment to the prosecution's case that a jury acquits an otherwise guilty person.

If the foregoing questions are satisfactorily answered, and it appears that a confidential informant will be able to provide good information, it does not mean that the investigator can relax. Once there is an identifiable confidential informant, new and different issues remain that, if ignored, can only add to the embarrassment of the investigator responsible for the informant's development, and even more so to the department or agency. Assuredly, they will only raise further questions about the informant's credibility.

For instance, it is the investigator and not the informant who decides how deeply the latter is to become involved in anything that even borders on possible criminal activity, and in what ways. True, informants frequently must be participants, whether active or passive, in order to establish and maintain relationships with the investigation's subjects. Even so, they must avoid becoming actual parties to the commission of crimes. Investigators responsible for handling informants cannot ignore the fact that an informant's active participation in any crime will greatly diminish both that person's credibility and the value of the information provided. Rest assured that defense counsel will make every effort to question an informant's character. Furthermore, informant participation in a crime for which a particular defendant is being tried also might open the door for defense counsel to argue that his or her client was entrapped. Successful or not, if that attorney can raise a reasonable doubt in the mind of but one juror, the result may be an acquittal or a hung jury.

Investigators who have and use confidential informants must be concerned about other control-related matters. These are issues based on the obvious need to protect their informants and their identities as well as themselves. Included among these concerns are clear and unmistakable instructions to informants reminding them that under no circumstances do they tell anyone about their relationships with investigators. To ensure that meetings between investigators and informants are not compromised, only the investigators choose meeting places. To further minimize the risk of compromise, lengthy telephone conversations between investigators and their informants must be avoided. The limits imposed on access to informants, also a matter of control and protection, were discussed earlier in this chapter.

Other pitfalls that conceivably can affect investigators' careers and be extremely embarrassing to their departments or agencies also must be avoided. For instance, do not forget that until an informant's reliability has been proved, those who are motivated by cash payments for information may report things for which there is no factual basis in order to get paid. Those who offer their services because they are affected by a cops-and-robbers syndrome may provide useless information in the hope of cementing their relationship and being made to feel that they are on the "inside" of an investigation.

A risk that can pose an even greater threat to investigators and their agencies are informants who, no matter how credible and for reasons known only to themselves, try to secretly record their conversations. In addition, when investigators and their informants are of the opposite sex, it is imperative that the former ensure that their relationships not become personal or entangling; in fact, even the slightest appearance of a personal relationship between the two must be avoided.

Aside from exercising good judgment in developing, using, and controlling informants, and making every effort to independently corroborate the information provided by them, the concerns cited here can assume even greater importance if, at time of trial, an informant's identity must be disclosed. Although prosecutors will try to protect informants' identities and avoid having them testify, they may not always be successful.

This lack of success is attributable to two factors, one of which is a clause in the Fifth Amendment to the U.S. Constitution granting to every accused the right to confront his or her accusers. The other is the very nature of trials in our courts, which are based on an adversary system. That may result in a judge ordering a confidential informant's appearance.

It has been held that although fairness to a defendant may require disclosing a confidential informant's identity, this is not an absolute. A judge's decision following defense counsel's motion for disclosure has to balance the public interest in protecting the flow of information against a defendant's right to prepare a defense. The question of what constitutes a proper balance in each case depends on the particular circumstances of that case.[14]

Consequently, although it may impose an added burden on investigators, in dealing with confidential informants, it is better for them to proceed on the assumption that disclosure may be required than that it will not be. However, this in itself does not justify a failure to develop and use confidential informants. A few examples, based on actual investigations, help illustrate not only some ways in which confidential informants can be used, but also some of the advantages and disadvantages that can be encountered when they are.

❖ **Case 9-11**

The Boston Police Department applied for a search warrant for drugs and guns based on information from a confidential informant of "dubious integrity." The information was not corroborated. The search was executed at the wrong address on March 25, 1994, by breaking down the door to the apartment of a 75-year-old minister who was chased, subdued, and handcuffed during the process. He went into cardiac arrest and died. Following this incident, the investigator responsible for the informant was criticized for having become personally involved with the informant and was suspended for fifteen days. On April 23, 1996, the City of Boston agreed to pay the deceased's widow $1 million.[15]

❖ **Case 9-12**

U.S. government agencies use their traditional intelligence efforts to keep abreast of the activities of an estimated eight hundred right-wing groups that espouse antigovernment sentiments in all fifty states. However, they also reportedly get help from private human rights groups that track the so-called fringe right with their own networks.[16]

❖ Case 9-13

On February 23, 1996, the FBI arrested a former U.S. Army enlisted man on charges of espionage. He had worked at the National Security Agency's headquarters from 1964 to 1967. Oleg Kalugin, a former Russian KGB officer in Washington, D.C., in his book, *The First Directorate: My 32 Years in Intelligence and Espionage Against the West,* had referred to a young soldier who spied for Russia and after leaving the NSA used KGB money to finance his education. Despite this, the man was able to elude detection until some time in 1993, when his former wife informed the FBI of his activities.[17]

❖ Case 9-14

Despite the untiring efforts and resources of the FBI, postal inspectors, and ATF over more than seventeen years, the Unabomber case investigation had not yet identified a suspect. It was not until early in 1996, when an anonymous confidential informant, acting through an attorney, provided information to the FBI, that Theodore John Kaczynski was taken into custody. Subsequently, the informant's identity was disclosed by the news media; it was the suspect's brother.

❖ Case 9-15

John Gotti, identified as the head of New York City's powerful organized crime Gambino family, was tried and acquitted three times, notwithstanding the time and resources that had been devoted to an ongoing investigation. However, in 1992, Gotti was convicted in a U.S. District Court for the Southern District of New York due in large part to the FBI's success in developing and using Sammy "The Bull" Gravano, who had been Gotti's "right-hand" man, as an informant.

❖ Case 9-16

Information provided to federal agents by a confidential informant helped lead to the April 26, 1996, arrest of two members of the right-wing Georgia Militia, an antigovernment group, who were charged with conspiracy and possession of materials sufficient to make more than twelve pipe bombs.[18]

❖ Case 9-17

In 1982, the Reverend John Burgess, pastor of a Carthage, Mississippi, church and part-owner in a culvert sales business, refused to do business with county supervisors who offered to buy pipe and supplies from him in return for kickbacks on the purchase price. His refusal put his business in jeopardy financially. In 1984, he approached the FBI offering his help in fighting what appeared to be widespread corruption at both the state and local levels. He not only permitted undercover FBI agents to pose as salespeople, contact customers, make sales, and participate in giving kickbacks, but he also met corrupt officials, made deliveries, and gave kickbacks all at considerable personal risk to himself. As a direct result of Reverend Burgess's service as a confidential informant, seventy-five state and county officials were charged.

Case 9-17 also shows how the work of undercover investigators, instead of confidential informants, can be used to develop evidence. In fact, there will be times when circumstances may dictate use of this investigative technique in lieu of trying to develop confidential informants. To further illustrate this point, it is worth looking at what had been a forty-month undercover investigation of the Chicago Board of Trade and Chicago Mercantile Exchange, until the FBI went public in January 1989.

During that time, five special agents worked in the Board of Trade's pits as professional traders, and on foreign currency matters at the Mercantile Exchange. As a result of their efforts, forty-eight employees were indicted in August 1989. Twenty-one of the defendants either pled guilty or were convicted.

SUMMARY

Criminal investigators know well that aside from physical evidence found at crime scenes, a major part of their work consists of a search for information. Although searching for information is equally true of civil inquiries, the process in criminal cases tends to be much more complex.

Information can be developed from a number of sources. It is true that many of the sources of information available to investigators in the form of certain records and documents are not available to the general public, including private-sector investigators. However, the latter do have access to certain public records, and depending on the nature of their work, they should avail themselves of that access. By the same token, all investigators should remember that a good deal of information, much of which can be found in libraries, is generally available and should be used to the fullest extent.

People also can provide information. Those who are in positions either to furnish information that otherwise might not be readily available or to corroborate that gotten from other sources, and whose identities need not be kept confidential, often can be excellent sources of information. They need to be developed very much like confidential informants, but unlike the latter, their activities are not controlled and their availability should not be restricted to only one or two investigators; they should be available to all departmental or agency personnel.

The very term *confidential informant* is indicative of the sensitivity involved with activities or persons that fall into this category. One of the important aspects of being an investigator involves report writing. That various investigative techniques are generally known does not alter the fact that those used in a particular investigation should not be disclosed in a report. Whether information is derived from a court-authorized telephone tap, bug, pen register, or mail cover, the method employed needs to be protected. This is done by reporting the information as having come from a confidential informant of known reliability.

When dealing with confidential informants, the question of reliability is of the utmost importance; it is something that no investigator can afford to assume. In reporting information furnished by informants, investigators are obligated to indicate if that particular informant is of known reliability. Investigators may have had sufficient contact with certain persons to know that they are indeed reliable. However, in some cases, the relationship may be too new, and the informant has to be identified as being of unknown reliability. In still other cases, there may have been times when informants provided some information that was good and some that was not. This, too, needs to be reflected by referring to the informant as one who has on occasion offered reliable information.

The term *confidential informant* obviously must be used when investigators report information furnished by people. Since persons, including public-spirited citizens, may hesitate to volunteer to become confidential informants, it is incumbent upon investigators to develop those who either are or might be in positions where they can obtain and make available information about known or suspected criminal activities. However, in doing so, the fact that an informant's identity may have to be exposed during a trial represents a risk that cannot be ignored.

Some people, in a spirit of public service, will agree to become informants, but as a practical matter, most will come from among known criminals. Regardless, investigators responsible for developing individual informants should be aware of the person's motives. This is important since motivation may affect both the individual's reliability and the investigator's ability to control the informant's activities.

Occasionally, the very nature of a particular investigation—its sensitivity, the possible need for special skills, and the needed resources to conduct a successful inquiry—may be such that using confidential informants in the more traditional sense of the term is unwise or impractical. There also may be time-consuming factors in complex investigations. The investigation may have ramifications that will require someone who understands the type of activity involved, is flexible enough to be able to adjust to any new developments that might arise, and has the ability to blend into the scene without arousing the subjects' suspicion. It also may be a situation in which both the person in charge of the case and the prosecutor's office believe that firsthand rather than secondhand information will be needed to get a conviction. Under these circumstances, thought has to be given to the possible use of police or federal agents in undercover roles.

REVIEW QUESTIONS

1. Name the two principal categories of sources of information.
2. What kinds of people can be used as sources?
3. Are all sources of information equally available to both public- and private-sector investigators?
4. What is the difference between a source of information and a confidential informant?
5. What motivates people to become confidential informants?
6. Should all investigators in an agency have access to all informants, or should access be controlled?
7. Are all confidential informants necessarily reliable?
8. Why must investigators who deal with confidential informants control their informants?
9. Is it permissible for investigators to develop and maintain personal relationships with their confidential informants?
10. Under what circumstances should the use of undercover police officers or federal agents be considered?

NOTES

1. "Private Groups Lead Charge in War on Far Right," *New York Times,* April 14, 1996, p. E3.
2. "Officials Say Gang Broken by 21 Arrests," *New York Times,* September 30, 1995, pp. 21, 23.
3. "Fingerprints Link Suspect to Bombing, Officials Say," *New York Times,* August 5, 1995, p. 23.
4. "Brooklyn Killing Is Linked to a Kidnapping in Seattle," *New York Times,* September 7, 1995, p. B3.
5. "The Late Mr. Rosenberg Left a Mystery Behind," *New York Times,* November 21, 1995, p. B4.
6. "U.S. Details Evidence in Brink's Robbery Arrests," *New York Times,* November 14, 1993, pp. 1, 40.
7. "Though Hunt for Suspect Was Vast, Chance Proved Crucial for Capture," *New York Times,* January 2, 1995, p. 10.
8. "3 Men Held in Slaying of Immigrant," *New York Times,* September 20, 1995, pp. B1, B4.

9. "Woman's Quest for Fame Ends in Death in the Night," *New York Times,* August 7, 1992, p. B3.

10. "After 30 Years, New Clue Pursued in Unsolved Killing," *New York Times,* November 30, 1995, p. B11.

11. "Hotel Clerk, Bus Employees Provide Clues," *The Boston Globe,* April 8, 1996, p. 12.

12. "The F.B.I. Goofed; The C.E.O. May Pay," *New York Times,* April 14, 1995, pp. D1, D4.

13. *United States v. Dennis,* 183 F.2d, 201, 224 (2d. Cir. 1950).

14. *Roviaro v. United States,* 353 U.S. 53, 58–61 (1957).

15. *The Boston Globe,* April 24, 1996, pp. 1, 25.

16. "Private Groups Lead Charge in War on Far Right," *New York Times,* April 14, 1996, p. E3.

17. "Ex-G.I. Arrested on Charges of Spying for Soviet Union," *New York Times,* February 24, 1996, p. 6.

18. "U.S. Seizes 2 Georgia Men With Ties to Paramilitary Group," *New York Times,* April 27, 1996, p. 9; "Ga. Militia Members Face Bomb Charges," *The Boston Globe,* April 27, 1996, pp. 1, 8.

Chapter 10

❖

Locating
and Interviewing
Witnesses

Chapter 3 discussed the characteristics of good investigators, among them dedication and a combination of persistence and patience. These traits permeate all phases of investigative work, but they can be sorely tried when it comes to the task of locating and interviewing witnesses. Dictionaries and *Roget's International Thesaurus* make little distinction between interviews and interrogations other than that the latter tend to be more formalized.

To locate and interview witnesses is essential to and an integral part of most investigations. To say that doing so is relatively easy oversimplifies the process. To better understand the difficulties that can arise in locating and interviewing witnesses, we first must look at the types of persons that may be encountered and some of the problems that may be found in dealing with them.

LOCATING WITNESSES

A definition of the word *witness* in *Webster's New World Dictionary* is "a person who saw, or can give a firsthand account of, something." Consequently, in other than homicide cases, victims qualify as witnesses, and they obviously should be the easiest ones to find and interview. This is based on the premise that once victimized and having called the police, they will stay at the crime scene and be available not only to the first responders, but also at a later time to investigators. Neither is it surprising that when complaints are made to federal agencies, where responses may not occur as speedily as with police departments, locating victims and witnesses is reasonably easy.

The fact that persons file complaints does not necessarily mean that they will readily agree to interviews. Victims may have been traumatized by the event, and they want the authorities to act speedily, yet until they are interviewed, they may not fully understand that as victims they also are eyewitnesses who will be expected to appear and testify at time of trial. Faced with this reality, victims' reluctance is understandable; they are fearful.

For example, a rape victim may feel that having to testify against her assailant in open court will force her to relive her nightmare. Merchants, forced to pay tribute to gangs of neighborhood thugs to prevent their businesses from being vandalized and customers harassed, may be afraid lest they become victims of even greater crimes. However, despite their reluctance and possible fear, once a complaint has been made (unless it was done anonymously), investigators at least know where to find the complainant or eyewitness.

Locating other witnesses may not be as easy. It is a mistake to assume that most witnesses, other than victims, will come forward freely, and once found, helping them overcome their reluctance or fear may pose a real challenge for the investigator. True, some will believe that as good citizens they are obliged to make themselves available; others may do so out of a sense of excitement. What becomes a matter of genuine concern to investigators is the knowledge that there may be potential witnesses whose reluctance or fear prevents them from making themselves known or volunteering information. A special effort must be made to identify and locate those persons. Equally important is the need to identify persons who may in fact be witnesses and who have not come forward, not out of reluctance or fear, but because they do not realize they may be in a position to be helpful. Consequently, locating witnesses can be an arduous, time-consuming task.

We already have discussed how investigations are initiated and who conducts them, noting that among the tasks to be done by patrol personnel who first respond to criminal complaints is to identify and locate witnesses. For the most part, patrol personnel are not the ones who conduct in-depth interviews; neither do they initiate a search for possible witnesses other than those persons whom they find at the scene upon their arrival. However, they can and often do assist in that effort under the direction and supervision of the investigator to whom the case is assigned.

The search for possible witnesses whose identities are not made known to investigators, whether because they do not want to become "involved," they are afraid, or they do not realize that they have information, calls for the utmost patience and perseverance. That identifying and locating these witnesses can be time consuming does not excuse the failure to try. The neighborhood canvass must be initiated, usually with the help of patrol personnel. This can mean going door-to-door and ringing doorbells, sometimes at odd hours, asking questions, and hoping that once such witnesses are located and identified, they will agree to be interviewed and to testify at time of trial if necessary.

Suppose a corner drugstore is robbed, shots were fired, and witnesses in the store say there were three robbers, but they have no idea how they left the scene. Diagonally across the street is an apartment building. The possibility that some of the tenants may have seen or heard something of potential value to the investigators should not be ignored. This will mean contacting everyone who lives in the building to see if they might have seen or heard anything that might be relevant. It does not mean contacting only tenants whose apartments face the street or intersection; it means contacting all of them. It is possible that some of them may have been on the street at the time of the robbery, and that they saw or heard something of interest. If this requires returning to the building one or more times, so be it. Parenthetically, although a neighborhood canvass is a logical starting point in looking for possible witnesses, other means should be considered. Cooperative members of the news media can help by featuring stories about the incident and urging people with information to contact the investigators.

INTERVIEWING WITNESSES

In some situations, initial contact may be by telephone, but regardless of how witnesses are identified and located, they must be interviewed. As for the interviews, good investigators take nothing for granted. They know that although privacy and minimal disruption during an interview are essential, the cooperation of possible witnesses is imperative. Therefore, interviews should be scheduled for a time and place to which the witness agrees even if it is to be at night, on a holiday, or on a weekend at the person's home.

An investigator's communications skills can be a major factor in whether or not the interview will succeed. Since their first priority is to get information, interviewers must control their interviews and keep witnesses focused. Their ability to put interviewees at ease can help witnesses overcome their reluctance or fear. It helps to open interviews by thanking the person for agreeing to meet. Showing empathy for any concerns the witness may have is also helpful, as is discussing generally what happened and what the witness may be able to contribute. If interviews are conducted at the investigator's office, the offer of a cup of coffee or tea can help relieve some of the possible tension.

Sometimes the anxiety to get as much witness information as possible, in as short a time as possible, can cause problems for both investigators and prosecutors. This can occur when investigators are not sufficiently alert for potential difficulties while conducting witness interviews.

For instance, when interviewed, did witnesses appear to be mentally competent? Were they physically present and conscious when the incident occurred so that they personally know what took place? Did they show signs of possibly being under the influence of either alcohol or drugs? Is it likely that what they believe they saw or heard was influenced by environmental factors such as rain, fog, snow, or distance from where the event took place? Are there personal factors, such as their ability to see or hear, that need to be considered? Do witnesses tend to offer different versions of what occurred? Are there any whose own versions tended to change during the interview? Did their statements seem to be based on fact or on perception? In other words, investigators must recognize that witnesses, even eyewitnesses, can be mistaken in terms of what they will relate during an interview.

The importance of these questions cannot be overemphasized. The answers give investigators valuable insight into the reliability of witnesses in terms of helpful information that they will provide and their potential as credible witnesses at time of trial. Consequently, investigators who are good interviewers must be equally good listeners. Illustrative of this is an article in the June 1984 *FBI Law Enforcement Bulletin,* which states that "One can obtain more accurate and complete information in interviews through simply listening."[1] The same article goes on to say that "Listening has become an important part of interview and interrogation training of new agents at the FBI in Quantico, Virginia. . . . Experience has shown the best listeners to be the best interviewers."[2]

However good they are as listeners, good investigators know that they are not infallible. Therefore, they always allow for the possibility that they may want to reinterview witnesses. To do this without seeming incompetent or risking embarrassment, they will do two things when closing an interview: they will thank the person for his or her help and express the hope that the person will not mind should the investigator find it necessary to contact him or her again for additional assistance.

Of course, one of the things in which criminal investigators are most interested is information that either identifies or will help identify the perpetrator. This often becomes a multistage pursuit. Unless a victim or witness actually knows the subject, investigators have to rely on a physical description followed by a look at mug shots, which, if unsuccessful, may be followed by developing a composite drawing made by an artist or by using a composite kit. The hope is that either an examination of mug shots or the making of a composite will result in an arrest and that witnesses ultimately will have a chance to pick the perpetrator out of a lineup.

That stage of the investigation related to identifying a perpetrator must be handled with great care, partially because witnesses questioned for descriptive data often find it difficult to provide accurate information let alone details. Remember that in having witnessed a crime, most people also have been traumatized. Thus in their anxiety to help, they may be receptive to investigators' suggestions in making an identification. This must be avoided. Furthermore, though the average person may have little trouble distinguishing race and sex, many other characteristics, such as height, weight, eye color, scars and marks, clothing, and kinds of weapons, are less easy to recall. If witnesses are unsure of characteristics like these, it is difficult to provide accurate information for use in flash description broadcasts to radio patrol vehicles in the hope of effecting an early apprehension.

However, once an arrest has been made, placing the suspect in a lineup for viewing by witnesses has to be considered. In doing so, investigators need to be aware that in some jurisdictions a subject's attorney is entitled to be present during a lineup viewing. Whether applicable or not, it is imperative that investigators avoid saying or doing anything that might be construed as trying to influence witnesses.

As for the lineup, no matter how many witnesses there are, they should be allowed to view the lineup only one at a time. This is done to ensure that all witness identifications are made independently. What's more, in preparing a lineup, investigators must ensure that its composition neither singles out nor otherwise focuses undue attention on the subject. This means that every person in the lineup must be of the same race and sex as the suspect, have the same general physical characteristics, and be wearing the same type of clothing.

The latter factors also apply at those times when witnesses are asked to try to make an identification based on a photographic lineup. This procedure differs from an examination of mug books in that investigators select a few photographs to be examined by witnesses much as they would an actual lineup instead of having them look at a seemingly unlimited number.

That one or more witnesses may make an identification during either type of lineup, no matter how certain they may be, does not excuse a failure to continue to search for, collect, and preserve physical evidence. This need assumes increased importance in view of the conclusion of a 1987 study that showed that almost 80,000 trials held in a year in the United States rely primarily on eyewitnesses. And a 1993 review of 1,000 cases in which defendants were convicted and later found not guilty indicated that eyewitness errors were the single largest factor, with flaws having been found to exist in both types of lineups.[3]

The foregoing considerations do not justify discontinuing a search for witnesses, and once found, the witnesses have to be protected against various concerns. For example, in April 1996, the news media petitioned a U.S. District Court judge to unseal documents submitted by the FBI in support of its search warrant application in the Unabomber case—a petition that was denied because of concern that, if granted, witnesses might be compromised and bothered by the news media.[4]

Witness protection may be justified, particularly in high-profile cases, but it becomes even more important in cases when there is fear of intimidation. Prosecutors in some jurisdictions have reported increases in victim and witness intimidation. In fact, some consider intimidation a factor in an estimated 75 to 100 percent of violent crime cases committed in gang-dominated neighborhoods.[5]

Several factors increase the chance of intimidation. Among them are the violent nature of the underlying crime, a victim's or witness's prior personal relationship with the perpetrator, the latter's geographic proximity to the victim or witness, and vulnerability that is culturally based. This would be the case with victims or witnesses who are members of children's or senior citizens' groups, or among recently arrived or illegal immigrants, all of whom tend to be easily victimized.[6] Further, the means used to intimidate are equally varied and include explicit threats of physical violence, actual violence, property damage, and such indirect methods as nuisance telephone calls.

The following cases indicate the roles of witnesses, and how in some situations their versions can affect inquiries for which they supposedly can provide information. These cases make it clear that not all witnesses are trustworthy.

❖ Case 10-1

In 1992, the case of a New York City police officer charged with fatally shooting a drug suspect was presented to a grand jury. Among the allegations made against him were statements from two sisters who reported having witnessed the entire incident. However, aside from some inconsistencies and self-contradictions in later statements to the police, an examination of the scene clearly showed that it would have been physically impossible for the sisters to have seen what actually happened at the time of the shooting.[7]

❖ Case 10-2

On the night of January 5, 1993, three guards at the Rochester, New York, Brinks depot were confronted and robbed by two men in ski masks; one guard was taken "hostage." The latter, arrested November 12, 1993, as a party to the robbery, when first interviewed told investigators that he had been kidnapped in a large U-Haul van with an overhead door. The other guards said the vehicle was a minivan, a fact confirmed on the basis of tire tracks found at the scene.[8]

❖ Case 10-3

At the time of the December 30, 1994, killings at two abortion clinics in Brookline, Massachusetts, witnesses described the assailant as a tall man wearing black clothes, armed with a .22 caliber semiautomatic rifle—information that proved helpful as the investigation and search for the subject took shape.[9]

❖ Case 10-4

On May 10, 1976, a woman was fatally shot; witnesses at the scene identified the subject, who was not apprehended until August 16, 1995, when his fingerprints for access to a bank account matched old police records. However, the earlier witness identification established his role in the homicide.[10]

❖ Case 10-5

A Los Angeles photographer charged with murdering a model in November 1995 was considered a suspect in a 1993 incident because of the similarities between both cases, and because witnesses had seen him with the earlier victim on at least two occasions.[11]

❖ Case 10-6

On February 27, 1996, a woman was critically injured by a carjacked vehicle fleeing from the police. A witness to part of the carjacking was able to describe a white Maxima containing two men that followed the carjacked automobile and to provide the police with three digits of the Maxima's license plate. This enabled the police to narrow the possibilities and arrest three men two days later.[12]

❖ Case 10-7

Jan Philipp Reemtsma, scion of a wealthy German family, was kidnapped March 25, 1996, and released on April 26, 1996, after payment of a $20 million ransom. The victim was able to give police a partial description of the vehicle used and a partial license plate number. As a result of the description, the police received more than 200 tips. The police also had a recording of a conversation with one of the kidnappers. Although the conversation was in German, the victim told the police that his kidnappers spoke to him in English, and they also spoke English among themselves.[13]

❖ Case 10-8

Witnesses reported seeing a white male in his 20s, wearing blue jeans, a white sweatshirt, and a white baseball cap, running away around 3:45 A.M. on April 29, 1996, shortly before a fire broke out that resulted in an estimated $1.6 million in damage to housing on Boston's Beacon Street.[14]

In some of these cases, witnesses were able to provide useful information; in others, it is too early to tell how helpful their information may prove to be. In any event, it is unwise to conclude that all witness information leads to a successful conclusion and prosecution, or even that investigators, despite their patience and diligence, always find at least some witnesses from whose information they can hope to develop additional leads. This is illustrated in the two cases that follow.

❖ Case 10-9

On March 8, 1966, a 7-year-old girl was stabbed to death in Elizabeth, New Jersey; twelve people saw either her murder or assaults on two other schoolgirls only minutes before. In October 1995, information from a woman, not a witness, prompted the police to reopen the case and reinterview some of the original witnesses.[15]

❖ Case 10-10

On September 17, 1995, the body of a female jogger who had been beaten to death was found in New York City's Central Park. Detectives spent all of September 19 stopping joggers, bicyclists, and skaters near the crime scene in an effort to find witnesses, but to no avail.[16] Over a period of thirty-five days, a team of about fifty detectives interviewed more than 100 homeless people living in and around the park in their continued search for witnesses, and possibly the perpetrator.[17]

The need to search for and find witnesses is obvious; it also is important to seek out those who may not have actually witnessed an incident, but who nevertheless may be able to contribute useful information. However, the success in locating people is meaningless if what they know remains unknown to investigators and, in criminal cases, to prosecutors.

Once identified and found, people have to be willing to speak with investigators and tell them whatever they can, but in many respects, the key to getting that information depends largely on the interviewer's personality and skills. An interviewer who is personable, open, friendly, considerate, and understanding can put people at ease.

Unlike custodial interrogations, discussed in Chapter 14, persons interviewed for information, including possible leads, are not given the Miranda warning, but they should be told why they are being questioned and how they might be able to help. However, in asking for their help, as with any lineup, interviewers must take care to avoid asking questions that are or give the appearance of being designed to influence the answers.

Once persons being interviewed know why, it often is helpful to begin with an open-ended question, such as what can they tell the interviewer about the incident. After the person has finished speaking, interviewers will start to ask more direct or specific questions in order to get additional information or to clarify statements already made by the person.

Good memories are attributes of good investigators, but they are no substitute for ensuring that interviews are recorded. Some investigators will make detailed handwritten notes during interviews to help them with the interview process and to make certain that what eventually will be recorded in their investigative reports is accurate.

Other investigators prefer to tape-record interviews. In choosing this method, one needs to be aware of some potential drawbacks. Anticipating an interview's length is difficult. If witnesses have a lot to say, this may mean a break in the process while one tape is removed and replaced by another. However, this time-out also means a break in the person's train of thought and can result in a loss of focus. The damage, though not necessarily irreparable, is something of which interviewers need to be aware. In any event, if the choice is taping, asking witnesses if they object to the recording is a courtesy that can help the relationship between the parties and thus put witnesses at ease. However, if they do object, it is better to use handwritten notes than risk alienating witnesses.

SUMMARY

Locating victims as witnesses in most crimes, homicides aside, is relatively easy, but one cannot assume that being victims always makes them receptive to being interviewed or willing witnesses at time of trial. They may not want to relive the incident, they may be intimidated, or both. Finding other witnesses may be much more difficult. This may be partially due to their not wanting to get involved, their not realizing that they have information that would be useful to investigators, or their being intimidated. If some victims are reluctant to testify in court, it is easier to understand why others, with helpful information, hesitate to answer investigators' questions or appear as witnesses at a trial. Nevertheless, investigators must be ready to deal with and overcome such obstacles.

When crimes are reported to the police, as distinguished from federal agents, the task of identifying victims and other witnesses usually falls to the patrol personnel who first respond. They need to remember two things: not everyone with useful information will come forward voluntarily, and not all eyewitness information is accurate. Despite this, it is the job of patrol personnel to elicit descriptive data about the perpetrator(s) so that it can be broadcast on the chance that an early arrest will result. They also can be called upon to help the lead investigator with whatever additional effort must be made to locate all possible witnesses.

In-depth interviews generally are conducted by investigators rather than patrol personnel. They, too, must keep certain precepts in mind. First is the importance of being good listeners. Second, in all witness interviews, they need to determine, as best they can, witness competence and reliability. Whatever the amount of physical evidence and case preparation, if at trial, defense counsel can raise questions in jurors' minds about witness competence or reliability, the case may well be lost.

Establishing that a crime has been committed is one thing; hoping that witnesses can furnish enough descriptive information about a suspect to warrant that person's apprehension is another. Despite some of the pitfalls associated with eyewitness identifications, once a suspect is in custody, investigators have to try to positively connect that person with the offense or, at the very least, with the crime scene. Such identification precedes subsequent investigative efforts to link the suspect to the crime through the collection and preservation of physical evidence.

The most common practice is to place a suspect in a lineup and bring in witnesses, each separately viewing the persons in the lineup in the hope that a positive identification can be made. Alternatively, witnesses can view a photographic lineup for the same purpose. Already existing questions regarding the accuracy of eyewitness identifications only adds to the responsibility of investigators in ensuring that absolutely nothing is done that could be even remotely construed as suggesting an identification to witnesses in any form of lineup.

Of the many facets of criminal investigations, the two that offer the best chance for developing leads are crime scene searches and information from witnesses—thus the emphasis on locating and interviewing the latter. Investigators must remember to be good listeners and to inform witnesses that it might be necessary to recontact them. They also should accept the idea that although many witness interviews will be productive in helping to identify suspects, and possibly convicting them, there also will be more than a few unproductive ones.

Establishing good rapport with witnesses makes for better interviews. Open-ended questions followed by specific ones can be the most productive, but as with lineups, investigators must avoid suggesting answers. No matter how satisfactory an interview from the standpoint of the information gotten, the results must be recorded in the form of either handwritten notes or on tape.

REVIEW QUESTIONS

1. Why is it relatively easy to locate victims?
2. What are the reasons that victims or witnesses hesitate to be interviewed and to agree to testify?
3. Is it realistic to assume that other witnesses will come forward voluntarily?
4. Aside from getting information, what other factors should be considered when interviewing witnesses?

5. Is it possible for persons to not know that they may have information that would be useful to investigators?

6. What conditions lend themselves to witness intimidation?

7. To what extent is intimidation considered serious in terms of its impact on victims and other witnesses?

8. Is it important for investigators to be good listeners during interviews, or is it enough for them to be skilled questioners?

9. Is it permissible to have all witnesses present at the same time for the purpose of viewing a lineup?

10. What precautions must investigators take in dealing with witnesses in any kind of lineup or when interviewing them?

NOTES

1. Edgar M. Miner, "The Importance of Listening in the Interviewing and Interrogation Process," *FBI Law Enforcement Bulletin,* Vol. 53, No. 6 (June 1984), p. 13.

2. Ibid., p. 16.

3. "Studies Point to Flaws in Lineups of Suspects," *New York Times,* January 17, 1995, pp. C1, C7.

4. "Judge Denies Media Access to Documents on Suspect," *New York Times,* April 11, 1996, p. B10.

5. Kerry Murphy Healey, "Victim and Witness Intimidation: New Developments and Emerging Responses," National Institute of Justice, *Research In Action* (October 1995).

6. Ibid., p. 3.

7. "Overwhelming Evidence in Police Shooting," *New York Times,* September 12, 1992, pp. 23, 25.

8. "U.S. Details Evidence in Brink's Robbery Arrests," *New York Times,* November 14, 1993, pp. 1, 40.

9. "Though Hunt for Suspect Was Vast Chance Proved Crucial for Capture," *New York Times,* January 2, 1995, p. 10.

10. "Fingerprints Reveal Suspect on the Run from '76 Killing," *New York Times,* August 19, 1995, pp. 1, 22.

11. "Man Charged in Murder Is Linked to 2d Killing," *The Boston Globe,* November 30, 1995, p. 66.

12. "3 Held in Carjacking That Hurt Teen-Ager," *New York Times,* March 1, 1996, p. B2.

13. "German Police Hope Clues Lead to Capture," *The Boston Globe,* April 29, 1996, p. 7.

14. "Back Bay Fire Origin Is Called Suspicious," *The Boston Globe,* May 1, 1996, p. 57.

15. "After 30 Years, New Clue Pursued in Unsolved Killings," *New York Times,* November 30, 1995, p. B11.

16. "Possible Witnesses and Tips Are Focus of Jogger Murder Investigation," *New York Times,* September 20, 1995, p. B4.

17. "Evidence Is Elusive in Central Park Jogger Killing," *New York Times,* October 23, 1995, p. B3.

Chapter 11

❖

Surveillance
and Intelligence

Our earlier reference to intelligence was as a trait of good investigators; here, we use the word with regard to the collection of information. Consequently, from an investigative viewpoint, surveillance and intelligence, though different, tend to complement each other since their goals are the same. For instance, surveillance in its various forms can be used for a number of purposes and in a wide range of investigations. One is to learn about the activities of those being surveilled. By the same token, since there can be no effective intelligence operations without collecting information, at least some surveillance is almost unavoidable in intelligence gathering.

At one time, surveillances were limited to collecting information by watching over or keeping someone or something under observation. As technology evolved and became more adaptable for law enforcement use, surveillances were able to expand to include listening as another way to gather information. Thus, these developments made it possible to use surveillance to support some aspects of intelligence gathering whether for strategic or tactical purposes. Of course, intelligence operations involve more than collecting information. Unless that information is properly analyzed, the data collected are worthless.

Although we deal with the intelligence aspect later in this chapter, perhaps the differences between its strategic and tactical use should be clarified now. To illustrate the former, suppose a U.S. government employee who has access to classified information is suspected of spying on behalf of an unknown foreign government. The identity of that person's contact, the identity of the receiving government, and the nature of the information being passed must be determined. Developing a strategy for that purpose requires collecting and analyzing a wide range of data about the victimized agency, the types of sensitive information it possesses, which of its employees have access to that information, and the government or governments that would benefit most from getting it. In this case, the name of a likely suspect gives investigators a point of departure. However, without spending the possibly considerable time needed to collect and analyze all the other information, the likelihood that the case will be brought to a successful conclusion is minimal.

Tactically speaking, let's say there has been a robbery, and hostages have been taken. Two types of information could prove to be extremely useful. Information about the location's design and layout might enable the police to enter the premises without detection, surprise the robber, and free the hostages with little risk and no injuries or deaths. However, even if access is out of the question, information about the robber could prove helpful. It might suggest a motive; indicate if the perpetrator has a criminal record and, if so, for what offenses; reflect drug or alcohol addiction; and provide insight into the robber's personality and whether or not there is reason to believe the hostages really are in danger. Tactical intelligence also might identify a close relative or friend who could be brought to the scene to reason with and try to convince the robber to give up peacefully.

A third example, showing the use of surveillance as well as of strategic and tactical intelligence, involves a kidnapping with a $1 million ransom demanded. The authorities are notified. The kidnappers give the victim's family specific instructions regarding the time and place where the ransom is to be left. The investigators' primary objective is the victim's safe return, but they also want to arrest the kidnappers, recover the ransom, and collect enough evidence for the prosecutor to be able to convict them.

Knowing the time and place for the ransom drop allows the investigators to reconnoiter the area and decide not only on how best to put it under surveillance, but also to develop a strategy for keeping the person who makes the pickup under observation once the site is cleared. A person picks up the ransom and leaves the scene in an automobile. The license plate number enables the investigators to identify the person to whom the vehicle is registered; this information then can be used to try to learn about that individual. The data may prove helpful tactically.

In the interim, the person driving reaches his destination, parks the automobile in the driveway, and enters a single family house. Another vehicle is also parked in the driveway. Before entering, he looks around to see if anyone is watching. His behavior suggests that his associates and the victim are inside. The investigators now have an address from which they can get data regarding the owners or tenants. This intelligence may provide information that can be used to develop a strategy for dealing with the kidnappers without risking anyone's life. Then again, it may indicate the futility of trying to rescue the victim other than by a forced entry. In that event, the fact that the investigators can see the house and its surroundings may give them a tactical advantage in gaining entrance, rescuing the victim, arresting the kidnappers, and recovering the ransom.

The preceding illustrations are designed to show how surveillances can be used and to clarify the differences between strategic and tactical intelligence, but one still needs to understand more about surveillances and intelligence gathering in general. Police and federal agencies constantly collect information since in many ways it is the lifeblood of their work.

PHYSICAL SURVEILLANCE

Surveillances, for the most part, do not just happen. True, there are some exceptions such as a physical surveillance that can be undertaken quite quickly, and with limited resources, but as a general rule, far more is involved than an investigator simply deciding to initiate a surveillance. To illustrate a quick but limited surveillance, on December 24, 1949, a reliable confidential informant called the Chicago FBI office to report that his office's Christmas party would be breaking up shortly. This meant that one of his coworkers, who was the subject of an investigation and under surveillance away from work, would be leaving his office before the scheduled surveillance agents would be going on duty. Since the surveillance normally was handled by two agents working in one automobile, the squad supervisor simply directed two agents then in the office to institute the surveillance until they could be relieved by the two who were scheduled.

Similarly, there can be times when an investigator believes that an occasional physical surveillance of a subject either may provide useful information about the person's activities or may suggest additional investigative leads. In reality, such surveillances are limited in time, and the resources needed consist of the investigator who has the case, another investigator, and an automobile.

However, many times, whether a surveillance is for the purpose of watching over or listening to someone or something, or collecting intelligence, a variety of resources and a good deal of planning are required. This may be true whether the surveillance is a one-time physical surveillance of limited duration or a long-term fixed or electronic surveillance. As a result, aside from the relatively rare exceptions cited, individual investigators may suggest a need for a surveillance, but the decision to proceed will be made by their superiors.

Consequently, investigators seeking approval for surveillances should be prepared to justify their requests. Toward that end, they first must be able to clearly articulate the surveillance's objective, namely, what will it accomplish? Is it to be for the purpose of establishing a violation of one or more criminal laws, or merely to gather enough information to satisfy the probable cause requirement for a search warrant application? Will it help identify suspected associates in a criminal enterprise, or is it intended to help locate persons or places? Is it to develop tactical intelligence about persons and places before the execution of a search or arrest warrant, or is it to collect strategic intelligence on the activities of illegal groups or organizations?

These are not the only questions for which answers are needed. Regardless of the purpose, investigators have to understand that no matter how seemingly worthy the goals, resources will be required. If the demands on the department's or agency's resources exceed the hoped-for benefits, the proposal may be rejected.

The needed resources may be financial, or they may relate to personnel and equipment needs. For instance, will there be expenses of any sort? If so, in what amount? As an example, suppose a fixed or electronic surveillance will make it necessary to rent space; how much will it cost? Will there be possible payments to informants or to others whose help may be needed at some stage of the surveillance? As for personnel and equipment resources, how many investigators and vehicles will be required? Will handheld radios or any specialized equipment be needed? Is the surveillance itself to be fixed, moving, or technical? If moving, will it be on foot, in automobiles, or a combination of the two; will a loose or a tight surveillance offer the best results? If a physical surveillance will involve movement by the subject and the surveillants, will added personnel and vehicles be needed in order to detect any possible countersurveillance? If a fixed surveillance, will scopes, binoculars, or cameras be needed? If technical, will it be a wiretap or some other type of audio surveillance; will it also use video? What kinds of recording equipment and how many people to operate the equipment will be needed? Will pen registers or mail covers be used?

Considering the multiple resource-related issues involved with most types of surveillance, logic dictates that their need and availability must be discussed and resolved before any approval can be given. Although this applies to almost all types of surveillance, other factors also need to be considered when moving physical surveillances are contemplated.

For example, an objective common to all surveillances is the collection of information; therefore, it is obvious that nothing of value will be learned if the subject detects the surveillance. Thus when physical, moving surveillances are undertaken, every effort must be made to minimize the risk of the surveillants' detection. Toward that end, the personnel and vehicles assigned must blend into the scenery of the location(s) in which the subject may be found. Today's investigative agencies recognize the importance of this kind of blending, something that has not always been true.

For example, despite its successes, FBI surveillances during the 1940s and 1950s, part of the Hoover era, were by no means easy. Between the dress code imposed on special agents, and the limited makes and colors of bureau automobiles (most often black or dark green Fords, Buicks, and Pontiacs), it is surprising that so few surveillances were detected since there really was no blending. Yet during one evening surveillance that took place on the Mall in Washington, D.C., realizing that male special agents (before female agents were appointed), sitting or walking alone, would be conspicuous and too easily detected, females from the field office stenographic pool were asked to volunteer to accompany agents so as to give the appearance of couples. Today, the problems of single-sex agent personnel or limited makes and colors of automobiles no longer exist. Blending aside, perhaps a few real-life cases can help illustrate the extent to which resources are or can be factors in planning surveillances.

The preceding paragraph's surveillance took place on the Mall between the Washington Monument and Lincoln Memorial. It required enough agents (and stenographers) to be able to observe the subjects at any point along the Mall. There also had to be communications equipment so that those on foot could be in touch with each other and with agents in automobiles at various locations around the Mall area. If not, the latter would be unable to continue surveilling the subjects once their meeting ended and they went their separate ways.

During the "cold war," the number of persons to be kept under surveillance reached a point where FBI offices with the greatest numbers of such subjects found it prudent to set up separate surveillance squads. This was deemed advisable to ensure the availability of whatever personnel and equipment resources might be needed to effectively cover the activities of those being kept under surveillance.

FIXED SURVEILLANCE

Although possibly with reduced numbers, these same concerns about personnel and equipment availability arise when physical and fixed surveillances are used to complement each other. This combination tends to be used as a way of keeping a suspect place or activity under surveillance, with investigators and automobiles away from the immediate vicinity so that those seen leaving the area can be kept under observation.

On the other hand, if a decision is made to use only a fixed surveillance, rather than a technical one, fewer people will be needed. This is due to the one location and the likelihood that the hours of operation will be somewhat limited. Even so, in such cases, the locations under surveillance must be monitored by at least two people per shift in direct communication with other personnel in case conditions change unexpectedly, necessitating a request for additional investigators. Otherwise, fixed surveillances may not serve any meaningful purpose.

TECHNICAL SURVEILLANCE

Technical surveillances, that is, those based on using telephone taps or other forms of electronic interception, call for more than the necessary equipment resources. This is true no matter where the monitoring devices are to be located. The very nature of technical surveillances is such that there must be sufficient personnel to monitor whatever activity occurs whenever it occurs. Consequently, this may mean coverage twenty-four hours a day, seven days a week.

Of course, if it is believed that a technical surveillance is warranted, it is important to remember that implementation will require an application for and receipt of a court order authorizing installation of the appropriate equipment. As a rule, if investigators can satisfy the court that there are good reasons for such installations, the authority will be granted.

The proposed use of technical surveillances raises three questions. First, since equipment installations for such surveillances require covert entries into certain specified premises, what circumstances will justify seeking authorization? Second, if the installations can be made only by means of covert entries, do the entries themselves violate the Fourth Amendment's prohibitions against unlawful searches and seizures? Third, if they do not, do investigators need court authorization to enter in addition to the authority to install the equipment?

As for justification for a court order's issuance, the focal point for federal investigators (state courts tend to follow similar procedures) is the Omnibus Crime Control and Safe Streets Act of 1968, which authorizes wiretaps and other kinds of electronic surveillance.[1] This statute was amended by the Electronic Communications Privacy Act of 1986[2] with respect to the procedure to be followed to obtain a federal ex parte order authorizing the interception of wire or oral communications.

The process, similar to that used for a regular search warrant, calls for a detailed affidavit application setting forth the reasons for the requested order and what the investigators hope to achieve if it is granted. Federal applications must be approved by either the attorney general of the United States or his or her specific designee, and upon presentation to the court, authority will be granted only on the basis of the facts in the application reflecting the following:

1. That there is probable cause to believe that an individual is committing, has committed, or is about to commit a particular offense as set forth in 18 U.S.C. 2516.

2. That there is probable cause to believe that particular communications regarding the offense can be obtained by means of an intercept.

3. That normal investigative procedures have been tried and failed, or there is reason to believe that they will fail if tried, or they would be too dangerous.

4. And except as provided in subsection (11), there is probable cause to believe that the facilities from which, or the place where the communications are to be intercepted, are being used, or are about to be used, in connection with the commission of such an offense, or are leased to, listed in the name of, or are commonly used by such persons.[3]

As for the second and third issues, in 1979, the U.S. Supreme Court held in *Dalia v. U.S.* that the Fourth Amendment does not prohibit per se a covert entry performed for the purpose of installing otherwise legal bugging equipment.[4] The Court also ruled that the Fourth Amendment does not require that a Title III electronic surveillance order include a specific authorization to enter covertly the premises described in the order.[5] The question of how best to proceed was considered to be within the discretion of those who would execute the court's order.[6]

The foregoing relates to bugging, that is, the installation of one or more devices that allow investigators to intercept telephone or other oral communications. However, another form of technical surveillance mentioned earlier is the pen register. This is a device that records telephone numbers that are dialed by the person(s) under surveillance. Whether such an installation constitutes a search and thus requires a warrant was the question raised in *Smith v. State of Maryland,* decided in 1979, with the Supreme Court ruling that installing and using a pen register was not a search within the meaning of the Fourth Amendment, and therefore no warrant is needed.[7]

Yet another form of surveillance is the mail cover, consisting of nothing more than the U.S. Postal Service honoring a request to record the names and addresses of those persons or organizations sending mail to a particular addressee. Since mail passes through so many hands, and everyone who handles any item can read the information, the person to whom the mail is sent, and who is under surveillance, cannot realistically claim that he or she has any reasonable expectation of privacy. Mail covers can provide investigators with limited but worthwhile leads.

Although it is not uncommon for private investigators to conduct physical surveillances on behalf of clients in various cases, law enforcement agencies tend to do so primarily in connection with high-profile criminal cases. However, this is not to suggest that police and federal investigators cannot initiate short-term surveillances in other situations with good results. The illustration that follows shows how a witness, the combined use of other investigative techniques, and physical surveillance helped the police quickly close a case.

On February 27, 1996, a carjacking took place in New York City. Fleeing from the police, the stolen automobile's driver struck and critically injured a woman. A witness to part of the carjacking was able to give the police a description of a white Maxima (with two persons inside) that followed the carjacked vehicle as it fled, and three digits of the Maxima's license plate. Accessing the Department of Motor Vehicle's computerized database, investigators were able to narrow the number of vehicles possibly involved to fewer than twelve. Thereafter, surveillances on all the possibilities resulted in the February 29, 1996, arrest of three men who were charged with the crime.[8]

We previously noted that in many ways mystery genre literature and movies have given the general public a somewhat distorted picture of investigations by conveying the impression that crimes are solved quickly. There is further distortion when surveillances are depicted in motion pictures by infusing them with an aura of excitement, even when they are at fixed locations.

In truth, some physical surveillances can be boring. Sitting in a parked automobile for hours on end waiting for a subject to move is neither exciting nor glamorous; nighttime surveillances can compound the boredom. Consequently, there is a risk that a subject might start to move without being observed. This can be true whether the surveillance is a fixed one or a combination of moving and fixed.

Different types of surveillances will pose different problems that have to be considered. Technical surveillances involving the interception of oral communications require court approval, a surreptitious entry of the designated premises, the availability of the proper listening and recording equipment, its installation by technically qualified personnel, and a competent staff and secure place for monitoring. For instance, if it is likely that the intercepted conversations may be in a foreign language, then ideally personnel who know that language should be assigned to the monitoring location.

Although some fixed surveillances can be conducted from a van or comparable vehicle, they may have some limitations. Regardless of how well equipped the vehicle is with photographic equipment, binoculars or other sight-enhancing devices, and a two-way radio, the surveillance's length and location may be limiting factors. For it to be effective, the fixed location must afford the surveillants the greatest field of vision, but once chosen, no matter how innocuous looking the van or truck, any vehicle that is parked in the same location for an extended period is bound to attract attention. If this happens, the police may be called. If they know of the surveillance and do nothing, people become even more curious. If they do not know, they may respond and question the vehicle's occupants, and if the van does not move, the surveillance may be compromised.

In reality, the best base for a fixed surveillance, particularly one of any duration, is inside a structure such as an office or apartment building, a hotel, or a home. As with a vehicle's location, the monitors' field of vision is critical, but now other factors must be considered. First, since a fixed surveillance's length of time is imprecise, a specific term for the rental of space really cannot be agreed upon between the property's owner or manager and the department or agency that will conduct the surveillance. Second, the space will not be furnished in a more or less traditional way, and investigators will be coming and going at odd hours. Third, in an office building, night cleaners or other building personnel certainly cannot have access to the space; if a hotel room is to be used, housekeeping personnel must be kept out. These considerations make it obvious that the building or hotel manager is going to have to be taken into the department or agency's confidence. Therefore, before actually setting up the surveillance, once a suitable location is found, the owner's or manager's integrity, trustworthiness, reliability, and discretion must be determined. If the fixed surveillance is to be undertaken in a residential neighborhood, the same determinations must be made not only with regard to the best location for purposes of observation, but also with regard to the occupants of the house who will be asked if their premises can be used.

Issues to be addressed when the surveillance is physical and moving are different from those that are technical and fixed, and differences exist even within this kind of surveillance. True, surveillances generally are initiated for the purpose of obtaining information about the subjects of certain types of investigations and their activities, but on rare occasions physical or moving surveillances are used to prevent or disrupt activity or contact. If the objective is information gathering, the surveillance will be a "loose" or discreet one; if it is to deter or disrupt, it will be "tight." Thus the first thing to be decided is the type: loose or tight.

Although tight surveillance is easier, it must be done with care to minimize the risk of the subject alleging harassment. The surveillants make no effort to avoid detection; the subject knows he or she is being watched. To illustrate, a technical surveillance provided details for a proposed one-day meeting between two subjects of an espionage investigation. One, a Chicago resident, was to meet the other in Washington, D.C. A tight surveillance of the former, from his arrival until his departure, was to be undertaken by two agents using one automobile. One agent awaited the flight's arrival at the gate; the other stayed with the car, parked directly opposite the taxi line. From the moment the subject entered the terminal, he was aware that he was under surveillance. The agent on foot remained nearby when he used the telephone and followed him into and out of the men's room. The subject knew that his taxi into the city was followed. When he stopped at a coffee shop for something to drink, the agent on foot sat next to him. Within three hours, and without having his scheduled meeting, he returned to the airport and took the next flight back to Chicago.

Loose surveillances are more complex. We have discussed the importance of vehicles and personnel blending into the surrounding scenery, and the risk of compromise if one or more of the cars used is parked in the same place for an extended period, particularly in a residential neighborhood. In contrast, finding suitable parking spaces in commercial or other busy neighborhoods is no less problematic though in a different way. If subjects move on foot in areas with a high volume of pedestrian or vehicular traffic, the challenge for surveillants is to not lose them in that traffic while ensuring that they themselves remain undetected. Even more challenging is maintaining the surveillance when subjects use taxis or other forms of public transportation, or drive themselves, and they engage in tactics intended either to confirm that they are under surveillance or to lose the surveillance.

There is no question that surveillances are useful; the results can be rewarding. There have been any number of instances when they have provided police departments and federal agencies with tactical intelligence information that has enabled them to conduct successful rescue operations where hostages have been held. In other cases, information derived from surveillances has been a major factor in planning raids that have resulted in the recovery of stolen property, the seizure of evidence, and the arrest of criminals.

On the other hand, perhaps nothing better illustrates the usefulness and value of surveillances for strategic intelligence purposes than the impact that they have had on organized crime in the United States, particularly the Mafia, or as it also is called, La Cosa Nostra. Especially noteworthy was the joint use of physical and technical surveillances that enabled the FBI to develop Sammy "the Bull" Gravano as a confidential informant and the strategy that led to the 1992 conviction of John Gotti, head of the Gambino organized crime family in New York City, who had been acquitted in three earlier trials.

Of course, surveillances are not the only ways in which investigators collect intelligence information. Confidential informants, whose role we discussed in Chapter 9, can be sources of such information. By maintaining contact with their informants, investigators can have access to information about a range of activities with which the latter are familiar, or about which they possibly can learn. However, because the levels of informant reliability are not always readily apparent, information obtained from them requires a greater degree of confirmation than that which is developed by investigators themselves either through surveillance or going undercover.

No matter how information is gathered, the collection process itself is but one aspect of intelligence. Regardless of the sources from which it is obtained, it must be carefully analyzed to determine its usefulness. Then it must be made available to those investigators for whom it will have the most value or meaning. Investigators who have confidential informants should not assume that the only information to which the latter may have access is directly related to matters of interest to themselves. Informants may know of other types of activities that would be of interest and help to other investigators.

SUMMARY

Surveillances are used for a range of investigative purposes, and confidential informants can be useful in providing intelligence information, but in many ways surveillances and intelligence gathering are complementary. The former can be a source of information regarding various activities by enabling investigators to monitor the goings and comings, and certain communications, of those under surveillance. In other situations, they can help provide intelligence information that permits the development of strategies or tactics for use in dealing with those persons.

Physical surveillances can be moving, fixed, or a combination of the two. Technical surveillances involve intercepting communications through the use of telephone taps or bugging. For the latter, certain criteria must be met, and court authorization must be obtained for their installation. Investigators also may use mail covers or pen registers as other forms of surveillance.

Whether a surveillance is to be physical or technical, investigators proposing their use must be realistic and consider the value to be received in relation to the resources needed if the objectives are to be achieved. This is especially true of investigations in which long-term efforts will be required to obtain meaningful information. Although they tend to be exceptions, there is nothing to preclude the occasional use of short-term surveillances, but short term or long term, surveillances can provide leads and possibly intelligence information, help solve cases, and result in arrests in criminal investigations.

Both surveillances and confidential informants can be sources of intelligence information. In high-profile cases, a combination of the two can be most productive. Nevertheless, whenever the primary purpose is to obtain intelligence, strategic or tactical, the source's reliability must be determined, data collected must be carefully analyzed, and then it must be made available to those investigators for whom it will have the most meaning and value.

REVIEW QUESTIONS

1. What purposes do surveillances serve?
2. Explain the difference between a moving surveillance and a fixed one.

3. How can surveillances contribute to intelligence information gathering?
4. What is meant by a technical surveillance?
5. What factors need to be taken into account whenever investigators propose long-term physical or technical surveillances?
6. What three things need to be considered before initiating a technical surveillance?
7. What is meant by a mail cover?
8. Why must great care be exercised in tight surveillances?
9. Are surveillances the only means of collecting intelligence information?
10. What needs to be done with intelligence information before it can be used effectively?

NOTES

1. Title III, 18 U.S.C. 2510–2520.
2. Title III, 18 U.S.C. 2518.
3. Ibid.
4. *Dalia v. U.S.,* 441 U.S. 238 at p. 255.
5. Ibid. at p. 258.
6. Ibid. at p. 257.
7. *Smith v. State of Maryland,* 442 U.S. 735 at p. 745.
8. "3 Held in Carjacking That Hurts Teen-Ager," *New York Times,* March 1, 1996, p. B2.

Chapter 12

❖

Collecting
and Preserving
Evidence

Most legal battles, whether criminal or civil, are fought in our courts. Only one side can win; therefore, attorneys know that if they hope to prevail, their evidence must be stronger than that offered by opposing counsel. Although the need for good and substantial evidence exists in any litigated matter, its quality and quantity are of special significance in criminal trials for two reasons. First, to win civil cases, only a preponderance of the evidence is needed; in criminal matters, the prosecution must prove its case beyond a reasonable doubt. Second, this is as it should be since a criminal defendant's freedom, and possibly life, is at stake.

We examined the need to protect crime scenes, a primary source of evidence, in Chapter 8. In an earlier discussion of good investigators' characteristics, we noted that among them are patience, the power of observation, and attention to detail, all important in every phase of investigative work. These particular traits tend to assume even more importance when it is time to collect and preserve evidence, especially in criminal cases.

Good investigators, as well as government and private attorneys, know the importance of evidence; they know that without it there is no proof, and without proof there is no case. This is true whoever is responsible for an investigation. It is immaterial whether inquiries are made by a lawyer, a police detective or federal agent investigating a crime, an insurance company employee working on fraudulent disability claims, a security manager looking into a suspected conflict of interest, or a private investigator handling a divorce action.

No matter who collects evidence, that person needs to be mindful of the fact that more is involved than simply looking for and collecting it. Evidence offered at time of trial is subject to challenge. If it has been compromised or made suspect, either by the way it was handled during the collection or examination process, or while in custody pending trial, it may be suppressed by the court when offered. This is true of all evidence handling by investigators; extreme care must be exercised from the moment they first arrive at an incident scene. In other words, several steps beyond finding and collecting evidence are involved: how it is handled from the moment it is found and how it is protected while in custody call for the utmost attention and care.

To introduce evidence, the attorney offering it must first lay a foundation by showing its relation to the issue being tried. Thus the importance of taking good field or original investigative notes at the scene cannot be overemphasized. These notes must include the precise location where every piece of evidence was found, the time it was found and by whom, its description, a description of the type of bag or other container in which it was placed, and the way in which the evidence container was both sealed and marked. The notes also should indicate how the evidence was disposed of after it was collected. For instance, did the investigator put it into an evidence locker or was it hand-carried or sent to a laboratory for examination? Here we also need to note that not all forms of evidence lend themselves to being collected, let alone examined.

With that thought, let us consider some factors related to the very subject of evidence before discussing the collection and preservation processes. First, we need to distinguish among the different types of evidence. In Chapter 13, we discuss what can be done in the way of examining evidence and the categories of forensic science with which criminal investigators should be familiar.

TYPES OF EVIDENCE

There are six principal types of evidence: circumstantial, direct, hearsay, parol, demonstrative and real, and probative. Circumstantial evidence, which may be used more often than direct evidence, consists of facts that only indirectly help prove a main fact that is in question. To illustrate the difference between the two, suppose a home has been burglarized. If the wallet of a man who neither lives nor works there is found at the crime scene, the wallet would be circumstantial evidence in a case charging him with burglary. On the other hand, the testimony of a witness who saw that same man throw a brick through a window to gain entrance and the man's capture by the police while still inside would be direct testimony in support of the charge. The direct evidence, that is, the testimony offered by the witness, also would be testimonial evidence.

Hearsay and parol are other forms of testimonial evidence as distinguished from real evidence. Hearsay almost invariably is ruled inadmissible since the person offering it has no personal knowledge of what actually happened. Rather, he or she is relying on secondhand information that he or she has learned from others.

Parol evidence tends to come into play in contract matters. Like hearsay, it is inadmissible. For instance, two parties enter into a written agreement; they later come to a disagreement over the terms and then find themselves in court. One of them then tries to introduce in evidence an earlier oral agreement between the parties to contradict the subsequent written agreement's provisions. The evidence would not be admitted.

Both demonstrative and real evidence directly address the senses. Such things as weapons or tools used in committing a crime, recovered stolen property, injuries, and the results of DNA testing in a rape case all would be demonstrative evidence.

Probative evidence consists of facts used to actually prove other facts. As an example, a bookkeeper is charged with embezzlement through the medium of writing checks to himself and forging the employer's signature. The fact that the checks were written by him and that bank records show that amounts equal to the sums of those checks were deposited to the bookkeeper's own account on the same days that the forged checks were issued would be considered probative evidence.

Ruling on the admissibility of evidence is a matter for the courts, but it is important for investigators who interview potential witnesses to make certain that whatever they have to offer is based on their personal knowledge. Failure to make that determination can result in that person's testimony being ruled hearsay and inadmissible. This is a reflection on the investigator's competence; it also can prove harmful to the prosecution's case. This aside, the most valuable types of evidence for criminal investigators are circumstantial, direct, and demonstrative or real; and the search for demonstrative or real evidence must be handled with great care. Of course, being careful goes beyond preventing possible contamination or compromise. At the heart of the search for real or demonstrative evidence is the need to ensure that whatever of value is found will be admissible at time of trial.

For any evidence, real or testimonial, to be admissible, it must satisfy certain criteria. Generally speaking, it must be relevant to the matter being tried. It also must be material; that is, it must be something that is substantial and that can properly influence a trial's results. Any evidence obtained in violation of any provisions of the Constitution relating to due process, or a person's right to a fair trial, will be suppressed.

One would expect to find at least some evidence at a crime scene. Then, too, if a quick arrest occurs, the subject can be searched for any weapon that can be used to effect an escape, tools or other instruments used to commit the crime, and any fruits of the crime. Realistically, however, there also are times when an investigation produces leads that suggest the need to look for evidence in places other than the primary crime scene or what the subject has in his or her possession at the time of arrest. Incident scene searches were discussed in Chapter 8.

FOURTH AMENDMENT RIGHTS

It is true that good investigators will not ignore even what may seem like a remote possibility in their continuing search for evidence. It also is true that they will do so in accordance with established legal principles. First and foremost is the Fourth Amendment to the Constitution of the United States, which reads as follows:

> The right of the people to be secure in their persons, houses, papers, and effects, against unreasonable search and seizure, shall not be violated, and no warrants shall issue, but upon probable cause, supported by oath or affirmation, and particularly describing the place to be searched, and the persons or things to be seized.

Therefore, searches of other than the crime scene, of the subject at time of arrest, and possibly of some other crime scenes require investigators to apply to a court of proper jurisdiction for a search warrant. The warrant's application must be accompanied by an affidavit, completed by the investigator, that sets forth the specific place to be searched, the probable cause or reasons on which the request for the warrant is based, and what it is hoped the search will produce. If the application is approved and a warrant is issued, it should be executed as soon as possible. Generally speaking, warrants are to be executed only during daylight hours. If execution is to be at night, that must be stated and justified in the application, and authorized by the warrant itself when issued.

When questions arise about an unauthorized nighttime search, any evidence recovered will be suppressed. This is illustrated by a situation that occurred in New York. The apartment of a defendant, accused of rape, was searched under a warrant to be executed between 6 A.M. and 9 P.M. Investigators recovered a large stick and pieces of bedding and clothing. Defense counsel's motion to suppress the evidence on the ground that the search was made after 9 P.M. was granted when the judge noted that no request had been made for a nighttime warrant. Subsequently, the evidence was ruled admissible when the investigator who executed the warrant produced his notebook in which he had indicated that the search actually began around 6 P.M. the day after the rape allegedly occurred.[1]

As might be expected, there have been court challenges to the admissibility of evidence. Not surprisingly, many of them have been based on questions about either an affidavit or application or a warrant's validity.

For instance, in 1933, the U.S. Supreme Court held that although an officer's affidavit for a search warrant stated his belief that certain goods subject to seizure were located at the defendant's home, it merely reflected that belief but without any facts to support it. Consequently, the absence of probable cause rendered the warrant invalid.[2]

In contrast, considering an attack on an affidavit for a search warrant based on factual inaccuracies, the Supreme Court in 1964 ruled that where those alleged inaccuracies "were of only peripheral relevancy to the showing of probable cause and, not being within the personal knowledge of the affiant," they did not go to the affidavit's integrity.[3]

The Fourth Amendment's criteria make it imperative that investigators applying for search warrants not lose sight of what must be included in their affidavits. They must do more than satisfy the issuing judge that probable cause for a search does in fact exist. They also must be able to describe with particularity the place to be searched and the objects for which they are looking. For instance, if they want to search apartment 200 at 1836 Avenue X in the hope of finding a .357 magnum revolver used in a homicide, asking for a warrant to search 1836 Avenue X to look for a handgun would not be sufficiently specific.

As previously noted, if investigators want to ensure that any real evidence found by them will be admitted at time of trial, then aside from primary crime scene searches and those incidental to arrests, they must apply for and get a warrant before proceeding with a search. In this respect, even the question of what constitutes a search has been litigated.

In 1924, the U.S. Supreme Court defined a search as a government trespass into a constitutionally protected area.[4] However, forty-three years later, the word *search* was redefined to include any government action that intrudes into an area where a person has a reasonable expectation of privacy.[5]

Despite the Supreme Court's repeated rulings that the Fourth Amendment's protections apply only to agents of government, they should not be ignored by either private-sector investigators or those in the public sector with whom they occasionally may work. This raises two issues that can have a bearing on the admissibility of evidence resulting from searches conducted by private persons.

First, that searches and seizures by private persons, whether security personnel or private investigators, may not violate a person's constitutional rights or render recovered evidence inadmissible does not necessarily mean that their conduct is acceptable. For example, although virtually all states, California among them, afford retail merchants some degree of protection against lawsuits charging false arrest and false imprisonment, the California courts have held that the state's Merchants' Privilege Statute does not grant security officers an unlimited right to search.[6] Neither would a person necessarily be precluded from bringing a civil action for an invasion of privacy. Thus even private-sector investigators' searches may not be immune from liability.

The second issue relates to searches conducted by private persons at the request or even suggestion of government investigators. It is not unusual to find close working relationships between some private security personnel and the police, sometimes to the extent that the former consider themselves members of the law enforcement community. As we noted, if they conduct searches on their own initiative, the fact that they might be subject to a lawsuit on privacy grounds does not necessarily render any evidence recovered inadmissible or prevent them from turning it over to the police. However, if there is the slightest indication that private persons conducted a search at the request or suggestion of police officers or federal agents, the so-called silver platter doctrine is invoked, and whatever evidence was found as a result of such a search will be suppressed. This is to prevent government investigators from using private persons to get evidence for them that they themselves would be unable to obtain lawfully.

We already have noted that even when search warrants are issued, certain restrictions may be imposed upon the investigators who will execute them. An example is the need to get specific authorization for a nighttime search. Another would be getting a "no knock" warrant, which waives the need for officers to identify themselves before entering for the express purpose of reducing the risk of evidence destruction or officer injury. However, these are not the only possible restrictions.

Suppose a robbery victim shot and wounded the perpetrator. The investigators, having access to the victim's gun, want a ballistics examination made as further evidence connecting the suspect to the crime. To do this, they obviously need the bullet lodged in the suspect. Owing to the intrusive nature of the procedure for the bullet's recovery, application is made for a search warrant. The question is, will a judge issue a warrant under such circumstances? The answer will largely depend on the judge to whom, and the jurisdiction in which, the search warrant's application is made.

When the question was raised in Georgia, the answer depended on the extent of the surgical intrusion. It was believed that if the intrusion were considered minor, a court might authorize it.[7] Arkansas and New York courts have taken similar positions holding that if surgery for a bullet's recovery posed a substantial risk to a defendant, getting a judge's approval was highly unlikely.[8]

With the extent of intrusion a factor considered by a judicial officer deciding whether to approve a search involving a person's body, what would be the likelihood of approval for a nonconsensual blood test? Such a situation arose in California.

After an automobile accident, one driver, suspected of having been driving while under the influence of alcohol, refused a police request for a blood sample that could be analyzed for its alcohol content. He said this would violate his Fifth Amendment privilege against self-incrimination.

The U.S. Supreme Court ruled that though the privilege is intended to protect persons against being forced to give testimonial evidence against themselves, it does not apply to matters involving physical evidence, and a blood test performed by a physician in a hospital, following accepted medical procedures, does not violate a person's due process. The Court continued,

> The integrity of an individual's person is a cherished value of our society. That we today hold that the Constitution does not forbid the states minor intrusions into an individual's body under stringently limited conditions in no way indicates that it permits more substantial intrusions under other conditions.[9]

COLLECTING EVIDENCE IN CRIMINAL CASES

For many years, investigators searching for physical evidence tended to focus on crime scenes, on a suspect's place of work or home, and, depending on the nature of the crime, on the suspect and possibly the victim. Today's searches necessitate looking beyond the usual sources, and consideration of other items that may have been in the care of or used by suspects. The significance of this is reflected in the prosecution's opening statement at the trial of Ramzi Ahmed Yousef, charged with having conspired in 1995 to kill several thousand travelers by planning the bombing of a number of American jumbo airliners. The prosecution observed that data retrieved from the defendant's laptop computer contained airline schedules of United, Delta, and Northwest Airlines flights as intended targets, a timetable for midair explosions, and a draft of a letter claiming responsibility for the bombings.[10]

No matter where investigators look for physical evidence, the collection process must be meticulous. To ensure that no possibility is overlooked, it also has to be methodical. In Chapter 8, we discussed what must be done to protect crime scenes; we also noted that some police departments and federal agencies now have crime scene specialists whose job it is to scour such scenes for the express purpose of collecting evidence, making certain that it is properly identified, preserved, and forwarded for laboratory analysis where appropriate. In departments that do not have such specialists, it is the investigators' responsibility to deal with this issue.

When searching for and collecting evidence, no assumptions should be made, and nothing should be considered insignificant. Important as it is to be methodical, it also is important to be flexible enough to give priority to collecting any items that may have evidentiary value but that also lend themselves to deterioration or change. This might be the case with liquids, or even some solids if the search scene is outdoors and the weather looks threatening.

Collecting evidence requires investigators to handle evidence. Wearing thin latex gloves when collecting evidence is best. In addition, investigators must make certain that they themselves do nothing that will either alter the state of the evidence or possibly destroy other items that may have some value. For instance, handguns should not be picked up by inserting a pen or pencil in the barrel since that could scratch the lands or grooves and affect a later ballistics examination; neither should embedded bullets be pried out of walls or floors since the instrument used could scratch them with the same result. It is better to carefully cut out the area adjacent to the bullet and let the laboratory examiners extract it. Handguns should be handled by using the thumb and forefinger, and touching only the rough or grained part of the grip. Glasses or other hard, smooth surfaces, such as telephones, that may have fingerprints on them, should not be picked up with a handkerchief since that could either destroy the prints or render them useless for comparison purposes.

Investigators must avoid doing anything that risks compromising or altering evidence in ways that will prevent or interfere with later laboratory or other examinations. However, being careful is no excuse for failing to mark evidence in a way that will allow them to positively identify it as evidence found by them when they are asked to do so at trial. Those who do not properly mark evidence for later identification will find their credibility and professionalism challenged by defense counsel and questioned by jurors.

Ideally, the investigator's personal form of identification should be placed on the recovered item. This is doable with such things as weapons, burglary tools, and bomb-making equipment. They have hard surfaces and are large enough to allow an investigator to place a unique or personal form of identification on the object. Initials or some specific marker used by the investigator and, size permitting, the date and time that the evidence was found should be the minimum required for identification purposes. Once done, if size permits, the item should be protected by being placed in a suitable container and sealed whether for storage in an evidence locker or submission to a forensic laboratory. Each item will dictate what constitutes a suitable container. For example, for some items, such as a handgun, knife, burglary tools, a glass, or recovered jewelry, clear plastic bags may be suitable. On the other hand, paper bags are better for clothing since the items might have trace evidence that otherwise could be lost by adhering to the sides of plastic bags. For blood or other liquids, sealed, clear plastic or glass vials should be used. In any event, certain basic rules should be followed for the collection of physical evidence: each item should be placed in a separate, fresh, clean, leak-proof, sealable container and kept away from direct sunlight and heat; and biological specimens should be kept under refrigeration except while being transported.

Of course, not every bit of evidence lends itself to such treatment for identification purposes. Certainly, neither hairs nor fibers, or other forms of soft goods, can be marked the same way as hard and larger objects. Nevertheless, they also must be handled with care lest their texture is affected in a way that conceivably would have an impact on laboratory examinations. As an example, the preferable ways for collecting trace evidence would include using a completely clean, uncontaminated vacuum cleaner, using adhesive tape, or shaking an object on which there might be trace evidence over a large, clean sheet of white paper. Tweezers or other suitable means also can be used. Regardless of the method, once picked up, the items must be carefully placed in appropriate containers.

Despite an investigator's personal identifier on evidence, when possible, all bags or containers in which evidence is placed also must be marked for identification. The case or file number, date, time, place of collection, and investigator's name should be noted. If another investigator was present and observed the collection of any item, his or her name also should be listed as a witness to the collection.

Meticulous attention to detail also begins another process, generally called maintaining the chain of evidence. This is to ensure that nothing happens or is done to any item of evidence that could be prejudicial to a defendant's right to a fair trial. To maintain the chain of evidence, there must be a log or other record that will show strict accountability for every single item, who handled it and when, what was done with it, and where it has been kept from the time it first was found by the investigators. Unfortunately, there are times when improperly handled evidence can be embarrassing, and even result in an acquittal of a person who otherwise might have been found guilty.

Jurors who spoke with the news media after the 1995 O. J. Simpson trial made no specific mention of the way the Los Angeles Police Department collected physical evidence. Nevertheless, certain admissions by prosecution witnesses, and the testimony of some defense witnesses, at the very least succeeded in calling into question the way in which some of the physical evidence was collected.

Other examples of poor evidence handling follow.

❖ Case 12-1

In the 1995 murder prosecution of Calvin Broadus (the rap singer also known as Snoop Doggy Dogg), a Los Angeles County deputy district attorney told the jury the victim's bloody clothes could not be offered in evidence since they had been destroyed by the police.[11]

❖ Case 12-2

On August 3, 1993, the body of James Jordan, father of basketball star Michael Jordan, was found near the North Carolina–South Carolina state line. During the ensuing murder trial, a South Carolina Law Enforcement

Division agent testified that he could not say conclusively whether the .38 caliber bullet exhibited in court was the one removed from the victim. When cross-examined, he said that it could have been fired from fourteen different brands of firearms, including a Smith & Wesson, the type found in the defendant's home. (If the bullet had been marked with a personal identifier when removed from the deceased, even if this required the investigator's presence during the process, this would not have been an issue.) Another agent, who supervised the trace evidence unit, admitted on cross-examination that he had failed to see a hole in the victim's shirt despite the medical examiner's testimony that a gunshot wound to the chest puncturing the aorta was the cause of death, and that burying the victim's clothes was not the best way to preserve evidence.[12]

❖ Case 12-3

A child was kidnapped from a Hollywood, Florida, mall July 27, 1981; two weeks later, his severed head was found in a canal 120 miles away. The body was never located. Otis Toole was a prime suspect. While jailed in 1983 awaiting trial in a fatal arson case, Toole told the police he wanted to talk about a child that he had killed in the Ft. Lauderdale, Florida, area. As a result, the police took bloody carpet scraps from Toole's car and trace amounts of blood from a machete that he said he had used to sever the child's head; however, the police subsequently misplaced the evidence.[13]

One cannot say too much about the importance of physical evidence. In some cases, even seemingly small or isolated items can prove most useful. Unfortunately, in others, the process of searching for and collecting evidence occasionally can be extremely difficult. Chapter 3 cites patience as one of good investigators' many attributes. We mentioned it again at the beginning of this chapter because this trait assumes such great importance when collecting evidence. What follows are more examples of patience, of how evidence is collected and can be used effectively to help solve some cases, and of investigators' inability to close other cases notwithstanding their efforts over time. Some of these examples also highlight the importance of integrity and objectivity.

Let us first look at a few cases, some as yet unsolved. The night of July 3–4, 1954, Marilyn Sheppard was murdered; her husband, Dr. Sam Sheppard, was convicted and given a life sentence. At a retrial ordered twelve years later, he was acquitted; no one else has ever been arrested let alone convicted. In 1996, their son reopened the investigation hoping to prove his father's innocence. At the trial, he learned that police said there were no signs of a forced entry, yet a police officer found pry marks on the basement door. Furthermore, investigators found a trail of more than thirty blood spots leading from the bedroom, where the murder occurred, to the basement, but Sam Sheppard had no cuts.[14]

March 8, 1966, a 7-year-old girl was stabbed to death in Elizabeth, New Jersey. Twelve people witnessed either the murder or assaults on two other schoolgirls minutes earlier and less than a mile from the stabbing. The police found the $1.50 hunting knife used to stab the victim, but no fingerprints. They also got a physical description of the perpetrator, who disappeared. During the latter part of 1995, a 60-year-old woman's tip, and the resurfacing of eight witnesses, caused the police to reopen the case in the hope that it now could be solved.[15]

The body of a female jogger who had been beaten to death was found under a stone bridge in New York City's Central Park on September 17, 1995. Investigators looking for evidence faced a number of problems. The body apparently had been left lying unnoticed overnight in a stream, and rushing water after heavy rain may have washed away potentially crucial physical evidence. The rain may have muffled the victim's screams; it also meant that fewer people, who might have seen or heard something, were in the park. The medical examiner was doing DNA, toxicology, and histology testing on the victim, and on September 19, detectives questioned a number of joggers, bicyclists, and skaters who may have seen or heard anything the night of September 16.[16] After thirty-five days of exhaustive investigation that included using helicopters, scuba divers looking for any hair or fiber evidence that might have been washed into the stream, and about fifty detectives who followed more than 300 telephone tips, no arrest had been made. In addition to looking for witnesses, police department criminologists had examined scraps of cloth as well as paper and rubbish found near the crime scene without finding a single shred or fiber of forensic evidence. However, investigators had determined that the attack took place near the Lasker Rink at about 6 A.M., September 17, and the victim then was dragged down a 20-foot embankment where her assailant tried to rape her. The victim suffered two cracked teeth and had cuts on her hands and arms showing that she had tried to defend herself.[17]

During October 1995, an act of sabotage caused an Amtrak train to derail in Arizona; a train crewman was killed, and a number of people were injured. The cause was the removal of bolts from a steel joint connecting two rails, and use of a piece of wire to bypass a warning system. Aside from a note found at the scene claiming responsibility in the name of the "Sons of Gestapo," the removal of the connecting bolts, and bypassing of the warning system, FBI evidence response teams found no other physical evidence despite conducting a detailed search of the wreckage and surrounding countryside in a mile-square area.[18]

More recently, and still unsolved, was the kidnapping of Jan Philipp Reemtsma, a member of a prominent German family that paid a $20 million ransom for his release. Kidnapped in front of his home on March 25, 1996, and released on April 26, Reemtsma was able to provide the police with a partial description of the automobile used and of its license plate number. The police also had a recording of one of the kidnapper's voices with the conversation in German although the victim said that the kidnappers spoke English both to him and among themselves.[19] In May, one suspect reportedly had been caught, but the other remained at large.

In contrast to the foregoing, let us look at some other cases where the evidence collected has proved most helpful. In 1993, several New York City firefighters were injured when a Molotov cocktail was thrown into a fire truck's cab. However, a fingerprint lifted from a gasoline can by members of the police department's crime scene unit helped solve the case.[20]

As part of the World Trade Center bombing investigation, the FBI searched suspects' residences and a storage locker where bomb-making chemicals were kept. They uncovered a considerable amount of evidence. The fingerprints of the first subject arrested were found on a black plastic bottle containing shotgun powder, a 50-pound bag of ammonium nitrate, a brown bottle of another chemical, a glass beaker, another plastic bottle, and a bottle of a propellant. They also found Jordanian and Iraqi currency. At the home of another subject, they found a plastic bag containing bullets, a gun clip, and materials linking him to a defunct company that had been the subject of a fraud investigation. Searching a third subject's apartment, the FBI found a jacket and a piece of wood with substances on them that were consistent with the household chemicals used to make the World Trade Center bomb.[21]

The night of January 5, 1993, two men wearing ski masks and armed with handguns robbed the Rochester, New York, Brinks' depot of $7.4 million in cash. They confronted three guards and took one, in handcuffs, as a hostage. On November 12, 1993, the FBI arrested three suspects, one of whom was the "hostage," and recovered about half the stolen money, a good deal of which was still in Brinks' bags. Aside from the recovered funds, evidence developed as a result of surveillance, and inconsistent statements by the hostage, other physical evidence was helpful. For instance, the hostage said he was kidnapped in a large U-Haul van with an overhead door, but the other two guards said a minivan was used. Tire tracks at the scene indicated a minivan, and they were similar to those made by a 1984 Plymouth Voyager owned by another one of the three men arrested. Furthermore, there was evidence showing that in March the latter had opened bank accounts in different names using $25,000 in cash although neither he nor his wife were working. He also was seen buying a number of postal money orders, some of which were for amounts of up to $4,000.[22]

The decomposed body of a woman who had been raped, strangled with a cord, and dead at least a week was found in a tractor-trailer parked in an isolated waterfront area in the vicinity of New York City's West Village. She had on a moderately priced jogging outfit and expensive running shoes and seemed to have been in good physical condition and to have maintained a healthy diet. Her nails were neatly manicured; her teeth were in good condition. She had no identification, and no one fitting her description had been reported missing. From the jogging suit manufacturer, investigators learned that at least 3,000 had been made, the last in 1992. Some had been sold in New York's Rockland County, but most had been shipped to the West Coast.[23] Having no success in identifying the victim on the basis of their own records and her fingerprints, a copy of the latter was sent by fax to the New Jersey State Police computerized system, where the victim was identified as someone who had applied for a New Jersey security guard's license.[24] In October, a New Jersey man, who had been seen with the victim, and who tried to withdraw money from an automatic teller machine with the victim's bank card the day after the murder, was arrested.[25]

A duffel bag containing a .22 caliber handgun, receipt from a gun shop, several ammunition clips bought on December 29, 1994, and a fingerprint left behind by a man who killed two and injured several others during his December 30 assaults on two different Brookline, Massachusetts, abortion clinics, helped with his identification and arrest.[26] This evidence also played a part in his subsequent conviction.

During late July 1995, a woman was found stabbed to death; a neighbor was suspected. Searching for evidence, an investigator found a bloody fingerprint on a beam in the victim's cellar. It matched one of the neighbor's fingerprints based on a set of his prints taken on July 24 and resulted in his arrest.[27]

Size aside, not all types of physical evidence can be "packaged" and retained for trial. Imprints or impressions, such as those made by footprints, tire tracks, and tool marks, can be evidence, but they obviously cannot be put into sealed containers for preservation. Among the evidence found at the Rochester, New York, Brink's robbery crime scene were tire tracks. Impressions found at a scene must be included in scene sketches, photographed, and whenever possible, casts of plaster of Paris or an equivalent material should be made, then marked for identification the same as other evidence.

Forms of physical evidence other than those already cited also have helped investigators. A combination of testimonial and physical evidence led to the August 25, 1995, arrest of a New York City business executive on charges of rape, sodomy, and possession of a dangerous weapon. On March 24, 1995, he lured a 19-year-old girl to his office under pretext of offering her a job. He and the victim took the elevator to his office, which she could not remember although she recalled the floor. A surveillance video camera in the building's lobby, its tape, and the victim's description of her assailant helped identify the man. Investigators then got a search warrant for the office. In executing it, they found a pornographic film that had been shown to the victim, and the knife described by her as being used to get her to submit. They also found that the victim's description of the office where the attack occurred matched that of the office where the subject was arrested, and that he was wearing a ring that the victim had described to the detectives.[28]

A two-and-a-half-year investigation by U.S. Customs, led to the September 1995 raids of factories, warehouses, and shops in New York City and Los Angeles. Officials found evidence of a Korean organized crime ring's operation that included the overseas manufacturing of clothing, handbags, and sporting goods with counterfeit labels for sale in the United States. This venture was described as part of a $300 billion illegal business.[29]

On March 4, 1996, the owner of a delicatessen located in New York City's lower Manhattan was killed with a .25 caliber gun while being robbed. On March 7, two police officers found a disassembled .25 caliber automatic near 96th Street, some distance from the scene of the shooting. Recalling the March 4 incident, they sent the weapon to the department's ballistics laboratory. After testing, it appeared to be the gun from which three shell casings were recovered following the homicide.[30] Westchester County Sheriff's Department detectives, hearing that this weapon was the same caliber as one used to kill an Elmsford, New York, motel clerk, sent three shell casings that they had collected as evidence to New York City for examination; another match was made.[31]

Searching for evidence at the scene of a Denver, Colorado, hit-and-run death, detectives found a piece of an automobile described as "cosmos black," a part of a $56,000 BMW. With a BMW dealer's help, they learned that it came from a 1995 BMW 540i Sport, of which there were only three in the entire state. This enabled them to identify a suspect.[32]

On April 19, 1996, a Teaneck, New Jersey, police officer, who also worked part time as a Sears, Roebuck & Co. security officer, was shot and killed while entering his automobile to make a deposit for Sears. Examining the crime scene for evidence, investigators found a copy of *Reader's Digest* with a mailing label on it. The addressee was a woman who gave detectives information that helped lead to the arrest of two men on April 26, one of whom was a friend of hers.[33]

Following a sixteen-month "sting" operation, on May 22, 1996, ATF and Customs agents in the San Francisco Bay area seized as evidence $4 million in weapons that had been smuggled into the United States. Illegally imported were 2,000 AK-47 fully automatic rifles from the People's Republic of China.[34]

Earlier in this chapter, we noted the physical evidence found in the FBI investigation of the World Trade Center bombing. In Chapter 9, we cited the records examined by the FBI and INS in connection with their search for those responsible for the crime. Aside from fingerprint evidence collected during the investigation, investigators examined telephone records and airline passenger manifests, a work permit application completed by one of the subjects who was arrested in Jordan on August 1, 1995, and the INS records relative to his October 18, 1989, admission to the United States on a student visa,[35] all of which constitute physical evidence.

In September 1995, three men suspected of being part of a gang smuggling Chinese immigrants into the United States and of killing one of them in Brooklyn, New York, were arrested in Milpitas, California. New York City detectives, looking for evidence possibly related to the Brooklyn crime scene and perpetrators, examined the public utility records for the apartment where the killing occurred. Based on the name of the person given on those records, they were able to track that subject and his two accomplices to Milpitas.[36] These records are evidence that can be used.

The bodies of two women cousins were found beaten to death on May 17, 1996. Investigators had reason to believe that one of the victims had questioned a home health care worker about $600 worth of forged checks, and the latter retaliated. Although the worker was released after her first interview, her bank records were reviewed as part of the investigation. Investigators discovered three checks deposited to the worker's account, each for $200, as well as the forgery of the checks themselves. Confronted with this evidence, the home health care worker confessed to the forgeries and the deaths of the two victims.[37]

These examples tell a good deal about collecting physical evidence. Investigators and the attorneys with whom they work, whether on criminal or civil cases, are well aware of the importance of evidence in cases that are to be tried. However, investigators need to appreciate the fact that evidence also can provide leads that can help identify parties and, in criminal cases, lead to arrests. Bear in mind that in criminal investigations the search for evidence is not always limited to the crime scene; neither is it always obvious. Hairs and fibers, or bits of dirt or paint flecks found at the scene of a hit-and-run accident, also are of evidentiary value. Various types of records often are useful in providing leads and as evidence. Sometimes evidence found during an investigation may even prompt a subject to confess, as illustrated in the home health care worker case.

COLLECTING EVIDENCE IN OTHER TYPES OF CASES

Although we have focused largely on collecting evidence in criminal cases, do not ignore the need to collect evidence in other types of investigations. For instance, if an aircraft crashes, NTSB investigators look for evidence at the crash site that will help them determine the accident's cause. In the process, they make every effort to recover both the flight data and cockpit voice recorders. They also collect as much of the aircraft itself as possible in the hope that with the pieces they can reconstruct both the airplane and what caused it to go down.

Although private-sector security directors, who either conduct or supervise investigations for their employers, are neither law enforcement officers nor licensed private investigators, they should not dismiss the importance of evidence collection. Theorizing that their cases are confined to the workplace, unless the employer seeks a criminal or civil trial solution, and that the same high degree of care exercised by the police or federal agents need not be followed, is shortsighted. Employers may prefer to resolve errant employee problems administratively, but nothing prevents employees who believe they have been wrongfully terminated or disciplined from suing to right their perceived wrong. In that event, employers cannot successfully defend themselves without evidence developed during the investigation that led to the administrative action.

Two examples illustrate the value of evidence as it applies to corporate security investigations. Both cases involved conflicts of interest; the terminated employees elected to sue their employer. The employer successfully defended itself in both instances with evidence collected during the investigations.

In one, evidence clearly showed that a manager had been using the employer's computer and time to develop three noncompeting businesses of his own. Confronted with the voluminous evidence that had been collected, he admitted his guilt and was terminated. However, he then filed a complaint with the state's commission against discrimination. Instead of a formal appearance before a hearing officer, the employer chose to submit a copy of its internally conducted investigative report with the carefully collected and preserved evidence attached. The actions against the employer were dismissed.

In the second case, the employee sued the employer in court alleging wrongful termination. Again, an internal investigation had been conducted. Evidence carefully collected and preserved showed not only that the employee had given help to a competitor of his employer, but also that he had abused his company-issued telephone credit card to make international calls in connection with a noncompeting business of his own. At the trial's conclusion, the jury found for the defendant employer.

FINGERPRINT EVIDENCE

Earlier in this chapter, we discussed in rather general terms the collection process and the need for investigators to exercise extreme care to avoid altering or destroying the evidentiary value of items found. Nowhere is this need greater than when dealing with embedded bullets and fingerprints.

Fingerprint evidence is invaluable as a means of positive identification. That many things on which they can be found are portable, such as a glass or telephone, is immaterial; they still must be lifted and preserved so that they can be offered in evidence at time of trial. The importance of lifting and preserving fingerprints increases when dealing with items on which they may be found, such as window glass in a burglary or a countertop in a robbery, that do not lend themselves to easy removal for either laboratory examination or production in court.

Although investigators themselves rarely are involved with classifying and searching fingerprints for purposes of identification, they are very much involved in looking for and lifting fingerprints at crime scenes. On occasion, they also may take the fingerprints of persons arrested for crimes. Therefore, owing to the important role of fingerprint evidence, it is only logical to consider some peripheral, yet allied, matters before discussing how they should be lifted and preserved.

First, there are three principal types of fingerprint patterns: arches, loops, and whorls, each having additional breakdowns such as plain and tented arches and radial and ulnar loops. Whorl patterns may consist of plain whorls, central pocket loops, double loops, or accidental whorls. Before any set of fingerprints can be searched, either manually or by using automated fingerprint processing, they must be classified. It is during the latter process that allowance is made for scarred patterns, amputations, or fingers missing at birth.

Next, positive identification is made when fingerprints found at an incident scene are compared with either a set of fingerprints on file or those of a known person whose fingerprints have been taken, and a sufficient number of identical characteristics are found to match. Of course, if those on file or just taken are of poor quality, making such an identification may be extremely difficult if not impossible.

Consequently, it is critical to not only take and submit readable fingerprints for identification, but also to lift and preserve good clear prints from objects. This means that personnel responsible for fingerprinting persons must avoid causing problems for those who ultimately must decide whether a positive identification can be made. Six problems can affect the process:

1. A failure to fully roll fingers from side to side, or to ensure full inking from joints to tips, will result in a failure to reproduce the details of each finger.

2. If fingers are allowed to slip or twist when being rolled onto fingerprint cards, smears, blurs, or false-appearing patterns will be the result.

3. To use writing or similar ink instead of properly thinned heavy black printer's ink will produce patterns that are too light or too faint for classification, or else the ink may run.

4. Failure to thoroughly cleanse the fingers of the person being fingerprinted of perspiration or foreign substances or to cleanse the inking apparatus of foreign substances may result in some distortion in the appearance of ridge, core, or delta detail.

5. Fingerprint ridge details may be either obliterated or obscured if too much ink is on the apparatus plate.

6. Not having enough ink on the apparatus plate may result in ridge details that are too light to be counted or traced.[38]

We now turn to the search for, lifting of, and preservation of fingerprints. Do not limit searches by looking only for those prints that may be obvious, such as in grease, dust, or other substances. Look for latent fingerprints, that is, those that are not readily visible, as well. Thus the search for fingerprints must cover everything on which they may be found.

Some items on which fingerprints can be found can be examined at the scene. However, others may need to be examined in a laboratory environment. This is particularly true of some objects on which prints may be found only through the use of chemical methods such as iodine vapor, ninhydrin, silver nitrate, or cyanoacrylate fuming, also called the "super glue procedure." It also is true of prints that become available when ultraviolet rays or laser radiation are used. In these situations, the investigator is responsible for ensuring that the item or items are properly packed for shipment in order to avoid any risk of change to the patterns. Fingerprint evidence being sent for examination must be packed so that no surface on which there may be latent prints is in contact with any other surfaces; neither should cotton or cloth ever be placed in contact with them.

In looking at items that can be processed for fingerprints at the site, such as drinking glasses, telephones, tools, an automobile involved in the commission of a crime, or other items on which prints may be found, investigators should wear either thin latex or light cloth gloves. They also should be careful to handle the objects being examined only by their ridges or by surfaces that would not accept latent impressions.

The examination itself is a three-stage process: dusting for fingerprints followed by photographing and lifting them. For dusting, contrasting powders should be used: gray on dark backgrounds, black on light ones. Using a fine ostrich feather, camel hair, or nylon brush that has been dipped into a small amount of powder, the surface being examined should be brushed very lightly until a fingerprint contour becomes visible. At that point, the brush strokes should be in the same direction as the print's ridge detail. An alternative method may be to use an atomizer. When the fingerprints are clearly visible, they are photographed with a fingerprint camera.

The third step involves lifting the prints. Just as contrasting powders are used to raise prints, so is contrasting tape used to lift them. White or black tape, with the adhesive side placed against the powder, is used. Fingerprints raised with gray powder on dark surfaces are lifted by using black tape; white tape is used to lift those raised with black powder.

When lifting prints, care must be taken to avoid any possible smearing. This applies both to the actual lifting of the prints and to covering the tape with celluloid to ensure that the fingerprints are preserved.

A New York City Police Department investigation in early June 1996 illustrates how fingerprints can contribute to solving crimes. In the space of eight days, four women had been victimized: one had been killed, one savagely beaten, another beaten and robbed, and the fourth brutally beaten in suburban Yonkers, New York. Detectives lifted a set of fingerprints at the homicide scene. Sent to the department's Identification Bureau for a search, they matched those of a man arrested in March for jumping over a subway turnstile. When taken into custody for the killing of the one victim, the subject admitted his guilt in the other three attacks and gave detectives information that would not have been known to anyone other than the assailant.[39]

In Chapter 8, we noted the proper marking and identification of all evidence found at crime scenes; we also have discussed the care with which evidence must be handled during the collection phase. Some items may need nothing more after being seized than secure storage until needed for trial; others may have to be submitted to a laboratory for further examination to determine their actual value as evidence.

Earlier in this chapter, we spoke of the importance of preserving the chain of evidence. This requires investigators to be every bit as careful of how laboratory submissions are made as they are in the collection process itself. Items must be packed in ways that will not compromise or call into question the validity of submissions; sufficient information must accompany submittals so that proper examinations can be made with a minimum amount of handling by and exposure to laboratory personnel. This is true whether they are to be delivered directly to laboratories by investigators or sent by other means that will ensure speedy and confirmed delivery.

As we have said, each bit of physical evidence, whether for laboratory examination or not, must be identified by investigators so that they can confirm in court that the item being offered in evidence is in fact what they found during their investigation of the case. Ideally, the investigator's personal or unique identifier should be marked on the particular item itself. Although this can be done on solids, the actual markings must be made in ways that will neither interfere with any laboratory examination nor in any way significantly alter the item's evidentiary value. In addition, identifying data must be placed on each container in which evidence is placed regardless of whether that container is a plastic or paper bag, a glass vial, or a wood or metal container.

Hairs and fibers found by themselves—that is, those not adhering to another piece of evidence—should be picked up with tweezers and placed on a small, clean piece of paper carefully folded to prevent any chance of breakage or loss before being placed in clear plastic bags. This prevents their clinging to the bag itself or being contaminated.

When submitting soft goods for examination, such as clothing items, each piece should be carefully and separately wrapped in clean paper with the contents and other identifying data noted on the outside. Under no circumstances should two or more items be wrapped together. For example, in rape investigations, each item of clothing worn by the victim at the time of the assault, and each item of the subject's clothing that may have been worn at the time of the rape, must be wrapped separately in a clean paper bag before being put into a larger container for shipment.

If more than one item of evidence is being sent for laboratory examination, each separately packaged piece should be placed in a single, secure, carton or box of a size and strength that will ensure the undamaged delivery of the contents. A memorandum or other form of instruction, addressed to the laboratory that is being asked to conduct the examination(s), should be attached to the outside of the container. It should include the investigator's name, department or agency and address, case file number, case name, and a brief description of the nature of the incident. If precautions should be taken by laboratory personnel in handling any items of evidence, such as bloody garments where the possibility of incurring an infectious disease exists, this, too, should be clearly stated in the shipping document. It also is advisable to place a copy inside the container in case the one on the outside is damaged or lost in transit.

Since investigators know what prosecutors will need to prove a person's guilt in any given case, they also are in a position to know just what types of examinations need to be performed. Therefore, they also should include in the transmittal what they would like to have done with each piece of evidence. This serves two purposes: it permits the direct dispatch of individual items of evidence to that section of the laboratory that will do the examining and facilitates the examination process, and it helps preserve the chain of evidence by reducing the number of people handling the items. Laboratory personnel, who may be called as witnesses at time of trial, then can testify with respect to their findings as well as the receipt and condition of the packaging of the items examined by them. This helps deflect defense counsel suggestions that evidence was tampered with or contaminated.

SUMMARY

The importance of evidence cannot be overemphasized regardless of the type of investigation. However, for it to be useful, it must be obtained lawfully, it must be relevant, and it must be material. Therefore, aside from evidence found at crime scenes or while searching suspects in custody, all other searches and seizures, whether of evidence or persons, must conform to the provisions of the Fourth Amendment regardless of whether the evidence is direct or circumstantial, physical or testimonial. In other words, the right to search and seize is clearly limited.

Investigators (and prosecutors) prefer working with direct evidence; however, more times than not they are obliged to concentrate on finding circumstantial evidence. In reality, it is the sufficiency of high-quality admissible circumstantial evidence that often results in convictions in criminal cases.

Circumstantial evidence can encompass a wide range of items. Some, such as hairs, fibers, paint or glass chips, drops of blood, or barely visible pieces of dirt, can be so small as to be easily overlooked by impatient, hurried, or careless crime scene searches. Others can be large, or even immovable, yet they may be a source of evidence that has to be collected and preserved. This might be true of fingerprints on an automobile used in a kidnapping, or on a marble countertop at a robbery scene. Just as fingerprints can be raised, lifted, and preserved as evidence, so can tire tracks or footprints be preserved for use as evidence by making plaster casts of them. Investigators must be made aware of and able to apply the various techniques that can be used to detect, collect, examine, and preserve evidence.

Circumstantial evidence is worthless unless and until it can be linked to both an offense and a suspect. This phase of an investigation is a task for laboratory personnel, yet their work is directly affected by the way in which evidence is submitted to them and what they can do with it. Furthermore, even the slightest break in preserving the chain of evidence may prove disastrous for a prosecutor if defense counsel uses that break to raise a reasonable doubt about a defendant's guilt in the mind of but one juror. Therefore, investigators must make certain that, from an investigation's opening until evidence is introduced at trial, they have done their part to establish and maintain that chain. This begins with the evidence collection process. When laboratory submittals are involved, it extends to the evidence's proper packaging, preparation for shipment, and transmittal for examination.

REVIEW QUESTIONS

1. What are the criteria for the admissibility of evidence in criminal cases?
2. Distinguish between the amount of evidence needed to prove a criminal case and that needed to prove a civil one.
3. With which of the six principal types of evidence do investigators most often work?
4. The Fourth Amendment deals with two issues; what are they?
5. Once investigators have obtained a search warrant, can they execute it at any hour of the day or night of their choice?

6. How can tire tracks or footprints be preserved as evidence?

7. Why is it not all right to use a knife or other sharp instrument to remove a bullet embedded in a wall?

8. How should trace evidence be collected and protected?

9. What is meant by protecting the chain of custody?

10. Letters of transmittal used to send evidence to a laboratory for examination should include what information?

NOTES

1. "Ruling in Favor of a Suspect Puts State Judge Under Fire," *New York Times,* February 2, 1996, p. B3.

2. *Nathanson v. United States,* 290 U.S. 41.

3. *Rugendorf v. United States,* 376 U.S. 528 at p. 532.

4. *Hester v. United States,* 265 U.S. 57.

5. *Katz v. United States,* 389 U.S. 347 (from Justice Harlan's concurring opinion at p. 361).

6. Any intrusion into a defendant's person or effect is not authorized as incidental to a citizen's arrest or under the Merchants' Privilege Statute. *People v. Zelinski,* 594 P. 2d. 1000.

7. *Creamer v. State,* 192 S. E. 2d. 350, 353; *Allison v. State,* 199 S. E. 2d. 587.

8. *Bowden v. State,* 510 S. W. 2d. 879; *People v. Smith,* 362 N. Y. S. 2d. 909.

9. *Schmerber v. California,* 38 U.S. 757.

10. "Plot of Terror in the Skies Is Outlined by a Prosecutor," *New York Times,* May 30, 1996, p. B3.

11. "Evidence Missing in Rapper's Trial," *The Boston Globe,* November 28, 1995, p. 30.

12. "Evidence Handling Assailed in Jordan Father's Death," *The Boston Globe,* January 11, 1996, p. 12.

13. "Loss of Evidence Impeded Inquiry Into Boy's Death," *New York Times,* February 18, 1996, p. 30.

14. "In Life of Notoriety and Pain, Son Tries to Solve His Mother's Murder," *New York Times,* March 26, 1996, p. A12.

15. "After 30 Years, New Clue Pursued In Unsolved Killing," *New York Times,* November 30, 1995, p. B11.

16. "Possible Witnesses and Tips Are Focus of Jogger Murder Investigation," *New York Times,* September 20, 1995, p. B4.

17. "Evidence Is Elusive in Central Park Jogger Killing," *New York Times,* October 23, 1995, p. B3.

18. "F.B.I. Studies Note for Clues on Derailment," *New York Times,* October 11, 1995, pp. A1, A16.

19. "German Police Hope Clues Lead to Captors," *The Boston Globe,* April 29, 1996, p. 7.

20. "Anatomy of a Murder Scene," *New York Times Magazine,* January 28, 1996, pp. 42–45.

21. "Fingerprints Being Studied in Bomb Case," *New York Times,* May 20, 1993, pp. B1, B4.

22. "U.S. Details Evidence in Brink's Robbery Arrests," *New York Times,* November 14, 1993, pp. 1, 40.

23. "After a Slaying, a Question Is Asked: Who Was She?," *New York Times,* September 25, 1994, pp. 39, 45.

24. "Police in 2 States Trace Identity of the Young Victim of a Slaying," *New York Times,* September 28, 1994, pp. A1, B2.

25. "Man Is Held in Strangling of Woman," *New York Times,* October 29, 1994, p. 23.

26. "Though Hunt for Suspect Was Vast, Chance Proved Crucial for Capture," *New York Times,* January 2, 1995, p. 10.

27. "Neighbor Is Charged in Somerville Killing," *The Boston Globe,* July 26, 1995, pp. 1, 4.

28. "Executive Charged with Raping Job Applicant," *New York Times,* August 26, 1995, pp. 21, 23.

29. "Agents Raid Counterfeiters of Apparel," *New York Times,* September 28, 1995, pp. B1, B3.

30. "Police Find the Gun Used to Kill Deli Owner," *New York Times,* March 8, 1996, p. B5.

31. "Gun Used on Deli Man Is Tied to '95 Killing," *New York Times,* March 13, 1996, p. B3.

32. "Scion of Rich Family in Colo. Is a Suicide," *The Boston Globe,* March 21, 1996, p. 3.

33. "Two Held in Death of Officer at Hackensack Sears Store," *New York Times,* April 27, 1996, p. 29.

34. "Chinese Sought in Plot to Import Arms to the U.S.," *New York Times,* May 23, 1996, pp. A1, A10.

35. "Fingerprints Link Suspect to Bombing, Officials Say," *New York Times,* August 5, 1995, p. 23.

36. "3 Men Held in Slaying of Immigrant," *New York Times,* September 20, 1995, pp. B1, B4.

37. "Health Aide Is Accused in Killings of 2 Women," *New York Times,* May 26, 1996, p. 29.

38. *The Science of Fingerprints (Rev. 12-84),* U.S. Department of Justice, Federal Bureau of Investigation.

39. *New York Times,* June 14, 1996, pp. A1, B5.

Chapter 13

❖

The Laboratory

We have discussed the collection and preservation of evidence, and in both Chapter 12 and earlier ones, we noted that some police departments and federal agencies use personnel specially trained for that purpose. We have also emphasized the importance of preserving the chain of evidence, but to merely collect and preserve evidence serves no purpose in criminal investigations unless it can be linked to the crime that is being investigated. Establishing that linkage is the role of laboratory and allied personnel.

Notwithstanding the significant contributions that forensics can make to both investigations and the ultimate trial of suspects, one has to understand that the subject is not without controversy. At the February 1996 annual meeting of the American Academy of Forensics Sciences, Dr. Henry Lee, head of the Connecticut State Police Crime Laboratory and a frequent expert witness at trials, commented on the impact lawyers, the police, the media, and some forensic scientists themselves have on this aspect of the investigative process. Dr. Lee said, "Under the name of truth and justice, the lawyers can do anything to scientists." As for the police, he said, "Once they make up their mind on a particular theory, you have to go along. . . . When forensic scientists find some evidence that does not fit the theory, something must be wrong." As for the media, Dr. Lee remarked that "They report an event without facts or without all the facts with such intensity to force the viewer to think what the reporter or commentator wants you to think, and we forensic scientists suffer." Neither did he spare his peers when he said that some scientists will testify to anything for money: "You do have professors who know nothing about forensic science and testify."[1] His comments about forensic scientists are particulary noteworthy because in November 1995 the U.S. Department of Justice's inspector general announced the appointment of five forensic scientists to inquire into allegations that the FBI Laboratory was biased in favor of prosecutors.[2]

Dr. Lee's observations about lawyers and the media should not come as a surprise. One hopes attorneys will conduct themselves ethically, yet those same ethical standards also require them to provide their clients with the best defense possible, including efforts to raise enough reasonable doubt in jurors' minds to win an acquittal by attacking the prosecution's offers of physical evidence. As for the news media, their role and impact on investigations, particularly in high-profile cases, has been discussed in earlier chapters. At the same time, since everyone associated with any investigation, whether as a member of a police department, federal agency, or forensic laboratory, should be objective from the investigation's inception to its conclusion, those who represent our criminal justice system should be greatly concerned with Lee's comments about the police and certain members of the scientific community.

Most, if not all, physical evidence eventually is submitted for laboratory or related examination. Some police and federal agencies have their own laboratories; others do not and submit evidence for examination to outside organizations. Big-city and state police departments frequently do their own examinations. Smaller departments tend to submit evidence to their state police laboratories. Although federal agencies may have their own specialized laboratories, and do their own examinations, the two most often called upon for help by local or even state police departments are ATF and the FBI.

ATF has three laboratories that conduct examinations related to explosives, bombings, arson, and illegal firearms trafficking. In addition to servicing its own agents, these facilities will provide support to state and local police departments in major case investigations.

At one time, the FBI Laboratory willingly conducted examinations for any law enforcement agency that sought its help, including laboratory personnel appearing as witnesses. However, as an increasing number of local and state departments established their own laboratories, and the FBI's own workload increased, this policy was modified. Evidence that has been, or will be, subject to the same type of technical examination by other laboratories or experts will no longer be accepted; neither will the FBI Laboratory accept referrals from other crime laboratories capable of conducting the same examination. Its position on reexamination has been taken to make certain that any evidence received by the FBI Laboratory is in its original condition so that the findings can be properly interpreted and meaningful testimony can be ensured. This is done to maintain the

FBI crime laboratory. (*Courtesy* FBI)

chain of custody and the integrity of the evidence. The refusal to accept referrals allows the laboratory to make better use of its own resources for the benefit of both those agencies whose cases are accepted and its own investigative needs.

Before discussing specific cases that will help illustrate the effectiveness of laboratory examination, it is important to understand what the term *forensic science* encompasses. There are two principal categories of forensic science: criminalistics and forensic medicine. However, aside from what each of these covers, there may be other functions that, though not necessarily scientific, come under the laboratory umbrella, such as the FBI's Translation Unit and Behavioral Science Unit.

Paul L. Kirk, a leading criminalist, has defined criminalistics as "the science of individualization."[3] This involves the recording, scientific examination, and interpretation of the smallest details of physical evidence with a view to identifying a substance, an object, or an instrument. It includes connecting evidence found at a crime scene by comparing it with a known specimen obtained from a suspect, reconstructing the way in which an offense was committed, developing evidence that may clear a suspect, and making expert testimony available at time of trial. Criminalistics covers such different topics as chemistry, firearms, photography, toolmarks, fingerprints, voice spectroscopy, questioned documents, and polygraph or lie detector examinations.

In contrast, forensic medicine deals with such diverse issues as pathology, serology, toxicology, odontology, and psychiatry. Although investigators may have at least some understanding of psychiatry, and how it can be helpful under various circumstances, other facets of forensic medicine may need clarification if they are to be properly used and of benefit to them. In fact, without data provided by certain types of forensic medicine examinations, solving cases involving questionable deaths would be nearly impossible.

What can investigators hope to learn from the results of pathology examinations? The time, cause, and manner of a victim's death can be determined in homicides, including the type of weapon or other instrument used to kill. Examining pathologists can let investigators know if injuries found on the deceased were postmortem, that is, after death, or antemorten, before death. They also can help by identifying the age, sex, height, and weight of victims and the age of mutilated or decomposed bodies and of skeletons. Furthermore, they can determine a deceased's virginity, defloration, pregnancy and delivery, and whether or not an act of sodomy took place.

Forensic serology deals with blood. It can distinguish between human and animal blood, and it can determine human blood types. In investigations in which the cause of death is not readily apparent, toxicology examinations can determine the origins and properties of poisons. This is done by chemical analysis, the action of a poison on humans and animals, and what conditions would have produced the results. In addition to identifying a poison that was used, the toxicology examination can let investigators know the amount used, and whether a particular poison would be lethal in that amount.

In some homicides or sexual assaults, there may be bite marks on the victims. If so, forensic odontology examinations can be helpful. They deal with teeth, denture, and bite marks; they can connect a particular bite mark to a particular person; and forensic odontologists can estimate a person's age. Equally important, forensic odontology can help identify a person when other means of identification, such as fingerprints, are unavailable. As an example in criminal investigations, in March 1995, the New York City Police Department used dental records to identify a homicide victim who had been burned to death.[4] Forensic odontology also has been used successfully to identify victims in noncriminal investigations, most notably following airplane crashes and other accidental deaths.

Although forensic meteorology is an aspect of neither criminalistics nor forensic medicine, investigators should be aware that on occasion it may be helpful. For instance, forensic meteorologists can assist in

New York City Police Crime Laboratory. (*Courtesy* New York City
Police Department)

evaluating footprints found in snow, determine the extent of visibility at
the time an incident occurred, discern whether severe weather might
have been expected or was an "act of God" that could not have been antic-
ipated, deduce whether or not slippery conditions had existed for a long
enough period before an accident to have allowed property owners to deal
with the hazard, know at what distance screams for help could have been
heard, or based on air conditions and evaporation rates, discover how long
a body might have been floating in a bathtub.

A high-profile 1991 criminal case helps illustrate forensic meteorology's role. William Kennedy Smith was on trial for rape in Florida. Her-
bert Spiegel, at that time a meteorologist on the faculty of Dade (Florida)
Community College, was called as an expert witness and asked to determine if there actually was a beach at the time of the alleged attack,
whether the visibility was sufficient for people on the beach to have been
seen from the Kennedy family's house, and if the victim's screams might
have been heard above noises made by the wind and waves. His response
was that there was a beach that night; it had been bathed in light by an
unobstructed full moon directly overhead; the action of the waves was
moderate; and the fact that the wind was blowing toward the Kennedy
house would have made it easy to hear a person's cries for help.[5]

Earlier in this chapter, we mentioned that in addition to its criminalistics examinations, the FBI Laboratory has translation and behavioral science units. The former, staffed with personnel capable of translating foreign languages into English, provides assistance in bureau cases
as well as in those in which other agencies need help because they have
encountered a language problem. As an example, a local police department raided a suspected bookmaking operation; however, all the book-
maker's records were kept in an unfamiliar form of writing. The materi-

als were sent to the Translation Unit and found to be in Yiddish (a language that uses the Hebrew alphabet). They were translated, returned to the sender, and resulted in a conviction.

In 1981, the FBI's Institutional Research and Development Unit undertook an in-depth cost–benefit study of what was then referred to as the Psychological Profiling Program. A questionnaire was developed and sent to all officials and detectives at any law enforcement agency that had used the profiling services. Recipients included city, county, and state police departments; sheriffs' departments; FBI field offices; highway patrols; and state investigative agencies. Data were sought in connection with murder, rape, kidnapping, extortion, threats, child molestation, hostage situations, and accidental death and suicide determination cases. The closing report of the analysis, completed in December 1981, stated, "The evaluation reveals that the program is actually more successful than any of us realized. The Behavioral Science Unit is to be commended for their outstanding job."[6]

The Behavioral Science Unit has been an effective ally for local, state, and federal investigators in a wide range of cases in which there has been physical evidence, yet little else to help identify the perpetrator or even the type of person who would commit a particular crime in a certain way. It has proved especially adept in its ability to provide support services to police departments confronted with serial cases such as rapes, murders, and arson fires. Among some of the high-profile serial murder cases in which the unit has made a significant contribution are those of Wayne Williams (Atlanta, Georgia, child-killing), Jeffrey Dahmer (who cannibalized his victims), and Ted Bundy (whose victims were college coeds).

In Chapter 12, we took note of a murder investigation in which investigators could not positively link certain evidence to a suspect because of the way in which that evidence had been handled during the collection and examination processes. In contrast, a great deal can be learned about innocence as well as guilt from evidence that has been properly collected, preserved, examined, and documented.

An excellent example of this, and of the value of forensics, occurred in New York City. In September 1992, based on separate inquiries by the district attorney, New York City Police Department, FBI, *and a criminologist and pathologist hired by the deceased's family,* a grand jury cleared a police officer in connection with the fatal shooting of a suspect in a drug investigation. Despite what two sisters who claimed to have witnessed the incident told the police, the separate inquiries showed the following:

1. The sisters alleged that the victim was on his back on the floor when shot by the officer. Bullet fragments, wounds on the deceased's body, and an impact mark on a marble pillar in the lobby where the shooting took place confirmed that the deceased was standing when he was shot.

2. Ballistics, powder burns on the body, pathologists' reports on the wounds, and two slugs recovered at the scene also confirmed that the officer fired two shots, not three as claimed by the sisters.

3. The sisters said the officer savagely beat the deceased. The medical examiner, and the pathologist retained by the deceased's family, said that their examinations showed that the deceased had two bruises, both consistent with the officer's version of what happened.

4. An examination of the place from which the sisters claimed to have witnessed the incident showed that they would have had to be lying prone to have seen anything, and even then they could have seen only feet and legs.

5. Playing four minutes of tape-recorded police radio transmissions confirmed the officer's version that he was frantically calling for help because of fear for his own life.[7]

In this illustration, forensics helped establish innocence. In another New York City case, forensics resulted in a man being charged on February 28, 1996, with murdering his estranged wife by shooting her once in the head, then placing the gun in her hand to make it look like a suicide. There were no eyewitnesses to the killing, which took place on January 13, 1996. The husband claimed the victim shot herself even as he tried to prevent her from doing so. However, the examination showed that the location of the wound was not in her temple, but rather above and behind her ear. According to Charles J. Hynes, the Brooklyn, New York, district attorney, these factors were among those that "determined conclusively that the fatal wound was not consistent" with the husband's account.[8]

Let us now consider some of the specific ways in which criminalistics can provide investigators with useful, if not always conclusive, information.

FINGERPRINTS

From a forensics viewpoint, developments have further enhanced the use of fingerprints for identification purposes. The number of characteristics required before two sets of fingerprint impressions can be considered sufficient for a positive identification varies among different countries, but prior to 1973 the U.S. standard required a minimum number of twelve identical points. However, after the International Association for Identification completed a three-year study, it concluded that "no valid basis exists at this time for requiring that a pre-determined number of friction ridge characteristics must be present in two impressions in order to establish a positive identification."[9] This obviously eases the burden on those who search fingerprints and determine that a positive identification has been made.

Another factor has been the development of a computerized search of basic fingerprint characteristics through the use of the Automated Fingerprint Identification System (AFIS). Before automation, the identification process was both tedious and time consuming. Persons taken into custody were fingerprinted, and then the prints had to be searched to see if an earlier set of those prints was on file. Whether submitted to the FBI's Identification Division or a state or local identification bureau, the prints had to be classified before any search could be made. Classifying, searching, and making an identification were done manually. Although AFIS has not eliminated the human factor in classifying fingerprints, and confirming that two sets are in fact identical when it appears that a match has been made, it represents a major contribution in accelerating the search aspect of the process.

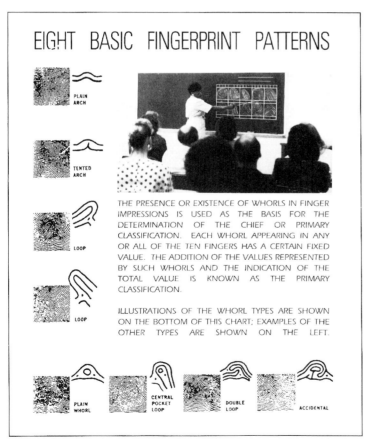

(*Courtesy* FBI)

Also helpful has been the use of new reagents for the development of latent fingerprints. *Webster's New World Dictionary* defines *reagent* as a term used "in chemistry, a substance used to detect or measure another substance or to convert one substance into another by means of the reaction which it causes." The significance of ninhydrin, although first prepared in 1910 by Siegfried Ruhemann, an English chemist, was unappreciated and largely unnoticed in the field of forensic science. It was not until 1954 that its use as a fingerprint developing reagent was first reported. It was found to react with the amino acids normally secreted from the sweat glands in fingers.[10] Researchers at the National Institute of Justice and elsewhere have discovered how to enhance ninhydrin's properties by way of structural modifications so that two complementary reagents, identified as 2-THIN and 3-THIN, now develop better fingerprint properties.[11] Investigators also have succeeded in using heated Krazy or Super Glue to form a vapor that attaches itself to the proteins and fats found in fingerprints.

Evidence of the importance of forensics, and of fingerprints, is found in a statement by a senior investigator in the World Trade Center bombing, who said: "Forensics are the key to any bombing case. You look for fingerprints, nitrates, a lot of lab stuff." In Chapter 12, we discussed that case with respect to the collection and preservation of evidence, noting the number of incriminating items found by the FBI on which two suspects' fingerprints were found. A look at some other cases in which fingerprints have been found helps further illustrate their evidentiary value.

❖ Case 13-1

A partial fingerprint and Krazy or Super Glue led to the identification and arrest of a man suspected of committing eleven rapes in four New York counties; the most recent having occurred on May 3, 1993, in Yonkers, New York. Part of his modus operandi or MO (the way in which he committed his crimes) was to disable victims' telephones. On May 3, he left a partial print that Yonkers Police Department laboratory technicians were able to bring into focus using Krazy Glue vapors.[12]

❖ Case 13-2

Discussing evidence collection in Chapter 12, we took note of a 1994 New York City homicide investigation in which the decomposed body of a woman found in a tractor-trailer remained unidentified for more than a week; no one filed a missing person's report that might have helped identify her. The New York City Police Department, having searched its own fingerprint files manually without success, sent a fax copy of the victim's prints to the New Jersey State Police. Using an AFIS, they quickly identified the deceased on the basis of fingerprints taken when she had applied for a security guard's license.[13] Once her identity became known, the investigation proceeded and a former boyfriend was arrested.[14]

❖ Case 13-3

On May 10, 1976, a woman was fatally shot during a drive-by shooting. A suspect, identified by witnesses at the scene, fled New York, changed his name, married, fathered two children, and was gainfully employed in South Carolina. During the summer of 1995, he was fingerprinted for access to his employer's bank account. Sent to the FBI's Identification Division, the prints matched those on his old police records. On August 16, 1995, he was taken into custody in South Carolina by the FBI and New York City detectives.[15]

❖ Case 13-4

A teenager was arrested on July 25, 1995, in connection with a neighbor's stabbing death. A Massachusetts state trooper, conducting a crime scene search, found and lifted a bloody fingerprint from a beam in the victim's cellar. The suspect had been questioned and fingerprinted on July 24; the bloody print matched one of his.[16]

❖ Case 13-5

Carrie Hope Feinberg disappeared the evening of January 13, 1996; on June 3, 1996, her partially clothed, bound, and gagged body was found floating in the Merrimack River near the Haverhill, Massachusetts, docking area. She had been gagged with silver duct tape. Using a nitrogen freezing technique, the Massachusetts State Police found a fingerprint between the tape's cover material and the adhesive. It matched one of a former boyfriend, who was arraigned for her murder on June 24, 1996.[17]

To further enhance and expedite the identification process in criminal cases, in November 1995, the FBI announced that it was setting standards for a computerized picture file of criminals. The head of the bureau's advanced technology unit said that in a few years the new standards would allow the FBI to expand an existing fingerprint and criminal history database to include not only electronic photographs of people taken at the time of their arrest, but also of scars, marks, and tattoos. According to Stan Zack, the unit chief, "The FBI will serve as the storage repository for the states. . . . We provide the common denominator that allows us to become the link."[18]

Important as fingerprint identification is to criminal investigations, it would be a mistake to not recognize its investigative value in helping identify persons killed in accidents or other disasters. Formation of the

FBI's Disaster Squad resulted from a 1940 commercial airline crash in which an FBI agent, a stenographer from Mr. Hoover's office, and an official of the U.S. Department of Justice were among those killed. An FBI team was sent to the site to help locate, identify, and recover their bodies, and to offer their assistance in identifying other crash victims, a practice that has been continued since that time.

DNA

In Chapter 1, we saw how the Will West–William West incident at the federal penitentiary at Leavenworth, Kansas, resulted in recognizing the singular nature of fingerprints for the purpose of positively identifying people. In that same chapter, we also learned that though deoxyribonucleic acid (DNA) was discovered in 1868, scientists were slow to appreciate its role in heredity. As a result, it was not until 1985 that the scientific community realized that portions of DNA structures of certain genes could be as unique as fingerprints for identification purposes. According to Alec Jeffreys, who with his associates at Leicester University made this discovery, the chance of two persons having the same identical DNA patterns is between 30 and 100 billion to 1.[19]

However, using DNA as an investigative tool has not been without controversy, primarily regarding testing techniques. In 1988, the FBI initiated a research effort to perfect a method for testing by its laboratory, and to establish the scientific validity and reliability of the testing process so that it could withstand the legal challenges that were to be expected.[20]

That same year, Yale H. Caplan, writing in *Academy News* for the American Academy of Forensic Science, commented that it was vital that laboratories conducting DNA tests have stringent quality control in their procedures, and that experts testifying on the subject of DNA should be conservative in their use of statistical data. He also wrote that the transfer of the testing techniques from a few highly specialized laboratories then performing the tests, to crime laboratories throughout the country, would require training, and that stringent quality controls, certification, and proficiency testing would have to be included.[21]

Efforts have been under way since 1992 to deal with the concerns expressed by Caplan. In that year, a report by the National Research Council's Committee on DNA Techniques in Forensic Science strongly endorsed the idea of a certification program for DNA analysts. Following issuance of that report, the National Institute of Justice announced its support of a project undertaken by the American Board of Criminalistics to develop written certification tests for five forensic science specialties, namely, forensic biology (which subsumes a DNA specialty), drug identification, fire debris analysis, hair and fiber analysis, and paint and polymer analysis. A pilot test, consisting of a minimum of 150 questions per

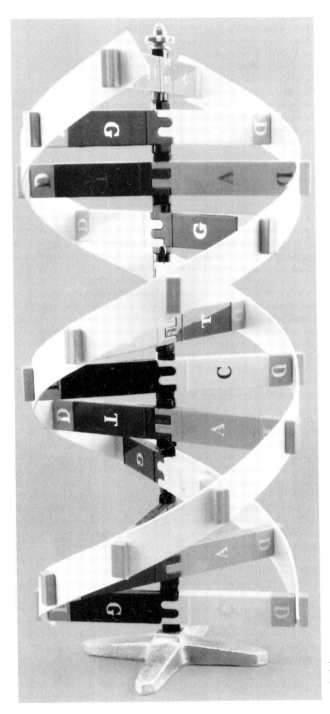

Model DNA strand showing polynu-
cleotide chains and hydrogen bonds.
(*Courtesy* FBI)

specialty, was given in conjunction with the 1994 meeting of the American Academy of Forensics. Among other things, those to whom certification would be granted would not only have to take continuing education courses, but also submit to recertification on a cyclical basis.[22]

The importance of such a program is illustrated by a Massachusetts Superior Court judge's action in connection with DNA testing performed relative to the defendants in five murder trials. The test results were ruled inadmissible in all five cases not because of any questions about the scientific theory of DNA testing, but rather because the court was concerned about the methods used by the private laboratory chosen to do the tests. It believed that either the procedures were insufficiently rigid or the laboratory failed to use accepted testing techniques.[23]

DNA testing necessarily must be done by qualified laboratories. However, with respect to such testing, investigators must be made aware of two things. They need to know what sorts of biological evidence are suitable for DNA analysis since the procedure is not without limitations. They also have to understand the extent to which DNA test results can affect their own work.

DNA analysis can be performed on only certain biological specimens. Blood can be analyzed if white cells are present; hair can be used for test purposes if the root is present. Bone, urine, and saliva can be tested, as can skin but only if nucleated epithelial cells are present. Thus despite limitations, investigators may have ample opportunity to obtain biological evidence and submit it for DNA testing.

However, finding such biological evidence and submitting it for DNA testing does not relieve investigators of their obligation to pursue all other leads. Relying solely on laboratory procedures and ignoring other avenues of investigation is no different from completely relying on a subject's confession, without independently developing corroborating evidence, only to have that confession repudiated. In either case, jurors will see investigators as lazy or incompetent, and the prosecution's case may suffer irreparable damage. Therefore, notwithstanding DNA testing, and regardless of the strength of the test results, investigators still must look for additional evidence with which to independently corroborate the subject's participation in the crime, or at the very least to show that the subject had both a motive and an opportunity to commit it.

The importance of DNA tests, and what they can contribute to both criminal investigations and the criminal justice system, is illustrated by a U.S. Department of Justice announcement that it was increasing its efforts to make DNA tests as common as fingerprints and to help accelerate the development of a national DNA data bank. According to a Justice Department report, in the last few years, twenty-eight men who had been convicted of rape, some of whom had been sentenced to death, were freed after DNA tests proved their innocence. Jeremy Travis, director of the National Institute of Justice (the Justice Department's research unit), observed that DNA has the power to "both exonerate the innocent and identify and convict the guilty." The continuing need to professionalize crime laboratories is emphasized, particularly for DNA testing. Barry C. Scheck, a professor at the Benjamin Cardozo School of Law, notes that every year since 1989, when DNA analysis was first admitted in evidence, the FBI Laboratory has found that about 25 percent of the primary suspects in sexual assault cases, whose DNA has been tested, have been exonerated. Scheck also has remarked that the problem lies not in DNA testing itself, but rather with the occasionally poor quality of the work done by police technicians.[24]

Specific cases in which DNA testing has been used may help us better understand its real and potential value.

❖ Case 13-6

On May 30, 1995, an unattached left leg, clad in a size 7½ military-style boot, two socks, and an olive-drab blousing strap used by military personnel to snug the cuffs of fatigue trousers over boot-tops, was found at the site of the bombed-out Oklahoma City Federal Building. At first, the state's medical examiner concluded that it belonged to a white male in his 30s. However, more sophisticated tests performed by the FBI Laboratory identified the leg as that of a 16- to 30-year-old black woman. One of the bombing's victims was 21-year-old Lakesha Levy, a black woman member of the U.S. Air Force.[25]

❖ Case 13-7

Anthony Shea was indicted on February 22, 1996, in connection with the August 4, 1995, robbery of a New Hampshire bank; he also was identified as a suspect in an armored car robbery in which two guards were shot and killed. In committing the bank robbery, two masked men forced their way into the building by smashing a window. It was believed that one or possibly both may have cut themselves going through the window since blood samples were collected from inside the bank and the alleged getaway vehicle. DNA tests conducted by the FBI Laboratory showed that Shea's blood matched those samples.[26]

❖ Case 13-8

In 1980, a California court sentenced Kevin Lee Green to fifteen years to life for beating his wife almost to death and killing their unborn baby. His wife testified against him although initially she did not remember the attack; he claimed he had been out and found her unconscious when he got home. Having received thousands of DNA test results from state files, the sheriff's crime laboratory was updating its computer database. In doing so, it found a match between blood from the Green case and one Gerald Parker, a convicted rapist in prison for a parole violation. Additional blood was taken from Parker for confirmation; he then was charged with the Green crimes.[27]

QUESTIONED DOCUMENTS

In any number of investigations, questioned documents, material typed, printed by computer, or written or printed by an individual, may be found. All lend themselves to laboratory examinations that can help investigators focus on the most likely suspects. However, if questioned documents have been typed or printed by computer, investigators are in a situation not unlike that of finding biological evidence that can be tested. They still must develop additional evidence to help prove that a suspect either committed the offense or at the very least had the motive and opportunity to do so.

Proof of a suspect's involvement is much easier when questioned documents are either handwritten or hand printed. As stated by Lee R. Waggoner in the June 1984 issue of the *FBI Law Enforcement Bulletin,* "Handwriting examination is one of the few forensic sciences in which a particular individual can be identified to the exclusion of all other persons."[28] However, as with other submissions for laboratory examination, laboratory personnel must depend on the quality and quantity of the materials submitted for examination by investigators.

For example, a masked man gives a bank teller a handwritten note saying the teller will be shot unless his demand for all the cash in the teller's drawer is met and no alarm is sounded. The teller complies; the robber escapes. The investigators have three things with which to work: the film from the bank's security camera, the robber's MO, and the note. Based on the film and MO, a suspect is identified and taken into custody. These factors alone will not prove this person committed the robbery, but the necessary proof may be found by a laboratory examination comparing his handwriting with that of the note's author. What steps have to be taken as a condition precedent to a laboratory submission?

Handwriting samples or exemplars are not considered testimonial evidence, so getting them from suspects does not violate the Fifth Amendment as regards protection against self-incrimination. By the same token, certain criteria must be satisfied before laboratory personnel can make a positive identification on the basis of handwriting.

Being able to submit known samples for comparison with the bank robbery note would be ideal, but since criminal investigators rarely work under ideal conditions, other exemplars have to be obtained. In getting them, there must be enough known samples to show the person's writing habits in relation to the questioned writing. In other words, investigators have to get known exemplars that can be compared successfully with the writing in question. To do this, the collected samples must be representative of the individual's normal writing habits and contain a sufficient number of the same words, letter combinations, and names as appear in the questioned document. The exemplars also must be gotten using the same types of writing instruments and format as those found on the document in question.[29]

Handwriting and fingerprints helped New York City detectives link Heriberto Seda, arrested on June 18, 1996, for shooting his sister, to a series of assaults, including three deaths, dating back to 1989. After his arrest, he scrawled and signed a statement for the police. Several letters in his signature and a symbol on his statement prompted a detective, who had worked the so-called Zodiac shootings, to have Seda's fingerprints checked. They matched those found in the earlier Zodiac investigations. This detective noticed the way in which Seda wrote certain letters, underlined words, and drew the symbol and recalled that fingerprints had been found in three of the earlier cases.[30]

FIREARMS

The use of firearms is not confined to homicides and assaults; they also can be used to commit other crimes, such as robbery, in which the weapon may or may not have been fired. When a firearm has been fired, a major part of the laboratory's work is to try to establish a connection between bullets or cartridge casings found at the crime scene or in a victim and a particular gun. The laboratory also can be helpful in trying to determine the type of weapon used. It also can check weapons for safety features and trigger pull, determine if the weapon has been fired recently, check a suspect's hand for evidence of gunpowder residue left when the gun is fired, and possibly restore serial numbers that have been removed from a weapon.

In earlier chapters, we touched upon the role of ballistics in connection with investigations, but not primarily from the forensics viewpoint. A laboratory's ability to connect crime scene evidence to a particular weapon, or even type of weapon, can provide investigators with important leads. When such weapons can be linked to a particular person, the prosecution's case obviously is strengthened. But ballistics has more than these uses, and they are best illustrated by examples.

On March 4, 1996, Abe Lebewohl, owner of New York City's well-known Second Ave. Deli, was killed with a .25 caliber handgun during a robbery in lower Manhattan. On March 7, two New York City police officers found a .25 caliber disassembled automatic near 96th Street at the Central Park Transverse. Recalling the March 4 case, the disassembled gun was sent to the police department's ballistics laboratory. There it was determined that it apparently matched the three shell casings found at the scene of the homicide.[31] When Westchester County (New York) Sheriff's Department detectives learned that the caliber of the weapon recovered in the Lebewohl investigation was the same as that used to kill an Elmsford, New York, motel clerk, they sent three recovered shell casings to the New York City Police Department's laboratory for a ballistics examination, where it was determined that the same gun had been used in both killings.[32]

Two men were killed with a shotgun in Boston on June 16, 1996; shell casings were found at the crime scene. Ten days later, the Lincoln (Massachusetts) Police Department arrested the driver of a van that was being driven erratically. A shotgun was found in the van. The defendant was charged, and bail was set. Since he could not post bail, he was held in jail, and the shotgun was sent for a ballistics examination. The laboratory matched it with the shell casings found at the scene of the June 16 homicides. Detectives also spoke with people who knew the subject and reported having seen him with the weapon.[33]

Another way in which ballistics can aid investigators is illustrated by a fatal shooting that occurred on a New York City subway platform the night of July 4, 1996. An unarmed man was shot by a police officer; five shots were fired. The victim, who apparently had been running away from the officer, had been shot in the back. Early ballistics tests showed that a spray of bullets hit the floor and walls of the subway station in the direction in which the victim had been moving, thus raising questions about the justification for the shooting itself.[34]

HAIRS AND FIBERS

Forensic examination of hairs and fibers, and even of dust or the contents of a vacuum cleaner bag, sometimes referred to as trace evidence, can provide valuable help not only in terms of leads, but also in that they may be able to link a suspect to a particular crime. They can be of evidentiary value in assaults, murders, breaking and entering, rape, burglary, robbery, and kidnapping cases, among others. Hair may be found on instruments used in assaults and murders, or where either suspects or victims have brushed up against or had contact with hairy or furry objects, including animals. Hairs and fibers also may be found on persons or items of clothing in rape cases.

Since hairs resist decomposition and putrefaction, laboratory examinations may help identify both living and deceased persons. However, on the basis of hair examination alone, it cannot be said that such evidence originated with a particular individual. Nevertheless, examination can be useful by helping to either eliminate or limit certain possibilities. It can distinguish between animal and human hair. If the hair is of human origin, it is usually possible to say whether it is from a person of the Caucasian, Negroid, or Mongoloid race, or if the person is of mixed race. Furthermore, examination can determine with a good deal of accuracy the region of the body from which hair has been removed, and whether it was forcibly pulled or fell out. It also can distinguish between natural and dyed or bleached hair.[35]

Hairs and fibers were key factors that helped connect Wayne Williams with the murder of twelve children in the Atlanta (Georgia) area.[36] They also were important in a New York City investigation in which the defendant was accused of killing three young females. Police laboratory tests matched one of three strands of hair found with the hair of one of the victims. Fibers found on all three matched fibers found either in a vacuum cleaner located in the defendant's apartment or on a spool of red thread that another test showed had been in the apartment.[37]

MISCELLANEOUS CRIMINALISTIC EXAMINATIONS

Discussing the arrests made after the Rochester, New York, Brink's depot armed robbery, we noted that the "hostage" kidnapped by the robbers told the FBI that he had been transported in a large U-Haul type of van with an overhead door, but tire tracks found at the scene indicated that the vehicle used was a minivan. Casts of the tracks, taken and submitted to the FBI Laboratory for examination, were found to be similar to those that would be made by a 1984 Plymouth Voyager Minivan like the one owned by one of the three subjects arrested on November 12, 1993.[38]

In earlier chapters, we cited the investigation of the World Trade Center bombing. In addition to fingerprints, laboratories played a vital role in identifying either explosive devices or their components. However, a technical consultant also was able to provide evidence of a different, and increasingly important, type at the trial of one of the defendants. One of the charges against Ramzi Ahmed Yousef at the time of his 1996 trial related to plans to blow up aircraft of American airlines in Asia.

In presenting its case, the prosecution alleged that the bombing of a Philippine Airlines plane was a test run for those attacks, and it led to the January 7, 1995, search of Yousef's Manila apartment by the Philippine authorities. At that time, they found not only a bomb-making operation, but also a laptop computer. On July 9, 1996, a Philippine National Bureau of Investigation technical consultant testified that when he examined the computer on January 9, 1995, he was able to retrieve files from its hard drive even though some of them had been deleted. Among the data retrieved by him were airline schedules, money transfers, identification photographs, a "threat letter," and other textual materials.[39]

Perhaps nothing under the criminalistics umbrella is as controversial as the polygraph, or lie detector. Advocates of its use argue that

Polygraph examination. (*Courtesy* FBI)

despite some possible shortcomings, it is helpful; opponents contend that it serves no real purpose. Nevertheless, and even though most courts still refuse to admit the results of polygraph examinations into evidence, they are used by some investigative agencies as an aid.

The controversy is not new. Appearing in 1964 before a subcommittee of the Committee on Government Operations of the U.S. House of Representatives, which was interested in the workings and results of polygraph examinations, Dr. Joseph F. Kubis, a professor in Fordham University's Department of Psychology, stated that lie detectors did not prove facts, they merely indicated whether a person believed what he or she said.[40] In his testimony before the same body, Dr. H. B. Donovan, a psychiatrist, expressed the opinion that lie detection was not a valid procedure.[41] On one occasion following a study of the polygraph's effectiveness, it was estimated that it is only 70 percent reliable.[42]

Certainly its use in connection with the Central Intelligence Agency's investigation of Aldrich Ames, one of the highest-profile espionage cases in U.S. history, seems to support the notion that the lie detector is unreliable as an investigative tool. Ames, a CIA employee spying for the Union of Soviet Socialist Republics (USSR), learned he was to take a polygraph examination on May 2, 1986. Afraid of being found out, he sought the KGB's advice and was told to "Get a good night's sleep, and rest, and go into the test rested and relaxed. Be nice to the polygraph examiner, develop a rapport, and be cooperative and try to maintain your calm." Ames passed; ironically, the only suspected deception on the examiner's part dealt with a truthful answer to a question that Ames was able to explain.[43] When Ames was again examined by the CIA on April 12, 1991, the polygraph indicated that some of his answers were deceptive. He was reexamined on April 16 by a different examiner and passed.[44]

FORENSIC MEDICINE

Earlier we discussed in general terms different aspects of forensic medicine that can make significant contributions to the investigative process. Autopsy results can prove helpful in various ways by what they reveal; they also can help investigators focus on what they may be able to eliminate. The tragic July 17, 1996, explosion of TWA Flight 800 with 230 on board, enroute from New York to Paris, can be used to help illustrate the point. The aircraft went down in Long Island Sound shortly after takeoff.

Although the explosion reportedly was witnessed by a number of people, it was impossible to tell initially whether the cause was accidental or criminal. This, in turn, raised a jurisdictional question discussed in Chapter 7. Since the initial assumption was that this was an accident, primary investigative responsibility lay with the NTSB. The FBI would cooperate but play a subordinate role until it might become evident that the explosion was caused by a criminal act. In that event, the NTSB and FBI roles would be reversed. Therefore, determining the actual cause was important if the investigation was to be properly focused and proceed without any loss of valuable time or momentum. Although careful examination of any downed aircraft's recovered parts is essential to a determination of cause, examination of passenger and crew corpses also might offer some clues.

After some of the first autopsies, Dr. Charles Wetli, the Suffolk County (New York) medical examiner, reported the cause of death was "predominantly massive blunt force injuries" that had resulted from either impact with objects inside the cabin or deceleration. He also said that based on twenty autopsies completed by examiners, using X-rays to look for signs of missiles or projectiles typically associated with an explosion, and that could be trapped by bodies, no evidence of a bomb had been found.[45] Subsequent examinations, after the recovery of 100 whole bodies and numerous body parts, failed to reveal any signs of microscopic traces of metal such as one might expect to find if a bomb made of metal or having metallic parts had been used. Neither, according to Dr. Wetli, were any of the bodies or body parts charred as would have been the case if a bomb had been in the passenger cabin.[46]

Although the precise cause of the explosion had not yet been determined as of July 20, 1996, the initial but admittedly incomplete autopsy results tended to discount the use of a bomb made of metal or metallic parts, or of a bomb in the passenger cabin. Consequently, from a jurisdictional viewpoint, investigative responsibility remained with the NTSB. It would continue until either contradictory evidence was developed during additional autopsies or recovered parts of the aircraft itself showed that the explosion's cause was a criminal act.

Although not precisely forensic medicine, one might nevertheless consider the relatively new field of psychological profiling under this heading. As the name itself implies, profiling deals with an individual's characteristics and thought processes based on the most thorough examination of crime scenes and evidence collection that tend to indicate how a particular person thinks.

Even though this investigative aid has made significant contributions to the solution of certain crimes, a regrettable but often necessary condition precedent to the use of psychological profiling is evidence that the crimes being investigated appear to be part of a series. This is because repetitive behavior provides profilers with insight into the subject's thought processes. Once investigators have reason to believe that they are confronted with a serial criminal, as might be true after a number of rapes or homicides, the technique can be used. Of course, even in certain cases in which serialization is not a factor, such as a kidnapping or bank robbery where hostages are taken, psychological profiling may help investigators find ways in which to achieve a nonviolent resolution to a situation.[47]

SUMMARY

Although a failure to thoroughly examine crime scenes, or carefully handle and protect evidence, can adversely affect the outcome of a trial, the inability to connect evidence to a particular defendant and offense will negate any consideration of prosecution. Furthermore, since the evidence found and used to convict in so many crimes is circumstantial, a nexus between the offense and defendant must be established. That task most often will fall to a highly qualified staff with access to a modern, well-equipped laboratory. Parenthetically, this same principle also may apply in civil litigation matters though on a smaller scale, and using private laboratories.

Illustrations used in this chapter represent but some of the forensic examinations that can be made. Laboratories with specialized equipment can make significant contributions to the investigative process. Using a spectrograph to burn material permits interpretation of the light that the burning process emits and makes it possible to identify even minute samples. Coloring agents that might be found in small quantities, such as in a piece of cloth or a paint sample, lend themselves to analysis by a spectrophotometer. Gas chomotography frequently is used to analyze plastics, illicit drugs, explosives, or other substances where there is a need to isolate liquids or gases from complex mixtures or solutions. Where the detection of trace elements is called for, as might be the case with glass, ashes, or other inorganic materials, a mass spectrometer can separate and record ions according to their characteristic masses. In addition, examinations can be invaluable in investigations where toolmarks, wood, firearms, and a possible need for voice identification are involved.

Consequently, it behooves criminal investigators to familiarize themselves, at least in general terms, with laboratory capabilities. That can help to both reduce the risk of a possible break in the chain of evidence and expedite the examination process since it will ensure the direction of evidence to the appropriate laboratory section(s). Of course, this also means understanding the difference between criminalistics and forensic medicine, and what each of these fields can contribute not only to solving crimes, but also to suggesting additional investigative leads.

In terms of criminalistics, as already noted, many and varied types of laboratory examinations are available. Furthermore, the field is not static; new techniques can be and are developed and used. They can help investigators not only link crimes to suspects, but also eliminate seemingly likely suspects, thus narrowing the field. Then, too, other types of assistance can help investigators even though they may not fall under the criminalistics umbrella. Examples would include foreign language translations and forensic meteorology.

Forensic medicine can contribute in many ways. Its role is not necessarily limited to establishing the cause and means of death or injury, or the identification of deceased persons. It can help isolate or eliminate certain factors related to death or injury, and it often can provide investigators with leads to be pursued. In addition, although not necessarily considered part of forensic medicine, investigators should not ignore the closeness between that field and psychological profiling, and what leads the latter may be able to suggest under a given set of circumstances.

REVIEW QUESTIONS

1. What is the primary purpose of forensic laboratory examinations in criminal cases?
2. Which two federal laboratories are used most by state and local police agencies?
3. Name the two principal categories of forensic sciences.
4. What does criminalistics involve?

5. What are the five main parts of forensic medicine?
6. How can pathology examinations help investigators?
7. With what does forensic odontology deal?
8. How can fingerprints help in noncriminal matters?
9. In what ways can forensic meteorology help investigators?
10. Is psychological profiling useful only in cases involving serial crimes?

NOTES

1. "Forensic Expert Says Profession Is Abused," *The Boston Globe,* February 22, 1996, p. 17.
2. "Team of Scientists to Investigate F.B.I. Chemist's Bias Claims," *New York Times,* November 9, 1995, p. A21.
3. Paul L. Kirk, "The Ontogeny of Criminalistics," *Journal of Criminal Law, Criminology, and Police Science,* Vol. 54 (1963), p. 236.
4. "Burned Body of a Woman Found at Brooklyn School," *New York Times,* March 10, 1995, p. B3.
5. "Quick, Watson! The Barometer! Of Microclimates and Crimes," *New York Times,* December 5, 1995, p. C10.
6. John Douglas and Mark Olshaker, *Mindhunter* (New York: Scribner, 1995), pp. 159–160.
7. "Overwhelming Evidence in Police Shooting," *New York Times,* September 12, 1992, pp. 23, 25.
8. "Husband Charged in Officer's Death," *New York Times,* February 29, 1996, p. B6.
9. Paul D. McCann, "Report of the Standardization Committee of the International Association for Identification," *Identification News,* Vol. 23, No. 8 (August 1973), pp. 13, 14.
10. S. Oden and B. von Hofsten, *Nature,* 173 (1954): 449.
11. *National Institute of Justice Update,* (September 1995) U.S. Department of Justice, Office of Justice Programs.
12. "Partial Fingerprint and Krazy Glue Lead to Rape Suspect," *New York Times,* May 22, 1993, p. 24.
13. "Police in 2 States Trace Identity of the Young Victim of a Slaying," *New York Times,* September 28, 1994, pp. A1, B2.
14. "Man Is Held in Strangling of Woman," *New York Times,* October 29, 1994, p. 23.
15. "Fingerprints Reveal Suspect on the Run from '76 Killing," *New York Times,* August 19, 1995, pp. 1, 22.
16. "Neighbor, 15, Charged in Somerville Killing," *The Boston Globe,* July 26, 1995, pp. 1, 4.
17. "Ex-Boyfriend's Print on Drowned Woman's Body, Court Told," *The Boston Globe,* June 25, 1996, p. 24.
18. "F.B.I. Setting Standards for Computer Picture File of Criminals," *New York Times,* November 5, 1995, p. 20.
19. "British Police Use Genetic Technique in Murder Arrest," *The Atlanta Constitution,* September 22, 1987, p. A3.
20. John W. Hicks, "DNA Profiling: A Tool for Law Enforcement," *FBI Law Enforcement Bulletin,* Vol. 57, No. 8 (August 1988) p. 3.

21. Yale H. Caplan, "Current Issues in Forensic Science: DNA Probe Technology in Forensic Serology: Statistics, Quality Control and Interpretation," *American Academy of Forensic Science, Academy News,* Vol. 18, No. 6 (November 1988) p. 11.

22. *National Institute of Justice Update,* (September 1995) U.S. Department of Justice, Office of Justice Programs.

23. *The Boston Globe,* March 12, 1996, pp. 15, 17.

24. "U.S. Has Plan to Broaden Availability of DNA Testing," *New York Times,* June 14, 1996, p. A12.

25. "Leg at Bomb Site is Identified, and a Body Will Be Exhumed," *New York Times,* February 24, 1996, p. 10.

26. "Recaptured Prison Escapee Indicted in '95 N.H. Bank Heist," *The Boston Globe,* February 26, 1996, p. 14.

27. "A '16-Year Nightmare' Comes to an End," *The Boston Globe,* June 22, 1996, p. 3.

28. Lee R. Waggoner, "Handwriting Evidence for the Investigator," *FBI Law Enforcement Bulletin,* Vol. 53, No. 6 (June 1984), p. 20.

29. Ibid., pp. 20–25.

30. "Police Say Brooklyn Suspect, 28, Admits Fatal 'Zodiac' Shootings," *New York Times,* June 20, 1996, pp. A1, B6.

31. "Police Find the Gun Used to Kill Deli Owner," *New York Times,* March 8, 1996, p. B5.

32. "Gun Used on Deli Man Is Tied to '95 Killing," *New York Times,* March 13, 1996, p. B3.

33. *The Boston Globe,* July 12, 1996, pp. 19, 28.

34. "Tests Raise Doubts About Justification of Shooting," *New York Times,* July 10, 1996, pp. B1, B3.

35. "Don't Miss a Hair," *FBI Law Enforcement Bulletin,* Vol. 45, No. 5 (May 1976), pp. 9–15.

36. Harold L. Deadman, "Fiber Evidence and the Wayne Williams Trial," *FBI Law Enforcement Bulletin,* Vol. 53, No. 5 (May 1984), pp. 10–19.

37. "Fiber Evidence Presented in Slayings Trial," *New York Times,* August 14, 1992, p. B2.

38. "U.S. Details Evidence in Brink's Robbery Arrests," *New York Times,* November 14, 1993, pp. 1, 40.

39. "Prosecutors in Bomb-Plot Case Turn to Suspect's Computer," *New York Times,* July 10, 1996, p. B2.

40. Hearing before a subcommittee of the Committee on Government Operations, U.S. House of Representatives, 91st Congress, 1st Session, April 29, 1964, p. 303.

41. Ibid., p. 302.

42. Lee M. Bunkey, "Privacy, Property and the Polygraph," *Labor Law Journal* 18 (February 1967), pp. 79–89.

43. Tim Weiner, David Johnson, and Neil A. Lewis, *Betrayal, The Story of Aldrich Ames, an American Spy* (New York: Random House, 1995), pp. 89–91.

44. Ibid., p. 163.

45. "Little Hard Evidence Found—Death Toll Is Set at 230," *New York Times,* July 19, 1996, pp. A1, B4.

46. *The Boston Globe,* July 20, 1996, p. A1.

47. John Douglas and Mark Olshaker, *Mindhunter* (New York: Scribner, 1995).

Chapter 14

Interrogating
the Subject

Thus far, we have discussed the various elements of an investigation, other than the interrogation of subjects. Those components collectively are designed to help investigators identify the person or persons responsible for committing the offense. Nevertheless, in many criminal cases, prosecutors must rely on circumstantial evidence to obtain convictions. Obviously, their jobs would be made easier if the investigators with whom they work could get confessions, or at least admissions, to further support that evidence.

Despite the importance of trying to get such corroboration, investigators need to be mindful of the limitations imposed upon them in this regard. Failure to do so can easily prompt a presiding judge to grant a defense motion to suppress a statement thus denying the prosecution the benefit that might have been derived from its admission in evidence. As a result, investigators need to understand not only the constitutional principles involved, but also the differences between suspects and subjects, and admissions and confessions.

SUSPECT OR SUBJECT?

In the early stages of an investigation following the commission of a crime, investigators will interview everyone who, in their opinion, might be able to contribute to a solution. As the inquiry progresses, they may begin to consider one or more persons as possible suspects, but they have little or no evidence to connect them to the offense. Consequently, during the early stages of the investigation, they conceivably may speak with someone who later may become a suspect and, eventually, even the subject of the investigation.

For example, in an earlier chapter, we discussed a case in which the decomposed body of an unidentified woman was found in a tractor-trailer in an isolated area. When she subsequently was identified, a former boyfriend, with a history of violence and sexual assault, was questioned three times and let go. However, at this juncture, he had become only a suspect, but following his third interview, investigators noticed discrepancies in his story and that he began to get nervous.[1] It was then that he became the subject. In other words, though his history and relationship with the deceased had made him a logical suspect, the inconsistencies noted during his interviews and his nervousness turned him into the investigation's focal point, and he became the subject of the investigation.

That a person's status may change from suspect to subject does not automatically convert any statements that he or she makes into an admission or a confession. Just as it is important to understand the difference between suspect and subject, so is it important to distinguish between a statement, an admission, and a confession.

STATEMENT, ADMISSION, OR CONFESSION?

In the foregoing example, despite the person's becoming a suspect based on his record and having known and had a relationship with the deceased, his merely acknowledging this information represents nothing more than a statement. If, on the other hand, he admitted to certain incriminating facts, such as being present at her death but denying that he actually killed her and not furnishing pertinent details, he would have made an admission. Had he acknowledged killing the deceased and provided investigators with all the details surrounding his involvement, he would have made a confession. Since anyone reading about a crime could offer to confess for any number of reasons, as has occurred on occasion, a confession must include details to ensure that the subject has, in fact, committed the offense.

LIMITS TO INTERROGATION

Understanding the suspect–subject and statement–admission–confession distinctions is important, but the need to fully understand the limitations imposed in trying to get subjects to confess is of even greater importance.

Otherwise, whatever confessions may be gotten will be ruled inadmissible when the prosecution attempts to have them admitted at trial.

A section of the Fifth Amendment to the U.S. Constitution states that no person "shall be compelled in any criminal case to be a witness against himself." Nevertheless, before the Supreme Court's decision in *Miranda v. Arizona,*[2] police investigators were not required to inform persons taken into custody of their right to remain silent, that if they made a statement it could be used against them in court, of their right to consult with a lawyer and have one present during interrogation, and that a lawyer would be appointed to represent them if they could not afford to hire their own. Thus it was not uncommon for the police to conduct custodial interrogations under less than favorable conditions in order to obtain confessions. There were prolonged interrogations and possibly other forms of duress with only subjects and investigators present; requests for an attorney might well be ignored. Although not couched in today's terms, there were times when police brutality was suspected even if it could not be proved, or the public simply ignored its existence.

Equally unfortunate in terms of seeking justice for those who were victims of crimes was the fact that more than a few defendants who confessed nevertheless were acquitted. Too often investigators concentrated on getting confessions without making any effort to independently corroborate newly acquired information, especially if it was provided by subjects. Then, at trial, defendants would repudiate their confessions alleging that they were given under duress in violation of the Fifth Amendment. These denials, if believed, could result in acquittals. Parenthetically, for many years prior to the *Miranda* decision, it was the FBI's policy to inform persons in custody of what are now referred to as the Miranda warnings.

The fact that any form of duress will vitiate a confession was addressed by the Supreme Court in *Michigan v. Tucker*. This ruling, citing three vital principles, stated that voluntariness is the constitutional standard for the admission of a confession in a criminal prosecution. First, a confession is inadmissible if it is not reliable, even if its reliability is unquestioned. Second, it is inadmissible if it was obtained by methods that are not consistent with basic ideas of fairness. Third, unless a confession is given freely and rationally by a subject, it will be inadmissible even though it is reliable.[3]

We have noted the possibility that during an investigation's early stages someone may be interviewed on the theory that he or she may be a witness. At that time, the individual is neither a suspect nor a subject. That interview is no different from any other described in Chapter 10. However, as the investigation progresses, it begins to appear that this person is a suspect, if not the focal point of the inquiry.

That an investigation develops a likely subject does not necessarily or automatically mean that that individual will immediately be taken into custody. Much will depend on the strength of the evidence developed up to this time. Although additional interviews may be conducted with that person, until he or she is taken into custody, the Miranda warnings need not be given, but they must be given prior to any custodial interrogation. Similarly, it is unwise to assume that under the circumstances any form of duress can be applied.

In view of this, though investigations seldom can be completed under what might be considered ideal conditions, it nevertheless is a sound practice, whenever possible, to defer a subject's interrogation until other aspects of the inquiry have been completed, or are near completion. By then the investigators, and the prosecutors with whom they are working, have an idea of the strengths and weaknesses of the case. This also puts interviewers in a much better position since their indication of a strong case, and intimate knowledge of detail, may cause the subject to confess. As an instructor once told a class of new FBI special agents, if an investigation has been thorough, and properly conducted in all respects, a subject's confession should be thought of as "icing on the cake" since there already should be enough evidence upon which a jury can convict.[4]

Nevertheless, certain preparations should be made before interrogations begin. In criminal cases, it is obvious that subjects must be in custody, and they must have been informed of their rights. Unless there is a clear indication that those rights are understood, and the person is willing to waive them in writing, no interrogation should be attempted.

Furthermore, private-sector security personnel may find it necessary to interrogate persons during noncriminal internal investigations conducted by them. Although the Fifth Amendment provisions against self-incrimination, upon which much of the so-called Miranda warnings are based, do not apply to private persons, security personnel conducting interrogations are well advised to keep two points in mind.

First, the principles regarding voluntariness announced by the U.S. Supreme Court in *Michigan v. Tucker*, cited earlier in this chapter, also have been adopted by state courts with respect to statements made to security personnel. As an example, in New York, confessions obtained by security personnel would be inadmissible in court unless made "freely, voluntarily, and without compulsion or inducement of any sort."[5] The second point is the need to avoid the possibility of subsequent litigation by a person from whom a confession is sought alleging false imprisonment. For instance, if investigators have been both thorough and careful in conducting an internal inquiry, informing a person that the office door is closed to ensure privacy and not restrict freedom of movement, that breaks for such personal needs as going to the toilet or getting something to drink are permitted, and that whatever he or she has to say is to be said voluntarily, they can do a good deal to help protect both the interrogators and their employers.

If in a criminal case a waiver is given to the investigators, the interrogation should take place in quiet surroundings, without interruption, and with all forms of distraction avoided. There should be a table or desk for the investigators' use, and adequate seating for them and the subject. Even though it is good practice for security personnel to tell persons being interrogated about breaks for reasons of personal comfort, it is imperative that representatives of government law enforcement agencies let subjects know at the outset that such breaks are permitted. Two investigators, whether the interrogation is conducted by law enforcement in a criminal case or by private security in an internal investigation, should be present throughout, one of whom acts as a witness to what was said and the fact that the subject's rights were respected. Furthermore, it is highly desirable that at least one of them should be of the same sex as the subject to minimize the risk of an allegation of sexual misconduct during the interrogation.

Investigators' dress and behavior should be businesslike. These are important factors in letting the subject know that they, not the subject, are and will be in control at all times. This means the lead investigator, not the subject, asks the questions, keeps matters focused, and keeps the subject from going off on tangents. To make certain that subjects not only fully understand the questions put to them, but also that their answers be equally understandable and rational, interrogators must avoid using language that is either above or below the subject's level of understanding.

Experienced investigators, preparing for interrogations, carefully review all of their notes. This helps them refresh their memories, focus on what information they hope to get from the individual, and better evaluate the truth of what they are told with regard either to details known only to them and the subject or to discrepancies or inconsistencies in what the latter says.

Despite this preparation, however, good investigators do not ignore lessons that have been learned over the years about the interrogation process. It had been a commonly accepted practice to approach interrogations armed with a series of prepared questions for which they wanted answers. This failed to take into account that in most cases people who are asked questions tend to provide little more information than what they feel is needed to answer those questions. Consequently, additional useful information in the subject's possession might be lost. This practice was universally accepted by law enforcement personnel, the FBI included, until 1984. In June of that year, an article in the *FBI Law Enforcement Bulletin,* dealing with interviews and interrogations, stated that:

> One can obtain more accurate and complete information in interviews through simply listening. . . . Listening has become an important part of interview and interrogation training of new Agents at

the FBI in Quantico, Virginia. . . . Experience has shown the best listeners to be the best interviewers.[6]

The concept of open-ended interviews, and giving subjects a chance to speak freely while interrogators take good notes, affords the latter opportunities to note discrepancies in individuals' statements.

As often happens, once investigators acquire more interrogating experience, they also tend to develop certain techniques with which they feel comfortable. This is not unimportant. Obvious discomfort on an interrogator's part may be communicated to a subject and convey the impression that the investigation is floundering because of a lack of hard evidence.

One approach used successfully by an investigator in both public- and private-sector interrogations, who firmly believed in being a good listener, was to open the interview by giving subjects some idea of the strength of the evidence against them, and then simply express an interest in hearing their side of the story. In some cases, subjects, realizing the case against them was strong, almost felt a sense of relief and confessed with little encouragement. In others, they saw this as a chance to try to mitigate their involvement by explaining why and how they committed the offense. It was only after they once finished their stories that they were asked follow-up questions so as to get specific details or clarify some seemingly contradictory statements.

Others may feel more comfortable going into an interrogation armed with a list of specific questions for which they hope to get answers. This technique can be successful up to a point, but it also may deprive the investigator of an opportunity to get what might seem to be relatively unimportant information that, nevertheless, may be used at trial as defense counsel attempts to discredit a confession's validity.

Regardless of any one investigator's preferred methodology, in addition to being good listeners, experience has taught the importance of being good observers throughout the interrogation process. In other words, they listen to what a person has to say, but they also look at his or her body language, or nonverbal communication. According to Raymond L. Gorden, since the latter form of communication is done less consciously than is verbal communication, it may be a more powerful force in face-to-face interaction.[7] For instance, persons who do such things as constantly crossing and uncrossing their legs, who keep moving around in their chairs or looking away from the interrogator either while being questioned or answering questions, who keep licking their lips or fidgeting with their hair or glasses may be saying as much by their behavior as by their words.

Aside from all the other preparations made for an interrogation, investigators have to decide whether the entire proceeding will be taped or manually recorded by them. Both forms must include certain procedures, but tape-recorded statements require considerably more than ensuring that writing instruments and paper are available. If tape recording is considered preferable, the guidelines set forth in *State v. Driver* warrant consideration:

1. The recording instrument must be capable of taping conversations.
2. The operator who will do the recording must be competent.
3. The end product must be both authentic and accurate.
4. It cannot have any additions, deletions, or changes.
5. The tape should contain start and stop times, and be left on throughout the questioning period.
6. If the tape breaks while questioning is in progress, it should not be spliced. Instead, renew questioning with a new tape and indicate the new start time.[8]

If the interrogation is to be taped, the tape recording also should serve as a complete log of the interrogation. For example, the names of those present, who is conducting the interrogation, start and stop times and whether they represent the interview's beginning and end or interruptions for reasons of personal comfort or otherwise should be stated. If the interrogation is manually recorded, a separate interview log, containing the same information, should be kept by the investigators.

In addition to the start time, all statements, manual or taped, should note at the outset the date and place where the interview is being conducted. The opening paragraph, or oral introduction, also should contain words that clearly indicate the investigators have identified themselves, by name, title, and agency or department, to the person being interrogated, as well as a statement to the effect that no threats or promises have been made to the subject in order to induce a confession.

The foregoing apply to manually prepared statements, whether written by interrogators or subjects. A closing paragraph, indicating the number of pages that constitute the entire statement, should be added to preclude a later allegation that it was altered in any way. Furthermore, each of those pages should be signed, or at least initialed, by the subject. The last page should be signed by that person and witnessed by the investigators. Before signing, subjects should be asked to carefully read the entire document. Any corrections or changes should be made by the subject, in his or her own handwriting, and each should be initialed by the subject. Investigators may further authenticate taped confessions by having them transcribed and having these additional safeguards incorporated therein.

To illustrate the need for extreme care in getting confessions, we need but look at a 1996 trial related to the death of a New York City firefighter killed while fighting a fire on June 5, 1994. A subject was identified, taken into custody, interrogated, and confessed to having set the fire. He then was charged with arson and second degree murder. However, when the case was tried, the defendant alleged that his confession had been coerced. He said he believed that he would be beaten if he failed to confess, and that he confessed while one investigator yelled at him and the other fidgeted with his holster in which he had his gun. Furthermore, he said the investigators had offered him three years in a mental institution if he would admit to setting the fire. Despite his confession, the jurors believed him; they acquitted him of both charges on July 1, 1996.[9]

There also may be times, however rare, when as a subject is being taken into custody, he or she immediately and voluntarily confesses to the crime. That this happened before the Miranda warnings were given will not vitiate the confession as long as its voluntary nature can be established.

SUMMARY

Circumstantial evidence often is the only evidence upon which a prosecution can be based; therefore, the ability to get a confession can add considerably to the strength of a case. When achieved, this goal most frequently results from an interrogation conducted by the investigators, a process that involves a good deal more than merely asking questions.

Some persons interviewed during an investigation as potential witnesses may, over time, evolve into suspects and, eventually, into subjects. The evolutionary process even may be based in part on a suspect's admission that, in turn, leads to his or her becoming a subject. It is only when the latter stage is reached, and individuals are actually taken into custody, that confessions are sought.

Taking someone into custody is critical both in trying to solve cases and to the possible impact of what follows on our criminal justice system. Over zealous investigators who, in their haste to question subjects, forget or ignore the fact that the essence of an admissible confession is its voluntary character, and who fail to observe legal mandates relative to the treatment of persons in custody, such as giving Miranda warnings, are unprofessional. Those who fail to independently corroborate details about an offense, relying instead on confessions, are both unprofessional and lazy. They do a disservice to themselves, their agencies, and above all to the very concept of justice.

Once a subject agrees to be interviewed, the investigators must control the interrogation. They need to feel comfortable with their chosen format for getting information, yet they also must be conscious of the importance of being good listeners and observers.

Realizing the impact that confessions can have on the outcome of a case makes it necessary for investigators to do more than what is called for in the preceding paragraph. They must also ensure the integrity and voluntary nature of those confessions. This is done by keeping an interview log, or orally incorporating comparable information in a taped interrogation, and by inserting opening and closing paragraphs in each written or transcribed confession as evidence that the subject was neither threatened nor otherwise coerced into confessing.

REVIEW QUESTIONS

1. Can a potential witness become an investigation's subject?
2. At what point does a suspect become a subject?
3. Distinguish between an admission and a confession.
4. When must a subject be advised of his or her rights?
5. How did *Miranda* change the interrogation process?
6. Do private investigators have to inform subjects of their rights before questioning them?
7. What is the constitutional standard for a confession's admission in a criminal case?
8. Why should investigators independently corroborate information instead of just relying on confessions?
9. What standards need to be followed for taped confessions?
10. What does a subject do to make changes or corrections in a written or transcribed confession?

NOTES

1. "Man Is Held in Strangling of Woman," *New York Times,* October 29, 1994, p. 23.
2. *Miranda v. Arizona,* 384 U.S. 436 (1966), 16 L. Ed. 2d 694, 86 S. Ct. 1602, 10 A. L. R. 3d 974.
3. *Michigan v. Tucker,* 417 U.S. 433 (1974).
4. Advice given to a 1948 class of new special agents of the FBI, of which the author was a member.
5. *People v. Frank,* 52 Misc. 2d 266, 275 N. Y. S. 2d 570.
6. Edgar M. Miner, "The Importance of Listening in the Interview and Interrogation Process, *FBI Law Enforcement Bulletin,* Vol. 53, No. 6 (June 1984), pp. 13, 16.
7. Raymond L. Gorden, *Interviewing: Strategy, Techniques and Tactics,* 4th ed. (Florence, KY: Wadsworth, 1987).
8. *State v. Driver,* 38 N. J. 255 (1962).
9. *New York Times,* July 2, 1996, pp. B1, B2.

PART III

❖

PRINCIPAL TYPES
OF INVESTIGATIONS

Part I introduced the subject of investigations by looking at their historical background, who conducts them, good investigators' characteristics or personal traits, exactly what investigations are, and how they are initiated. Part II discussed the many components of an investigation. Part III examines a wide range of incidents or activities that warrant investigation. It focuses on matters that investigators are most likely to encounter with the greatest frequency. It does not purport to cover every possible type of inquiry. Neither is it a step-by-step technical manual on how investigations are conducted, since virtually all inquiries in reaction to an event have many common elements.

Most of what follows concerns investigating various crimes, some violent and some not. Some are offenses against persons; others against property. Some, particularly those involving violent crimes or major losses, will, simply by virtue of their high profiles, put additional pressure on investigators for quick solutions, as previously pointed out. At the same time, it also is important to acknowledge that not all investigations involve criminal activity. With that in mind, Chapter 18 looks at some noncriminal investigations that are likely to be encountered by both public- and private-sector investigators.

The ultimate objective of any criminal investigation is fourfold: a solution that then results in an arrest, a trial, and the perpetrator's punishment. However, in reality, the investigator's goal is limited to the solution and arrest phases. Prosecutors handle the trial phase and hope they can get defendants convicted; courts mete out the punishment. Despite this, investigators dare not ignore the importance of their own roles and actions if the prosecutors with whom they work are to get convictions. They have to remember that once it has been alleged that a crime was committed, it is their job to prove the allegation's truth, namely, that a crime was in fact committed.

Statutes that designate a particular offense to be a crime also set forth the elements that constitute the offense. They are a combination of a definition and an outline of what specific acts must be proved to establish that crime. For example, precisely what act or acts would be needed to prove a robbery was committed?

Here one must not forget that despite the underlying commonalities of criminal statutes in the United States, each state has its own criminal code. Therefore, elements may vary from state to state and include further refinements if state laws have different degrees of severity under the umbrella of a particular offense. To illustrate, robbery in every state requires proof that the subject committed a larceny, that is, the taking of the property of another person, but robbery is distinguished from larceny because it also involves the use or threatened use of force. However, a state also might elect to establish different degrees of robbery, each with its own distinguishing elements for which there would have to be proof. For instance, robbery in the third degree might be limited to the forcible theft of property. To prove second degree robbery, one might need to show that there was another participant in the commission of the crime, or that the perpetrator(s) caused physical injury to any person who was not a participant, or that what appeared to be a firearm was displayed. First degree robbery, the most serious, might further require proof that any deadly weapon, not only a firearm, was used.

Consequently, investigators first must develop enough evidence to satisfy each of those elements that together constitute a particular crime. Once there is proof that a crime has been committed, investigators have to be able to show that the act that actually caused the particular injury or loss under investigation was the work of one or more persons.

Investigators also should be familiar with the expression *corpus delicti* or the "body of the crime." Often used in connection with the commission of crimes, it is related to the elements set forth in the statute and refers to the facts that prove a crime has been committed.

Notwithstanding the use of the word *body,* surely a key factor in homicide investigations, in practice the term has a broader meaning. As an example, if a building is destroyed by a set fire, the "body" would be the fire and that it was caused by an act of arson.

As a further introduction to the chapters that compose Part III, it seems only fitting to briefly cite three rather celebrated investigations that bring together much of what was discussed in Parts I and II. First is the February 1993 World Trade Center bombing case; second, that of the Unabomber, an investigation first opened as a result of an incident that happened in May 1978; and last, the July 1996 loss of TWA Flight 800 with 230 passengers and crew aboard.

These cases illustrate a number of points discussed in several earlier chapters and confirm that all reactive investigations, criminal or other, have much in common. Among them are investigators' personal traits; the need for cooperation when jurisdictional matters are in question; the importance of incident scene searches; the use of sources of information, confidential informants, and witnesses; how evidence is collected and preserved; and the contributions forensic laboratory examinations can make to an investigation. These three cases will be discussed in greater detail in Chapters 15 and 18.

Chapter 15

❖

Crimes of Violence

In this chapter, we examine crimes of violence and how they are investigated. Although some of the offenses discussed may at first seem to be crimes against property, and are even classified as such for crime-reporting purposes, they are considered here because of the possible effect on the victims of the violence associated with these offenses.

HOMICIDES AND ASSAULTS

By definition, both homicides and assaults involve one person attacking another. As a practical matter, the only real difference between them is that homicide victims are killed, whereas assault victims are not. Assaults range from relatively simple cases in which, despite the victim's fear, no physical contact occurs, through an assault and battery, in which contact occurs, to an assault with intent to kill. The most serious assaults may leave the victim near death. Because of the similarities between homicides and assaults, their investigative techniques also are similar.

There are five principal categories of death, not all of which involve some form of criminal activity: murder, manslaughter, accidental, suicide, and natural. Murder and manslaughter clearly are crime related. As a rule, accidental deaths and suicides are not, but the circumstances surrounding them may be sufficiently suspicious to justify an investigation to confirm the absence of any criminal activity. Deaths attributable to natural causes rarely require any form of inquiry other than that made by medical personnel.

The most serious of all crimes are homicides: the death of one person caused by another's actions. It makes no difference whether the death resulted from a deliberate act, self-defense, or an accident. The homicide investigator's task is twofold: to develop the evidence needed to determine the category into which a homicide falls, and to prove that a particular person is responsible for that death. This is true even if there is conclusive evidence that the death resulted from an act of self-defense or an accident.

There are levels of seriousness under the general heading of homicides; the most serious is murder. Murder statutes usually distinguish between first and second degree. Most first degree murder charges require proof that a person who caused another's death did so knowingly and with premeditation or malice aforethought. There also are some states where a person who causes the death of another while committing a felony (referred to as felony-murder) can be charged with first degree murder despite the lack of premeditation or malice; in others, the charge would be murder in the second degree, a less serious offense. In most jurisdictions, second degree murder is charged when death is caused by a person who knowingly intended to inflict serious physical injury, but not to kill.

Manslaughter, like murder, may have a dual classification: voluntary and involuntary. Voluntary manslaughter involves one person killing another intentionally, but under extremely stressful conditions as in the heat of passion or while in a rage. An example would be two people having a very heated, emotional argument. One becomes so enraged that he chokes the other to death. Death caused by a failure to act with proper caution is involuntary manslaughter. A motorist who causes the death of a child while speeding through a clearly marked school zone would most likely be charged with involuntary manslaughter.

As we noted, the circumstances surrounding accidental deaths and suicides may call for an investigation to determine whether a crime has been committed. Suppose a person is killed in an accident that took place while riding as a passenger in a friend's automobile. To say the death was accidental assumes facts without looking for them. Is the conclusion justified? Information about the weather, road, and the driver's condition and behavior at the time of the accident might indicate the death was a case of involuntary manslaughter.

A person who takes his or her own life commits suicide. But do the circumstances surrounding the death clearly indicate that the deceased killed him- or herself? Is it possible that it is a homicide made to look like a suicide? Discussing crime scenes in Chapter 8, we took note of a New York City case that at first seemed to be a suicide, yet finding a 1/2-inch screw on the victim's bed made the detectives hesitate to classify the death as such; after a four-month investigation, two arrests were made.[1]

Investigating autoerotic deaths can be especially troubling to law enforcement personnel since they may closely resemble a suicide. *Webster's New World Dictionary* defines *autoerotism* as "sexual sensation arising without external stimulus, direct or indirect, from another person; self-generated sexual activity directed toward oneself, as masturbation." Consequently, if the means used by the deceased to reach a desired level of stimulation involve some form of bondage, or the use of a ligature, a self-inflicted autoerotic death can result. However, the use of a ligature also opens the door to the possibility that the death is a homicide and raises questions about the actual cause. Only a medical examiner can determine if the victim's death was an accident, a suicide, or a homicide. Nevertheless, the element of uncertainty in autoerotic death cases means that the scene of such a death must be treated as a crime scene pending receipt of an autopsy's results. Only if the medical examiner rules the cause of death to be a homicide is further investigative involvement justified.

The circumstances surrounding accidental deaths may necessitate conducting an inquiry to eliminate the possibility of a homicide. Although the actual cause of all deaths must be determined by a physician, if the apparent cause is questionable, at least some investigation may be helpful. For instance, a corpse is found in a hotel room bathroom; there is a broken glass and a good deal of blood. The police are called. Is this a suicide, a homicide, or an accident? Although a medical examiner's autopsy finds that death was caused by a massive coronary, the police investigation indicates that the death was accidental; the deceased had gone to the bathroom for water with which to take medication that had been prescribed for his condition. The glass broke in his hand, cutting an artery.

In addition to recognizing the various forms of death that may be encountered, it is important to understand that although most homicides involve one victim and one perpetrator, this is not always the case. There also are such crimes as serial and mass murders, each posing different problems.

One person responsible for multiple deaths in a single incident or within a very short time is a mass murderer. The fact that those responsible often are quickly identified and caught does not lessen the need for thorough crime scene searches to collect and preserve evidence, as well as to identify, locate, and interview witnesses and others who can provide meaningful information.

In contrast, a single person who kills multiple victims, with either long or short intervals of time between each victim, is a serial murderer. Serial murderers kill repeatedly, but they also tend to commit each of their crimes in a similar way. Although victims may be randomly chosen, there are times when serial murder investigators will detect patterns. The Wayne Williams case, cited in Chapter 13, is a good example. Of twelve victims with whom Williams was associated, all were black males ranging in age from 10 to 28, and eight were under 20. Furthermore, although one died from a blunt trauma to the head and one was stabbed, the remaining ten died from asphyxiation or strangulation.

The difficulties encountered in investigating serial murder cases may be compounded by a delay in recognizing the existence of a strong probability that there is but one perpetrator. Several deaths may have occurred over time, with lapses between each, yet their connection may be obscured until a particular MO becomes apparent. A further delay in recognizing a serial murder case may occur when, despite similarities in the killings, victims have been found at different sites, or even in different jurisdictions. Some of the more notorious serial murderers, the number of their victims, and the time frames during which they killed, follow:

> Albert Henry De Salvo, aka (also known as) "The Boston Strangler," thirteen victims, 1961–1962
>
> Juan Corona, twenty-five victims, 1970–1971
>
> Theodore Bundy, wa (with alias) Ted Bundy, aka "The Love Bite Killer," at least thirty-six victims, 1974–1978
>
> John Gacy, wa Jack Gacy, thirty-three victims, 1975–1978
>
> David Berkowitz, aka "Son of Sam," five killed, seven injured, 1976–1977
>
> Wayne Williams, twenty-eight victims, 1979–1981
>
> Donald Harvey, thirty victims, 1984–1987

Obviously, a first homicide, and even succeeding ones, will be investigated as would any killing until it may appear that a serial murderer is at work. It is then that police agencies can benefit from the FBI's help in two ways. One is to ask for the assistance of the bureau's Investigative Support Unit, formerly called the Behavioral Science Unit, in developing a psychological profile of the killer. The unit's work was discussed in Chapter 13. The other is to avail themselves of the work of the FBI's Violent Crime Apprehension Program, or VICAP.

Although an MO can be helpful in any number of cases, John Douglas, who until his retirement was the chief of the FBI's Investigative Support Unit, has suggested that there is a difference between an MO and a perpetrator's "signature" in serial murder investigations. According to Douglas, an MO is learned behavior, and as such, it is a dynamic that can change as criminals learn how to improve their technique from each of their earlier offenses. In coining the word *signature* and distinguishing it from an MO, Douglas states that the former, unlike the latter, does not change. For instance, if a criminal dominates his or her victims, inflicting pain or provoking begging or pleading, it is a signature that expresses that individual's personality; it is something the perpetrator needs to do.[2]

All homicide and assault investigations pose certain questions for which investigators must seek answers. One that needs to be addressed in these cases, including what appear to be questionable suicides or accidents, is motive. In other words, what prompted a person to kill or commit an assault, to take his or her own life and possibly that of another?

The search for answers differs in more clear-cut cases such as murders and manslaughter as opposed to suicides or murder-suicide investigations. In suicide and murder-suicide cases, investigators look for evidence of poor health, problems with a marriage, an emotionally damaging experience such as the death of a loved one, a divorce, loss of employment, or remorse over something the suicide may have done and regretted. Investigators may also look for evidence of significant financial problems, or of children possibly seeking revenge against parents.

True, medical personnel determine the actual cause of all questionable deaths. However, the police most likely will be the first responders to the scene of a suicide or murder-suicide. Not knowing the cause, they must act as they would to protect any crime scene. This includes looking for evidence that would tend to confirm or deny that the death was a suicide. Did the deceased leave any notes for relatives or friends explaining why he or she chose death? The police search for what may have been the agent or instrumentality used to kill, such as a gun, sharp instrument, drugs, or poison, or is the apparent cause hanging, the use of gas, or jumping from a building.

Investigators working a suspected suicide or murder-suicide case must approach the inquiry as a possible murder until the probability of the latter has been ruled out. To illustrate: assume a suicide note is found; its authenticity has to be established. This may require a laboratory examination of the document to look for possible fingerprints (other than those of the deceased) and to determine the document's age. If it is in longhand, is it the deceased's writing? If typed or done with a computer, does the typing or printing match a machine to which the deceased had access? Relatives or friends to whom the note was addressed have to be interviewed, not only to help establish the document's authenticity, but also for any information they can offer about the deceased's situation, including his or her frame of mind, that might reinforce the probability that this is a suicide rather than a homicide. Investigators cannot ignore the fact that what seems to be a suicide, or even a murder-suicide, may actually be a homicide, and they must act accordingly until suicide can be confirmed.

We have taken note of mass and serial murders and suicides and murder-suicides. However, as a practical matter, most death-related and assault investigations will tend to focus on single incidents that have resulted in death or injury, usually to one person, even though there may be multiple perpetrators. Regardless, the importance of motive is common to homicides, suicides, and assaults. We already have said that motive must be taken into account in trying to distinguish between homicides and suicides. There is no guarantee that a motive will surface in every murder and assault, and perhaps in some manslaughter investigations, but learning that one possibly exists often can provide early leads.

What, then, are some of the underlying reasons that will prompt one person to deliberately kill or assault another? Among the most common causes of criminal homicide are

Anger

Revenge or jealousy

Profit

Felony-murder

Killing in self-defense

Murder-suicide

Random killing

Sex and sadism

Investigators responding to any criminal homicide or assault have to concentrate on five matters: the victim, the weapon, the witnesses, the general area in which the incident took place, and the collection and preservation of evidence. In earlier chapters, we emphasized the importance of each of these, but the need to get medical care for assault victims cannot be overemphasized. This is true whether the injuries are minor or so severe that the victim is comatose and the prognosis unfavorable.

Victim identification is imperative. Assault victims, unless comatose, can provide the necessary information; homicide victims obviously cannot. In homicides, such things as a driver's license or other form of identification, or witness identification, should be considered leads, not positive identification. A homicide victim's bone structure can provide information about the deceased's sex, height, and even age; evidence of surgery may help with identification. However, to positively identify a victim, only fingerprints, DNA testing, dental work, or a confirmed identification by relatives, close friends, or coworkers should be relied upon. Until victims can be positively identified, the scope of the investigation will be extremely limited.

In conjunction with a detailed examination of the crime scene, including evidence collection, the time of the victim's death must be determined. Perhaps one or more witnesses can help in this regard; otherwise, it has to be established on the basis of medicolegal or other evidence. Because of the importance of crime scenes from an evidentiary point of view, if it appears that the incident leading to the victim's death occurred somewhere other than where the deceased was found, the primary scene also must be identified, located, and thoroughly searched.

In addition to establishing the victim's identification and approximate time of death, both the cause and means of death have to be determined. The apparent and actual causes of death may differ, and it is the medical examiner, not the investigator, who really determines the cause and means on the basis of an autopsy. For instance, a corpse is found on a beach, there are no outward signs of a homicide, and the apparent cause of death is drowning. However, the autopsy report or protocol says no water was found in the deceased's lungs. This indicates the person was dead when his or her body went into the water. The report also states that a small puncture wound was found behind and below the victim's right ear, and that traces of cyanide were found in the deceased. This, and other information already accumulated, tells the investigators that the deceased was the victim of a homicide. In turn, they now can begin to develop a tentative theory of a possible motive, the reasons for the death, and leads in their search for likely suspects.

The nature of homicides necessitates working backwards. To determine what happened and how it happened is one thing, to find out who is responsible is another. To do the latter, investigators have to attempt to recreate the last hours of the victim's life. This will include visiting the deceased's home and place of work, and interviewing people who knew the victim well enough to answer questions about his or her personal habits. This re-creation also may be helped by the autopsy report in terms of possible sexual activity or by noting the contents of the victim's stomach and the stage of digestion. In other words, what was the deceased doing, where, and with whom, in the hours before being killed.

Various underlying motives for a homicide have been mentioned, but understanding motivation is no substitute for asking pertinent questions and getting answers. What are some of the questions for which answers are needed? In many homicides, victims and their killers know each other; they also may be related. Therefore, one of the first questions is, who benefits from the victim's death? Interviewing relatives, close friends, and possibly certain coworkers may provide some insight, so may an examination of any letters or diaries that the deceased kept. Being able to trace the ownership of any physical evidence found at the crime scene also may prove helpful.

Important as these steps are, other equally valuable leads may be developed by checking various sources of information. They should not be overlooked since they might contain data about previously recorded significant activities.

For instance, police department and court records may contain 911 calls reporting noisy neighbors, someone repeatedly disturbing the peace, spousal abuse, or stalking. Credit records might show a history of unpaid bills, credit problems, defaults on loans, or bankruptcy. The deceased's bank may have information indicating unusual changes in accounts or banking habits. Insurance companies with which the deceased's life was insured might have recently been instructed to make changes in the beneficiaries of his or her insurance policies. Information indicating that the deceased made or talked about making changes in a will may be revealing. Employment information, such as job changes and the reasons for them, the nature of recent but significant business transactions, or the contents of a safe deposit box may prove to be of use. In any event, the more data available, the easier it is to focus on a possible motive. Determining a possible motive initially can, in turn, help narrow the investigation's focus to those persons who would seem to be the most likely suspects.

Detecting a motive is not always easy. In fact, during the first phase of a homicide investigation, there might seem to be multiple motives for the deceased's death. However, even when one or more seemingly valid motives exist, investigators must remember that motive alone does not equal guilt, but it may be a factor in terms of developing a theory upon which to proceed. It also is important to remember that just as motive is a consideration in all crimes, not only homicides and assaults, so is the matter of opportunity. But again, having the opportunity to commit a crime, by itself, does not prove guilt.

Occasionally, the question of motive can be elusive because so many people might have reason to commit murder. This point is illustrated by the Rosenberg case.

> Sometime after 5:30 P.M. November 9, 1995, L. Richard Rosenberg was killed by a single gunshot wound to the upper torso that caused internal hemorrhaging. There were rumors, neither confirmed nor denied by the police, that he also had been stabbed repeatedly, his throat had been slit, and he had been shot three times. Rosenberg, a builder and developer, was described by a former employee as "abrasive and rough," and by others as having enemies in many places. He reportedly spoke out frequently against both labor unions and tenants' groups. During the course of the investigation records in the office of the County Clerk for Dutchess County, New York, revealed that between 1987 and the date of his death, Rosenberg was the plaintiff in over sixty cases, and the defendant in twenty-two. He also was the plaintiff in a number of other cases in which suit was brought under one of his corporate names. Based on the information developed the New York State Police were in the process of interviewing all of Rosenberg's former and current business associates as well as every resident of his 834 unit apartment complex.[3]

In contrast, there also may be times when motive and opportunity are sufficiently obvious for investigators to be able to focus on a logical suspect. This is illustrated by another case.

May 17, 1996, two women were found beaten to death in their home. Cousins, one 75, the other 84, they had employed a home health case worker who was questioned by the police during the early stages of the inquiry and released. However, as the investigation continued the police began to theorize that perhaps the younger victim, believing that the home health case worker had forged about $600 worth of checks, questioned her, thus prompting the case worker to return to the house to retaliate. With that in mind they examined the case worker's bank records and found a pattern of deposits. Three checks, each for $200, made payable to the worker, had been forged and deposited to her account. Confronted with this evidence the worker confessed.[4]

Of course, the apparent absence of motive or opportunity should not automatically eliminate suspects. Suppose that a wife, in a seemingly ideal marriage, is found murdered in her home. There are signs of a burglary and struggle, but strangely enough, nothing was stolen. Title to most of the couple's assets is in the husband's name, and his insurance benefits from his deceased wife's life policy are less than $25,000. Furthermore, at the time of the incident, the husband was out of town on business. Given these facts, there is no apparent motive for murder, nor does it seem as if the husband would have had an opportunity. Nevertheless, to eliminate him as a suspect at this time without further investigation would be improper. Maybe he had a motive unknown to any relatives or friends, such as another woman with whom he wanted to live, and he purposely planned his trip to establish an alibi after hiring someone to kill his wife and make it look like a burglary while he was gone.

In Parts I and II, we discussed the characteristics of good investigators, how investigations are initiated, and the various elements that, when they come together, can result in successful inquiries. What can be achieved through the practical application of a combination of these factors, not only in homicide and assault cases but also in others, can be illustrated by sampling actual cases and showing the various steps that may have to be taken during an investigation.

❖ Case 15-1

Around 1:15 A.M. July 29, 1992, the nude body of a nameless teenage girl was found stuffed into a plastic garbage bag, dumped during the night in a parking lot in the Chelsea district of New York City. She had been shot in the head. Detectives working the case reviewed missing persons' reports in an effort to identify the victim. Within one or two days, they took the family of a missing person, whose description fit that of the deceased, to the morgue. The family identified the victim as an 18-year-old aspiring actress, model, and dancer from Brooklyn. Initially, thinking that the victim might have been a student at the Fashion Institute of Technology, investigators checked the school's records, but they could not confirm her status. However, they did learn that she had been acquainted with several students who, when interviewed, told the detectives about a man who had approached them posing as a theatrical agent and promising to introduce them to important people in the arts. On August 6, 1992, a deliveryman, who was obsessed with the victim for two years and who allegedly lured her while in the guise of a theatrical agent, was arrested.[5]

❖ Case 15-2

On June 20, 1996, the Pennsylvania authorities arrested a man in connection with the earlier death of a 30-year-old father of two. Twenty years earlier, on June 2, 1976, the men, who were friends, had gone skeet shooting. The deceased reportedly was killed when he fell and caused his shotgun to fire into his chest; the death was ruled an accident. A short time later, the widow and the friend, who allegedly had been in a relationship before the time of the accident, married and moved out of state. The victim's father had his suspicions. Despite the passage of time, he persuaded the authorities to exhume his son's body and reexamine the evidence. On reexamination, it was determined that the deceased had been too far from his gun, and the friend had been too close to the victim, for death to have occurred as described by the deceased's friend. In 1992, the Pennsylvania State Police sent the subject's boots, taken from him two days after the incident, to the FBI Laboratory for examination. Blood found on them indicated that the friend had been physically close to the victim when the latter was shot, not 250 feet away as claimed. On April 29, 1995, the well-preserved body of the victim was exhumed. A pathological report concluded that based on the wound's shape and angle, and the absence of any evidence of burning associated with close-range gunshots, the deceased could not have accidentally shot himself. Furthermore, it also appeared that the victim had been shot while seated, as he would have been if he was throwing skeet, and not while running as claimed by the subject.[6]

❖ Case 15-3

On April 8, 1996, one Robert Shulman, confessed to killing and dismembering the bodies of five prostitutes over a five-year period. He was arraigned on charges of murder. The victims' arms had been cut off so that they could not be identified, but one, who had a tattoo, was identified by detectives as a known prostitute. This prompted them to interview other prostitutes who worked in the same area as the identified victim. Some remembered this particular victim driving away with a man in a light blue Cadillac who frequently was seen cruising the neighborhood. Two said they had been picked up by the same man in the same car and been driven to a particular house. This information led to Shulman's apartment in a house shared with three others, including his brother. The Cadillac was registered in the latter's name. Searching the subject's apartment, investigators found forensic evidence linking Shulman to the murders, for which he was arrested April 6, 1996.[7]

❖ Case 15-4

On June 20, 1996, a Staten Island, New York, man was charged with murder and linked to another killing and a wave of robberies of which the elderly were his victims. He was considered a suspect in a total of twelve incidents that occurred between December 28, 1994, and April 23, 1996. His MO was a factor in his arrest. Investigators learned that he would appear without invitation at the home of an elderly person, offering to do repairs. Once inside, he would bludgeon his victims and tie them up. On several occasions, he either pushed or threw them downstairs.[8]

In these cases, skillful investigators succeeded. Arrests were made, even if not always quickly, and certainly not without a lot of patience and hard work. The following additional examples illustrate investigations as yet unsolved, some of the frustrations often encountered, and the need for patience and perseverance if solutions are to be found.

❖ Case 15-5

In the fall of 1981, a 23-year-old female was found bludgeoned to death in her apartment. She was identified as a student at the Portsmouth (New Hampshire) School of Hair Design, and a regular at some of the city's clubs. A year later, a 21-year-old student at the same school, and club regular, also was found bludgeoned to death in her apartment. Both victims had hoped for modeling careers. The Portsmouth Police Department still considered both cases pending as of August 1996. More than twelve detectives assigned to these cases over time have interviewed about 200 people, among them the victims' friends, local troublemakers, and sailors from ships in port at the time of the murders. Shortly after the second killing, they narrowed their search and focused on one suspect. However, having neither a firm motive nor any physical evidence to link him to the murders, he has not been arrested and charged despite his continued refusal to provide an alibi.[9]

❖ Case 15-6

Karen Holmer, a young Swedish national, was last seen alive in and around a Boston club on June 22, 1996. Her body was found in two large plastic trash bags in Boston; the lower part of the torso was missing. Neck markings indicated strangulation with a rope or cord, not by hand. Investigators, believing this indicates the MO of a person who prefers to strangle with something other than his or her hands, considered two possible theories: (1) an accidental death caused by someone using bonding devices during sex, or (2) murder by a person who planned to kill the victim using a rope or cord. A partial fingerprint was found inside one of the two bags that held the body, but it did not have enough characteristics for an identification, and an effort was being made to improve it. If this could be done, a combination of the fingerprint and MO might facilitate a computer search for possible leads to suspects with similar criminal histories. Investigators also were trying to identify the bag manufacturer in the hope of learning if the bags were sold for commercial or retail use, and where they might have been bought.[10]

Although most of our discussion has been related to homicides, in effect the same techniques and procedures apply in assault investigations. In distinguishing between homicides and assaults, we noted that in the latter cases victims are not killed. Consequently, they may be able to help by either identifying their assailants or at least providing information that eventually will lead to their identification.

However, to assume that victims can or will help in all assault cases is wrong. Victims in comas caused by particularly vicious assaults are no better able to offer firsthand information about what happened than are homicide victims. If they did not see their assailants, they obviously cannot help identify them. The trauma caused by an assault may be so great that victims are reluctant to help for fear of being assaulted again, perhaps even more viciously. Therefore, these cases are best handled much the same as homicides. Investigators rely on their own skills and initiative, beginning with their arrival at the crime scene and continuing through the processes of collecting and preserving evidence, locating and interviewing witnesses, connecting evidence to suspects, and identifying and arresting the assailants.

What help some victims can and will offer should be accepted, but only as help, nothing more. Even though they were eyewitnesses to their own victimization, remember our earlier discussion of the risks that can be involved when eyewitness identifications prove faulty. If identification is considered the key to a successful prosecution, and the defense proves it to be inaccurate, the case will fail. As a result, investigators must never shirk their responsibility to *independently and objectively* corroborate all information and evidence that may be offered to them whether by victims or witnesses.

ROBBERY

We know there may be jurisdictional variations in what constitutes any offense, and investigators need to know the elements of offenses based on the statutes applicable to their states. But what constitutes a robbery in general legal terms? The American Law Institute's Model Penal Code states that a person is guilty of robbery if in the course of committing a theft that person (1) inflicts serious bodily injury upon another; or (2) threatens another with or purposely puts the victim in fear of serious bodily injury; or (3) commits or threatens to commit any felony of the first or second degree. An act shall be deemed "in the course of committing a theft," if it occurs in an attempt to commit a theft or in flight after the attempt or commission of the offense.[11]

Robberies have much in common with assaults. In both, the use or threatened use of force is a key factor, but robbery victims also are deprived of their property, or an attempt is made to do so. Because of the deprivation factor, robberies are considered crimes against property, yet if one allows for the victim's trauma, they are crimes against both persons and property.

Robberies tend to fall into one of three categories, but their targets are many and varied. Ambush robberies, such as purse snatching, generally are committed on a more or less random basis. They are unplanned and based on surprise. A likely, unsuspecting victim appears; the robber moves quickly and flees. More selective robbers may do some planning, but if they do, it tends to be minimal. Take a liquor store robber. There are five stores in a three-block radius; he chooses the one that seems to do the most business and plans the robbery for just before closing on a Saturday because that appears to be the busiest day of the week.

People obviously are victims, but so are businesses and institutions selected as targets. A person can be robbed on the street, while at home, or in a vehicle. Banks are targets, but so are filling stations; neighborhood convenience stores; drug, liquor, and jewelry stores; hotels; and many other types of commercial establishments. Occasionally, even museums and art galleries are targeted.

The third category of robberies are those that are planned. Victims are carefully selected, the details are well thought out, contingency plans are made, and there even may be one or more rehearsals. The January 17, 1950, Brinks robbery in Boston is a good example of a planned robbery.

We observed that in assaults, despite some exceptions, victims often can provide at least some information that eventually will help identify their assailants. The same is true in robberies, but knowing that not all witness identifications are necessarily reliable, robbery investigators cannot limit their questions to victims and other possible witnesses to the matter of identification. They also must learn as much as they can about the victims, the circumstances surrounding the robbery, and what was stolen. As with any crime, they must search for physical evidence.

For instance, if a bank robber's MO involved a written demand for money, the note and any fingerprints that might be recovered from it would be evidence. The countertop should be dusted for possible prints. If victims were bound, the materials used to bind them would be physical evidence. An injured robber might leave traces of blood. If robbers fire shots, whether to attract attention or facilitate their escape, the bullets would be evidence.

We previously discussed another example of a planned robbery, again involving the Brinks organization. It is the one that took place the night of January 5, 1993, at the Rochester, New York, depot. The requisite elements of robbery were present: the theft itself was a felony (the loss was $7.4 million in cash), and there was fear, for the robbery was committed by two men armed with handguns. We have used this case before to help illustrate different aspects of investigations; we now look at it for what we can learn about the scope and magnitude of a robbery investigation. But first we need to review the details of the crime, and of the subsequent arrests of three subjects accompanied by the recovery of a substantial amount of the stolen money.

The *New York Times* for November 14, 1993, reporting the November 12, 1993, arrests and recovery, stated that two men, wearing ski masks and carrying handguns, entered the Rochester Brinks depot the night of January 5, 1993, confronting three guards. They took not only the money, but also a handcuffed guard as a hostage, whom they dropped off five miles from the scene. The FBI interviewed the "hostage" and the other two guards. When interviewed, the former's confusing and inconsistent accounts of what happened, his four-day refusal to give investigators a deposition, his unwillingness to take a polygraph examination, and his provision of seemingly wrong and misleading information made him an early suspect. Among other statements, he said he was kidnapped in a large U-Haul van with an overhead door; the other two guards' statements, as well as tire tracks found at the scene, indicated a mini-van was used. Surveillance showed the "hostage" and the other two men arrested, apparently unemployed, meeting frequently, buying money orders, opening bank accounts, and paying cash for vacations in Hawaii and Florida. Tire tracks found at the crime scene were similar to those made by a 1984 Plymouth Voyager owned by one of those arrested November 12. In March 1993, this same subject opened bank accounts in various names with $25,000 in cash although neither he nor his wife was employed; he also was seen buying a number of postal money orders, some for amounts of up to $4,000. Of the three men arrested, one of whom was the "hostage," two were apprehended by the FBI in New York City, the third in Rochester. A large quantity of cash was recovered, and about half of the total taken was still in Brinks bags.[12]

This case illustrates a number of factors that were essential to its successful conclusion:

1. The need for patience and perseverance
2. The importance of teamwork with leads in Rochester and New York City
3. The need to pay close attention to what everyone interviewed says, remembering that a witness may become a suspect, and even a subject
4. The value of careful crime scene searches, the collection and preservation of physical evidence, and the contribution forensics can make regarding that evidence
5. The leads and evidence that surveillances can help develop
6. The information that can be obtained from records

Each of these factors contributed to the robbers' arrests and the recovery of stolen property. However, by no means are they the only investigative techniques that can be used with success. Given the right circumstances, undercover or so-called sting operations also can be used to good advantage in robbery cases. An example is a case worked jointly by the FBI and the San Jose, California, Police Department.

On February 29, 1996, after an eighteen-month investigation, a raid involving more than 500 police officers and FBI agents culminated in the arrest of more than 120 subjects. Another 45 had been taken into custody the day before. During the eighteen months, more than 400 Silicon Valley businesses had been robbed of computer chips. One firm alone suffered the loss of $9.9 million worth of computer parts. Most of the stolen chips did not have serial numbers, making them easy to sell and hard to trace. The robbers, depending on insiders for information about where and how to steal, used handguns, long guns, semiautomatic weapons, and a sort of paramilitary style in committing the robberies. They used duct tape and Flexicuffs to immobilize persons who were present. Law enforcement personnel, using video cameras and tape recorders, set up a phony storefront business in San Jose, buying only from invited vendors.[13]

Although the sting contributed to success in this case, so did many of the essential investigative techniques used in the Rochester case. Something else worth remembering in robbery investigations is the fact that just as video cameras and tape recorders were used in the San Jose sting, they now are used with increasing frequency by various businesses, not only financial institutions, that consider themselves likely robbery victims. Therefore, in addition to everything else that needs to be done in robbery cases, investigators should ask whether the victim has either video or time-lapse cameras installed. If so, the film should be taken for both the leads it may provide in helping identify the robber and its evidentiary value.

Of course, not all robberies are major cases. Some involve lesser amounts and a single subject. It also is worth noting, and admitting, that despite all the hard work that goes into any investigation, good luck also can play a role. That was true on March 6, 1996, when a woman walked into the Federal Savings Bank in Barrington, New Hampshire. She said she had a remote control device and threatened to detonate a bomb; she was given $5,503 and left. The bank held a mortgage on the subject's home, on which she had not paid, and which was to be auctioned that same day. Shortly before the scheduled auction, the subject made a payment on her mortgage at the office of a lawyer whose clerk became suspicious about her sudden ability to pay the same day the bank had been robbed. The police were called; they checked the bills' serial numbers and found the payment had been made with the stolen cash.[14] The clerk's willingness to tell the police of her suspicions played a significant role in the subject's arrest.

In Chapter 10, we discussed the importance of both finding and interviewing witnesses and the fact that not all witnesses will voluntarily make themselves known or be willing to testify. This may be especially true of witnesses to robberies, including victims, who should be the best witnesses of all. Robbery involves either the threat or actual use of force, and witnesses understandably are afraid. We also noted that at times witnesses may not realize that they have valuable information.

Since witnesses, always important, assume heightened importance in robberies whether the crime consists of a purse snatching or the theft of millions of dollars, good robbery investigators do not limit their interviews to persons who are identified as witnesses at crime scenes. True, going from door to door is time consuming and may prove unproductive, but it also can be very productive. The same person who may not have actually witnessed a robbery, or been in a position to get a good look at a perpetrator, may nevertheless be able to give a good description of a getaway car or escape route information.

Sting operations, questions about video or time-lapse camera film availability, and the special importance of locating and interviewing witnesses are investigative techniques that are particularly applicable to robbery investigations. However, to itemize each separate step in robbery cases would be redundant since much of what goes into all good investigations is generic and has been covered in detail in Parts I and II of the text.

SEX OFFENSES

To many people, the term *sex offense* means rape, certainly a violent crime. In some instances, such as the rape of a child where there may be no need to resort to threats or actual violence, the resulting trauma and impact on the victim may be comparable to violence. Statutory rape, in which an underage victim consents and force is not an issue, does not involve violence.

Although the *Bureau of Justice Statistics Dictionary of Criminal Justice Terminology* defines rape as the unlawful sexual intercourse with a female by force or without legal consent,[15] sex offense investigators have to be familiar with the rape statutes of the jurisdictions in which they work. For instance, in some states, rape without legal consent may apply to males as well as females. But rape is not the only sex offense subject to investigation. Consequently, there must be an awareness of the spectrum of crimes covered by this heading.

Statutes establish degrees of murder, manslaughter, and robbery, but essentially each is based on a common denominator. Sex offenses differ in that they are wide ranging. Furthermore, depending on the nature of a particular sex crime, investigators may find it both necessary and prudent to realign their investigative priorities. Crimes that are sex offenses include sexual assaults, exhibitionism, fetishism, "Peeping Toms," obscene telephone calls, indecent exposure, and even some forms of pornography. Forms of child abuse, including molestation and pedophilia, are also sex offenses.

Good investigators are sensitive to the needs of all victims, and to those of their families. Nevertheless, nowhere is that need greater than in sex offense investigations. Even victims who have suffered no physical injury are faced with severe emotional and psychological injuries. Sex crime victims also may suffer from embarrassment and guilt feelings. They ask themselves what they did wrong. These factors highlight the need for sex crime investigators to take advantage of continuing education programs from which they may benefit; they also are why increasing numbers of police executives now appreciate the contributions that women investigators can make in the specialized field of sex crime investigations.

Just as murder is the most serious of all homicides, rape is the most serious of all sex offenses. Whether a rape was an exercise of the assailant's power, a display of anger, occurred on a date, or was statutory, it poses a challenge. Obviously, the use of force and the resulting trauma mandate medical attention for the victim. In all rape cases, statutory included, establishing that a rape or sexual assault did occur will require a physical examination of the victim. However, although examining physicians can provide invaluable information about the victim's condition, they cannot state categorically that a victim was raped. That is a conclusion that, as a matter of law, must be left to a trial court.

In addition to providing information about the victim's condition, examining physicians can help investigators by collecting certain physical evidence. This would include semen specimens and pubic hair. Depending on where the assault took place, they also may be able to collect other physical evidence such as hairs, fibers, and even traces of dirt. Furthermore, the circumstances surrounding the rape may be such that the victim's clothes also are physical evidence that needs to be protected and preserved.

Despite any help gotten from physicians, investigators still must protect and scour the crime scene for additional evidence. There may be more than one crime scene. For instance, let's say the first victim–perpetrator contact occurred in a public place such as a restaurant or bar; then they left together in an automobile and drove to a park where the victim was forced out of the car and assaulted. There, hairs and fibers, dirt, and possibly tire tracks would become physical evidence. A condom might be recovered, and if so, it "can help prove corpus delicti, provide evidence of penetration, produce associative evidence, and link the acts of serial rapists."[16]

Each venue, the restaurant or bar, automobile, and park where the assault took place, is a crime scene. Interviewing people who may have been at the place where the victim and perpetrator first met might provide information about the assailant or possibly confirm that the two of them were seen together. The vehicle and park where the rape took place are possible sources of physical evidence.

Obviously, the victim's interview is critical. She may be seriously injured, and she is traumatized, angry, and ashamed. Initially, the victim is the only one who can provide details about what happened, where it happened, and what preceded the assault. Interviewing investigators, whether male or female, must be sensitive, considerate, sympathetic, understanding, and patient. They also must be alert for signs of the victim's state of mind at the time of the rape since the question of consent versus feeling psychologically if not physically threatened may become an issue at a later trial.

In all criminal cases, investigators want complete details as soon as possible. However, in rape investigations, they may have to be satisfied with an initial interview to be followed by one or more in-depth interviews. Therefore, the goal of the first interview should be to obtain information about the following:

1. The best physical description of the assailant. In addition to information normally sought about perpetrators, the act of rape is such that perhaps the victim saw scars or marks that are not usually exposed to public view.

2. Specific information about the place or places where the rape took place. For instance, was it in an automobile, office, bedroom, hotel room, or park?

3. The names of possible witnesses. Persons who can do nothing more than attest to the fact that they saw the victim and perpetrator together nevertheless should be viewed as witnesses.

4. Information about and descriptions of any weapons or vehicles used.

5. The circumstances that led up to the assault.

6. Information volunteered by the victim regarding the perpetrator's behavior or specific acts.

The victim's condition and willingness to speak will be factors in the initial interview and affect the amount of detail that can be gotten. Although it is perfectly proper in later interviews to go over items already covered, additional information also should be sought. Anything said or done by the perpetrator could be important, especially if there is any indication that this incident was the work of a serial rapist. It might be indicative of his MO, and the additional data could be helpful to the FBI's VICAP, mentioned in Chapter 13.

Three New York City rape cases are helpful in showing how victim information may lead investigators to conclude that a serial rapist is at work. In each, the victims were fair-skinned, petite young women living in the same general area, and all of them gave detectives the same physical description of their assailant.[17] The similarity in the victims' appearance caused investigators to believe that the assailant was a serial rapist. Although the crime scenes were searched for fingerprints, semen, and pubic hairs, the commonality of the victims' appearance, their descriptions of their assailant, and his apparent confinement of his activities to a particular area are valuable leads.

Other rape victim information also could prove helpful, especially if the rapist used a condom. For instance, did the victim recently have consensual sex, and if so, did her partner use a condom? If a vaginal lubricant was used, what brand was it? Does the victim use any other external or internal vaginal products and, if she does, what brands are they?[18] However, when asking these questions, investigators must make it clear that neither are they questioning the victim's truthfulness nor are they simply curious about the victim's sex life. They need to explain that the answers may help if a suspect who used a condom is taken into custody.

Any woman who says no to having intercourse means just that, *no.* And at the inception of a rape investigation, no assumptions should be made about the truthfulness of the victim's complaint based on her dress or lifestyle. Even prostitutes can be and are raped.

Once a suspect is identified, every effort must be made to collect the clothing worn by him at the time of the assault so that it can be submitted for forensic examination. Unless the subject is speedily caught while wearing the clothes described by the victim, a search warrant for his home has to be obtained. In that case, and if a condom was used during the act, condoms should be included in the search warrant application.[19]

In most rape cases, the victim is the sole witness. Nevertheless, not having other witnesses to the actual assault does not excuse failing to at least interview people who may be able to put the victim in the company of someone preceding the time of the rape. Witnesses of this sort may be particularly helpful in date rape cases. To illustrate, the victim says she was raped at a party. Her physical examination and evidence show signs of force and sexual activity. By interviewing others who were at the party, investigators may learn nothing more than that the victim and a man were seen leaving the room together for a time and, when they returned, the victim looked disheveled and upset. The ability to link the victim and the man is by no means conclusive, but it gives investigators a good lead on which to work.

Of course, rape or rape-homicide are not the only sex crimes. Other and less serious offenses occur. Among them are the activities of exhibitionists, fetishists, "Peeping Toms," obscene telephone callers, or those who engage in acts of indecent exposure or pornography. They upset and embarrass their victims, but they seldom are physically threatening. Information gotten from victims of these offenses, except for obscene telephone call and child abuse cases, and a review of MO files often help investigators make arrests and close cases. As for obscene telephone calls, despite the caller's anonymity, carefully questioned victims occasionally can provide information that eventually will help identify the perpetrators.

Not surprisingly, the most difficult sex offense investigations tend to be those related to children, principally incest, pedophilia, exploitation, and child abuse (physical or psychological). Getting evidence to prove a crime against a child can be more difficult than developing evidence in adult victim cases. For investigators to use terminology that can be understood by persons questioned in connection with any crime is important, but that importance is heightened in child-related sex offense investigations.

This added difficulty can be caused by more than possible terminology problems. First, in many cases, the perpetrator may be either a family member or a friend, or someone whom the child knows and trusts. Second, there may be questions about a child victim's reliability and credibility as a witness. Here, a child's age may be a significant factor. Parenthetically, although it is the prosecutors' job to question witnesses, they often will ask investigators for an opinion about witness credibility and reliability. In any event, even when children understand questions, they may be reluctant to answer out of fear, misguided love, or both.

Knowing the nature of the various offenses makes it easier to understand why child victims tend to hesitate when questioned. For instance, incest is not just intercourse between the sexes; it is intercourse between persons who are considered to be too closely related by blood. The degree of closeness is defined by statute. Consequently, if incest occurs between parents and children, the latter may not object because they are too young to know it is wrong, or parents tell them it is "our secret," or a child knows it is wrong but is afraid to tell anyone, including the other parent. Incestuous relationships may continue for years without any family members or friends ever being told, let alone the police.

Pedophilia is a form of sexual perversion involving children. Put another way, pedophiles prefer children as their sex objects. As with incest, pedophiles often turn out to be adults whom their victims trust and respect, such as members of the clergy or teachers. Pedophiles often rely on this trusting relationship to prevent their victims from informing others. In some cases in which victims have come forward, they have done so years after they first were victimized.

Exploitation occurs when children are used for pornographic activities or prostitution. These children frequently are runaways. Finding themselves without even minimal resources for survival, without food to eat or a place to sleep, they accept what they perceive to be offers of friendship from adults who, in return, use various physical or psychological threats to force them to participate in pornographic acts or prostitution.

In discussing how investigations are opened, we said there needs to be a predicate. The predicate in exploitation cases often is a call from a concerned parent reporting a missing child. Obviously, a detailed physical description of the child, including what he or she might have been wearing, and information about any relatives or friends with whom the child might have, or attempt to have, contact are needed. Information about interests or skills also may prove helpful. If a case is opened on the basis of a referral from another department or agency, the investigation most likely will begin with a visit to bus depots, shelters, or other places in the city to which newly arrived children most likely would gravitate. Known and suspected exploiters need to be located and questioned, as do established confidential informants.

Once found, exploitation victims must be carefully and thoroughly interviewed. However, since these children generally are old enough to understand the questions put to them, and there is no blood or other close relationship between the victim and the exploiter, there are fewer obstacles to overcome than in incest or pedophilia cases. The results of detailed interviews can lead to crime scenes. Warrants can be obtained and searches conducted for evidence linking the victim and the exploiter. In conducting searches in cases of this sort, remember that it is likely evidence will be found providing additional leads involving the exploitation of other victims.

When incest or pedophilia inquiries are initiated, questioning victims is unavoidable. As with all victim interviews, privacy and the lack of distractions must be assured. The circumstances and victim's age and level of understanding may make it advisable to have present an adult with whom the victim is comfortable, but obviously not the suspect. To minimize the risk of terminology problems, investigators may find it useful to give children dolls with which to show just what happened. As with exploitation cases, one often finds that pedophiles have multiple victims. Therefore, this avenue of investigation should not be ignored. If there is evidence of additional victims, even if not necessarily current, the leads should be developed and pursued.

Because of the physical or psychological impact on children, the most serious child-related offenses involve abuse. As with incest and pedophilia, those responsible for child abuse often are either parents or other adults who have a close relationship to the victims. Since they obviously are not going to report their abusive actions, most child abuse investigations are opened on the basis of the suspicions or complaints of third parties such as physicians, social workers, neighbors, or possibly other relatives of the victims. Increasing numbers of states now have laws requiring certain categories of persons, such as health-care professionals, lawyers, and social workers, to report suspicions of child abuse.

Although some of these professionals may have reason to suspect a child has been or is being abused, emergency room physicians are the ones most likely to detect actual signs of abuse. When abusive behavior reaches the point that there suddenly is fear for a child's life, the abuser may feel a need to get medical help and will take the child to the nearest hospital. Examining physicians will examine the child and take a medical history, which help the doctor diagnose and treat the illness. As a result, it is important in these cases for investigators also to be able to recognize the symptoms of child abuse and to understand what signs physicians look for to confirm suspicions of abuse.

Injuries are of special concern when inconsistent with the parents' explanation or when there does not seem to be a reasonable explanation. Examples would include skin damage resulting from cuts that do not appear to have been accidentally caused; bruises; cigarette or other burns; skeletal fractures, that is, bone damage, including painful movement and deformity; brain damage evidenced by coma, convulsions, or retardation; and internal injuries as indicated by shock, abdominal pain, or signs of internal bleeding.[20]

Inconsistencies in the explanation of how injuries occurred, or explanations that are illogical in terms of the actual injury, will raise questions in the examining physician's mind. So will delays in getting help for injured children, which is unnatural, finding injuries unreported by parents or guardians, or those that appear to have been caused at different times. Neither is it common to find infants with bruises or broken bones, or older children with bruises, the nature of which would most likely result from being whipped with a belt, rope, or electric cord.

The known eyewitnesses in child abuse cases are the abused children and their abusers. The abused children may be too young to speak. If not, as victims of abuse, they may be afraid to talk. The likelihood of finding other eyewitnesses is minimal. Consequently, as with so many other types of investigations, the case will have to be built primarily on circumstantial, and possibly some physical, evidence. Among those to be interviewed will be doctors, other health-care professionals, and social workers who may have had some direct contact with the victim and the abusers, as well as neighbors and any other persons who may be able to provide helpful information.

Difficult as physical child abuse cases are, there at least are visible signs of that abuse. The same cannot be said when children are the victims of psychological abuse. Despite the problem's seriousness, cases of this kind are rarely reported let alone investigated unless a child's delinquent or antisocial behavior becomes so bad that it is considered harmful to the child or to the community.

As with physical abuse, the only eyewitnesses are the psychologically abused children and their abusers. The problem often is compounded by the parties failing to recognize what is happening. Even if the children do, and are old enough to speak to investigators, there is no assurance that they will. By the same token, since the circumstances that would prompt police involvement require some form of delinquency, even if the result of psychological abuse, the initial investigation would focus on the delinquent acts themselves and who was responsible for them. Once children are identified as perpetrators, unless their behavior has caused death or injury, or significant property damage, the likelihood exists that the matter would be referred to an appropriate social agency. Psychological abuse as a contributing factor would not by itself necessarily justify any further police role.

ARSON AND BOMBINGS

Among the several definitions of violence found in *Webster's New World Dictionary* are "physical force used so as to injure or damage; roughness in action" and "a use of force so as to injure or damage; rough, injurious act." Certainly these definitions apply to acts of arson and bombings. Although arson, like robbery, is considered a property crime for reporting purposes, in reality its impact on victims also makes it a crime against persons. The same is true of bombings, even when no one is injured or killed.

The foregoing aside, arson and bombings have much in common. An explosive device may be used to start an intentionally set fire, or a deliberately set fire may cause an explosion. In both cases, there is damage; there also may be injuries or death. There also are similarities in their investigation. First, when there is a fire of unknown origin or an explosion, investigators start by examining the scene and available evidence, and eliminating possible causes. Second, the nature of both arson fires and bombings often leaves little physical evidence of a starting or triggering mechanism that can be traced to a logical suspect.

What, then, constitutes an act of arson? Arson statutes may differ from state to state and include deliberately caused explosions. However, acts of arson generally include any fire or burning in a building or other property protected by law (possibly including motor vehicles); the fire must have been intentionally set as distinguished from one caused by accident, negligence, or an act of nature; and an individual must have set or caused the fire to be set, or done something to further the act. Arson, like certain other offenses, is considered by the degree of the crime's seriousness; it may be simple or aggravated arson. If set without danger to life or risk of injury, it is simple arson. On the other hand, if the intention is to destroy or damage property by fire, by explosion, or by using any other type of device, thus placing people in danger of losing their lives or being seriously injured, and that risk of death or injury could have been reasonably foreseen by the perpetrator, it is aggravated arson.

A simple arson can become an aggravated one. Suppose vandals think it would be fun to start a fire in an abandoned building. Setting the fire would be an act of simple arson, but if the building is destroyed, or a firefighter is killed or seriously injured fighting the fire, it becomes aggravated arson. That the vandals did not intend to destroy the building is offset by the fact they could have reasonably foreseen that the fire department would respond to put out the fire, and that in doing so, there would be a risk of injury or death.

Criminals are motivated, and those who start fires or cause bombings are no different although their motives may be. However, even with the elements in mind, investigators first must determine the cause of a fire or explosion. They have to eliminate acts of nature or accidents as possible causes before they start to look for motives in fire and explosion cases. In other words, can acts of nature or accidents be ruled out? For instance, a house fire caused by a lightning strike is an act of nature; a restaurant fire caused by an uncontrolled grease fire in its kitchen is an accident. So is a grain storage bin explosion if caused by accumulated grain dust. Nevertheless, since combustion results from a combination of fuel, oxygen, and a source of heat, as investigators look for the possible cause of the fire or explosion, they also look for any evidence of materials that might have been used to start and help spread a fire.

Once acts of nature or accidents are ruled out, the cause is of unknown or suspicious origin, and it becomes a matter for investigation. Motive and opportunity now have to be considered; so does the question of whether the perpetrator was an arsonist or a pyromaniac. What are the most likely motives for deliberately starting a fire or causing an explosion? High on the list is financial gain, including an attempt to defraud an insurer, avoid payment of obligations, or eliminate a competitor. Intimidation may be a motive, particularly when an organization has labor problems or is being pressured to "cooperate" with or "employ" the services of organized crime. Emotional reasons, such as revenge, jealousy, spite, or hatred cannot be ignored. Yet other motives might be an attempt to conceal another crime, vandalism, and pyromania.

To recognize these as the principal motives for arson fires and the explosions that may accompany them is one thing, but it also is important to understand that the motives for terrorist bombings will be different. Both international and domestic terrorists often resort to bombings to intimidate or express their hatred of governments or other groups, to extort funds that they need to continue and expand their operations, or for revenge. The bombings are intended to further their political or social agendas. It is not unusual for investigators to get some help in many of these cases by the need of terrorists to obtain publicity to achieve their goals. Consequently, if terrorist bombings are in behalf of organizations rather than individuals, the group responsible may well use the news media to identify itself.

Being able to distinguish between arsonists and pyromaniacs also can be helpful. Arsonists do not randomly select targets or start fires; pyromaniacs do not engage in planning and target selection. Arsonists want to achieve maximum damage; pyromaniacs want to see something burn. Arsonists know that they must carefully plan, be able to start the fire deep inside the victim's premises, and ensure its rapid spread. In contrast, pyromaniacs start fires to satisfy their need for either excitement or sexual gratification. For success, arsonists' plans include the careful selection of ignition points, plants, and trailers; pyromaniacs are inclined to use as fuel whatever materials are handy.

Considering the motives for arson, unless a fire is the work of a professional arsonist, the perpetrator's MO may be of only limited value since there is no pattern to suggest leads other than those developed in connection with this one case. This is not necessarily true when pyromania seems to be the cause. Here, looking for patterns, the MO may prove helpful. Therefore, in addition to the steps normally taken in arson inquiries, a review of earlier reports of suspicious fires should be undertaken. Whether those cases have been solved or are pending, evidence that such fires occurred at certain times of day, days of the week, in certain neighborhoods, or certain kinds of buildings may help bring the inquiry into focus.

Getting information through interviews and record checks is essential to all investigations. In arson and bombing cases, two initial and invaluable sources of information are the person who discovered and reported the fire and the responding fire department personnel. If there was an explosion before flames were noticed, information about the color of the flames and the smell of the smoke can help eliminate natural acts or accidents as causes. Firefighters can be especially helpful with respect to the color of the flames and smell of smoke.

In addition, they can identify the point of origin, provide information about charring and burn patterns, and assist with a search for items that could have been used to start the fire. This would include timing devices, matches, cigarettes, and candles, as well as trailers to help a fire's spread. Notwithstanding interviews with the person who discovered and reported the fire and firefighters, others at the scene also must be identified and interviewed. Photographs should be taken, including photographs of onlookers in suspicious fire investigations.

The building's owner or manager and people who worked in the building must be interviewed. They may have information that suggests a possible motive. Of course, owners or managers who hire arsonists obviously will not be helpful. On the other hand, if they have been threatened, they may be afraid to talk. Employees may not know anything useful. Competitors should be interviewed for whatever they can offer. They may know that the victim was having financial problems, or they themselves may have been threatened by labor racketeers trying to get a toehold in their industry.

When interviewing owners, managers, employees, competitors, and neighbors, be alert for any indication that substantial amounts of merchandise or other tangible assets had been removed from the premises shortly before the fire. Further, were there any radical changes in the organization's operating hours, or in terms of who did or did not have uncontrolled access to the premises? Had any unusual activities or incidents occurred recently?

Interview persons at insurance companies and financial institutions who have done business with the apparent victim. Examine the victim's insurance and financial records. Were there any recent and significant increases in insurance coverage? If an owner or manager becomes a suspect, his or her personal records, as distinguished from the business records, also should be examined. Information about personal credit, including bankruptcies, ownership of a home and other valuable assets, liens, and divorce or nonpayment of alimony or child support proceedings, may provide evidence of a motive.

All criminal investigations are challenging, but perhaps none pose the unique problems found in arson cases. Despite the help given by firefighters at the scene, collecting physical evidence for forensic examination and trial purposes can verge on the impossible. For instance, delay in reporting a fire delays extinguishing it, and all traces of its incendiary origin may have been consumed. Although a fire's cause is suspicious, the crime scene may have been hosed down, or its contents moved, before physical evidence can be properly collected and recorded. Using a timing device to start a fire gives a perpetrator a chance to establish an alibi.

Debris, or a building's collapse, may cover or destroy evidence of arson. Even weather conditions can be a factor. On the one hand, extreme heat can cause volatile accelerants to evaporate, whereas on the other, freezing adds to the difficulty in searching for evidence. Perhaps at least some of the complexity of investigating arson can be made a little easier to understand by looking at a few actual solved and unsolved cases.

❖ Case 15-7

A New York City fire lieutenant died as a result of a February 24, 1992, clothing store fire. On February 27, 1995, the store owner and two other men were arrested and charged with setting the fire to collect insurance. The owner also was charged with witness tampering with respect to the testimony given to the grand jury by former store employees. The delay in arresting the subjects was attributed to the trouble encountered in following a "paper trail" and developing evidence that would stand up in court. According to the indictment, the owner had moved a large quantity of merchandise from the store shortly before the fire, and afterwards he falsely claimed that the destroyed goods resulted in a $100,000 loss.[21]

❖ Case 15-8

A December 1995 clothing store fire in New York City's Harlem section killed eight people, including the perpetrator, who shot himself. He had participated in demonstrations outside the store before the fire prompting the police to consider the possibility of a conspiracy, but they found no evidence to support that theory. Although neither the store nor the building owner was under investigation for the fire, investigators were looking into possible safety violations by the owner, among them a sprinkler system that had been turned off and a rear exit door that had been bricked up.[22]

❖ Case 15-9

A fire destroyed a major part of Malden Mills, located in Methuen, Massachusetts, in December 1995; damage and allied losses were estimated at between $400 and $500 million. Absent any evidence of arson, investigators theorized that the cause could have been a boiler fire or explosion, an exploding electrical transformer outside the building, the rupture of a high-temperature oil heating system used to manufacture a particular fabric, or a small fire that led to an explosion of fabric dust. Although they also agreed that the possibility of arson could not be ruled out until their inquiry, which would require site excavation among other things, was complete, an extremely harsh winter forced them to delay excavation until April 1996, since a large part of the initial work would consist of "carefully combing the remains of the building with rakes, shovels, and even small hand tools."[23]

❖ Case 15-10

A story in the *New York Times* for February 19, 1996, dealt with a fire at a Brooklyn, New York, chop shop in which a firefighter was killed. In addition to the illegal construction, investigators found that during an attempt to switch vehicle identification numbers on a stolen automobile, a fuel tank was dropped spilling gasoline on the floor, and grinding machine sparks ignited fumes from the spilled gasoline.[24]

❖ Case 15-11

On April 29, 1996, four five-story apartment buildings on Boston's famous Beacon Street suffered fire damage estimated at $1.6 million. Damage was so extensive that investigators would not be able to start collecting debris in search of the cause, or looking to see if an accelerant was used, until staging had been erected to prevent the buildings' collapse. In the meantime, reliable witnesses told an arson squad investigator they had seen a white male in his 20s, wearing blue jeans, a white sweatshirt, and a white baseball cap, running from the scene shortly before the fire broke out, and he kept running when they tried to stop him.[25]

Bombing investigations, like murders, can be categorized as either single incident bombings or the work of serial bombers. Like arson cases, they can be complex. For example, based on the lapsed time between bombings, it may be difficult to determine whether a given bombing is a onetime incident or the work of a serial bomber. A bomber may be able to function for years before a discernible MO leads investigators to conclude that they are looking for a serial bomber. Looking at a few actual cases helps illustrate not only this point, but also the complexity of bomb investigations and the nature of the physical evidence for which searches must be made.

On May 7, 1982, a Brooklyn, New York, woman was killed as she opened a parcel that contained an elaborately made bomb. It consisted of .22 caliber bullets placed inside a hollowed-out cookbook. Her son was arrested, but charges were dropped owing to a lack of evidence. On October 15, 1993, a vacationing resident of Staten Island, New York, suffered minor injuries from an exploding package that had been sent to him. On April 5, 1994, a Brooklyn woman was critically injured when a letter bomb, addressed to her brother, exploded. On June 27, 1995, a woman residing in Queens, New York, received minor injuries when she opened a package delivered to her grandparents' home. On June 20, 1996, a Brooklyn man was unhurt when he opened a small parcel addressed to his wife and triggered an explosion. In all these cases, .22 caliber bullets were fired through a short barrel, the device had been packaged in a brown padded bag, the same triggering mechanism had been used, and each device consisted of three barrels with two going one way and one another. Although the U.S. Postal Inspectors wanted to do additional testing, New York City detectives were convinced that one person was responsible for all five bombings.[26]

At the beginning of Part III, we took particular note of three high-profile cases involving explosions. Two were bombings; one turned out not to be. They were the 1993 World Trade Center bombing, the opening of the Unabomber case in 1978, and the 1996 explosion of TWA Flight 800. The investigation of the first led to the conviction of four Middle Eastern terrorists in a U.S. District Court. The government's case was "built on myriad small details" that included thick volumes of telephone records showing constant contact among the defendants, airline tickets and boarding passes, computer disk searches, DNA tests, fingerprint analysis, forensic examinations that found traces of chemicals on clothing, vehicle rental contracts, videotapes, parking stubs, bomb-making formulas, and a large plastic trash can, examination of which uncovered evidence that seemed to indicate that it had contained the actual explosive used in the bombing.[27]

The Unabomber case illustrates not only the complexity of bombing investigations, but also the need for investigators to be patient and persevering, cooperation among investigative agencies, the value of sources of information and informants, the importance of all searches, and the use of forensics. The predication for this investigation, later designated the Unabomber case, was the May 25, 1978, explosion of a bomb that injured one person at Northwestern University, Evanston, Illinois. Between then and April 24, 1995, fifteen more bombings occurred. Altogether, they caused three deaths and twenty-two injuries, three of which were classified as either serious or severe. On April 3, 1996, UNABOMB Task Force members detained Theodore J. Kaczynski and executed a search warrant on his Montana home.

That this investigation had been pending for almost eighteen years amply illustrates the investigators' dedication and persistence, and the cooperation among the FBI, ATF, and Postal Inspection Service is evidence of the value of teamwork. However, what were the ways in which sources of information, warrant-authorized searches, and forensics contributed to Theodore Kaczynski's transformation from suspect to subject?

Among the many pieces of evidence found and examined during this investigation were fingerprints, typewriter imprints, and unexploded devices. The paper on which the subject wrote his various messages was analyzed; in one instance, traces of writing otherwise invisible to the human eye were uncovered. Saliva from stamps on letters mailed to victims and news organizations was subjected to DNA analysis. A psychological profile of the subject was develped, and computers were used to compile lists of possible suspects. A special telephone line resulted in the receipt of more than 20,000 tips. Scrap metal dealers were interviewed and, based on the type of some of the packaging used, lists of persons employed by companies that deal in artificial human limbs were scrutinized. Data provided in 1987 by a person who saw a man placing a bomb gave investigators a physical description of a likely suspect.[28]

The ability of investigators to find and link bits and pieces of information is critical to all successful investigations, both criminal and noncriminal. However, since we can learn a good deal about this from the Unabomber case, a closer look at what was done there is warranted. In doing so, remember not only that this case, dealing with sixteen bombs, was pending for almost eighteen years, but also that it had leads in Illinois, Utah, Tennessee, California, Washington, Michigan, Connecticut, and New Jersey.

The initial information leading to Kaczynski as a suspect was provided by his brother, and the investigation then focused on him. As it progressed, application was made for a search warrant of the Montana cabin in which he lived and worked. Among the items found during the warrant's execution were the following:

Chemicals and other materials that could be used to make pipe bombs

Ten three-ring notebooks with diagrams for destructive devices and sketches for containers that could be used to conceal and transport them

Handwritten notes in Spanish and English

Containers of potassium chlorate, sodium chlorate, sugar, zinc, aluminum, lead, and silver oxide, all of which could serve as fuels and oxidizers

Cell batteries and electrical wire to provide the power needed to cause a detonation

Logs of experiments with regard to pipe dimensions, and combinations of explosive materials relative to weather conditions

A partially completed pipe bomb

Various tools that would be needed to convert the materials found into pipe bombs

Three manual typewriters, one of which may have been used to write a 35,000-word manifesto that was sent to both the *New York Times* and the *Washington Post* with a demand that it be printed

Two live bombs, one of which was virtually identical with a bomb that had been used in one of the fatal attacks

Handwritten notes that might have referred to some of the victims, and an original of a letter sent by the Unabomber to the *New York Times* in 1995

Having collected these various items of evidence, it became necessary to connect them to both Kaczynski and the sixteen bombs that were part of the Unabomber investigation. Learning that Kaczynski could write in Spanish explained the Spanish and English handwritten notes, but for the most part, the task of connecting him to the evidence and the bombs was one for a laboratory.

Preliminary laboratory examinations determined a number of relevancies. First, in addition to bomb design and construction similarities, bomb fragments found at crime scenes matched evidence found in the cabin. For comparison purposes, the analysis focused on microscopic marks that had been left by cutting tools, such as wood-carving knives and wire cutters found in the cabin. Second, preliminary tests of the three manual typewriters confirmed that the type on one matched the type of the manuscripts sent to the news media.[29] In addition, reportedly among the papers taken from the subject's home were references that appeared to relate to some of the Unabomber's victims. According to NBC News, one entitled "Hit List" included the words *Airline Executive, Geneticist,* and *Computer Industry;* among the known victims were an airline executive, a geneticist, and people associated with computers.[30]

The foregoing were not the only items linking the subject to the bombings. On April 15, 1996, U.S. District Court Judge Charles Lovell, who authorized the warrant for a search of Kaczynski's home, released an inventory of what was found. Aside from what was set forth earlier, other items found were addresses of corporate executives, street maps of San Francisco, and bus schedules. Also taken as evidence were a hooded jacket, a blue zippered sweatshirt with a hood, and two pairs of plastic glasses. All appeared to be similar to the clothing and sunglasses described by a witness who observed a person leaving a bomb in a Salt Lake City parking lot in 1987. In fact, the latter information was the basis for a description of the Unabomber and a sketch furnished to law enforcement agencies and the news media.[31]

Next, once Kaczynski became the subject, and being mindful of how long the Unabomber had been active, an effort had to be made to trace his travels over the years. The finding of maps and bus schedules would be yet another connection since three bombings were in the San Francisco Bay area, two were in Sacramento, California, and five of the bombs had been mailed from northern California. Furthermore, on the basis of hotel records, investigators were able to confirm Kaczynski's presence in Sacramento on dates when some of the bombs were mailed from there. Nevertheless, the long-term trace process meant that other hotels and homeless shelters at which Kaczynski might have stayed, as well as bus stations, bookstores, and libraries that he might have used along principal routes going from his Lincoln, Montana, home to Salt Lake City and a number of California cities also had to be canvassed.[32] Of course, the ultimate success or failure of this investigation will be determined when the case is tried in court.

An example of an even more complex investigation is the case of TWA Flight 800, which exploded shortly afer departing New York for Paris the night of July 17, 1996, killing all 230 aboard. Three different theories were advanced as possible causes: a massive mechanical failure occurred; a bomb was on board; the aircraft was shot down by a ground-to-air missile. If the cause was a bomb or missile, the explosion would have been the result of a criminal act and justifies examining that phase of the investigation here. If it was due to mechanical failure, the disaster was an accident, and we consider this possibility in Chapter 18.

Absent a clear indication that the cause of the explosion was anything other than an accident, the primary investigative responsibility was vested in the National Transportation Safety Board, assisted by the FBI and ATF; if it later appeared that a criminal act was the cause, responsibility would shift to the FBI. Since the aircraft went down at sea, the U.S. Navy was asked to handle the attempted recovery. The multiple possible explanations dictated that the only logical way to proceed would be by process of elimination in the hope that physical evidence would help determine the actual cause.

This meant that the aircraft's pieces, including the flight data and cockpit recorders, and other debris would have to be recovered and carefully examined. In addition, radar tapes of the takeoff would have to be reviewed, and a search would have to be made for anyone who might have witnessed the explosion.

Adding to the complexity was the fact that earlier in the week in which the explosion occurred, a letter was faxed to an Arabic newspaper warning of an attack, and the morning after the incident, a Tampa, Florida, television station received a telephone call from someone who claimed responsibility.[33] These leads also would have to be followed up. Although none of the three theories could yet be ruled out, the fax, the telephone call, and the fact that the aircraft was a Boeing 747, considered one of the safest and most reliable, made the idea that the cause was a massive mechanical failure less credible.

If a bomb or missile did cause the explosion, what was the motive? The fax and telephone call might suggest an arbitrary act of violence by Middle Eastern terrorists, but could it have been the handiwork of a homegrown militia group? Was it the result of an act to defraud an insurance company, a personal matter involving one of the passengers, or a suicide? Difficulties encountered in determining the actual cause, coupled with these questions for which answers were needed, made it advisable for the FBI to initiate a concurrent criminal inquiry even though the NTSB would continue to have primary investigative responsibility. However, if in fact a bomb or missile downed TWA Flight 800, the likelihood that it was a terrorist act cannot be discounted. We pursue the criminal aspects of this investigation under that heading.

TERRORISM

Just what is terrorism? The Vice President's Task Force on Terrorism defined it as "the unlawful use or threat of violence against persons or property to further political or social objectives. It is generally intended to intimidate or coerce a government, individuals, or groups to modify their behavior or policies."[34] From a U.S. government legislative viewpoint, terrorism would include

1. Hijacking or destroying a foreign aircraft outside the United States and taking refuge in the United States
2. Employing violence against any passenger on board a civilian or government aircraft
3. Committing a crime against a federal official
4. Interstate travel or the use of foreign transportation to commit murder or assassinate someone
5. Training foreign nationals how to use firearms, munitions, or explosives
6. Murdering a hostage
7. Kidnapping, assaulting, or murdering a U.S. citizen outside the United States if the person suspected of such activity is returned to the United States

From an investigative perspective, one also needs to consider what constitutes an act of international terrorism. Andre Bossard, the former executive director of the International Police Organization (INTERPOL), has defined international terrorism as follows:

> A terrorist act is considered international if the objectives of the terrorist concern more than one country; action starts in one country and ends in another, or is prepared in one country and perpetrated in another; victims are citizens of different countries or are members of international organizations; [or] the acts damage more than one country or international organization.[35]

The inherent and insidious nature of terrorism suggests that investigators should have some appreciation of its scope. In addition, they dare not assume that acts of domestic terrorism are nonexistent. In 1985, there reportedly were 1,103 criminal explosions or attempts in the United

States, in 1994, there were 3,163. Seventeen were aimed at local, state, or federal agencies in 1990, fifty-one in 1994. Pipe bombs are among the most commonly used devices. Solving these cases is made more difficult by the absence of taggants (microscopic chemical tracing elements) in gunpowder used to make the bombs, and the failure of Congress to mandate their inclusion. The benefits that would be derived become evident if one looks at the Swiss government's experience. There taggants are required and have been used by the police to track suspects in more than 500 bombings since 1990.[36]

General investigative jurisdiction for terrorist acts rests with the FBI, but in many cases, the investigation will be handled by a task force that may include other federal as well as state and local police agencies. Although other cases are in reaction to a committed offense, the imminent risk of death or serious injury that tends to accompany terrorism heightens the importance of a proactive approach to prevent terrorists from carrying out their work. However, effective proactivity requires good intelligence gathering. Therefore, every effort must be made to develop reliable confidential informants. It even may become necessary to have undercover investigators try to infiltrate the group under investigation. Liaison with private human rights groups that are concerned with and track the activities of fringe right-wing groups also can be helpful. Nevertheless, important as intelligence collection is in such cases, the process itself is not always an easy one in view of the legal constraints placed upon certain of its aspects.

Before beginning investigations of terrorist activities, we need to be aware of three things:

1. The kinds of people that tend to become involved in terrorist activity
2. The types of organizations that engage in terrorist activity
3. The types of activities in which they engage

No one profile fits all terrorists. For those active in behalf of Armenian or Puerto Rican groups or the Jewish Defense League (JDL), young, naive people who are considered expendable are used for most "front-line" operations. Other tasks are handled by those who are older, better educated, and possibly more dedicated. This is especially true of those in the Middle East where, in the late 1960s and into the 1970s, a majority of terrorist organizations were made up of both males and females who were flexible, college educated, well trained, urban, multilingual, well traveled, reasonably sophisticated, disciplined, and middle class. Coincidentally, in the 1970s, tactical training for the Japanese Red Army was provided by the Popular Front for the Liberation of Palestine (PFLP). By 1988, Middle Eastern terrorists prone to attacking Western interests were more likely than not to be poorly educated, from very large families, unskilled, unemployable, illiterate, rural, undisciplined, poorly trained male refugees, between 17 and 23, who had grown up as members of street gangs.[37]

It is interesting to compare these profiles of Middle Eastern terrorists with the general profile of radical right-wing groups found in the United States, such as the Covenant, the Sword and the Arm of the Lord, the Aryan Nations, and the Sheriff's Posse Comitatus. Members of these groups tend to belong to a radical religious majority, have limited educations, be immature, and have experienced social or economic failure. In age, they may range from teenagers to senior citizens. In contrast, their leaders generally are well educated, dedicated, articulate, and representative of the racial and ethnic orientation of a majority of the population of the United States.[38]

On the basis of more current information, it has been estimated that more than 800 right-wing groups with antigovernment sentiments operate throughout the United States. They consist of militias, white supremacists, neo-Nazis, skinheads, survivalists, and constitutionalists. Many are connected to each other not only by the Internet and fax machines, but also by the belief they share in a Christian identity.[39]

Hostage rescue team training, FBI Academy, Quantico, VA.
(*Courtesy* FBI)

By no means are the groups already named the only ones. There also are the Puerto Rican Independence Movement, which includes the Armed Forces for National Liberation, the National Liberation Movement, Revolutionary Commandos of the People, and the Organization of Volunteers for the Puerto Rican Revolution. In addition, there are Armenian Nationalist organizations such as the Armenian Secret Army for the Liberation of Armenia, Justice Commandos for the Armenian Genocide, Armenian Revolutionary Army, and Avengers of the Armenian Genocide. Among the principal Middle Eastern groups, one finds the Abu Nidal Organization, Palestine Liberation Front, and Popular Front for the Liberation of Palestine—General Command. Other terrorist groups, some still active and some inactive, are the Italian Red Brigade, German Red Army Faction, Action Direct in France, the Irish Republican Army, and the Basque Separatist Movement in Europe, the Japanese Red Army in Japan, and various organizations in some Central and South American countries.

Aside from groups of the ideological right already named as operating in the United States, one finds the Ku Klux Klan, Freemen in Montana, and the American Nazi Party. That most of these organizations do not have a profit motive, claiming instead that they are motivated by their purported desire to correct alleged political, social, racial, or economic injustices, does not alter the fact that their activities violate the law.

Equally important is the need to recognize terrorist organizations operating in the United States that claim no such motives. Instead, their activities focus on the use of intimidation in order to profit and control. Included among them are the El Rukins, the Crips and the Bloods, the Asian Triads and Tongs, and motorcycle gangs. Some of these gangs originated in cities such as Chicago, New York City, and Los Angeles, but there also are signs of expansion through the opening of "branches" in other communities across the country.

Terrorists engage in a wide variety of activities and use intimidation as a principal means of achieving their objectives. Thus it comes as no surprise that among their most common activities are conspiracy, bombing and arson, assassination, kidnapping and hostage taking, robbery, extortion, hijacking, and skyjacking. In Chapter 16, we see that some domestic terrorist groups, whose motivation is profit, also are involved with controlled substances.

Unlike domestic terrorist organizations, international terrorists get financial and logistical support, in addition to safe havens, from certain countries. In fact, some of their activities might be described as "state sponsored." This can pose problems for investigators not only in terms of making arrests but also in collecting evidence. For instance, beginning around 1990, high-quality, counterfeit U.S. dollars, made with the same rag content in the paper used and containing some of the same features as authentic ones, began to appear. Some of this money was being used by people with ties to terrorist organizations. Although aware of this, as of early 1996, the U.S. government still did not have sufficient evidence to publicly accuse Iran of printing the money, and Syria of sanctioning its distribution.[40]

To further illustrate some of these difficulties and the extent to which investigators must go in searching for and collecting evidence, Ramzi Ahmed Yousef was suspected of masterminding New York City's 1993 World Trade Center bombing. He also was suspected of terrorist activity in Thailand, and he was active in the Philippines and Pakistan. Yousef, taken into custody in 1995, was subsequently extradited from Pakistan to the United States.

Opening Yousef's May 1996 trial in U.S. District Court, on a charge of conspiracy to kill an untold number of air travelers in 1995 by placing bombs on a dozen American jumbo jetliners, the prosecution referred to data retrieved from Yousef's laptop computer, including schedules of United, Delta, and Northwest Airlines flights (intended targets), a timetable for midair explosions, and a draft of a letter claiming responsibility for the bombings. As the trial progressed, note was taken of the 1995 bombings of a Manila theater and a Philippine Airlines plane. According to the prosecution, it was these incidents that led the Philippine authorities to the discovery of a bomb-making operation in Yousef's apartment.

In testifying, a technical consultant for the National Bureau of Investigation, the Philippine equivalent of the FBI, stated that in addition to retrieving the airline schedules, he found a record of money transfers, identification photographs, a "threat letter," and other text. Furthermore, he said the retrieval of the files was from the computer's hard drive, that some had been deleted, but that he himself had not made any entries.[41] Indicative of the care and attention that must be paid to collecting and examining evidence from an investigative perspective, merely recovering Yousef's laptop during the search of his apartment would have proved nothing without the retrieval of the data stored on the hard drive. The trial ended with his conviction.

Most criminal cases tend to be individualized. Notwithstanding the ability of investigators to link one person or organization to a particular offense or series of crimes on the basis of an MO, signature, or intelligence, there is not the same degree of association that appears to exist in terrorist cases. In this respect, the latter are unique because of the possibility of such association either between groups or acts. Illustrating such a possibility is an item from the April 16, 1996, edition of the *New York Times.*

April 15, the University of South Florida announced that final examinations at its Tampa campus would be given a week early due to the receipt of a letter containing a threat to blow up an administration building and kill a white, female professor on April 29. The letter also mentioned Ramadan Abdullah Shallah, a former adjunct professor of Middle East politics, who left the campus in 1995 to become the leader of the Islamic Jihad. Sent to a Tampa newspaper on March 25, it was signed "The One, The Leader of the War Purges," a previously unheard of group described as "a diverse group of extremist individuals" with connections to Jihad and Hamas, both Middle East terrorist organizations. However, the letter also contained a reference to the April 19, 1995, Federal Building bombing in Oklahoma City for which two men are in federal custody.[42]

Cases like this place investigators on the horns of a dilemma. In this one, for example, the mention of Shallah and the fact that the signatory group apparently has ties to Middle East terrorist groups clearly suggest an investigative lead that must be pursued. By the same token, does the reference to the Oklahoma City bombing indicate some connection, is it mentioned for no purpose other than to emphasize the university's vulnerability compared to that of a government building, or is it only an expression of admiration for the bombers? Although information about the letter's sender is sparse, and there is no obvious connection, the possibility that one might exist cannot simply be dismissed. At the very least, there must be an effort to find out more about the senders.

To assume that all terrorist acts are the work of sizable organizations is a mistake. Neither is it realistic to theorize that the results of those acts are indicative of the number of perpetrators involved. For example, despite the magnitude of the Oklahoma City bombing, the evidence indicates that it was the work of two men. Consequently, all terrorist acts must be thoroughly and meticulously investigated. This point is clearly made in the case of the bomb that exploded July 27, 1996, at the Atlanta (Georgia) Centennial Olympic Park, where a large crowd was gathered at the time of the explosion.

Witnesses had to be identified and their accounts recorded. An installed special "tip" line generated more than 600 calls; each had to be evaluated and possibly pursued. A warning call to Atlanta's enhanced 911 system from a pay telephone before the detonation occurred enabled investigators to identify the telephone from which the call was made and send it to the FBI Laboratory to see if fingerprints could be recovered. Components of the device, a pipe bomb, also were sent to the FBI Laboratory for examination and the possible recovery of fingerprints. Based on the recorded call, the caller was described as a "white male with an undistinguished accent." Investigators hoped that information provided by witnesses and the tip line calls also would give them enough information to permit production of a composite drawing of a suspect.[43]

We have mentioned the downing of TWA Flight 800 as possibly having been caused by a bomb. If proved true, the further possibility that the explosion was an act of terrorism could not be ignored. As of October 7, 1996, there were some signs that a bomb caused the explosion, but from an evidentiary standpoint, there was insufficient evidence to categorically say that a crime had been committed. Nevertheless, the investigation would continue on a two-track approach with the NTSB pursuing the theory that a massive mechanical failure, which we discuss in detail in Chapter 18, caused the accident. Simultaneously, the FBI and other law enforcement agencies would go forward with the idea that a bomb, possibly placed on board by terrorists, was responsible. If one assumes the latter scenario to be the most likely, how far afield must investigators go in trying to learn not only who might have caused the explosion, but also why? A look at what occurred between the night of July 17, 1996, when the flight went down, and July 28, is enlightening.

During that time, a Joint Terrorism Task Force was organized. The FBI interviewed close to 1,500 people, including all those who were directly involved with the aircraft's servicing. They placed under surveillance New York area known supporters of terrorist groups and undertook an examination of databases for reports on possible suspects and of recent travels by terrorists. Confidential informants were contacted on a worldwide basis. A master file was created to store all information and leads, and a chart of the most likely suspects, listing both those considered as obvious choices and those seen as long shots, was drawn up. Research was begun on prior terrorist attacks with particular attention being paid to significant dates during recent years on which attacks had been made or Islamic militants had been executed, such as the hanging of five by the Egyptian government on July 17, 1993. In addition, information was sought not only with regard to a possible "lifeguard" flight (an urgent shipment of emergency supplies of medication or other health care–related needs) that might have bypassed security and been placed on board at the last minute, but also whether twenty-seven unclassified diplomatic pouches were X-rayed before being placed on the aircraft. The Task Force took note of the 349 passengers who arrived on board from Athens, where the flight to New York originated, and of those boarding in New York for Paris. Steps were taken to develop complete financial and personal profiles of everyone who boarded in New York, and to verify the passenger list on the chance that someone boarded using a false name. Prosecutors began to issue subpoenas for certain basic records.[44]

The World Trade Center bombing that resulted in the conviction of four men with ties to Middle East groups is another example of the extent to which investigators must go in cases of terrorism. It was pointed out that the government's case was "built on myriad small details."[45] Among the evidence presented were volumes of telephone records showing constant contact on the part of the parties, airplane tickets and boarding passes, the results of computer disk searches, DNA tests, and fingerprint analyses, reports on chemical traces found on certain articles of clothing, rental contracts, videotapes, stubs for parking, bomb-making formulas, a large plastic trash can, parts of which indicated that it seemed to have contained the actual explosive.

Earlier in this section, we cited some of the complexities of terrorist investigations and things of which investigators have to be aware. We also have used examples to illustrate the scope and magnitude of such investigations. However, additional factors must be kept in mind regarding terrorism. There are questions about terrorist organizations themselves, and about investigative techniques applicable to these cases, over and above those normally followed in all criminal inquiries.

Any investigation into terrorist activity when there is reason to believe it is sponsored by an organization must take into account the group's goals as the motivating factor and its tactical approaches to achieving its objectives. The importance of learning how the organization is structured, how members communicate with one another, and about its desire and aptitude for creating violence is undeniable.

Crime scene searches; collecting and preserving evidence; subjecting physical evidence to laboratory examination; and identifying, locating, and interviewing witnesses obviously are mandatory. In this respect, much of the approach to the investigation will be dictated by the underlying offense; that is, whether the crime was robbery, kidnapping, a bombing, extortion, and so on. However, when crimes are associated with terrorism, victims and witnesses need to be interviewed and reinterviewed to ensure that not even the smallest bit of information is missed. Statements must be obtained, and each of their stories must be confirmed.

Of course, identifying the party responsible for the act or acts is the investigation's prime objective, but when it appears that more than one person may be involved, their identities, and those of any coconspirators, also must be learned. Physical and electronic surveillances must be considered. All suspects must be investigated relative to their associations, their history, and the possibility of getting them to cooperate with the investigation. Persons on the fringe who may be inclined to aid and abet acts of terrorism also should be identified.

A last word on terrorist investigations. Ensuring that the evidence collection process satisfies all legal requirements is imperative in all cases, but it assumes even more importance when terrorism is involved. This is because, regardless of the questionable merits and tactics employed in behalf of their causes, terrorists may claim their motivation is based on perceived political injustices, they were exercising First Amendment rights, and the process used to collect evidence violated the Fourth Amendment's safeguards. Further, since some evidence collection may involve confidential informants, both investigators and prosecutors should not ignore the likelihood of a challenge to informant credibility if informants are called as witnesses at trial.

SUMMARY

In all investigations, one logically assumes the investigators need a point of departure. However, in criminal cases, whether they involve acts of violence or other offenses, they often have to begin their work with multiple starting points in mind. First, without knowing the elements of the crime under investigation, it is hard to know what evidence will be needed to prove not only that an offense was committed, but also that the subject committed it. Next, they must consider the variations of different crimes. For example, homicide includes murder and manslaughter; further distinctions are made between first and second degree murder, or voluntary and involuntary manslaughter. Occasionally, investigators have to resort to using a process of elimination. Are they dealing with a homicide or a suicide, an arson or an accidental fire? In looking for likely suspects, they ask themselves who possibly had a motive, and finding one, did that person have an opportunity to either commit the offense or have it committed?

All criminal investigations, whether or not violence is a factor, involve certain basic steps. Crime scenes must be searched for physical evidence. Once collected, that evidence must be sent for laboratory examinations. Victims and witnesses must be identified and interviewed. Sources of information have to be checked, and confidential informants contacted. The MO has to be carefully considered. It is essential that all information obtained from victims, witnesses, subjects, and confidential informants be independently corroborated. Using one or more forms of surveillance may prove helpful. Depending on the nature of the primary offense, such as large-scale, well-organized, gang robberies, or even certain types of white-collar crimes, sting operations may be productive. Cooperation among different investigative agencies often is helpful even though jurisdiction is clearly defined and their active participation is not needed.

However, in addition to these standard techniques, other resources are available in violent crime cases. For instance, we know that in most cases victims also are witnesses who are interviewed for whatever information they have. This obviously is not true in homicide or other suspicious death inquiries, and the circumstances surrounding the death may be such that there are no apparent witnesses. If so, it nevertheless is incumbent upon investigators to go door to door, ring doorbells, and ask questions in the hope that someone may have seen or heard something that will be useful.

Most important in death cases are the medical examiners. They can do more than help identify victims; they often can provide a number of invaluable leads. Investigators need to know the cause of a questionable death; was it a homicide, an accident, a suicide? If a homicide, autopsies may find some physical evidence. By no means unimportant is the fact that they frequently can tell investigators how victims spent the last few hours of their lives, information that in itself can be helpful. Medical examiners also can determine if death was accidental or a suicide, in which case criminal investigators can close the case.

The techniques used in assault cases are similar to those used in homicides. One objective is to try to apprehend assailants as quickly as possible. However, it is a mistake to assume that since assault victims are alive they will be able to provide valuable information to investigators. They sometimes can be helpful, but at other times victims may have survived yet been so badly injured that they are comatose. If this is the case, they are no better able to make a direct contribution to the investigation than are homicide victims.

This is not true of victims, and possibly witnesses, in robbery investigations. Here they certainly can be interviewed for information; however, there are considerations that need to be borne in mind. First, the very trauma of being a robbery victim, or witness for that matter, when there has been the threat or actual use of force, may make it hard for them to provide accurate information or physical descriptions, or they may be too afraid to do so. Nevertheless, there is a sense of urgency in getting the best possible physical description of the robber or robbers in the hope that this will lead to an early arrest. For other details about the crime itself, reinterviews within a reasonably short time may prove more productive. Among the questions to be asked are those about anything said by the robber or robbers, a noticeable foreign or regional accent, names that were possibly used, signs of familiarity with the victim or scene, and colloquialisms that were used. The answers may provide leads.

Second, in robberies as in homicides, there may be witnesses or others who have useful information but who will have to be sought out. Do not count on people volunteering; many do not want to become involved. Again, crime scenes must be carefully searched for physical evidence that may have been left behind, including such things as fingerprints, notes, a piece of clothing, hairs or fibers, shell casings or bullets, or binding materials. If a robber was injured while committing the crime, there also may be blood.

Sex offenses are traumatic experiences for victims. Therefore, investigators must be sensitive to victims' feelings and needs. This is true in all cases whether the victim has been raped or is an abused child. Victims must be interviewed, crime scenes searched for physical evidence, and whatever is found has to be collected and subjected to laboratory examination. Just as medical examiners make significant contributions in questionable death cases, physicians who examine sex offense victims also can provide useful information, but remember that their testimony alone is insufficient. In rape cases, they can testify about evidence of intercourse, the condition of a victim's clothes at the time of examination, and about contusions and abrasions found. They cannot say that the victim was raped; that is a conclusion of law. Similarly, they can offer their professional opinions about child abuse based on their findings, but they cannot state categorically that a child was the victim of abuse.

One might think arson and bomb cases would be relatively easy to solve. In truth, they are among the most difficult. Although first responders to the scene may find the circumstances surrounding the fire or explosion suspicious, the possibility that the cause was accidental or an act of nature must be ruled out before a criminal investigation begins. Once the process of elimination has been completed, and it appears a crime has been committed, the investigation will focus on the questions of who had a motive, who had the opportunity to set the fire or cause the explosion, or who would possibly hire someone to act in his or her behalf.

It is unwise to assume that there will be a quick solution and arrest simply because there is evidence that a fire or explosion was deliberately caused, and that some one person had a motive and an opportunity to act. As with all criminal cases, for solutions, arrests, and the ultimate punishment of perpetrators, investigators and prosecutors need more than a hunch; they need physical evidence. However, in arson and bomb cases, the fire or explosion itself may have been of such intensity as to destroy the minute pieces of physical evidence that would at least provide leads if not an actual link to a suspect, or weather conditions at the time may have caused a deterioration to or alteration of such evidence. Consequently, in arson and bomb cases, a search for a paper trail is essential.

A deliberately set fire may cause an explosion, but there also are explosions that are not preceded by fires. Bombs are used to destroy, kill, or seriously injure. Bombings tend to be the work of terrorists, whether domestic or international, fairly sizable or very small groups. Investigators follow what might be called generic techniques. They search crime scenes, interview surviving victims and witnesses, collect and examine physical evidence, use sources of information and confidential informants, and look for paper trials or other similar evidence. But here the use of physical and electronic surveillance, the possible use of undercover investigators, and the role of intelligence gathering should not be ignored.

REVIEW QUESTIONS

1. What is meant by the term *corpus delicti?*
2. Why must investigators know the elements of a crime?
3. From an investigator's perspective, what is a principal difference between a homicide and an assault?
4. Is a suicide a homicide?
5. What are the elements of robbery?

6. What is a key consideration in looking for homicide or arson suspects?
7. In what types of cases can medical examiners and doctors be most helpful?
8. Can a prostitute be raped?
9. What three things are needed to have combustion?
10. Are all terrorist groups both large and international?

NOTES

1. "Tiny Clue Prevents a Slaying from Being Listed as a Suicide," *New York Times,* August 27, 1995, p. 34.
2. John Douglas and Mark Olshaker, *Mindhunter* (New York: Scribner, 1995), p. 251.
3. "The Late Mr. Rosenberg Left a Mystery Behind," *New York Times,* November 21, 1995, p. B4.
4. "Health Aide Is Accused in Killings of 2 Women," *New York Times,* May 26, 1996, p. 29.
5. "Woman's Quest for Fame Ends in Death in the Night," *New York Times,* August 7, 1992, p. B3.
6. "Doctor Faces Murder Charge in '76 Killing," *New York Times,* July 28, 1996, p. A18.
7. "Man Arrested in L.I. Killings of 5 Prostitutes," *New York Times,* April 9, 1996, pp. B1, B5.
8. "Man Seized in Wave of Killings and Robberies," *New York Times,* June 21, 1996, pp. A1, B2.
9. "A Killer May Be Walking Among Them," *The Boston Globe,* July 10, 1996, pp. 21, 24.
10. "Evidence Shows Rope or Cord Was Used in Nanny's Killing," *The Boston Globe,* July 11, 1996, p. 25.
11. *American Law Institute Model Penal Code, 1985* as proposed at the May 24, 1962, Annual Meeting of the American Law Institute at Washington, D.C., p. 145.
12. "U.S. Details Evidence in Brink's Robbery Arrests," *New York Times,* November 14, 1993, pp. 1, 40.
13. "Chip Thieves Are Arrested After a Sting in California," *New York Times,* March 1, 1996, p. A10.
14. "Woman About to Lose Home, Accused of Heist," *The Boston Globe,* March 23, 1996, p. 26.
15. *Bureau of Justice Statistics Dictionary of Criminal Justice Terminology,* 2nd ed. (Washington, D.C.: U.S. Department of Justice, Bureau of Justice Statistics, 1988).
16. Robert D. Blackledge, "Condom Trace Evidence: A New Factor in Sexual Assault Investigations," *FBI Law Enforcement Bulletin,* Vol. 65, No. 5 (May 1996), pp. 12–16.
17. "Grappling with Serial Rape Cases," *New York Times,* February 13, 1994, pp. 41, 44.

18. Robert D. Blackledge, "Condom Trace Evidence: A New Factor in Sexual Assault Investigations," *FBI Law Enforcement Bulletin,* Vol. 65, No. 5 (May 1996), pp. 12–16.

19. Ibid.

20. *Child Abuse Prevention Handbook* (Sacramento, CA: California Department of Justice, 1982), pp. 7–9.

21. "Arrests Made in '92 Blaze That Killed a Firefighter," *New York Times,* February 28, 1995, p. B3.

22. "No Conspiracy Found in Fire that Killed 8," *New York Times,* February 27, 1996, pp. B1, B6.

23. "Mill Excavation to Take Month," *The Boston Globe,* April 30, 1996, p. 38.

24. "2d Man Charged in Blaze That Killed a Firefighter," *New York Times,* February 19, 1996, p. B3.

25. "Back Bay Fire Origin Is Called Suspicious," *The Boston Globe,* May 1, 1996, p. 57.

26. "Brooklyn Bomb Tied to 14-Year Series," *New York Times,* June 22, 1996, p. 22.

27. "4 Are Convicted in Bombing at the World Trade Center That Killed 6, Stunned U.S.," *New York Times,* March 5, 1994, pp. 1, 28.

28. "Federal Agents Detain Man Who Is Believed to Be Unabomb Suspect," *New York Times,* April 4, 1996, pp. A1, B12.

29. Compiled from *New York Times,* April 5, 1996, p. A24; April 9, 1996, pp. A1, A18; April 13, 1996, pp. 1, 10.

30. "Cabin Said to Yield Document Titled 'Hit List'," *The Boston Globe,* April 10, 1996, p. 3.

31. "Evidence Listed in Unabomb Case," *New York Times,* April 16, 1996, pp. A1, A19.

32. "Hotel Records May Forge Link in Unabomb Case," *New York Times,* April 8, 1996, pp. A1, B8.

33. "Little Hard Evidence Found—Death Toll Is Put at 230," *New York Times,* July 19, 1996, pp. A1, B4.

34. *Vice President's Task Force on Terrorism* (Washington, D.C.: U.S. Government Printing Office, 1986), p. 2.

35. Andre Brossard, *Transnational Crime and Criminal Law* (Chicago: Office of International Criminal Justice, University of Illinois at Chicago, 1990), p. 21.

36. "Terrorism Now Going Homespun as Bombings in the U.S. Spread," *New York Times,* August 25, 1996, pp. 1, 36.

37. Thomas Strentz, "A Terrorist Psychosocial Profile Past and Present," *FBI Law Enforcement Bulletin,* Vol. 57, No. 4 (April 1988), pp. 13–19.

38. Ibid.

39. "Private Groups Lead Charge in War on Far Right," *New York Times,* April 14, 1996, p. E3.

40. "Super-Counterfeit $100's Baffle U.S.," *New York Times,* February 27, 1996, p. A10.

41. "Prosecutors in Bomb-Plot Case Turn to Suspect's Computer," *New York Times,* July 10, 1996, p. B2.

42. "Threat Prompts University to Hold Tests a Week Early," *New York Times,* April 16, 1996, p. A19.

43. "With Scores of Tips, and Photos, Bomber's Description is Emerging," *New York Times,* July 29, 1996, pp. A1, B6.

44. Compiled from *New York Times,* July 28, 1996, pp. A1, A19, and July 29, 1996, pp. A1, B4.

45. "4 Are Convicted in Bombing at the World Trade Center That Killed 6, Stunned U.S.," *New York Times,* March 5, 1994, pp. 1, 28.

Chapter 16

Other Crimes

In this chapter, we discuss a variety of nonviolent offenses, among them fraud and white-collar crime, burglary, larceny, motor vehicle theft, and crimes involving dangerous drugs and controlled substances. Even though all but those offenses related to controlled substances involve a deprivation of property, they nevertheless have distinguishing characteristics. Although people are the actual victims in each case, the offenses generally are referred to as property crimes with the exception of those involving drugs. As with all criminal investigations, violent and nonviolent, victims and possible witnesses have to be identified and interviewed, crime scenes searched, and evidence collected. However, despite these commonalities, there also are some differences. They are found in the way these cases are handled, in terms of the expected results, and with respect to the pressures applied for quick solutions. Let us consider each.

Interviewing violent crime victims and often other witnesses can produce leads and other useful information about the crime. Victims and witnesses also may help identify perpetrators. The autopsies of homicide victims can provide important information about the deceased as well as leads based on physical evidence taken from or found in the deceased. In contrast, in many property crimes, there is no direct confrontation between victims and victimizers; neither are there other witnesses.

As for results, expectations for solutions tend to be a good deal lower. Several factors contribute to this, not the least of which is the absence of witnesses. Then, too, in some cases, such as fraud or white-collar crimes, perpetrators may be helped, and investigators hampered, by a delay in reporting the offense. Some victims may not realize what has happened until they have suffered significant losses; others may be too embarrassed to report their victimization. The amount of physical evidence found in some nonviolent crimes may be very limited, and the complexity of evidence collection in cases in which computers have played a part cannot be discounted. In addition, unlike investigators, for whom solutions mean the recovery of victims' property *and* the perpetrators' arrests, victims deprived of property by nonviolent means frequently are more concerned with recoveries than they are with arrests.

Finally, the pressures applied to investigators to quickly solve nonviolent crimes are not as great as in violent crime cases. This is largely because, with the possible exception of significant white-collar crimes, major drug cases, or celebrity victims, property crimes are not especially newsworthy. On the other hand, violent crimes attract the attention of the news media, politicians, and consequently, the general public, all of whom expect immediate results. In fact, even in major fraud and white-collar crime and drug cases, the news media and local politicians often first learn of the investigation when agencies and prosecutors announce indictments and arrests.

That there may be a lower expectation in terms of results, and less pressure for quick solutions, does not absolve investigators of the need to put forth their best efforts to apprehend those responsible and, where possible, recover victims' property. This calls for an understanding of how these nonviolent crimes occur. Investigators invariably have questions for which they seek answers, and they have to decide on the best investigative techniques to be used.

FRAUD AND WHITE-COLLAR CRIME

The term *white-collar crime* was first introduced by Edwin Sutherland, who defined it as "a crime committed by a person of respectability and high social status in the course of his occupation."[1] Today's white-collar criminals still tend to be respectable people, but "high social status" no longer is a condition precedent to an offense that can be committed by either men or women. Perhaps in today's environment, a better definition would be that of a nonviolent offense committed for profit. Further, since white-collar crimes involve some form of deception, concealment, misrepresentation, or abuse of trust, investigators may find it more helpful initially to focus on particular activities rather than on individuals, and to concentrate on getting the cooperation of victims.

Fraud and white-collar crimes are similar yet different. The main types of fraudulent offenses consist of bunco and "con" (confidence) games, so-called bank examiner frauds, the use of checks and credit cards to defraud, and consumer and business fraud. Examples of white-collar crimes include insider trading, embezzlement, computer crime, and money laundering.

The elements of fraud may vary from state to state, but generally they require a criminal intent to deprive a rightful owner of property by concealing the perpetrator's objective, and relying on the victim's naivete, negligence, or compassion. For instance, in bunco and con game cases, victims are led to believe that by giving money to someone, usually a stranger or possibly a casual acquaintance, they will get an unusually high rate of return on their investments. Bank examiner frauds involve soliciting cash from victims by showing fake bank examiner credentials and claiming that money is needed to catch a bank employee suspected of wrongdoing. Using counterfeit checks or credit cards to buy items for which vendors never will be paid is fraud.

To assume that only individuals engage in fraudulent activities is a mistake; some businesses do so as well. One example is the so-called bait-and-switch sale. Certain goods are advertised to attract customers who then are given various reasons for the unavailability of the advertised goods; instead, they are sold other more expensive items. Other examples include unneeded repairs of an item or charging customers for new parts and making the repairs with used ones.

Those white-collar crimes related to insider trading tend to get the most publicity. These involve the money-making purchase or sale of publicly traded stocks on the basis of information not yet known to the general public. To illustrate, a law firm paralegal is working on the proposed purchase by one of his employer's clients of another company; the stock of both companies is publicly traded. The outcome is not in doubt, and the acquired firm's stock will increase in value upon consummation. Only key executives of the two organizations and involved law firm personnel are aware of this. Seeing an opportunity to make a lot of money quickly, the paralegal tells a few select friends, and he and they each buy 1,000 shares of the about-to-be acquired firm's stock at $10 a share; with the acquisition's completion, each share's value is $25. The paralegal and his friends each have quickly made $15,000 on their original investments as a result of inside information.

Embezzlement rarely attracts publicity, except in cases involving large sums of money or when either victims or embezzlers are well known in the community. Just as a relationship of trust exists in insider trading cases, so is it an element in embezzlement. For instance, an employee who misuses employer funds entrusted to his or her care for personal benefit would be an embezzler. Withdrawing money from an account over which the employee has control in order to buy a new automobile would be embezzlement.

Considered white-collar offenses, computer crimes can consist of some form of fraud, embezzlement, or larceny. Obviously, the key distinction is

Winding Trails of Insider Tips

After an insider told a friend of a pending takeover bid for the Norton Company, the Securities and Exchange Commission says the information passed through nine generations of tippees, all of whom now face charges. Some of the same people were also charged in an unrelated takeover, of Motel 6, in which the SEC says tips passed through seven generations of tippees. Here is the SEC's version of how tips in the two 1990 deals reached the six people who heard about and traded on both tips.

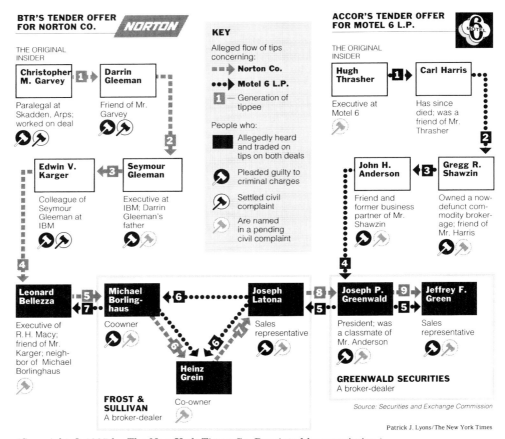

(Copyright © 1995 by The New York Times Co. Reprinted by permission.)

the use of a computer with which to commit the offense. Many computer crimes, like other nonviolent offenses, are not publicized unless the victims are well known, large sums of money have been stolen, or there has been access to, if not the theft of, sensitive information. Computer crimes also are particularly susceptible to late reporting. Occasionally, this is due to a victim's embarrassment, but more often it is due to the inherent nature of much computer crime in that there may be extended periods during which victims are unaware of what is happening.

Money laundering frequently is associated with organized crime, and thus it is somewhat likely to attract publicity. Nevertheless, it is a white-collar crime that either makes money earned from illegal activities appear as if it were earned legitimately or disguises the sources from which the illegal funds were derived. The ability to detect and follow paper trails is essential to all money laundering investigations as evidenced by the tools provided by the government for the purpose of combating the problem.

The U.S. Congress originally enacted the Bank Secrecy Act in 1978. Its four principal requirements are as follows:

1. Bank records must be kept for not less than five years.

2. Financial institutions must file reports with the Internal Revenue Service on all currency transactions of more than $10,000.

3. Currency or Monetary Instrument Reports must be filed with U.S. Customs whenever any currency or other monetary instrument valued at more than $5,000 is brought into or taken out of the United States.

4. Persons who have accounts of $5,000 or more on deposit in foreign banks must file a Foreign Bank Account Report.

That many of the basic techniques employed in violent crime cases also apply in nonviolent crimes does not mean that all the latter investigators will have the benefit of working from a crime scene in the more accepted sense of the term. For instance, a fraud perpetrated through the use of a telephone call does not really include a crime scene although a crime has been committed. Consequently, in fraud investigations a first step is to obtain a detailed description of the offense. In other words, how was the crime committed? This can be gotten only through victim interviews. Throughout these interviews, it is important to be sensitive to both the victims' losses and their possible embarrassment because they contributed to those losses.

Victims' backgrounds should be considered. They may suggest why a particular person was selected. That, and the MO used, may help identify likely suspects. At the same time, considering how many frauds are perpetrated, and perpetrators' mobility, certain types of documentation can prove useful not only in tracking and eventually locating the latter, but also in prosecuting them. Such documentation includes handwriting samples found on such diverse items as signed sales slips, applications for credit or credit cards, and rental car agreements. Driver's license data used in renting cars, or for identification when making certain purchases, can provide leads. License plate numbers on service stations' charges and descriptions of rental cars used by subjects are of evidentiary value, as are credit card imprints on airline, hotel, and restaurant charges and car rental contracts, and possibly serial numbers or other descriptive data on sales slips.

Most credit cards are issued by or through banks. Therefore, when they are used to perpetrate a fraud, the issuing banks, or those whose stolen or counterfeited cards were used in the scheme, are the victims. In fact, it has been estimated that, worldwide, banks and credit card companies lose \$3 billion annually.[2] Consequently, victimized banks almost invariably will give investigators any help they can.

White-collar crimes are different from most other crimes. The predication for their investigation tends to vary depending on the nature of a particular offense. Complaints about insider trading may be based on unusual purchases or sales of publicly traded stocks of companies, especially if rumored to be involved with the acquisition of or sale to another firm. Embezzlement or bribery or kickback investigations often are the result of an employer's suspicions. Computer crime investigations tend to be opened when a victimized organization notices what seems to be unusual activity affecting its database or operating system. Inquiries into money laundering may be predicated on bank examiners' reports or filings required by the Bank Secrecy Act.

As is true of all investigations, regardless of the basis for the complaint, the complainants must be thoroughly and carefully interviewed. Details about what first aroused their suspicions and about the suspect activity must be obtained. In virtually all these types of cases, there is a paper trail or some other form of documentation that must be secured and protected for its evidentiary value. Other aspects of these investigations will follow, but first, and with the foregoing as background, a look at a few actual cases may provide a better understanding of some of the different techniques used in fraud and white-collar crime cases.

❖ Case 16-1

In September 1995, a woman was arrested as she tried to buy a \$2,000 fax machine, a \$1,200 computer, and several other items with a counterfeit credit card that led to a five-month investigation by New York City, state, and federal agencies and resulted in a 200-count indictment against eight persons in February 1996. They were described as heading the largest credit card ring in the United States, with contacts here, in Europe, and in Asia and running a four-year multimillion-dollar scheme using stolen credit cards, making their own, and assuming the identities of unsuspecting credit card holders. They had managed to steal \$650,000 in goods and cash advances in ten months and had credit cards that would give them access to \$8 million. To assume the identities of legitimate credit card holders, the eight stole their credit card numbers from invoices. They then contacted credit reporting and mortgage agencies for information about these persons' credit histories, credit limits, and other personal data. Next, they diverted mail intended for those persons by filing changes of address with the U.S. Postal Service. In the ringleader's apartment, investigators found stolen invoices; both stolen and counterfeit Visa, MasterCard, American Express, and Discover credit cards; and equipment for making counterfeits, including holograms and magnetic tape, and embossing and encoding machines.[3]

❖ Case 16-2

At the end of February 1996, after a two-year investigation in which Russia's Ministry of Internal Affairs cooperated with the FBI, three Russian immigrants were charged with helping operate a sham company that had been paid to deliver to Russia, but did not, computer equipment and other goods worth $4.6 million. One organization that lost $2 million trying to import equipment through this company was a charity. The sham company's "office" was a postal box in New York City; its telephone number was an answering service. During the FBI Laboratory's examination of various documents provided by the Russian government, latent fingerprints were developed that enabled the bureau to identify the perpetrators.[4]

❖ Case 16-3

A telephone call from one victim to another questioning certain documentation used to secure a loan for one of the subjects led to the FBI's March 1996 arrest of two people and ended a scheme that defrauded eight international financial institutions of hundreds of millions of dollars over a two-year period. One subject, who had worked in the computer systems department for the Philip Morris Companies until 1992, approached a bank posing as a company official. He said Philip Morris needed money for a top-secret international project, and all contacts were to be made through him. He then submitted a so-called incumbency certificate bearing his own name and that of Philip Morris's assistant secretary. The latter said the certificate was "phony" thus prompting the call, which was monitored by the FBI, to the Philip Morris offices to arrange for a meeting. The subject posing as the company's assistant secretary then was arrested.[5] Later the *New York Times* reported that on June 5, 1996, this subject entered a plea of guilty to bank fraud and money laundering charges involving eight victims and more than $350 million.[6]

These examples of different fraudulent schemes clearly show that such charges can involve widespread rather than narrow investigations. Of course, fraud is but one kind of white-collar crime. Although other types also require a search for paper trails, the problems and the techniques used are somewhat different. We have seen the types of evidence for which investigators search in credit card cases. Contract documents and bank checks and the phony incumbency certificate played significant roles in the Russian and Philip Morris cases.

However, in some other white-collar offenses, such as bribery or kickback cases, investigators are faced with a unique situation. Unlike violent crimes, or fraud inquiries like those already cited relative to credit card use or counterfeiting, in bribery or kickback cases, crime scenes in the more traditional sense are nonexistent. Furthermore, victims tend to be the employers of either or both of the scheme's participants. Unless they know what is happening, they obviously cannot file complaints to trigger an investigation. Employers of persons who offer bribes or kickbacks, knowing of or approving these tactics as a way to get business, assuredly will not complain. As a result, investigations of this sort often are opened on the basis of an anonymous tip, or possibly because an ethical employee of one of the two involved organizations reports having been offered a bribe or having been solicited for a kickback.

In 1995, a J.C. Penney Company buyer was sentenced to eighteen months and fined $50,000 for accepting $1 million in bribes and kickbacks from vendors and sales representatives. In 1996, a former director of shopping center development and marketing for the Kmart Corporation was indicted for having accepted kickbacks, bribes, and other payments from firms with which Kmart was doing business. Among other facts investigators learned was that he had been given tickets to Superbowl games and limousine rides. It is not uncommon for buyers for retail establishments to receive "favors" that may range from dinners, to vacations paid for by vendors, to kickbacks.[7]

Investigations normally start with victim and witness interviews and crime scene searches, but this is not possible in bribery or kickback cases unless a complainant is identified. Absent an identifiable complainant, attention will focus on the person or persons named in the anonymous tip. As in any inquiry, the early questioning of suspects is imprudent since it may lead to the destruction of some physical evidence. By the same token, it is possible that disposing of other items of evidentiary value may be too difficult to accomplish, or they will be available from other sources.

Cooperative persons who have been offered bribes or who have been solicited for kickbacks are invaluable. Ways in which they can help investigators collect evidence, and prosecutors get convictions, were illustrated in Chapter 9. However, the question of how best to proceed arises when reliable persons willing to become confidential informants are not available.

Although bribery or kickback schemes take at least two willing persons to succeed, it often is easier to see telltale signs of such activity by focusing on the suspected recipient, especially his or her lifestyle. Knowing where suspects live and vacation, whether in owned or rented premises, the number and types of owned or leased motor vehicles they have, and even where their children, if any, attend school are worth noting. Are any of these inconsistent with their earnings? Credit records and bank accounts should be examined. Poor credit or large, frequent, and unexplained deposits from a single source may indicate their participation in illegal activities.

Investigations also must extend to the workplace. Suspects' personnel files and the nature of their assignments have to be considered. The former are a source for background information; the latter can be evidence that the individual is in a position to benefit from a bribe or kickback. Was the person's preemployment screening thorough? Are there some seemingly unanswered questions that might suggest prior involvement in unethical or illegal activities? Is the suspect's job one that lends itself to bribery or kickbacks? If it is, the person's work must be examined for possible patterns that appear to lend credence to his or her participation in one of these schemes. Although reference has been made to the susceptibility of retailers, by no means are bribes and kickbacks exclusive to that industry. The following cases illustrate both how far ranging bribery and kickback investigations can be and how they can disprove as well as prove guilt.

❖ Case 16-4

A packaging materials buyer for a manufacturer solicited kickbacks from two vendors; both agreed. Instead of cash payments, he sought other benefits. He asked one to buy him new tires for his automobile and choice tickets to popular sporting events. From the other, he asked for and got the occasional use of both a cabin cruiser and a luxury apartment. When his demands increased to a point that both vendors deemed excessive, they complained to the employer, admitted their complicity, and agreed to cooperate with the investigation. Each gave a detailed, signed statement setting forth how they had been approached, for what they had been asked, what they gave the buyer, and what business they got in return for doing so. As the case progressed, it also was determined that the buyer was a bad credit risk, an alcoholic, and a gambler, and he was paying alimony to a former wife and was supporting an unemployed girlfriend with whom he was living. In addition, the apartment they shared and the automobile he was driving were inconsistent with his salary.

❖ Case 16-5

A retired insurance company executive, who had been involved with choosing a well-known general contractor to build a 300,000-square-foot addition to his employer's corporate headquarters, also reviewed and approved all the contractor's change order requests for additional funds as work progressed. After he retired, a new employee, working on an alteration project, found that contemporaneously with the addition's construction, the retired executive had a new home built by the same general contractor, and the latter had never before built a single family home. This led to an investigation that showed that money to pay for the new home had been included in the change orders approved by the former executive.

❖ Case 16-6

Two unsigned letters alleged that a plant engineer was taking kickbacks from contractors doing work at his facility. An examination of his employment application showed that he had owned two businesses before he took his current job. Credit and court records showed that he had declared bankruptcy both times, yet within the last year he bought two other businesses in fields in which he had no experience. According to records at the Registrar of Deeds, he recently bought a home in an upscale neighborhood, but with a very small mortgage. A check of motor vehicle records indicated ownership of four luxury cars. Discreet neighborhood inquiries uncovered the fact that his four children attended private schools, and that he and his family had recently taken a four-week vacation cruise to Europe. His salary was $40,000 a year. The employer's purchasing policy for all labor and materials required competitive bids for work costing $3,000 or more. Upon examining all contract work for which the subject was responsible, a pattern emerged. He had awarded multiple sequential contracts for less than $3,000 to certain firms when in reality the composite work called for in each of these instances consisted of single projects, each with a total value of more than $20,000.

❖ Case 16-7

An employer received an anonymous letter alleging that a service manager in a highly technical area was getting kickbacks on several small contracts that he had awarded. The writer said the work could have been done more efficiently and cheaply in-house. Two things were readily apparent. First, the nature of the allegations indicated that the writer most likely was an employee working in the same field. Second, competent technical assistance would be needed to determine if the statements about the work itself had merit. Initially, since all the involved projects were for under $500, company policy had not been violated. While technically qualified persons carefully examined the completed projects, an effort to identify the anonymous complaint's author was undertaken. In the interim, the technical evaluation concluded that none of the work could have been done better or for less money in-house. Proceeding on the assumption that the author was an employee familiar with the work, the personnel files of everyone working for the manager were reviewed, and all these employees were interviewed. A review of the personnel files showed that one employee had twice been passed over for a salary increase. Examination of his handwriting resulted in a match with that of the letter's author. When reinterviewed and confronted with this information, the employee admitted his guilt.

Other examples of white-collar crime, worth noting because of their diversity, help illustrate how deeply investigators must dig in working such cases. The problems encountered often are compounded by the fact that the trusting relationship that exists between victim and perpetrator enables the latter to offend for some time without the victim becoming suspicious, let alone aware of the transgression. It also puts the offender in a position to destroy or manipulate physical evidence.

For instance, in May 1996, a thirty-two-year employee of the Brooklyn, New York, diocese pension office, and its manager with the authority to sign checks since 1990, was arrested for having written checks for $1.1 million to different firms with which the diocese did business, cashing them, and taking the money. The discovery was made during her absence on April 2. Her superior, looking at the March bank statement, noticed a $15,500 check to a company that had completed most of its work months before. The manager was the primary contact with outside companies, and about once or twice a month she would issue checks for bills that she claimed had been lost or accidentally destroyed.[8]

Not surprisingly, some white-collar crimes involve people working in the securities industry. Not all those investigations will necessarily involve law enforcement assistance. In early 1996, the National Association of Securities Dealers (NASD), a self-regulating industry body that oversees the activities of all U.S. stockbrokers, found a pattern that caused it to initiate an investigation of New York area brokers. People who failed the licensing examination in New York had passed tests taken outside New York. Investigators found evidence that some brokers had paid others to take the examination for them, one having admitted paying $2,500. They also found there were people who had never taken the examination yet had been working as brokers for more than a year.[9] Of necessity, this involved careful scrutiny of passing and failing examination results and how many who failed took the examination over, as well as interviews. Additionally, unlicensed persons who nevertheless claimed to be licensed stockbrokers also had to be identified.

In recent years, insider trading has become an increasingly serious problem. When suspected, these offenses require the involvement of either federal law enforcement or regulatory agencies such as the FBI or the Securities and Exchange Commission (SEC). On February 27, 1996, the president and chief executive officer of American Biltrite Inc. and a friend were ordered to pay fines and restitution totaling $27,000 to settle accusations that they had engaged in illegal insider trading. The SEC's complaint, filed in a U.S. District Court, alleged that in 1992 the president gave a friend information about a business venture not yet announced, prompting the friend to buy 1,500 shares of stock before it rose 25 percent when news of a joint venture became public. This allowed the friend to realize a $9,000 gain within forty-eight hours of the time of purchase.[10] Situations of this sort require investigators to look into sizable stock transactions involving publicly traded companies, both purchases and sales, preceding mergers, acquisitions, or joint ventures. They also have to interview stockholders to determine what made them buy or sell, if they have any personal contacts within the affected companies or possibly law firms representing them, and, if not, through whom they acted and the extent of that person's possible inside contacts.

As another example, in May 1996, a Bankers Trust Securities Company compliance officer was charged with securities fraud for having illegally traded shares of nine companies in 1994. It was alleged that he and a cousin used insider information to make $54,000 based on information gotten on November 17, 1994, from someone representing ITT Corporation in its acquisition of Caesar's World, which occurred in December 1994. The subject, who used at least two confederates and lied to both the SEC and his employer's investigators, bought money orders and took them to a broker's office to finance the purchase of call options.[11]

Even in white-collar crime cases, there may be times when methods normally associated with burglary and larceny inquiries prove useful. A 1996 FBI sting operation resulted in forty-six persons being charged with securities fraud and conspiracy. Low-priced stocks of tiny companies were being offered for sale. Some of the firms hired promoters to urge people to buy their stock, and bribes were paid to brokers to get them to buy shares for their customers. Some of the bribes were paid in cash or shares of stock. As part of the investigation, the FBI opened its own small stock brokerage operation and soon was doing business with and collecting evidence on those who were charged.[12]

It is clear from the foregoing that it is impossible to try to simplify either the nature of fraud or white-collar crimes, or the techniques that must be used in trying to solve them. Equally clear in many of these cases is that one cannot overemphasize the importance of finding and following paper trails that eventually may constitute the only physical evidence that an offense was committed.

BURGLARY

In burglary cases also, investigators need to be familiar with the elements of the offense. And again, despite certain common characteristics, each state's burglary statute may vary, however slightly, from those of other states. Nevertheless, an acceptable definition of the offense is found in the *Dictionary of Criminal Justice Data Terminology,* published by the U.S. Department of Justice's Bureau of Justice Statistics. It defines burglary as an "unlawful entry of any fixed structure, vehicle, or vessel used for regular residence, industry or business, with or without force, with the intent to commit a felony or larceny."

Clearly, there must be evidence that the entry was unlawful, the place or object entered was regularly rather than occasionally used as a residence or for industry or business, and the entry was made for the purpose of committing a felony or to steal another person's property. Thus a person unlawfully entering a home to kill a resident could be charged with both homicide and burglary.

Burglary investigations have a unique quality. On the one hand, burglars often leave fairly good physical evidence; on the other, cases can be hard to close because witnesses are scarce, and the fruits of the crime are disposed of quickly. However, it helps if some of the factors that encourage residential burglaries are understood. Further, recognizing the telltale signs that may be indicative of the type of person who committed the burglary can provide useful leads.

Among the factors that experienced residential burglars look for are a collection of newspapers, mail, and possibly dairy products. Too many or too few lights left on, or none at all, and an empty garage with the door left open for extended periods of time also tend to indicate that the occupants are away. For the burglar, this is important; it looks like a chance to steal with a minimal risk of confrontation or apprehension.

With respect to burglars' characteristics, juveniles are more likely to enter poor or middle-class residences. This may also be true of drug addicts looking for money with which to satisfy their habits. These burglars are inclined to search haphazardly rather than methodically; what they take often is varied rather than specific. If they steal things other than cash, it is because they find the objects attractive, not because they attach any particular value to them.

Burglarized hotel rooms, like the burglaries of upscale homes, generally are the work of more experienced burglars. They focus on wealthier victims, and appreciating an item's worth they will take only valuable property. They make every effort to avoid being seen; they search the hotel room or home in a methodical way. In residential burglaries, they may unlock select doors, and even windows, to facilitate their escape in the event that the occupants return. Juveniles, addicts, or inexperienced burglars will not hesitate to break a window or glass door to get in; experienced burglars more often than not will use a specific type of tool for that purpose.

There usually is some physical evidence in burglary cases. This makes it imperative for both the first responders and investigators to exercise care to prevent the destruction or alteration of any of that evidence.

The search for and collection of physical evidence must cover points of entry and exit as well as the interior. It includes looking for such things as tool marks, fingerprints, imprints left on dirt or soft ground, dirt left inside, trace evidence, and even blood, especially if glass was broken to gain access.

Concurrent with victim interviews by investigators, patrol officers should go door to door to look for and identify possible witnesses who also can be interviewed. That neighbors may not have seen the burglary does not necessarily mean they did not see something unusual that warrants exploration.

Obviously, there will be questions for victims that only they can answer:

1. Is hired help regularly in the house, or have any repair people recently been in the house?

2. Who has keys, and have any been lost or stolen?

3. Is there anything about the timing of the burglary? Was there an obituary in a newspaper, or an item about the victim's expected attendance at a publicized event?

Postal Inspectors' burglary investigation. (*Courtesy* U.S. Postal Inspection Service)

4. Have there been earlier attempted burglaries, whether or not successful?

5. Get a list and detailed description of the stolen property; color photographs as well, if available.

6. Is there anything unique about any of the stolen property?

7. Who knew about the stolen property, and where it was kept?

8. Was anything else taken, such as a snapshot of a family member, or was anything disturbed, such as food or drink taken from a refrigerator? (If food was taken and only partially eaten, such as a piece of fruit, it should be treated as physical evidence and submitted for a forensic odontology examination.)

9. Was the stolen property insured? Were there any recent changes in the amounts of coverage?

The burglar's MO is of interest to burglary investigators. Knowing it, they will contact their confidential informants, pay close attention to other sources of information that might prove helpful, and start to identify suspects. Known or suspected fences will be contacted, and pawn shops will be visited, in an effort to trace the stolen property. Although most burglary complaints are legitimate, the fact remains that if none of the foregoing are productive, a discreet inquiry into the victim's background, particularly his or her financial condition, may be worthwhile. No matter how unlikely it may seem, burglary investigators cannot afford to simply discount the possibility of victim involvement.

LARCENY

An acceptable definition of larceny requires that an owner be intentionally deprived of the possession of his or her property, either permanently or for an unreasonable length of time, or that a perpetrator's intended use of that property will deprive the owner of its use. Intent is required in all crimes, but in larcenies, some courts call only for a showing of the thief's intention to deprive rather than requiring that he or she also intended to gain some personal benefit.[13]

The word *larceny* really is an all-inclusive term since it refers to stealing of any kind. It includes some thefts already discussed, such as confidence games, which are a form of fraud. We also have discussed embezzlement, a white-collar crime that involves the secret appropriation of either money or other property, most often by an employee to whom it has been entrusted. However, receiving stolen property and shoplifting also are considered larcenies.

The offense of larceny may take many forms, but the basic investigative approach is fairly standard. Although the crime scene must be identified and secured, unlike burglary the types of physical evidence for which to search will be a good deal different. Instead of looking for tool marks or broken glass, the items to look for may run the gamut from paper records to computer hardware and software. Of course, in both burglaries and larcenies, any recovered stolen property is physical evidence. However, it must be noted that cash is an exception absent other evidence linking it to the crime. Burglary and larceny also are distinguishable on the basis of their time of occurrence. Victims become aware of the former quite soon after they have taken place, but certain larcenies may be undetected by victims for an extended period.

All larceny victims must be thoroughly and carefully interviewed. They alone can provide information about the way in which the theft occurred, and only by getting those details can an MO be determined. With this information, the agency's MO files should be searched. Furthermore, since one objective of a larceny investigation is the recovery of the stolen property, victims must be asked for more than a general description of the property; they need to describe any unusual characteristics that will help identify that property.

The foregoing steps are critical in larceny cases. True, the basic techniques used to solve them are pretty much the same as those employed in other investigations, but a difference is worth noting. In thefts where there are no witnesses, the case solution rate tends to be low. Thus in these situations, when there is no descriptive data on possible suspects, what arrests are made often result from investigators' ability to first recover the stolen property, then work backwards.

Consequently, at the outset of many larceny cases, it is information rather than physical evidence that is needed for the investigation to go forward. Based on the MO, and any information possibly gotten from the MO files search, places frequented by thieves known to operate in the way in which a particular theft occurred might be put under physical surveillance. Confidential informants should be contacted for what they already know or might hear. With good descriptive data on the stolen property, pawn shops should be visited, and known fences questioned.

If the volume of reported larcenies is great enough, and the dollar value of the stolen property is high enough, a sting operation might be considered. However, in suggesting either a sting or long-term surveillance, investigators should borrow a page from the business world by thinking in terms of the benefits to be derived compared to the operation's cost. A successful sting or long-term surveillance requires an expenditure of both personnel and funds; therefore, using either or both has to be justified in relation to the hoped-for results.

Stolen mail and equipment recovered by Postal Inspectors from a letter carrier's home. (*Courtesy* U.S. Postal Inspection Service)

To illustrate, the New York City region had been plagued by a series of thefts from trucks and warehouses. In the opinion of federal officials, about $1 billion worth of consumer goods had been stolen from cargo shipments in New York and New Jersey. The involvement of both states prompted the FBI and New Jersey State Police to set up a cargo theft task force to identify professional cargo thieves whose primary targets were warehouses and truck shipments. The bureau also opened and operated for nineteen months a Garfield, New Jersey, business ostensibly engaged in buying stolen goods. Thieves would visit and negotiate a price for their goods. The objectives were to identify and arrest the thieves and collect evidence for prosecution. However, it also was important to avoid doing anything that would create a demand for stolen goods. Consequently, the only people from whom the business would buy were those identified as cargo thieves by undercover agents or confidential informants, and no more than one stolen load would be bought from any one thief. After recovering an estimated $38 million worth of merchandise, more than sixty individuals and small gangs were arrested and charged on September 17, 1996.[14]

The fact that larceny cases often have to be worked in reverse, that is, the goods are recovered before investigators can look for suspects, adds to the importance of learning as much as possible about the stolen property's characteristics so that it can be identified. This is especially true in the case of stolen art works, with which investigators may encounter additional complications, one of which is theft to order for purely private collectors. Since this minimizes the likelihood of recovery, it also greatly reduces the probability of an arrest and prosecution. However, this is not the only problem.

Experts estimate international traffic in stolen, smuggled, and looted art at between $4.5 and $6 billion a year, with a recovery rate of only 5 percent. In 1994, insurance companies paid claims of almost $1 billion for such losses in Great Britain alone. The low recovery rate in these cases is largely because art thieves know both their art and where to find markets for the sale of stolen or smuggled works. Then, too, defining what constitutes stolen art is problematic and compounded by the fact that from a historical perspective so much valuable art has been taken by the Roman, Hapsburg, and Napoleonic empires, the Nazi occupation forces, and the Soviet Army as "spoils of war."[15]

Despite these difficulties, among the leads to be pursued by stolen art investigators is contact with the FBI for data that may be available in the bureau's National Stolen Art File, a program implemented within the Laboratory Division in May 1979. The Stolen Art File consists of a computerized index of both stolen and recovered art as reported by local law enforcement agencies. It also contains data and photographs of art objects for which the origin and ownership are either unknown or in question. As of May 1989, when the file contained nearly 5,000 art objects, plans were underway to expand its capabilities, refine its computer coding, and improve both its speed and accuracy.[16]

Among the various steps already discussed relative to larceny investigations is contact with pawn shops, who by law must keep records of their transactions and known fences. In most cases thieves want to sell what they steal. Therefore, buyers or receivers of stolen goods also are parties to the theft and may be subject to arrest and prosecution. However, just as there is a need to show that the thief intended to steal, for the crime of receiving there must be a showing that the receiver had knowledge, or at least a reason to believe, that the property being offered was stolen. Without evidence to support this element of the offense, it is almost impossible to charge let alone convict anyone.

Shoplifting is larceny; the victims are retail merchants. Most often the subjects are detained on the premises, and the investigations are handled by the merchant's security officers or other store employees. Occasionally, they are conducted by the police, usually patrol officers. The detention of shoplifters is based on a reasonable suspicion that they have stolen merchandise for which they have not paid; therefore, they have in their possession what amounts to physical evidence. The recovery of that evidence, necessary for a prosecution, must be handled with great care, especially if the police are involved.

The stolen property's dollar value may be such that the offense is a misdemeanor, and the Fourth Amendment's warrant provisions on searches and seizures would apply if there is police involvement. That these provisions do not apply to private persons would not preclude an innocent person from suing the merchant for false arrest and imprisonment, and possibly for an invasion of privacy. As a result, shoplifting investigations must establish that one or more credible witnesses saw the subject taking the goods, for which he or she has no proof of purchase, the items are sold on the victim's premises, and they can be identified as the merchant's property by virtue of sales or price tags, labels, or some other positive means of identification.

MOTOR VEHICLE THEFT

Motor vehicle theft, which includes the theft of heavy equipment, is but another form of larceny. Although the elements may vary slightly from state to state, the crime of motor vehicle theft consists of the intentional taking or transporting of a vehicle by someone without the owner's permission. As for motive, the five main reasons to steal a motor vehicle are to go joyriding, sell it, use it for transportation in connection with the commission of another crime, strip it for its parts or as an act of vandalism, or chop it up and use or sell its components (called a chop-shop operation).

As with so many larcenies, witnesses will be hard to find. Therefore, once a theft has been reported, the focus is on the vehicle's recovery in the hope that it will contain at least some physical evidence that will lead to a suspect. The first step in the recovery process is to find the stolen vehicle; the second is to identify it.

Not surprisingly, patrol personnel usually are the ones who locate stolen vehicles by being both alert and observant. They look for vehicles whose driver's side door glass is broken or altogether missing, those with missing or damaged door locks or missing license plates or parts, or those parked away from the normal flow of traffic for a period of time. Other indicators that a vehicle may have been stolen would be an accumulation of parking tickets, clean license plates on a dirty vehicle or dirty ones on a clean vehicle, and mismatched front and rear license plates. In addition, a driver whose actions arouse suspicion may be operating a stolen vehicle, and a byproduct of stopping that driver may be noticing that the vehicle identification number (VIN) plate is improperly secured.

As for identification, at one time vehicles had motor numbers stamped into engine blocks. This necessitated developing a methodology to detect altered numbers. In 1954, U.S. manufacturers adopted a new system of vehicle identification numbers, and in 1968, they agreed to have them uniformly placed on the left side of the dash, where they could be seen through the windshield, and on the federal safety certification label that is found on either the driver's side door or the doorpost. Some few exceptions were made for luxury vehicles. Of greater importance to investigators is the fact that as of October 1997, VINs also will be required on front and rear bumpers, front fenders, rear quarter panels, doors, hoods, and trunk lids.

Since VINs are listed on motor vehicle registrations, the information should be available from victims. Being able to match VINs on stolen vehicles with those recovered is essential for identification purposes. A VIN consists of a combination of numbers and letters, each with its own significance. They are used to denote the following:

Nation of origin

Manufacturer

Specific make

Type of restraint system

Car line

Body type

Engine description

A digit for checking purposes

Model year

Assembly plant

Production sequence

The normal assumption is that a vehicle actually has been stolen, not that the owner has disposed of it to collect insurance, or to avoid payments owed or repossession by a finance company. Consequently, victim interviews and the ways in which victims respond are especially important. Significant questions for which answers must be obtained are as follows:

What is the license plate number, and what is the vehicle's description, including information about any noticeable dents or scratches, cracked or broken glass, and the type or types and location(s) of radio antennae.

Is the vehicle's registration kept in the vehicle itself or on the owner's person?

Where did the victim last see the vehicle?

Who was the last person to use it?

When last seen, was the vehicle unlocked, and were the keys left in the ignition?

Who other than the victim was permitted to operate it?

Was that person the operator at the time the vehicle was reported stolen?

Does the victim owe any money on the vehicle to either a bank, finance company, or mechanic?

Is the vehicle equipped with any special equipment such as wheels, tires, a sound system, or lights?

Are there any decals or other similar items displayed in any windows or on bumpers?

Were there any items in either the glove compartment or trunk that would help identify the vehicle?

A recovered stolen vehicle must be treated as a crime scene and processed accordingly. If it was broken into, there may be tool or other marks; it must be dusted for fingerprints. A search should be made for possible hairs or fibers, cigarette butts or chewing gum in ash trays, or papers of any kind that the thief might inadvertently have left behind that may offer leads that will help with his or her identification. If the thief gained access by breaking glass, some traces of blood may be found. All recovered physical evidence needs to be carefully collected and preserved, and when appropriate, submitted for laboratory examination.

Any combination of physical evidence that may be collected and a recovered vehicle's condition may suggest likely suspects. For instance, a vehicle recovered reasonably close to where the victim left it, with such things as candy wrappers or beer cans inside, might point to joyriding as the motive. One found in an out-of-the-way location with virtually no damage other than that caused when it was stolen, or one that was deliberately set on fire, may well have been used as transportation in connection with the commission of another crime. The theft of well-maintained, undamaged, popular makes or styles may signal the careful selection of motor vehicles by a gang that steals to order for resale and possibly export. In many ways, the MO of the latter type of thief is not too dissimilar from that of one who steals automobiles for stripping or chop-shop operations.

DANGEROUS DRUGS AND CONTROLLED SUBSTANCES

There are different levels of activity and different crimes connected with dangerous drugs and controlled substances. The range of offenses extends from an individual's use through manufacturing and importing with possessing for sale and wholesaling in between. Although many gangs and individuals engaged in the drug trade do not hesitate to use violence, and users can die from too pure or impure narcotics or an overdose, the underlying crimes are not classified as violent.

Some drug offenses, such as those involving users or possibly even street-corner pushers, frequently can be and are dealt with by patrol officers or plainclothes personnel. However, the nature and level of some drug activities may require not only a high degree of skill and sophistication on the investigators' part, but also the cooperation of federal, state, and local agencies. This is particularly true of cases involving major importers, manufacturers or processors, wholesalers, and distributors. This broad category includes organizations whose primary activity revolves around controlled substances. It also applies to others, such as organized crime groups (which we examine in Chapter 17), whose involvement with drugs is but one of their many so-called business enterprises.

Owing to the nature and varying levels of activity, it is helpful to know something about both the main categories of drugs and the organizations involved with their ultimate distribution and sale. First, not all drugs are illegal per se. However, real concern arises when otherwise legal narcotics are used by individuals to the extent that they become physically or psychologically dependent upon them. For example, a physician's prescribing the temporary limited use of morphine to deaden a patient's pain, or cough syrup with codeine to help a patient deal with a bad cough, is not illegal. Neither is there anything illegal about drinking tea, coffee, or cola beverages, all of which contain caffeine.

Drugs and controlled substances generally are classified into five main categories: cannabis, narcotics, stimulants, hallucinogens, and depressants, each with one or more subdivisions.

Cannabis	Marijuana, hashish, hashish oil
Narcotics	Opium (from which morphine and codeine are derived), meperidine, hydromorphone
Stimulants	Nicotine, caffeine, amphetamine, methamphetamine, cocaine
Hallucinogens	LSD, Ecstasy, peyote, psilocybin mushrooms
Depressants	Barbiturates, benzodiazepines

Investigators are primarily concerned with organizations or persons considered to be major manufacturers or importers. Manufacturing and importing tend to go together, but the ways in which drugs are imported can vary. They can be hidden on aircraft and ships for recovery upon arrival or brought into the country by crew members who may be able to bypass U.S. Customs.

Next they focus on wholesalers, who may cut pure narcotics to increase volume and profits, and subwholesalers. The former can make distribution of multiple kilos of drugs; subwholesalers sell in single kilo quantities. Below subwholesalers are local dealers who buy in single kilos and then sell fractions thereof to street dealers, often referred to as

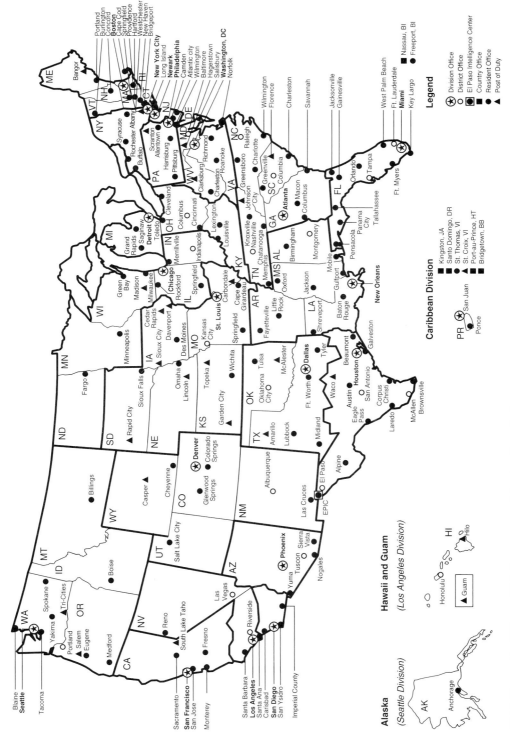

DEA Domestic Offices. (U.S. Department of Justice, Drug Enforcement Administration)

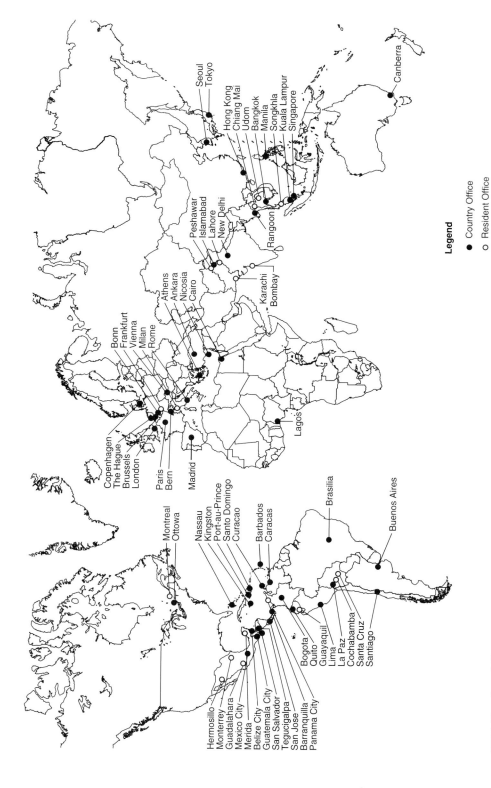

DEA Foreign Offices. (U.S. Department of Justice, Drug Enforcement Administration)

Clandestine drug laboratory crime scene.
(*Courtesy* Drug Enforcement Administration)

street-corner pushers. At the bottom of the rung are the runners, who make deliveries, and the lookouts, whose job it is to alert their bosses when they see or suspect a police presence in the area.

Most investigations are in response to a report of a specific crime. In contrast, drug investigations are proactive. They are designed both to prevent the sale and use of drugs and to arrest the sellers or users. The wide acceptance of this approach does not mean that the elements of the offenses of selling and using are identical in all jurisdictions. Degrees of seriousness for other crimes tend to be based on such factors as the perpetrator's intent and the severity of the victim's injury or loss. In drug cases, quantity is a key factor, particularly in relation to the arrest of street dealers and users. For example, suppose an arrested person has in his or her possession 10 grams of cocaine. In some states, the only charge for so small an amount might be illegal possession; in others, the charge might be possession with intent to sell or distribute.[17]

An acceptable investigative technique in street dealing cases is for undercover officers to buy and then arrest the seller, or to be wired so that the entire transaction can be monitored, and possibly even recorded, by other investigators who then make the arrest. If used, great care must be taken for two reasons. First, there can be considerable risk to the buyers if sellers suspect that they are police officers, let alone that the entire transaction is being overheard. Second, under these circumstances, it is highly probable that sellers will claim entrapment. Therefore, if under-cover personnel are to make the buy, to defend against such an allegation, they will need to show the defendant's predisposition to commit the crime.

The covert nature of drug activities and the tight controls exercised over those involved with drug dealing organizations mean that successful investigations largely depend on investigators' ability to get information and develop intelligence. They need to find out about the sources of the drugs, the methods used to supply the various sales organizations, and what networks are used for their distribution. They also have to be able to track money received and spent by those organizations. In essence, there are but two ways in which to get this information: by developing confidential informants or inserting undercover personnel into the orga-nization. Although there obviously is an element of risk to either course of action, it may be less if informants can be used.

Users, lookouts, runners, and street dealers are potential informants. Arrested, they may be willing to cooperate in exchange for a reduction in the charge, but only prosecutors, not investigators, can agree to such arrangements. However, realizing that lookouts, runners, and even street dealers are low-level members of the enterprise, investigators look for persons who may be higher in the organization and can possibly be devel-oped as informants. Persons without any apparent means of support who nevertheless spend money freely for such things as clothes, cars, travel, and entertainment, and especially those who occasionally use forged doc-uments to hide their true identities, may be at the supplier level, and their development could prove most helpful.

As for the investigation itself, information may be gotten from a complainant, victim, or even a witness to a transaction, but information without actually having a controlled substance as physical evidence is vir-tually useless for purposes of prosecution. That prosecution may be impossible under these circumstances does not lessen the need to protect those sources of information.

Both electronic and physical surveillances are appropriate in these investigations. As we discussed earlier, any decision to employ either or both must take into account the resources that will be required if the surveillance is to be productive. Even if the resources are available, it is important to acknowledge that the results may be quite limited in view of the known use of word and hand codes and signs by those engaged in the drug trade. Despite these limitations, it may be possible to learn how lower-level operatives communicate with each other and with the next higher level. If this can be done, it may eventually lead to records on beepers, pagers, and telephone numbers used, which in turn, may lead to still more useful information.

Whether undercover investigators or confidential informants are used, their main goal should be to get information about street sellers' contacts and their sources of supply. In this connection, it is important to remember that though every effort is made to develop reliable informants who are compensated for their information, reality dictates that in drug cases in particular they occasionally may provide information that either is not true or is based on the informant's personal hidden agenda. Consequently, investigators should not act solely on the basis of informant-provided information; there should be independent corroboration.

At the outset of our discussion of dangerous drugs and controlled substances, we noted the frequent need for collaboration among agencies. This is due to the complexity of major drug investigations, the fact that drug trafficking may affect several jurisdictions, and the need for good intelligence. As a result, a task force approach may be the best and most effective solution, but only if at the time of its creation the lines of authority and areas of responsibility of each component are clearly delineated.

Drug cases, like all criminal investigations, need to be conducted with a view to the ultimate prosecution of the subjects. Therefore, for purposes of prosecution, these inquiries have to establish more than the ways in which dangerous drugs and controlled substances are moved. They also need to identify both those who actually do the moving and those who are in charge of or directly responsible for the particular operation.

To illustrate how far reaching drug activity can be, and the importance of investigators making full use of their resources, on October 1, 1996, the U.S. Attorney in Brooklyn, New York, announced that forty people, believed to be members of a crack-cocaine ring run by the Lucchese crime family, had been arrested. The ring reportedly was controlled by one James Galione, a "made" family member who took control in 1992. Particularly interesting was the fact that this appeared to be the first time that an organized crime family was involved with street-level drug dealing. The New York City Police Department and federal agencies, working together, relied on wiretaps, accounts of former drug dealers who cooperated with them after they themselves had been arrested, and surveillances.[18]

SUMMARY

The techniques used in working nonviolent crime cases are much the same as those employed in cases of violent crime. Crime scenes must be defined and protected, victims and witnesses located and interviewed, and evidence collected and preserved. However, despite the fundamental similarities, some differences do exist. Nonviolent crime victims may be unable to provide physical descriptions of perpetrators because either they had no face-to-face meeting or too much time passed between any such meeting and the realization that they had been victimized. There may not be any witnesses. This can make it more difficult to devlop good leads. Then, too, except for the occasional high-profile fraud or insider trading case, or cases involving celebrities, nonviolent crimes rarely attract so much attention that investigators feel pressured to solve them quickly.

In violent crimes, burglaries, or even motor vehicle thefts, tangible forms of physical evidence may be found at the crime scene. Such evidence may not be readily apparent in fraud or white-collar crimes since it tends to consist of records either in hard copy or on computer disks. But once located, those records can provide leads that must be pursued and that eventually may lead to the subject's identification and apprehension.

Burglaries and larcenies are different. Like all investigations, whether of violent or nonviolent crimes, the inquiry's departure point is the crime scene and a search for physical evidence. The physical evidence found in these cases may be greater than that found initially in fraud and white-collar crimes. The goal in burglaries and larcenies is twofold: to recover the stolen property and arrest those responsible. As a result, even if a burglar's or thief's MO is recognizable, investigating these offenses often means concentrating on the recovery as a way of getting to the subject. Sting operations may be helpful in solving burglary and larceny cases if there is enough activity to justify allocating the necessary resources. As a rule, case closings based on solving nonviolent crimes tend to be low. They are even lower when the stolen property consists of works of art since these thefts often are made for private buyers, not for public display.

By definition, motor vehicle thefts are larcenies. Unlike other larcenies, however, there rarely is a crime scene in the accepted sense of the term. If there is any physical evidence, it obviously cannot be collected until the vehicle is found. Intent, an element of the offense, may also be a factor in a vehicle's recovery and condition. For instance, there is a good deal of difference between stealing a vehicle to go joyriding, stealing for export and resale, and stealing for use in committing another crime.

All police agencies want to prevent crimes, but nowhere can they justify being proactive to the extent that they can in dangerous drugs and controlled substances cases. By the same token, but for organized crime investigations, nowhere is there a greater need for good intelligence. A wide range of investigative techniques are needed, including a collaborative effort on the part of affected agencies, the use of physical and electronic surveillances, and the possible use of undercover investigators or confidential informants. Although sound, firsthand information about both methods used and persons involved is highly desirable, agency supervisory personnel must carefully weigh the risks of undercover operations or informant use against the benefits as part of the decision-making process.

REVIEW QUESTIONS

1. Why are nonviolent crimes different from violent ones in how they are handled and the results expected?
2. What is a white-collar crime?
3. Give an example of a high-profile white-collar crime.
4. What are the main objectives of property crime investigations?
5. How can a business perpetrate a fraud?
6. Name the four main points of the Bank Secrecy Act of 1978.
7. Define burglary, and distinguish it from larceny.
8. What is a VIN?
9. What are the five principal categories of dangerous drugs and controlled substances?
10. Name three important bits of information that investigators have to get for prosecutors in drug cases.

NOTES

1. Edwin H. Sutherland, *White Collar Crime* (Hinsdale, IL: Dryden Press, 1949), p. 9.
2. "Authorities Break Credit-Card Fraud Ring," *New York Times,* February 8, 1996, p. B5.
3. Ibid.
4. "F.B.I. and Russian Police Cooperate to Bring Fraud Charges," *New York Times,* March 1, 1996, p. B5.
5. "Bank Official Tipped F.B.I. to Suspected Loan Scheme," *New York Times,* March 21, 1996, p. D2.
6. "Ex-Employee of Philip Morris Pleads Guilty to Bank Fraud," *New York Times,* June 6, 1996, p. D2.
7. *New York Times,* April 12, 1996, p. D2.
8. *New York Times,* May 8, 1996, p. B3.
9. *The Boston Globe,* July 10, 1996, p. 40.

10. "Insider Trading Costs Pair $27,000 in Fines," *The Boston Globe,* February 28, 1996, p. 47.

11. "Ex-Official of Bankers Trust Charged with Securities Fraud," *New York Times,* May 30, 1996, p. D3.

12. "46 Charged in Stock Fraud Sting by F.B.I.," *New York Times,* October 11, 1996, pp. D1, D4.

13. *Delk v. State,* 64 Miss. 77, 1 So. 9 (1880); *McIntosh v. State,* 105 Neb. 328, 180 N. W. 573 (1921); *State v. Slimgerland,* 19 Nev. 135, 7 P. 280 (1885).

14. "Agents Posing as 'Fences' Arrest 60 in Theft of Cargo," *New York Times,* September 18, 1996, p. B4.

15. "Art Theft Is Booming, Bringing an Effort to Respond," *New York Times,* November 20, 1995, pp. C11, C12.

16. Alice S. Cole, "The FBI's National Stolen Art File," *FBI Law Enforcement Bulletin,* Vol. 58, No. 5 (May 1989) pp. 10–12.

17. *U.S. v. Russell,* 411 U.S. 423 (1972).

18. "Officials Say Mafia Ran Crack Ring in Brooklyn," *New York Times,* October 2, 1996, p. B6.

Chapter 17

❖

Conspiracy
and Organized Crime

Any definition of the word *conspiracy* makes it clear that more than one person must be involved in a plan. Thus if two or more people plan to commit a fraudulent act, rob a bank, steal motor vehicles, or have a surprise party for a friend, they are participants in a conspiracy. Our concern, of course, is with those conspiracies that are directed toward the commission of a crime.

The tendency to associate criminal conspiracies with organized crime is understandable since the term *organized crime* clearly implies the involvement of two or more people. However, to think of conspiracies only in connection with the more traditional type of organized crime, such as the Sicilian Mafia, also known as La Cosa Nostra, the oldest and best-known organized crime group in the United States, is a mistake. To do so is to ignore other organized groups such as the Asian Triads, some with Tong connections, the Columbian drug cartels, Jamaican posses, outlaw motorcycle gangs, the "Russian Mafia," and various street gangs like the Crips, Bloods, El Rukins, and Vice Lords, some of which have begun organizing branches throughout the country. Consequently, we first need to consider conspiracies, then how they relate to both traditional and other organized crime groups.

CONSPIRACY

A criminal conspiracy consists of an agreement between two or more people to perform an illegal act, with a specific criminal intent, accompanied by an overt act in furtherance of the agreement. The Federal Criminal Conspiracy Statute requires proof that one or more of those persons agreeing to perform an illegal act did in fact do something to effect the object of the conspiracy.[1] For example, three people merely agreeing to rob a bank would not satisfy the requirements, but if one of them steals a car to be used in committing the robbery and escaping, the overt act element would be satisfied.

Does someone who knows of a plan to commit a crime, or who even approves of it, become a conspirator? No, not unless that person intends and agrees to cooperate according to a 1956 federal court ruling that held "Mere knowledge, approval of or acquiescence in the subject or purpose of the conspiracy, without an intention and agreement to cooperate in the crime is insufficient to constitute one a conspirator."[2] The need to show both a basic intention to agree and an act to effectuate the conspiracy's objective was reaffirmed in 1978.[3]

To illustrate this, arson of a clothing store in New York City's Harlem in December 1995 left eight people dead, one of whom was the perpetrator who had participated in demonstrations outside the store and later shot himself. Absent evidence linking his conduct in setting the fire to any other protesters, or to anyone who aided or directed him to start it, no conspiracy charges could be filed.[4]

There was no indication of gang involvement in the foregoing, but gang criminal activities have become a matter of increasing concern to law enforcement, and with good reason. In the spring of 1992, the National Institute of Justice sponsored a survey on gang crime. Police departments in seventy-nine of the largest U.S. cities and forty-three smaller ones were queried. All but seven of the largest cities and five of the smaller ones reported gang problems. Based on the responses, there were an estimated 249,324 gang members and 4,881 gangs reportedly responsible for 46,359 gang-related crimes and 1,072 gang-related homicides during the previous year.[5]

ORGANIZED CRIME

Law enforcement's primary goals are to prevent crimes, investigate those that have been committed, and apprehend those who are responsible for their commission. Nowhere is the emphasis on prevention greater than when dealing with organized crime, whether the organization is a traditional or a nontraditional one. This is largely due to the pervasive nature of their activities and their impact on society. As a result, to the extent that arrests can be made and charges can be filed for conspiracy, organized crime activity can be preempted.

This is by no means an easy task since proving a conspiracy requires evidence of both intent or agreement to commit a crime and an overt act in its furtherance, and there are practical and legal limits on what investigators can do. Among the resources available to them are electronic, physical, and photographic surveillances, and what might be called a form of sting by using reliable confidential informants or undercover personnel.

Among the most desirable resources for learning about plans are electronic surveillances and stings. From them overt acts can be determined, and moves can be made before the intended crime is committed. Although electronic surveillances can be initiated with careful planning and court authorization, their limitations must be recognized. They may be highly productive, but they also may be unproductive if conversations are guarded or unrelated to criminal activity. Therefore, the option of using reliable confidential informants or undercover investigators has to be considered.

In Chapter 9, we illustrated the value of good informants, yet developing them may not always be feasible when dealing with gangs or organized crime groups. Furthermore, their reliability may be questionable, or their own criminal records may be used by defense counsel at time of trial to challenge their credibility. In any event, when the use of either informants or undercover investigators is being considered, it is important to remember two things: the defense argument of entrapment, and the risk to informants or undercover personnel.

The U.S. Supreme Court has resolved the entrapment issue. If prosecutors can prove a defendant's predisposition to commit a crime, the entrapment defense will not lie.[6] For years, the Court repeatedly has recognized that deceptive strategies may be necessary when investigating "sophisticated crimes of a consensual nature," in these cases, referring particularly to drug transactions.[7] As for using confidential informants or undercover investigators as a means of getting information, no constitutional problem is encountered if someone misplaces his or her confidence in another person, which is a characteristic of undercover operations.[8]

Nevertheless, because of the personal risks inherent in any form of undercover activity, whether engaged in by informants or law enforcement personnel, the fifteen points comprising the guidelines established for their use at the federal level are worth noting.

1. What is the level of the activity's seriousness?
2. Are there any other techniques that could accomplish the same goal?
3. What is the likelihood of obtaining a viable criminal prosecution of substantial magnitude?
4. Is the proposal an efficient use of investigative resources?
5. Will the undercover operation produce evidence that can be used against the target?
6. What will be involved in the way of risk of harm or injury to innocent persons and undercover operatives?

7. Is there any possible civil liability on the government's part?

8. Is there any risk of harm to the reputations of innocent third parties?

9. Will confidential relationships be violated?

10. Will the target's entrapment and unauthorized government conduct be avoided?

11. How suitable are the confidential informants and undercover personnel for the operation?

12. What will be the type and degree of control exercised by the government's personnel over cooperating persons?

13. What roles are to be played by cooperating individuals and government agents?

14. What is the assessment of the overall plan in terms of minimizing the incidence of sensitive circumstances?

15. Do the plans create a risk of harm and intrusion?[9]

No matter the type of organization on which an organized crime investigation focuses, there are specific areas of interest. Learning about the group's organization, structure, and objectives, and how those objectives are reached, is important. Equally important is the ability to identify its members and to determine how influential are the persons whom the group controls or with whom it works.

The various ways in which street-gang members identify each other frequently can be used by investigators to identify specific gangs and their members. For instance, most commonly used are a particular style of dress, tattoos or other insignia, hand signals, and even graffiti. Gangs also tend to use graffiti to identify their "turf," or the geographic area that they control.

Street-gang graffiti is a form of intelligence for investigators, sometimes compared to information derived from organized crime telephone taps. A New York City incident shows graffiti's use for intelligence purposes in identifying a gang and its turf. A wall of Public School 149–207 bore the inscription: "HMC BK RTC" doodled over "Hit Squad Blood Gang 4-Life BRIMS." To the police, this was the Rolling Thirties sect of the Crips (RTC) saying that its turf had been invaded. For gangs, TOS means "terminate on sight"; 187, the Los Angeles Police Department's code for homicide, imported from California gangs, means murder.[10]

Collaboration by affected departments, sting operations, and undercover work can prove fruitful in dealing with gangs. The combined efforts of the FBI, DEA, Massachusetts and Connecticut State Police, and several northern Connecticut and western Massachusetts local police departments resulted in the April 12, 1996, arrest of thirteen members of the Diablos motorcycle gang, who were charged with being involved with violent drug and weapons activities. The sting was a fake motorcycle repair shop designed to attract gang members, who also were charged with murder-for-hire in conspiring to silence a police officer. An undercover FBI agent, posing as a "street tough," had been instructed by the alleged head of the Meridien, Connecticut, Diablos chapter to ensure that the man hired to kill the head of the Meridien Police Department's Narcotics Squad shot him in the head since he probably would be wearing a bullet-proof vest.[11]

Assuming that references to some crime groups as gangs means they lack organization or that their activities are limited is unwise. Some may take their cue from the Mafia on both counts, as was the case with a Queens, New York, group.

On June 19, 1996, after a two-year investigation by the FBI and New York City Police Department, a thirty-two-count racketeering indictment was handed down against fourteen gang members, all in their 20s. Among the counts were armed robberies, assaults, and arson fires during the preceding three years. The gang had semiautomatic weapons, police scanners, stolen automobiles used as getaway cars, and ski masks. Among the specific crimes charged were robbery (including four banks), arson, loan sharking, and assault. From the investigation, it was learned that this gang had managed to develop a criminal enterprise very much like the startup phase of better established organized crime groups, and the organization itself was not unlike a typical Mafia family. The gang's leaders tried to insulate themselves by recruiting people to commit crimes in their behalf while they avoided direct involvement.[12]

There is increasing concern with and a need to investigate Triads or Asian gangs' activities, some with Tong associations. Tongs, largely imported from China, are not new. Many, like the European guilds of medieval times, were organized to protect their members' interests. If one Tong's member offended a member of another so as to cause a "loss of face," a war would follow. Tongs still exist to protect their members. Those who feel the need for an occasional threat or use of force find a Triad relationship to be worthwhile.

Asian gangs engage in various activities, among them robberies, protection rackets, and smuggling immigrants and narcotics into the United States. They will kidnap, torture, extort, and murder to either increase their profits or strengthen their grip on those with whom they have contact.

Asian gang investigations are even more complex than those of other organized crime groups. The nature of their activities and the ways in which they deal with victims and victims' families instill so high a degree of fear that victims are afraid to complain. This also makes it difficult to recruit and develop informants. In addition, Asians are a rather closed society, preferring to keep embarrassing matters like criminal activities quiet and within the local Asian community. Finally, race and language problems can make it hard to initiate undercover operations.

Nevertheless, as the following two cases show, Asian gangs have been successfully investigated.

On February 23, 1996, eight racketeering indictments naming sixty-four New York City Chinatown gangsters were unsealed in a U.S. district court. Among the charges were smuggling more than 350 people into the United States from China since 1992 at a charge of $30,000 per person, having held more than 150 for ransom, and having tortured them until relatives or friends in this country or China paid the amounts demanded. They also were charged with kidnapping a woman and holding her until a $38,000 ransom was paid, murdering members of rival gangs, and the robbery and extortion of four businesses and restaurants in New York and New Jersey from which they got about $200,000.[13]

Less than a month later, on March 12, 1996, six Chinese immigrants from Fujian Province were indicted and charged with selling heroin and offering buyers significant discounts in return for forged passports that could be used to help smuggle illegal immigrants into the United States. In this case, there were authorized telephone taps, and Chinese-speaking investigators succeeded in infiltrating the group.[14]

Evidence of organized crime's existence in the United States, largely in the form of the Sicilian Mafia, goes back to the early 1900s. However, as time passed, and especially from 1920 to 1933 when the law prohibited the manufacture, importation, transportation, or sale of alcoholic beverages, other groups, mainly Irish and Jewish, appeared on the scene. Aside from bootlegging to satisfy the public's demand for alcohol, and occasional gang wars to protect their "territories," organized crime activity tended to focus on various forms of gambling and prostitution.

At the time, the federal government's main interest was bootlegging; it violated federal law, and taxes were not being paid on the profits earned. Otherwise, organized crime generally was considered a matter of local concern since police departments knew it existed and who the leaders were—so much so, in fact, that it was not unusual for some police personnel, judges, and politicians to be on a gang's payroll. Parenthetically, bribing the police and other public officials was, and still is, a hallmark of organized crime. Despite this awareness, it was not until the discovery of a meeting of Mafia bosses in upstate New York in November 1957 that law enforcement agencies, from the federal level downward, began to understand the threat that organized crime represented.

Prohibition's repeal eliminated the need for bootlegging, but not the Mafia. Prostitution remained a source of income. Gambling operations, including bookmaking, lotteries, and casinos, expanded both within and without the United States. In fact, New York area organized crime family involvement with the startup, development, and operations of the early Las Vegas casinos led to the establishment of Nevada's Gaming Commission in an effort to keep them out. These same families also were firmly entrenched in Cuba's casinos during Fulgencio Batista's presidency, before his overthrow by Fidel Castro. Loansharking, labor racketeering, and "consulting" also became lucrative activities. Initially, the older family heads avoided involvement with drugs. That began to change as younger members assumed leadership positions, as noted in Chapter 16 with the Lucchese family's involvement with street-level drug sales. Mob families continue to limit their competition. They also operate seemingly legitimate businesses as a front to give them a reportable source of income for tax purposes and for use in laundering money.

Concern with money laundering prompted a panel comprising members of the U.S. House of Representatives' Banking Committee to summon witnesses in February 1996. The latter testified that drug dealers and other criminals move as much as $500 billion a year through the banking system. Edward W. Kelley Jr., a Federal Reserve Bank governor, estimated that from $300 to $500 billion annually goes through U.S. banks.[15]

To better appreciate what organized crime investigations entail, one has to understand the Mafia's organization and the extent of its operations. The greater New York area is a good place to begin. Controlled by five groups, the Gambino, Columbo, Bonanno, Lucchese, and Genovese families, each has its own head or "godfather." The Genovese family has been described as the "Mafia's mightiest faction."[16]

According to Lewis D. Schiliro, Special Agent in Charge of the FBI's New York City Office's Criminal Division, the Genovese family's growing power within organized crime made it a priority target for investigation. This one family reportedly has about 300 "soldiers" or made members (those who have been sworn to secrecy) and another 1,000 associates who assist with its criminal activities. In addition to traditional organized crime activities, the Genovese family has been involved with extortion, labor racketeering in the construction industry, New York City's garbage hauling, and hiring practices for the Jacob K. Javits Convention Center. It also has influenced practices at the Fulton Fish Market, had a good deal of control over Little Italy's Feast of San Genaro, and has been involved with labor racketeering and extortion at both Port Elizabeth and Port Newark, New Jersey.[17]

A number of factors have contributed to the success of Mafia investigations, whether in the New York area or elsewhere. True, affected law enforcement agencies cooperated, but in reality it was a combination of investigative techniques that resulted in a number of key convictions, not the least of which was that of John Gotti, convicted of thirteen counts in a U.S. District Court in April 1992. Court-authorized electronic surveillances, physical surveillances, undercover personnel, and confidential informants all played a role.

Gotti, known as the "Teflon Don" because of the number of times he had been tried but not convicted, had engineered the death of his predecessor as the Gambino family head so that he could take over. The FBI used technical and physical surveillances, but developing Sammy "the

Bull" Gravano as a confidential informant and the information he provided were key to Gotti's 1992 conviction.

For years, Vincent Gigante was the suspected head of the Genovese family; he also was thought to be the most powerful Mafia boss in America. In addition to the Genovese organization's previously described activities, two indictments (one in 1990 and another in 1993) had been pending against him charging illegal payoffs relative to an ironworkers' union and conspiracy to extort involving window manufacturing and installation companies doing business with the New York City Housing Authority. The Genovese family also was considered to be the wealthiest of all the Mafia organizations in the United States.[18]

In the Genovese case, investigators had to overcome an obstacle completely different from anything encountered with Gotti, despite the cooperation of federal and local law enforcement and the use of well-recognized investigative techniques. Gigante had managed to escape trial allegedly because he was mentally incompetent. Under physical surveillance, he was seen wandering his neighborhood in pajamas and a bathrobe. However, on August 28, 1996, U.S. District Court Judge Eugene H. Nickerson declared Gigante mentally competent to stand trial on murder and racketeering charges calling his behavior an "elaborate deception."[19]

We already have discussed the principal areas of interest to organized crime investigators. However, with the end of prohibition and disappearance of the Irish and Jewish gangs that were in competition with the Sicilian Mafia, attention has focused on the latter. As a result, it pays to look at the organization's characteristics.

There is good reason to refer to each different group as a "family." First, each has a definite hierarchy. The "Don," or family head, is assisted by a "consigliere" or counselor; intermediate ranks oversee the work of the "soldiers." Each member takes an oath (omerta) that swears him to secrecy and obedience. Discipline is extremely tight; a breach can mean death. There may be a trial or initiation period for those chosen for membership to ensure their willingness to obey orders when told to commit a crime.

Membership is considered a career and is restricted; one does not simply decide to join. Applicants must be sponsored by an existing member, usually a relative or close friend, and satisfy the ethnic factor to qualify for the "Sicilian Mafia." Meyer Lansky, trusted by the various family heads and considered responsible for the Mafia's financial successes during the 1940s and 1950s, never became a made member because he was Jewish.

To assume that with Gotti's confinement and Gigante's trial the Mafia no longer is active or poses a threat would be a mistake. Although it is true, according to James Moody, a deputy assistant director of the FBI and former chief, Organized Crime Section, that it technically no longer operates in Philadelphia and has almost stopped being active in Milwaukee, St. Louis, and Kansas City, and that there has been a substantial reduction in the number of active family units, it nevertheless remains strong in the Buffalo, New York, area and active in New York, New Jersey, Boston, Los Angeles, and San Francisco.[20]

In addition to continuing investigations of Mafia activities, investigators now are confronted by Russian and Chinese organized crime families that, in many ways, are similar to the Mafia. Neither can the possibility of the Russians and Mafia working together be ignored. This has prompted the FBI to create squads focusing on Russian and Chinese activities much as they have on La Cosa Nostra. The Russian government's cooperation, gotten by the FBI's Legal Attache in Moscow, has proved helpful in learning more about Russian organized crime activity in the United States.

The FBI's New York Russian Squad, formed in May 1995, has received help from the Russian Ministry of Internal Affairs (MVD). Based on information received, there is evidence of Russian organized crime activity in New York, Denver, Miami, Los Angeles, and Boston, as well as in suburban New Jersey and Toronto, Canada.[21]

The Russian–Mafia connection is not new. Federal criminal trials in the 1980s found evidence of a relationship between the Columbo organization, one of New York's five Mafia families, and the Russians. However, illustrative of the value of informants was the 1996 testimony of Anthony S. Casso before the U.S. Senate's Permanent Subcommittee on Investigations. Casso, formerly the acting head of the Lucchese organization turned informant and was scheduled to testify about murders and violent conspiracies arranged by American organized crime families with Russian immigrant gangs. Among other subjects, he was to testify about how New York families used force to cash in on such activities as gasoline tax frauds and gasoline bootlegging developed by the Russians. The latter reportedly provided the brains behind these schemes, and the Mafia, the force. Michael Franzese, a Columbo family captain turned informant, also was to testify about a multimillion-dollar gasoline excise tax fraud devised by the Russian and Columbo gangs. A third informant, identified only as a Russian criminal, was scheduled to tell the subcommittee about Russian organized crime efforts to extort money from Russians playing in the National Hockey League. It appears that after the 1991 collapse of the Soviet Union more than 4,000 Russians came to the United States, where, operating mainly in New York and New Jersey, they engage in a range of crimes, particularly international drug trafficking and money laundering.[22]

These crimes are not the Russian Mafia's only interests. In June 1995, Vyacheslav Kirillovich Ivankov was arrested and, with four others, indicted on a charge of conspiring to extort $3.5 million from two Russian emigres. Ivankov was alleged to be more than a mere member of Russian organized crime; he reportedly was sent to the United States to manage and control Russian organized crime activities here.[23] On July 8, 1996, he and three codefendants were convicted of extortion by a jury in a U.S. District Court in Brooklyn, New York.[24]

Earlier in this chapter, we commented in general on Asian gangs and the nature of their activities, which include importing heroin and smuggling illegal Chinese immigrants into the United States. According to Moody, these operations are controlled by the Hong Kong Triads and Chinese American Tongs that, in the FBI's belief, use violent street gangs such as the Ghost Shadows and White Tigers as enforcers. The Triads, which predate the Sicilian Mafia, charge fees ranging from $30,000 to $50,000 per person for smuggling people into the United States. Investigators also have learned that three New York City Tongs are engaged in extortion, allegedly demanding as much as $100,000 for permission to open a restaurant, and $20,000 a week from those who want to operate gambling dens in Chinatown.[25]

Difficult as organized crime investigations are, those involving Asian organized crime are even harder. As with all organized crime investigations, surveillances alone are not enough. Efforts have to be made to develop confidential informants, and thought must be given to the possible infiltration of undercover personnel.

In this respect, Asian organized crime cases can pose unique obstacles. Risks to confidential informants and undercover investigators aside, developing informants or infiltrating a group is not easy. As we discussed earlier in this chapter, Asian gang investigations have to deal with the closeness of that society, racial differences, and language barriers. All can add to the hardships investigators have to overcome.

For instance, Asian society not only tends to be closed, it also is quite formal. Strangers, regardless of race, are not easily or readily welcomed, let alone accepted. Racially speaking, any number of investigators might be used for physical surveillances of Mafia families, but because of appearance one cannot expect investigators who are not ethnic Asians to discreetly participate in this type of surveillance. In fact, even ethnic Asians could be handicapped by language when wiretaps or electronic surveillances are used. Irrespective of race, an investigator fluent in Mandarin Chinese may find it difficult to fully understand Cantonese, and vice versa.

Parenthetically, the need for language fluency and the proper use of idiomatic expressions or colloquialisms is a significant factor not limited to Asian gang investigations. For example, there are differences between the Italian spoken in Sicily and that spoken in Northern Italy, or between Russian and Ukrainian. Consequently, important as language fluency is for investigators monitoring wiretaps or other forms of electronic surveillance, if a decision is made to infiltrate, it is critical. No matter the willingness of an informant or undercover investigator to become a member of an organized crime group where a foreign language may be spoken, the inability to converse in the correct dialect and use customary idioms or colloquialisms is more than a giveaway; it greatly increases the risk to both the investigator and the investigation.

SUMMARY

The nature of conspiracy makes such investigations difficult. First, the number of people planning a crime may be very limited despite the number that ultimately may be involved in its execution. Second, to prove a conspiracy, there must be evidence of an overt act in furtherance of the planned offense. Therefore, successful conspiracy investigations may largely depend on the use of electronic and physical surveillances, and possibly on information provided by confidential informants. Nevertheless, the possibility that a conspiracy investigation actually can help prevent the commission of a more serious crime should not be ignored.

Although conspiracy is not limited to organized crime gangs, the tendency is to associate it with them because of the number of people involved and because their activities are planned, often on a long-term basis. Then, too, just as there is a tendency to associate conspiracy with organized crime, people tend to associate the term *organized crime* with the Sicilian Mafia even though it actually applies to any criminal organization whose operations are controlled by a hierarchy. Therefore, whether investigating conspiracy as an offense by itself, or in conjunction with organized crime activities, the roles of street, certain motorcycle, and Asian gangs, as well as those of the Sicilian and Russian Mafia must be included.

These cases are not easy to work. Virtually all the characteristics of good investigators described earlier come into play. Victims of and witnesses to organized crime activities understandably are afraid to give information or otherwise cooperate. In fact, the fear may be so great that some victims will not even report their victimization. Under these circumstances, investigators must exercise other options, however limited, in trying to collect evidence.

Court-authorized wiretaps and other forms of electronic surveillance, supplemented by physical surveillance, can be invaluable. However, knowing that these techniques are used, organized crime groups have become more cautious regarding what they say, where they go, and with whom they are seen. This does not mean abandoning these investigative tools; it merely recognizes their limitations.

As a result, investigators resort to using other methods, one of which may be a sting. Although such operations can be very productive given the right conditions, investigators cannot ignore the resources that will be needed if a sting is to succeed. Success requires an investment of personnel, money, and time; therefore, before proposing the use of a sting, investigators should do a cost–benefit analysis that will justify the proposal.

Developing reliable confidential informants or using undercover investigators to infiltrate gangs, Triads, or families undoubtedly is the best way to get information and evidence about their activities; it also involves risk to the informants or undercover personnel. For one thing, their appearance must be consistent with that of the group members, and the possible need for foreign language fluency also has to be considered. If this is not done, and informants or undercover personnel are identified before arrests are made and trials begin, their likely deaths or serious injury cannot be ruled out, and the investigation will be compromised. If their use is disclosed at trial, defense counsel probably will allege entrapment and assuredly will challenge informants' credibility. Thus any decision to use informants or undercover investigators must be carefully weighed and thoroughly analyzed before proceeding.

REVIEW QUESTIONS

1. How many people are needed to constitute a conspiracy?
2. Is merely agreeing to commit a crime enough to constitute a conspiracy? If not, what else is required?
3. What is one benefit of conspiracy investigations?
4. Explain the usefulness of electronic surveillance in conspiracy investigations.
5. Is street-gang activity limited to big cities, or does it occur in smaller communities as well?
6. In what ways do street-gang members identify themselves?
7. What factors do the federal guidelines take into account in deciding on the use of confidential informants or undercover personnel?
8. Why are they important?
9. What organized crime groups exist in addition to the Mafia?
10. Under what circumstances can foreign language skills be critical to undercover investigators?

NOTES

1. U. S. C. A., Section 371.
2. *Cleaver v. U.S.,* 238 Fed. 2d 766, 771 (10th Cir., 1956).
3. *U.S. v. U.S. Gypsum Co.,* 438 U.S. 422, 443 n. 20, 98 S. Ct. 2864, 2876 n. 20, 57 L. Ed. 2d 854, 873 n. 20 (1978).

 4. "No Conspiracy Found in Fire That Killed 8," *New York Times,* February 27, 1996, pp. B1, B6.

 5. G. David Curry, Richard A. Ball, and Robert J. Fox, "Gang Crime and Law Enforcement Record Keeping," *Research in Brief,* NIJ, August 1994.

 6. *U.S. v. Russell,* 411 U.S. 423 (1972).

 7. *Lewis v. U.S.,* 385 U.S. 206 (1966); *Sherman v. U.S.,* 356 U.S. 369, 372 (1958); *Sorrells v. U.S.* 287 U.S. 435, 441 (1932).

 8. *Hoffa v. U.S.,* 385 U.S. 293, 302 (1966).

 9. Jay B. Stephens, "Setting the Sting, Minimizing the Risk," *Criminal Justice,* Vol. 1, No. 2 (Summer 1980), pp. 14–17, 38–39.

10. "Decoding Graffiti to Solve Bigger Crimes," *New York Times,* October 4, 1996, pp. B1, B7.

11. "FBI Net Snares 13 Members of Motorcycle Gang," *The Boston Globe,* April 13, 1996, pp. 13, 15.

12. "14 in a New Queens Gang Are Charged in 12 Crimes," *New York Times,* June 20, 1996, p. B3.

13. "64 Indicted as Gangsters in Chinatown," *New York Times,* February 24, 1996, pp. 23, 24.

14. "Heroin Indictments Link Drugs to Smuggling of Aliens," *New York Times,* March 13, 1996, p. B3.

15. "Mob Banking Activity Called Threat," *The Boston Globe,* February 29, 1996, p. 41.

16. "Secretive Genovese Clan Seemed Almost Immune from the Law," *New York Times,* August 29, 1996, p. B6.

17. Ibid.

18. "Strolls in Robe Notwithstanding, Mob Figure Must Stand Trial," *New York Times,* August 29, 1996, pp. B1, B6.

19. Ibid.

20. Peter Maas, "Who Is The Mob Today?" *Parade Magazine,* February 25, 1996, pp. 4–6.

21. Ibid.

22. "Former Lucchese Crime Boss Is to Testify on Russian Mob," *New York Times,* May 15, 1996, p. B7.

23. "Trial Looms for Man Held as Emigre Godfather," *New York Times,* March 17, 1996, p. 38.

24. *New York Times,* July 9, 1996, p. B3.

25. Peter Maas, "Who Is the Mob Today?" *Parade Magazine,* February 25, 1996, pp. 4–6.

Chapter 18

❖

Other Types
of Investigations

Many people, if not most, often equate the word *investigations* with crime although in Part I we noted that there are other types of inquiries. This tendency is largely due to two factors. First, if there is any aura of glamour or notoriety at all to investigations, it arises when crimes are committed against or by well-known victims or criminals, or an offense is particularly heinous. Second, aside from the results of scientific investigations, for which there is but a limited audience, criminal investigations are the ones most often reported by the news media.

Thus far, we have discussed violent and other serious offenses and organized crime, but other types of investigations are needed as well and are the subject of this chapter. In some cases, investigations may be necessary in order to assess the seriousness of a threat, which may or may not have criminal overtones. In others, even though no crime was committed, incidents such as accidents or corporate policy violations call for explanations and the identification of those responsible. Certainly employers' efforts to screen applicants for positions with their organizations are investigations.

THREAT ASSESSMENTS

If one recognizes the objectives of any threat assessment, one can see how they can prove useful in criminal as well as other situations. Threat assessments are designed to determine (1) the magnitude of any given threat, (2) the likelihood that the threat will become an overt act, and (3) its immediacy. Thus in many respects, threat assessments are a form of intelligence gathering. The investigator's goal is to collect credible information, not necessarily evidence. Depending on the nature of a given threat, a variety of sources may be used in the information collection process.

For example, if the threat involves a terrorist organization holding hostages that it threatens to kill at an hourly rate until its demands are met, how likely is this to happen? Known information about the group and its leaders, confidential informants, or undercover personnel could be among the sources needed to help assess the threat. A manufacturer hears rumors that employees at one of its suppliers may go on strike. If they do, it will threaten its own production; what is the probability of a strike, and how soon is it likely to occur? In this case, such diverse sources of information as industry trade associations, labor unions, and the news media might prove helpful.

Regardless of the circumstances, any perceived threat must be carefully evaluated in terms of its impact should it occur. Since knowing who the persons or groups posing the threat are can provide valuable insight into the entire situation, identifying them is of primary importance. Such information can be helpful in assessing the potential for violence, the immediacy of the situation, and the seriousness of the threat so that plans can be made to deal with it. In other words, intelligence may make it possible to manage both the activities of those making the threat and the level of risk to which intended targets will be exposed.

Intelligence or information gathering also is important with respect to undertaking threat assessments. Receipt of an actual oral or written threat is not a condition precedent to initiating a threat assessment. Information about the suspected activities of a person or group may be enough to justify a threat assessment. For example, a reliable confidential informant's report that a group plans to bomb a house of worship, without an overt act in furtherance of the plan's execution, is not a conspiracy, but it would be sufficient to undertake a threat assessment.

Threat assessments of all forms of criminal activities must be handled with great care since intelligence collection can involve more than surveillances or information from informants. Investigators must not ignore constitutional guarantees on the theory that they are merely assessing threats, not building a criminal case. This is particularly true of assessments involving persons or organizations perceived to be a threat because they are suspected of, but not necessarily tied to, terrorist activity. Activities limited to expressing political opinions, no matter how distasteful to the vast majority of people, are not considered a threat under our form of government, but there still has to be an assessment to determine whether anything more than an expression of opinion is likely to occur.

Regardless of the circumstances, investigators need guidelines in order to ensure that all threat assessments are made within the limits imposed by law. In other words, of what should a threat assessment program consist; who or what types of organizations should qualify as subjects of an inquiry for threat assessment purposes? It is important for all investigative agencies to develop criteria to justify an individual or organization becoming the focal point of a threat assessment.

The number of people involved has to be considered, but numbers alone are not enough. Background information about those people and their organizations becomes part of the assessment process. Affiliations or linkage between or among different groups, what each advocates, whether they have or had access to the resources that would be needed to carry out any threats, and the extent of their activities can offer insight into their motives, goals, and the seriousness of their threats.

Because threat assessments are sensitive, the unit within the agency responsible for collecting information about possible subjects and conducting the threat assessment investigation should be identified. Unit members also should make persons or organizations that might come into contact with or know about persons or groups that represent potential threats aware of the unit's existence. To avoid witch hunts that can be unfair to individuals and their organizations, and a waste of investigative resources, the unit also is responsible for educating those persons or organizations about the criteria that must be satisfied before concerns about potential threats are brought to the attention of investigators.

To effectively make threat assessments, investigative agencies have to be proactive. In some cases, assessments may actually help prevent a crime. In others, they may be able to greatly reduce the impact of a crime on a particular victim. In still others, they may show that no threat exists.

ACCIDENTS

Accidents occur daily, but not all are investigated. Most of those that are involve situations that have resulted in serious injury or death to persons, significant damage to or loss of property, or both. Accident investigators, whether their cases are related to motor vehicles, trains, or aircraft, look for answers to two main questions: what was the cause, and who was responsible? Motor vehicle accidents usually are investigated by local, sheriffs', or state police departments; those involving trains or aircraft are the province of the NTSB.

Some accidents are criminal; others are not. For instance, the death of a person in an automobile accident caused by a drunken driver is a crime; if the cause was a skid on icy pavement and hitting a tree, it is not. The cause, whether a crime or not, cannot be determined until the investigation is completed. Therefore, in principle, accident investigations are handled the same as criminal investigations.

This means surviving victims and witnesses must be identified, located, and interviewed. Accident scenes must be treated like crime scenes; they must be protected, carefully searched, and evidence must be collected and preserved. In many cases, investigators will find it necessary to have some, if not all, items of physical evidence examined by forensic specialists. In fact, the mode of transportation itself has to be treated as evidence and it, too, may have to be examined by specialists to see if the resulting accident was caused by a criminal act, a mechanical defect, or the operator's behavior, including the possible use of alcohol or drugs. Sources of information may prove helpful. In other words, all investigative techniques generally employed, including reconstruction of the incident, may be called into play in accident cases. This is illustrated in the following cases.

There was a hit-and-run death in Denver, Colorado, in 1996. The grille of the vehicle that caused the victim's death was found at the scene. Determining that it was from a BMW, investigators went to a BMW dealer who identified it as "cosmos black" from a $56,000 1995 BMW 540i. With that information, they learned there were only three such vehicles registered in all of Colorado. This narrowed the scope of the inquiry, and in one owner's garage they found a BMW 540i with damage that was consistent with the evidence found at and recovered from the accident scene.[1]

On February 9, 1996, three people were killed when two commuter trains crashed in northern New Jersey. Responding NTSB investigators checked the engineers' records, records of the equipment involved, braking systems, and speed.[2]

Among their findings, they learned one of the engineers had run a stop signal; also, he had previously been suspended for a total of 105 days for having failed to stop and for a derailment. In addition, his previous infractions included running stop signals twice and having once missed a station. He also had a vision color deficiency. Furthermore, his record showed that before this accident he had worked for fourteen and a half hours with only one four-and-a-half-hour sleep break. On February 8, he reported for work at 6:11 P.M., took his sleep break in a passenger coach car from 12:48 A.M. to 5:30 A.M., and was to have finished work at 7:30 A.M. However, he agreed to make an extra run; the accident happened at 8:40 A.M.[3]

Eleven people died as a result of a head-on collision between two trains on February 16, 1996. Among the initial findings were the fact that some of those killed might have survived if the trains' emergency exits had functioned properly, and the passengers on one train could not open some of the windows and doors. In searching for the accident's cause, NTSB investigators were trying to find out if a particular signal was yellow, which would have limited train speed to 30 miles per hour, or if it was green, in which case, the speed limit would have been 70 miles per hour. Since neither the trains nor the signaling equipment was defective, investigators would have to resort to analyzing computerized data recorders to learn the signal's color.[4]

A New York City subway accident on February 5, 1996, injured nine passengers. The NTSB investigation found the cause to be a variety of problems, the responsibility for which rested with the New York City Transit Authority.[5]

Among the most difficult and time-consuming accident investigations are those involving downed aircraft. This is due to several reasons, not the least of which is whether there are any survivors who can be interviewed. Then there is the question of whether the cause was pilot error; if so, was weather a factor? A possible mechanical failure cannot be ruled out, and on occasion neither can the possibility of a criminal act. When investigating aircraft accidents, every effort must be made not only to recover and identify all those aboard, but also to recover all the airplane's parts so that it can be reconstructed. Both can be critical in trying to determine cause.

According to the Federal Aviation Administration (FAA), a U.S. government agency, and airline industry sources, the search for clues takes the following into consideration:

1. *Structural deformation.* If recovered debris has holes, it frequently can be determined if they were caused from inside or outside the aircraft.

2. *Stress fractures.* These are indicative of the structural failure of parts before a crash; impact fractures would indicate a later occurrence.

3. *Discoloration.* When detected on metallic parts, it will vary in relation to the part's proximity to fire and the intensity of the heat.

4. *Dyes.* Some engine parts are dipped in dye when they are made. Thus if dye is found in the crack of a cracked part, it indicates that the part was defective when the aircraft was built.

5. *Chemical residues on debris and their patterns.* Explosive material might be embedded in debris in a characteristic or signature pattern.

6. *Elongated lightbulb filaments.* These would mean the lights were on at the time of the crash; the filaments would not be misshapen if the aircraft's electrical system failed before.

7. *Records.* Aircraft maintenance and service records and the personnel records of those performing the work and flying the aircraft at the time of the accident are needed.

8. *Flight data recorder.* This permits the creation of a computer simulation of the flight's final moments; an explosive device would leave a "signature sound" on the recorder. The cockpit voice recorder also would be examined as part of the flight reconstruction process.[6]

August 21, 1995, ASA crash, Carrolton, GA. (*Courtesy* Alan Pollock, National Transportation Safety Board)

The ways in which NTSB aircraft accident investigators consider multiple factors is best illustrated by citing several actual cases.

❖ Case 18-1

In November 1995, an American Airlines plane crashed near the Hartford, Connecticut, airport; the passengers and crew suffered only minor injuries. The investigation raised questions about the air traffic control system's performance. The radar system tracking the flight had issued a "minimum safe altitude warning" alert, yet the crew was not informed; neither did the system take into account a ridge 2.6 miles from the airport. In addition, although the night was stormy, the aircraft had been directed to the runway without the benefit of instruments to indicate the glide slope or diagonal path that would have taken it safely to the ground.[7]

❖ Case 18-2

In April 1996, a Cessna 177 B left California for a cross-country flight with a 7-year-old pilot, her father, and her flight instructor on board. It crashed killing all three while taking off from Cheyenne, Wyoming. Investigators found the instructor's hand and wrist had a pattern of injuries that suggested he was at the controls when the crash occurred. As for the cause, from a safety perspective, the aircraft was overloaded. Allowance should have been made for the fact that mountain air (at Cheyenne) is

July 1994 crash USAir Flight 1016, Charlotte, NC. (*Courtesy* Alan Pollock, National Transportation Safety Board)

thinner and lessens power. As a result, with the same number of passengers, baggage load, and fuel as when it left California, the aircraft might have been overweight.[8]

Not all criminal cases are solved; neither are all accidents. Nevertheless, it was hoped that a June 9, 1996, crash of a Boeing 737 would provide clues to two earlier, unsolved cases, one in 1991 and the other in 1994. In these two crashes, all aboard were killed; there were no deaths or injuries in the 1996 incident. Prior to the 1996 accident, it seemed that the earlier crashes might have been caused by an "uncommanded roll" of the 737s in which one wing would dip unexpectedly, but this was unconfirmed. However, the pilot of the 1996 flight reported feeling a "bump" on the airplane's rudder followed by a more substantial swing as the aircraft rolled to its right and crashed.[9]

The case just cited shows that when accidents are unsolved, the possibility that subsequent incidents may provide clues that will help solve the earlier cases should not be ignored. This is comparable to the approach taken by criminal investigators assigned cases involving serial killers or rapists who often leave clues that lead to their eventual detection and apprehension. The need for attention to detail is no less important in accident investigations than it is in criminal cases.

An example is a July 6, 1996, incident involving Delta Flight 1288's departure from Pensacola, Florida. The aircraft, an eight-year-old MD-88 jet, was about 1,500 feet down the runway when smoke was seen coming from its left engine, which then blew apart, causing a gash about 1 inch wide and 4 inches long across the airplane's side, killing two passengers and injuring others. Investigators found a 100-pound titanium hub inside the engine in two pieces with some of the fan blades still attached. At first, they considered the possibility that the problem was caused by either an internal problem or a foreign object, such as a bird, being sucked into the Pratt and Whitney JT 8D-217 engine. Delta had encountered four other disabling incidents since April 1996, not necessarily involving the same engine model, but two did involve MD-88s. The engine's pieces were collected for examination.[10]

The investigation found a 1-inch fatigue crack in a part of the blown engine, and it was to be tested in an effort to find out what caused that crack. The NTSB also was looking at the possibility that this same kind of flaw may have caused a similar part to fly apart and been responsible for a United Airlines crash in 1989. At the same time, investigators were examining Delta's maintenance practices, including the testing of the damaged fan hub, to see if an earlier oil seal leak might have contributed to the problem since the fan hub that broke apart had been installed on the engine in January because an oil leak had burned out a bearing on the original hub.[11]

Aircraft accident investigators also have to be patient. In 1994, an American Eagle turboprop, manufactured by the French company Avions

Transport Regionale, crashed at Roselawn, Indiana, killing all sixty-eight people aboard. On July 9, 1996, the NTSB reported the main reason was the failure of both the manufacturer and the FAA's French counterpart not only to tell the airlines, FAA, and pilots all that they knew about this particular aircraft's vulnerability to ice, but also to take corrective action.[12]

In 1989, Pan American Flight 103 exploded in flight over Scotland; everyone on board was killed. That this incident occurred over land helped investigators; their painstaking search for and collection of debris over a widespread area enabled them to find evidence that lent itself to forensic examination. From the latter, they were able to determine that the blast took place in a specific cargo bin containing checked luggage. That, in turn, made it possible to identify the city in which the luggage had been placed aboard the aircraft. They then determined that only a few passengers had checked baggage there, and one bag had been checked by a person who never boarded the flight. They also found a tiny chip identified as part of a bomb mechanism, thus indicating this crash was no accident. The evidence collected and analyzed provided leads and ultimately resulted in the identification of the terrorists responsible for this disaster.

One incident mentioned in Chapter 15's discussion of terrorism was the July 1996 crash of TWA Flight 800. The uncertainty of the cause and lack of sufficient evidence to indicate it was the result of a criminal act warranted considering this investigation in greater detail as an accident.

Primary responsibility for the investigation rested with the NTSB on the theory that the downing could have been caused by a major mechanical failure. However, two other theories, both of which would be crimes if proved true, also had to be considered: that a bomb had been placed on board or the aircraft had been brought down by a bomb or ground-to-air missile. Consequently, the FBI also became actively involved. In this case, unlike the Pan American disaster, the explosion happened over Long Island Sound, not over land, and investigators were faced with having to try to recover physical evidence from the water. There also was an urgency to the recovery effort since the ebb and flow of tides could scatter debris, and the longer aircraft components remained in salt water the greater the risk that corrosion and the water's movement could mask or even wash away traces of any explosives.

Despite these obstacles, with the U.S. Navy's help an estimated 95 percent of the aircraft was recovered within ninety days. Admittedly, what remained missing could include parts that could help determine the actual cause, especially such items as floorboard pieces, pieces from directly under the wings on both sides of the aircraft, an auxiliary fuel tank, and probes that measured the amount of fuel in the center tank.[13] Nevertheless, on November 20, 1996, James K. Kallstrom, Assistant Director in charge of the FBI's New York City office, expressed the belief that it was "mathematically less likely that a bomb or a missile" was responsible. He said that "From a logical standpoint, there is less of a chance we'll find what we need to prove a criminal act. . . . That is not to say we can't find bomb damage or missile damage in the missing 5 percent."[14]

The uncertainty notwithstanding, much can be learned from what investigators had found up to November 20. Although parts recovered as of August 11 showed no visible signs of bomb damage, they were submitted for laboratory testing to see if there were any possible traces of explosive residue. State-of-the-art explosives detection equipment used near the parts' recovery area indicated the presence of plastic explosives. Those components were sent to the FBI Laboratory for further testing. The findings could not be confirmed, possibly because the first readings were wrong, or they were not repeated when the parts underwent more sustained scientific procedures.[15]

In the latter part of August 1996, laboratory chemists found traces of PETN (pentaerythritol tetranitrate), an explosive component often found in plastic explosives and surface-to-air missiles, in part of a seat recovered from between rows 17 and 28. Nevertheless, like all good investigators, they refused to jump to a conclusion since (1) no other traces of PETN were found, (2) when used it generally is a key part of a detonator, not of a main explosive charge, and (3) no evidence had yet been found of "shock wave" damage that almost invariably accompanies a blast.[16]

Even though this finding was inconclusive, it meant an explosive device could not be ruled out as the cause. Coincidentally, one phase of the FBI's investigation focused on tracing this particular aircraft's whereabouts in the months before the crash. On September 19, 1996, investigators learned that on June 10, 1996, packages with explosives had been placed on board at St. Louis as part of a test for bomb-detecting dogs, but not in the same places as where the PETN traces had been found.[17]

In tracking the aircraft's previous whereabouts, the bureau found it necessary to contact law enforcement agencies in cities where the airplane would have been on the ground long enough for any of those agencies to have conducted the bomb detection dog tests since neither TWA nor the FAA had such data in its records. St. Louis was one of those cities. However, the record simply cited a "wide-bodied jet"; it did not include the tail identification number. Next, a check was made of gate assignment records for the test date, and the aircraft used was finally identified as having been TWA 800.[18]

Examination of recovered debris helped investigators eliminate some possibilities and consider others. The four recovered cargo containers were ruled out as places where a bomb could have been hidden. So, too, was the cockpit area since the glass covers on most of the pilot's gauges and the glass ceiling light over the stairwell to the plane's upper deck were unbroken. Recovered wreckage showed extensive fire damage. This would be expected regardless of what caused the aircraft to blow up, and it tended to focus attention on the center wing fuel tank. Even though it was virtually empty when the flight left New York, it still might have contained a sufficient amount of fuel to explode if it became warm enough to vaporize and something ignited it.

These were not the only leads followed. Within days of the crash, the FBI had interviewed approximately 1,500 people, and prosecutors started to subpoena certain basic records that might prove helpful. Among those interviewed were all service personnel who had any direct contact with the aircraft, and New York area known supporters of terrorist groups were placed under surveillance. A Joint Terrorism Task Force was set up, and a crash master file was created in which all information and leads would be stored. Confidential informants were contacted worldwide; recent travels of terrorist suspects were examined. Neither did investigators ignore the possibility that the crash was an act of violence by a domestic militia group, a case of insurance fraud, a personal dispute with which but one passenger was involved, or even a suicide. They asked if the "lifeguard" flight package placed on board at the last-minute, which would have been able to bypass security, and twenty-seven diplomatic pouches were X-rayed. Passengers who had arrived aboard the aircraft from Athens were interviewed, complete financial and personal profiles were created for everyone who boarded in New York, and the passenger list was scrutinized to see if anyone might have been using a false name. A similarity between the breakup of TWA 800, Pan American 103, and a 1985 bombing of an Air India flight led investigators to compare sounds on the TWA cockpit voice recorder with those on Pan Am 103's.[19]

Lacking any definitive mechanical cause for the crash, humans, including airport workers, others with access to the plane, and passengers could not be ignored as possible suspects. This prompted investigators to look for data that might signify sudden changes in individuals' personal or financial status, check records and to make inquiries based on tips provided by landlords, friends, and others. Among the items checked were passenger tax returns, insurance policies, credit records, employment histories, and court records relative to divorce or other legal proceedings. Eyewitnesses to the crash were interviewed. Since some reported seeing a flash of light heading toward the aircraft at the time of the incident, explosives and missiles at area military installations were inventoried to see if anything was missing. Pursuing these leads allowed investigators to eliminate several potential suspects.[20]

As in all accident investigations, an essential element to discovering a possible solution is the re-creation of the incident. In cases in which vehicles of any sort are involved, investigators attempt to reconstruct the particular type of vehicle to see what may have been responsible for or contributed to the accident. The recovery and examination of a 15-foot-long piece of TWA 800's left wing showed little to indicate a fire or soot in contrast to signs of severe burning found on recovered sections of the right wing. This seemed to support the theory that the explosion, whatever its cause, happened in the aircraft's right central section, close to where the wing and fuselage are connected. Examination of the four engines showed they were not a factor in terms of having malfunctioned or been hit by a heat-seeking missile.[21]

As reconstruction of TWA Flight 800 continued, investigators observed that many of the coach seats in rows 17 to 28 of the aircraft's right side had not been recovered, whereas those in other passenger cabin areas had been. This seemed to indicate that the explosion occurred in the general area of the missing seats, especially since what few seats had been recovered from those rows showed a great deal more burn damage than was found on seats from other sections. In the interim, bomb experts and metallurgists examined recovered metal parts for signs of pitting, characteristics that would indicate close exposure to an explosive.[22]

The process of elimination plays a role not only in criminal investigations, but also in accident cases. TWA Flight 800 was no exception. For example, NTSB investigators agreed with the FBI that there was circumstantial evidence that a bomb caused the crash, but their experience also led them to believe that lacking proof that a bomb was in fact involved indirectly supported the theory that an explosion in the center fuel tank would have been of sufficient force to destroy the aircraft.[23] Investigators also were concerned that with the passage of time metal parts not yet recovered might be so badly corroded by salt water that even if they eventually were found, critical evidence needed to show if the cause was a bomb, missile, or mechanical failure would be erased.[24]

More than two months after the incident, efforts to reassemble TWA Flight 800's midsection and center fuel tank continued but without any finding of obvious signs that a bomb caused the explosion. However, despite being able to reassemble 80 to 85 percent of the center fuel tank, large parts of the left and right sides, a fuel pump, and six internal fuel gauges still were missing. So were signs of microscopic pitting and cracking in metal shards that would be "one of the only indisputable signatures of a blast from high explosives."[25]

As noted before, adding to the complexity of the TWA Flight 800 investigation was the entire aircraft's submersion in water. This added to the difficulty of recovering parts, reassembling the aircraft, and determining the accident's cause. This does not mean that accident investigators invariably confront such obstacles. For instance, determining the cause of workplace accidents does not pose the same problems.

In 1970, Congress passed the Williams–Steiger Occupational Safety and Health Act, known as OSHA.[26] Responsibility for developing general and construction industry standards[27] to provide employees with a safe and healthful workplace, as well as oversight, was given to the U.S. Department of Labor. The act also authorizes states to develop their own programs subject to federal approval, one condition of which is that state standards must be at least as stringent as those of the federal government.

No matter whether employers are governed by federal or state standards, workplace accidents resulting in either serious injuries or death must be reported to and are investigated by OSHA compliance officers. Their findings can result in criminal as well as civil proceedings against errant employers, depending on the circumstances surrounding any given accident. The overwhelming majority of investigated accidents end up as civil matters. Nevertheless, the possibility that a criminal complaint may be filed mandates conducting the entire investigation with that thought in mind. Unlike so many other investigators, compliance officers' work is made easier by the fact that accident scenes, as well as workplace accident victims and witnesses, are easily identifiable and available to them. As we already have seen, this is something that cannot be counted on in strictly criminal cases.

When an accident is reported, the scene must be secured. Physical evidence must be collected, preserved, and when appropriate, submitted for laboratory examination. For instance, suppose employees are overcome by noxious fumes. The substance and containers from which it emanated would be evidence for laboratory examination; if the employees were wearing protective masks, the masks would have to be examined for possible leaks. If a large stationary piece of machinery is involved, such as a punch press used to shape metal, it would have to be examined on site for defects; photographs would have to be taken and identified.

Victims and witnesses must be identified and interviewed. Interview details can help investigators reconstruct how the accident occurred. Other areas of inquiry would be dictated in large part by the accident scene and nature of the incident itself. As an example, if it appears that victims contributed to their own injuries or death, investigators have to find out in what ways. Were they working under the influence of alcohol or drugs, or were they careless? If careless, had they been working excessively long hours before the incident occurred? If so, was it by choice or because the employer required it?

In reportable workplace accidents, investigators must look into the employer's compliance with the OSHA standards applicable to that type of activity, including the history of previously reported incidents. To illustrate, compliance officers look for the following:

1. Does the employer have an enforced safety program?
2. Are employees who fail to comply disciplined?
3. If hazardous or toxic materials are used in the workplace, are employees provided with suitable personal protective equipment and trained in its use? Are all containers properly labeled? Do employees understand the labels' significance? Have they been trained in the materials' proper use and storage?

4. If particular tools or machines are used, do they satisfy applicable OSHA safety requirements, are employees trained in their use, and are they provided with whatever personal protective equipment may be needed?

5. Were any involved machines or tools defective? If so, in what ways and for how long? Why did the employer permit their continued use? What action had it taken for their repair or replacement?

6. Has the employer had this or similar incident(s) occur before? If not, have there been other significant accidents, and of what did they consist?

7. Does examination of the personnel files of those involved in the accident reflect a history of on-the-job injuries, serious or other?

8. If the victim died, what caused the death? If it resulted from ingesting or inhaling a toxic substance, what was that substance?

9. If it appears that the fault lies with the employer, is there evidence to suggest mere failure to comply with the OSHA standards, or does it indicate willful disregard for employees' safety?

From the foregoing, it is clear that accident investigators follow the same principles as those who work criminal cases. Criminal investigators try to reconstruct how crimes were committed; accident investigators try to reconstruct the incidents' causes. In both situations, the scene must be identified and secured; victims and witnesses must be identified and interviewed. Physical evidence is searched for and collected, including documentation and other records. It then must be preserved and, where appropriate, subjected to laboratory examination.

APPLICANTS

Although criminal defense counsel occasionally hire private investigators, most criminal investigations are conducted by sworn law enforcement personnel. There are limitations to the former's work inasmuch as they do not have access to all the same resources that are available to federal, state, county, and local police agencies.

With respect to accident investigations, although the NTSB and OSHA compliance officers inquire into those incidents falling within their respective jurisdictions, there is nothing to prevent interested private parties from conducting their own investigations as long as they do not interfere with government personnel. As an example, if an airplane crashes, aside from cooperating with the NTSB, and absent signs of criminal activity, one expects the airline and aircraft's manufacturer to make their own independent inquiries as to the cause. Similarly, employers may conduct their own accident investigations even when there is OSHA involvement, and certainly nothing prevents them or their insurers from doing so when OSHA is not involved.

Unlike criminal or accident investigations, applicant investigations are the province of prospective employers. Notwithstanding their importance to those employers, particularly when positions of trust or unusual responsibility are at issue, decisions to investigate or not rest exclusively with employers. If investigations are to be conducted, their sufficiency will depend largely on the resources available to the investigators. Government investigators have access to many resources that are unavailable to the private sector, including corporate security personnel or private investigators.

The differences can be considerable. As an example, there is the matter of criminal history information. Private party access can vary from state to state, but no state allows the unlimited access available to government representatives. Despite these and other limitations that may be imposed on the private sector, the fundamentals of applicant investigations are the same regardless of who conducts them.

Applicant investigations begin with the completion of the application for employment. Responsibility for ensuring the form's adequacy and proper completion by applicants rests with human resources personnel, not investigators. However, applications that are inadequate because of either the forms themselves or the information provided by applicants are obstacles to meaningful investigations. Even if applicants submit resumes, employer applications still should be completed.

Resumes and completed applications should be compared for possible inconsistencies. Resolution of any discrepancies should be considered investigative leads. If there are no differences, or there are only properly completed forms with which to work, the first step is to verify the applicant's information. If a job requires proof of U.S. citizenship, human resources should ask applicants to obtain certified copies of birth certificates or produce their naturalization papers or valid U.S. passports. If citizenship is not required, human resources, not investigators, should verify legal entry into the country by asking applicants to produce valid documentation from the U.S. Immigration and Naturalization Service.

The scope of background investigations for local, county, or state government applicants tends to differ from those for federal applicants. The extent of preemployment screening at these levels is determined by either the state or political subdivision with which employment is being sought, and with the possible exception of policing positions, the process tends to be somewhat limited. Federal applicants are subjected to more thorough screening, the most stringent being for those seeking appointment to federal law enforcement, other investigative, or intelligence agencies. In addition to verifying birth, citizenship, education, and employment data for this group, criminal histories are checked; neighbors and personal references are contacted; and questions are asked about the applicant's character, associations, possible addictions, and loyalty to the U.S. government.

Members of the business community do the least thorough preemployment screening, if they do any at all. That applicant investigations are not justified either because applicants must be told of the inquiry or the jobs are deemed of minor importance, such as messengers for stock brokerage companies or school custodians, is shortsighted. Employers define the parameters within which any preemployment screening will be done, but investigators should know what to look for and where information will be found.

In conducting preemployment investigations, remember that when people are asked about other people, they frequently are reluctant to provide answers, whether investigators represent a government agency or private employers, and whether they show a badge, government credentials, or a business card. If applicant investigators do not put those contacted at ease, communication is inhibited, and the results will be less than satisfactory. Investigators must do more than identify themselves. They should make it clear at the outset that those about whom they are asking questions are being considered for positions of responsibility and trust; they are not in any trouble.

If there is an academic component, the college or university from which graduation is claimed should be contacted to verify attendance dates, grades, and the degree(s) awarded regardless of the applicant's provision of the information. An effort should be made to learn if the applicant ever was the subject of significant disciplinary action. It also may be advisable to contact a select few faculty members under whom the student studied for whatever information they can offer.

Previous employers should be asked to confirm dates of employment, job titles, beginning and ending salaries, and supervisors' or managers' names. The latter should be contacted for any meaningful information they are willing to provide. Applicants' stated reasons for leaving should be confirmed. Would the employer consider the applicant eligible for reemployment?

Credit records should be checked, if obtainable. Limited private-sector access to criminal histories does not preclude examining court records for information about criminal proceedings against applicants. However, if applicants appear to have been defendants in criminal cases, investigators should not reach any conclusions without a positive identification. It also is important to remember that even if there is such identification, the records pertain to only that particular court's jurisdiction. Civil court records should be checked for information about possible liens, bankruptcies, divorce actions, mortgages, ownership of realty, or restraining orders.

Despite their relationships, personal references, be they neighbors, coworkers, members of the clergy, or friends, often are good sources of information. Occasionally, they also can provide additional leads. Visiting neighborhoods where applicants live may be worthwhile. Does information already developed by the investigation appear to be inconsistent with the applicant's lifestyle? If so, fairness requires reconciling the differences. This may call for the investigator to interview the applicant.

If a position requires any form of licensing by the state, the licensing authority should be contacted not only to confirm that the applicants are in fact licensed, but also to determine whether they ever have been suspended or otherwise disciplined, if so, for what reason? Applications for positions that require licenses should ask applicants if they ever have been or are licensed to work in states other than the one in which they hope to work. If the answer is yes, those states should be contacted for confirmation and information about disciplinary action.

CONFLICTS OF INTEREST

Conflicts of interest are most often found in and investigated by sizable business organizations as violations of corporate policy. In today's environment, they may require a level of sophistication on the part of investigators that is not needed in other cases; they also may involve some rather delicate questions of law. These inquiries tend to be conducted by corporate security personnel, if a security department exists. Otherwise, private investigators may be retained.

Most businesses of any appreciable size have conflict of interest policies covering both actual conflicts and activities that have the appearance of a conflict. Many organizations with such policies consider the subject so important that they require all new employees to sign a statement acknowledging that they have read and understand the policy. Some even repeat the process periodically.

Although the offense is not a crime, the investigative approach taken is much the same as in criminal cases. First, there is a predication for the investigation; someone suspects a conflict, and the matter is referred for investigation. Second, crimes have their elements, and so do conflicts. Investigators must establish that a conflict of interest policy exists, that the employee knew of its existence and content, and that the activities engaged in violated or appeared to violate that policy. Third, the "crime scene" must be secured and searched; evidence must be collected and preserved. The search also must be extended in an effort to collect any existing materials of evidentiary value. Fourth, an attempt should be made to identify and interview any possible witnesses. Finally, the involved employee has to be interviewed. That the subject's identity is known to the investigator from the outset is a feature that distinguishes this type of inquiry from many crimes, and even from some other types of policy violations.

Conflicts of interest cases are not crimes, yet an employer's action following completion of an inquiry may well result in litigation. If that comes to pass, the outcome will depend on the evidence, whether injured employers or fired employees sue for damages, or the latter seek satisfaction from an administrative body such as a commission against discrimination. Consequently, the need to identify, protect, and search the crime scene without delay is critical. If this is not done, the subject may destroy evidence. If all, or even part, of the evidence is stored in a computer, this need for prompt action assumes added importance.

With respect to searches, failure to consider two important side issues may negate the impact of evidence found, and could give suspect employees yet another cause of action against their employers. In discussing the collection and preservation of evidence in Chapter 12, we noted the Fourth Amendment and its search warrant requirements, but in *Burdeau v. McDowell,*[28] the U.S. Supreme Court held that it applied only to government agents, not private persons. Therefore, searching employees' computer files, desks, work areas, or offices per se does not violate the Fourth Amendment. However, this means only that affected employees cannot sue their employers on constitutional grounds; it does not preclude suing for an invasion of privacy. Consequently, if there are to be any internal investigations, regardless of the basis for them, businesses should have a clear, legally sound policy and procedure covering searches and seizures.

Examples of conflicts of interest inquiries help illustrate the importance of quickly protecting the scene to obtain evidence, the types of evidence that may be found, and how extensive some investigations can be. In each, the employers had conflicts of interest policies. All new employees were required to acknowledge in writing their understanding of these policies. The companies also had well-defined, legally sound policies and procedures covering both internal investigations and searches and seizures.

One case involved a manager suspected of operating three businesses of his own on his employer's time and using the latter's computers. He was not suspected of competing with his employer. His superior referred the matter to security. The computer's use suggested the likelihood that his computer files would contain evidence, and they had to be protected. Consequently, arrangements were made to have them dumped immediately, making certain that any purely personal data, such as medical information, was not included. A review of his personnel file for possible leads turned up nothing of a questionable nature, but his computer files contained numerous copies of letters sent by him to various individuals and organizations soliciting business for one of his three enterprises. Having been informed of his rights at the outset of his interview, he nevertheless acknowledged being aware of the employer's conflicts of interest policy and of his having violated it.

After his dismissal, he filed a complaint alleging he was fired because of his country of national origin. The employer's defense consisted of evidence showing it had a conflicts of interest policy, the person's having acknowledged its existence both when hired and during the investigation's interview, and the data recovered from his computer files in accordance with clearly defined investigation and search policies. The Commission Against Discrimination found for the employer.

An internal audit of a multinational corporation's Hong Kong purchasing office raised questions in the auditor's mind about a buyer's possible conflict of interest. He immediately informed the corporate director of internal audit, who referred the matter to the corporate security director. In the interim, the auditor simultaneously got a short one-paragraph written "confession" from the buyer, and another from a secretary who, though not directly involved, knew what was going on. Both implicated the Singapore-based regional purchasing director. In the regional vice president's absence, neither was terminated nor even suspended. The auditor's imprudent action in obtaining the confessions while the buyer and secretary still had access to the office and the distance from corporate headquarters to Hong Kong with its attendant time difference were matters of concern from an evidence collection viewpoint. Getting the statements alerted the buyer and secretary to the fact that they were suspects; the time factor would give them a chance to destroy computer files that might contain evidence. This necessitated telephone instructions from corporate headquarters to immediately suspend and bar both from the premises in the hope that they had not yet thought to delete their files, and to have those files dumped and sent to corporate headquarters. Luckily, neither the buyer nor the secretary had as yet destroyed their files.

On examination, the secretary's files showed no evidence of involvement on her part. The buyer's files contained evidence not only of his and the regional purchasing director's involvement in a variety of conflicts, but also of the participation of two other managers, one in Bangkok and one at corporate headquarters. This evidence, the need to preserve and collect evidence from the files of the two new participants, and the geographic spread of the subjects meant that just as law enforcement agencies occasionally find it helpful to create task forces in criminal cases, a collaborative effort was called for here. Both the employer's Far East regional counsel, based in Australia, and a manager from corporate headquarter's Management Information Systems (MIS) division helped.

The corporate security director oversaw the investigation, examined all the data collected, and forwarded leads to the regional counsel and MIS manager. As with the first of the cases cited, the conflict consisted of doing personal business on the employer's time, with the latter's facilities, and in the purchasing director's case, planning his travels on corporate business around meetings scheduled for his personal activities. In addition to thoroughly examining the subjects' computer files, written consent was gotten from each to allow a search of hard copy files kept in their respective offices. Since all of them, including the headquarters-based manager, did some travel in connection with their jobs, their expense reports and travel schedules were examined to see if they had arranged to meet in pursuit of their joint personal business ventures. Following collection, examination, and evaluation of all the evidence, each subject was informed of his rights and interviewed; signed statements were gotten. Copies of the investigative report, with the supporting evidence, were submitted to the individuals' division heads and human resources for appropriate action. None of the individuals challenged the employer's decisions.

We previously took note of the U.S. Supreme Court's ruling that the Fourth Amendment does not apply to private persons. In Chapter 14, we discussed that part of the Fifth Amendment and the Court's 1966 decision in *Miranda v. Arizona,*[29] requiring that persons subject to a custodial interrogation by law enforcement personnel be told they need not make any statement, but that any statement they choose to make can be used against them in court. This decision also has been held to not apply to private persons.

Nevertheless, in the conflicts cases cited, the subjects, regardless of where they were based or interviewed, were informed of their rights. Each was told that the interview room's door was closed to ensure privacy, not restrict their movement; they could ask for a break to go to the toilet or get something to eat or drink; they were under no obligation to answer any questions asked of them; and they were free to leave at any time. Interview logs were kept. This modified Miranda warning, standard security department procedure for all interrogations, helped enhance the value of any statements made by showing they were given voluntarily.

The foregoing conflicts investigations were relatively simple in that they were limited to the employers' organizations, thus making evidence collection and subjects' interviews fairly easy. However, another inquiry illustrates this is not true in all cases.

This investigation was predicated on unsolicited information provided by a competitor's employee alleging that a sales engineer had helped the competitor by borrowing expensive technical equipment for the latter's use. The employee's personnel file was requested, and a name check of the competing firm's owner showed that he was a former employee. A review of both files indicated a history of a relationship between the two.

The manager of the branch from which the equipment had been borrowed was identified and interviewed. He said when the salesperson asked to borrow it for a customer, he refused the loan since the equipment's use was too complex for any customer to use by itself. With his help, a new employee in his branch, from whom the item had been borrowed, was identified and interviewed. In his statement, he said he thought the request strange, but since he was new, and the salesperson was a "big producer," he believed it best to lend him the equipment.

Details about the date of the loan, how the competitor got delivery, where the item was used, and how it was returned to the salesperson were confirmed by the confidential informant, who continued working for the competitor.

Since the company provided salespersons and certain other employees with telephone company credit cards, the calling records were examined. Those pertaining to the subject showed many calls to a number identified as the competitor's, including several around the time of the equipment loan. Physical surveillance confirmed meetings between the subject and competitor, and it also revealed the former spent most of his time at a business office in a neighboring town. The business name indicated it was a corporation and prompted a check of the secretary of state's records. They listed the subject as an incorporator and the current president, in itself a conflict of interest even if the company was not competing with his employer.

With the informant's information, the statements of the branch manager and the person who loaned the equipment, telephone credit card records, those of the secretary of state, and the surveillance results in hand, arrangements were made to interview the employee. He was informed of his rights, refused to be interviewed, and was fired. He then sued charging wrongful termination. Upon hearing the evidence at trial, a jury found for the employer.

CORPORATE POLICY VIOLATIONS

It probably is safe to say that all corporations consider criminal activities a policy violation. Significant crimes are referred to and investigated by the police. But aside from conflicts cases, which certainly are policy violations, it is not unusual to find minor crimes investigated internally in order to expedite the termination process. However, other policy violations must be investigated as part of an employer's disciplinary process. Thus inquiries predicated on suspected policy violations, minor crimes included, usually are conducted by security departments where they exist. That these matters are handled internally with a view to possible disciplinary rather than court action does not lessen their importance. This is supported by the employee action taken after discharge in two of the cited conflicts cases.

Employers rely on the results of internal investigations to dispose of policy violation cases. They do this without knowing whether affected employees will accept their decision or respond by taking some form of legal action. Consequently, these inquiries must be conducted as thoroughly, meticulously, and objectively as would be true in a major criminal investigation.

The fact that these investigations are conducted within the confines of the workplace, by employees on their employer's behalf, does not justify opening an inquiry without a good reason to do so. Normally, there will be a complaint alleging activity or behavior that is against the employer's rules. The first step in the process is to carefully interview the complainant and get not only all the details about the violator and what has been or is being done, but also the names of other employees (witnesses) who may be able to provide information on the subject.

The elements will dictate what must be proved. Therefore, after the interview, ensure that a policy dealing with the particular activity exists, that the conduct complained of, if true, violates that policy, and that the policy is one of which the employee should be aware. In addition, does the basis for the complaint suggest that there may be some physical evidence, or does it indicate that the only available evidence will be testimonial? If there is any indication that physical evidence exists, it has to be identified, collected, and preserved without delay.

If only testimonial evidence is available, all known witnesses must be interviewed, and detailed information, preferably in the form of signed statements, has to be obtained. Interview each witness separately. In addition to details, ask for the names of other possible witnesses; do not rely solely on the names provided by the complainant.

Review the subject's personnel file. His or her background, job performance, evidence of prior misconduct, or information indicating any kind of relationship with the complainant may prove helpful. It often is useful to review the complainant's personnel file. Internal investigative files should be examined to see whether the complainant has filed complaints about coworkers before; if so, against whom, with what frequency, and what was the disposition of those cases? Although no seemingly valid complaints should be ignored, it is important to recognize that chronic complainers do exist.

If the employer uses closed-circuit television to record any activities, tapes should be examined on the chance they may have caught the suspect employee's misbehavior. If this is not the case, testimonial evidence gotten from those interviewed may indicate the viability of using closed-circuit television surveillance in an effort to further document the alleged misconduct.

There are times when investigations of alleged policy violations involve more than interviews, and even taped evidence. What follows illustrates the point. The employer was a multinational corporation. One of its manufacturing plant managers received a letter from an employee accusing the site's number-three person of abusing his authority by having subordinates do work of a personal nature for him on company time and, occasionally, using company materials, clearly a policy violation if true. Because of the accused's seniority, the plant manager ignored the complaint.

Some time later, a retiree saw a write-up about the accused in a company newsletter that he received. He wrote the president alleging the accused was disloyal to the organization and detailing behavior similar to that contained in the complaint to the plant manager. The letter was given to the security director. He immediately reviewed the personnel files of the author and the accused, then arranged to interview the author. Aside from the file reviews showing that at one time the author's and accused's home addresses were the same, there was nothing derogatory in either one.

At the interview's outset, the author hesitated to speak. For the first time he said that the accused was a relative, and that he himself had participated in some of the misconduct. As a result, he would agree to talk only if his identity would be protected. The investigator, considering his options, agreed. Three hours later, he had learned about the unauthorized use of company vehicles, the names of some employees who had been verbally abused by the accused, of others who had done work for the accused on his boat on the employer's time, the nature of that work, and the accused's habit of lunching at the same place and returning to work "drunk."

The information had to be corroborated, but in ways that would protect its source. The personnel files and time and attendance records of all named employees were reviewed for background information; they then were interviewed. Employees' passes, used to take company or personal property from the plant, were examined. So were all data relating to the movement of company vehicles. The accused's company-issued telephone credit card records were reviewed. A physical surveillance for a week during his lunch hour found him drinking heavily; the bartender, discreetly interviewed, confirmed this as a daily occurrence. A good part of the work reportedly done on the subject's boat was visible during a harbor visit; photographs were taken. Arrangements were made for his interview. When he was confronted with the evidence, he resigned.

SUMMARY

Looking at the way in which noncriminal investigations are conducted makes it clear that the techniques employed are not too different from those used in criminal cases. This is true whether it is a matter of assessing threats, finding the cause of accidents, determining applicants' suitability, or enabling employers to act when any company policies reportedly are violated, including those dealing with conflicts of interest. People have to be identified and interviewed, and sources of information have to be checked.

Threat assessments are proactive and a form of intelligence collection. They consist of gathering and evaluating information upon which decisions can be based and can be useful to both government agencies and private employers. As with all intelligence gathering, the information is derived from multiple sources.

Informants often contribute, especially to assessments being made by law enforcement agencies, but various records and the general public also may be able to provide information. Although the private sector does not have the same degree of access to certain records that government agencies do, it nevertheless can get information from a wide variety of sources, possibly including informants who are employees. The fact that threat assessments per se do not necessarily lead to any immediate action does not mean that the constitutional or privacy rights of individuals or organizations can be ignored, particularly when government initiatives in assessing threats are involved.

Accident and criminal investigations are very much alike. Accident investigators must secure the scene so that evidence can be collected and, where appropriate, submitted for laboratory examination. This is true whether the particular incident involved a form of transportation or occurred at the workplace. Transportation accidents frequently require the recovery of parts and reassembly of the vehicle for careful examination and reconstruction of the accident. This is particularly true of aircraft.

Surviving victims and witnesses must be identified, interviewed, and their statements obtained. Circumstances may dictate inquiries into their backgrounds and personal lives. Persons suspected of having caused or contributed to accidents must be identified, their backgrounds must be looked at, and they must be interviewed. In addition to interviewing employers, businesses' accident histories need to be examined when work-place deaths or serious injuries occur.

Applicant investigations, based on job sensitivity not just on job title or access to assets, also require record checks and interviews to confirm data provided by applicants. Academic credentials must be verified when part of job descriptions. Former employers, including persons to whom applicants reported, and personal references, should be contacted. A look at pertinent public records needs to be considered.

Investigations of policy violations, conflicts of interest included, should be undertaken only in response to complaints and are governed by the elements needed to prove the offense. For some violations, evidence other than testimonial may be available. If so, the scene has to be secured and searched, evidence has to be collected, and violators' work histories have to be examined. Eventually, they must be interviewed. On occasion, confidential informants can offer useful information, and possible witnesses have to be identified and interviewed. Under certain circumstances, physical surveillances may prove helpful.

Except for threat assessments, it is conceivable that any one of these types of investigations could lead to some form of legal action against those responsible for their initiation. That action could be a civil suit or a complaint to an administrative agency. Consequently, all investigations, not merely criminal cases, must be conducted with the greatest degree of professionalism.

REVIEW QUESTIONS

1. Name the three objectives of threat assessments.
2. Since only assessments are involved, can constitutional safeguards be ignored?
3. Unless there are signs of sabotage or terrorist activity, who has primary investigative responsibility when train or airplane accidents occur?
4. Who conducts serious workplace accident investigations?
5. Why is it important to protect accident scenes?
6. In what ways are private-sector applicant investigations more difficult than those of government applicants?
7. Are private-sector applicant investigators completely foreclosed from access to criminal history data?
8. What evidence is needed to show a conflict of interest when employees allegedly are working on their own businesses on their employers' time even if they are not competing with their employers?
9. What are the elements of all company policy violation cases?
10. Is there less need for care, thoroughness, and objectivity in internal investigations when an employer elects to treat minor crimes as policy violations instead of referring them to the police?

NOTES

1. "Scion of Rich Family in Colo. Is a Suicide," *The Boston Globe,* March 21, 1996, p. 3.
2. "Engineer in Fatal Train Collision Had a Record of Running Signals," *New York Times,* February 12, 1996, pp. A1, B5.
3. "Engineer in N.J. Had a Record of Suspensions," *The Boston Globe,* February 12, 1996, p. 3.
4. "Investigators Citing Design Flaw and Engineer Error in Accident," *New York Times,* February 19, 1996, pp. A1, A9.
5. "Officials Dispute Federal Findings on Subway Safety," *New York Times,* March 21, 1996, p. B4.
6. "Looking for Clues in the Wreckage of a Plane," *New York Times,* July 19, 1996, p. B5.
7. "Safety Board Transcript Shows Pilot Knew He Was Crashing," *New York Times,* March 22, 1996, p. B6.
8. "Safety Mistake Cited in Crash of Girl's Plane," *New York Times,* April 13, 1996, pp. 1, 7.
9. "Investigators Look to June Mishap for Clues to Crashes of 737's," *New York Times,* July 3, 1996, p. A21.
10. Compiled from *New York Times,* July 8, 1996, p. A9; *The Boston Globe,* July 7, 1996, p. 2, and July 8, 1996, p. 3.

11. *The Boston Globe,* July 9, 1996, p. 6.

12. "Safety Board Finds Airplane Maker at Fault in 1994 Turboprop Crash," *New York Times,* July 10, 1996, p. A10.

13. "Doubts Grow About Finding Cause of Crash," *New York Times,* October 8, 1996, pp. B1, B2.

14. "Criminal Act Is 'Less Likely' In L.I. Crash," *New York Times,* November 21, 1996, pp. B1, B7.

15. "Detection Machine on Front Line," *New York Times,* August 13, 1996, p. B5.

16. "Trace of Chemical," *New York Times,* August 23, 1996, pp. A1, B6.

17. "Bomb Security Test on Jet Before Crash May Explain Traces," *New York Times,* September 21, 1996, pp. 1, 24.

18. Ibid.

19. Compiled from *New York Times,* July 28, 1996, pp. A1, A19 and July 29, 1996, pp. A1, B4.

20. "Quietly, Officials Seek Clues in Lives of Flight 800's Dead," *New York Times,* August 18, 1996, pp. 1, 48.

21. "Investigators Intensifying Search for Center Section of Jet," *New York Times,* August 20, 1996, p. B4.

22. "Many Seats Are Still Missing from a Section of Flight 800," *New York Times,* August 21, 1996, p. B5.

23. "A Shift in Focus for Crash Inquiry," *New York Times,* September 19, 1996, pp. A1, B8.

24. "Corrosion May Have Erased Vital Clues From T.W.A. Wreckage, Experts Worry," *New York Times,* September 27, 1996, p. B4.

25. Compiled from *New York Times,* October 4, 1996, p. B6, and October 2, 1996, pp. B1, B6.

26. 29 U. S. C. 657.

27. 29 C. F. R. 1901.1 to end.

28. *Burdeau v. McDowell,* 256 U.S. 465, 65 L. Ed. 1048, 415 S. Ct. 574, 13 A. L. R. 1159.

29. *Miranda v. Arizona,* 384 U.S. 436, 16 L. Ed. 2d 694, 86 S. Ct. 1602, 10 A. L. R. 3d 974.

PART IV

❖

ADMINISTRATION AND CASE COMPLETION

In Part I, we delved into the history of the investigative process, learned how investigations are begun, and looked at what it takes to be a good investigator. Part II discussed the elements or components of an investigation. To a large extent, they are the resources or tools with which investigators need to be familiar in order to do their jobs effectively. In Part III, we considered the different types of cases most often encountered by investigators. They included violent and nonviolent crimes, and instances when no crimes are committed yet inquiries have to be made.

Investigators like their jobs and the challenges with which they are confronted. They dislike the frustration that accompanies an unsolved crime. They know that every investigation that is started must be completed, and completion necessarily involves taking care of certain administrative matters. Cases have to be managed and reports written. Investigators would be happier if these various "housekeeping" tasks could be avoided, yet they also know each is a necessary part of the job. They find themselves working with lawyers, appearing in court when necessary, and learning how to gracefully accept decisions rendered by courts or administrative bodies with which they may not always agree.

Chapter 19

❖

Case Management

Effective case management revolves around a series of interrelated functions that largely depend on the individual investigators. Nevertheless, the roles of their supervisors and managers, as well as their department's or agency's executives, cannot be ignored. The department's or agency's management staff has the ultimate responsibility for administration. When it fails to discharge its responsibilities, case management, the organization, and the investigative processes suffer. Public-sector investigators can find themselves wasting precious time and effort looking for information that should be readily available in properly managed agencies or departments.

Conditions found in 1953 by the newly appointed chief of the State Department's investigations unit illustrate failures with respect to poor records and case management. U.S. passports are issued by the State Department; therefore, it also is responsible for investigating passport fraud cases. Passport fraud is a crime. Despite a unit chief, sizable headquarters supervisory staff, and special agents in charge of field offices, he found passport fraud investigations that had been pending for more than a year without so much as a memorandum in the file relative to their status. This evidenced a serious management breakdown that was soon changed.

In addition, as a result of unsubstantiated allegations first made at Wheeling, West Virginia, on February 9, 1950, by right-wing Senator Joseph R. McCarthy, to the effect that the State Department was riddled with Communists and their sympathizers, the department was in the throes of having to reinvestigate several thousand employees. The process consisted of headquarters supervisors going through employees' personnel files and writing individual letters setting forth leads to be covered by each of the appropriate field offices. This, too, was changed with a tenfold increase in output to the field.

These examples show the importance of management and executive roles, and how they can hinder or help field investigators by either denying them the availability of and easy access to helpful information or ensuring it. Well-organized records and management systems result in less wasted time and effort and allow investigators to focus on such essentials as getting much needed information from sources outside their organizations.

CASE MANAGEMENT

Records management really is an adjunct of case management. Its importance was expressed in 1983 by John F. Duffy, then president of the Police Executive Research Forum and Sheriff of San Diego (California) County:

> Additionally, police managers and executives should pay close attention to how criminal records are filed and organized to make sure that they are easily accessible by investigators and that they contain information that investigators need. To lose a case because a witness is not available is unfortunate; to lose a case because the detective cannot find information that the department already has in its files is inexcusable.[1]

Notwithstanding executive and managerial responsibility for the provision of good records management systems, actual case management rests with first-line supervisors and the investigators who report to them. Supervisors assign the cases that their investigators work. It is with this process that case management really begins. Supervisors know they are accountable to their superiors. In the final analysis, their performance is evaluated on the basis of their ability to ensure that leads are covered and cases closed in timely fashion. They also know each of their subordinate's ability to handle complex investigations and manage their cases. Consequently, prudent supervisors will not assign any one investigator more work than that person reasonably can handle.

An illustration is the way an FBI field office supervisor approached case assignments. An agent, only a little more than a year out of training, had fifteen complex cases assigned and worked surveillances. He also was translating materials sent from FBI headquarters. Another agent on the same squad, with more than ten years experience, had an average of seven cases assigned. When the newer agent asked his supervisor about this obvious disparity, he was told that even with relatively few cases the older agent had trouble meeting deadlines, but he had learned that regardless of his caseload, the younger one always met them.

Another factor supervisors need to keep in mind in assigning work is made more difficult because the degree of complexity is not always readily apparent to them at the time of case assignment. As investigations develop, some cases inevitably will prove to be more complex and time consuming than others. In criminal cases, the level of complexity may not become obvious until crime scenes have been examined for evidence, victims have been identified, and they and witnesses have been interviewed. This truism has been illustrated in any number of cases cited in earlier chapters. Neither is the issue of complexity limited to criminal investigations, as illustrated in Chapter 18 with particular reference to accident cases.

REPORT SUBMISSION

The next step in case management is the submission of reports. Each organization has its own standards with regard to when reports are to be submitted. However, supervisors are responsible not only for overseeing investigators' timely submissions, but also for carefully reviewing the reports for accuracy and possibly suggesting new avenues of inquiry.

Despite the supervisory role in case management, nothing that has already been said relieves investigators of their individual responsibility for managing the cases assigned to them, an important aspect of which is report writing. Whether reports can be deferred until cases are closed or interim reports must be submitted at specified intervals is a matter within an agency's discretion. Here one may find differences between police departments and federal agencies. One of a number of incentives in policing to move from uniformed to detective rank is that detectives have more discretion in doing their jobs. Although federal investigators also enjoy considerable discretion, concerning report writing, their agencies tend to have more stringent submission requirements. However, regardless of any report writing deadlines, investigations must not be allowed to languish, and those to whom cases are assigned have the primary responsibility for ensuring that they do not.

CASE ANALYSES

On occasion, individual case management in police departments may be difficult for newly promoted investigators. The transition from patrol officer to detective is not always easy. Patrol officers tend to focus on one task at a time; detectives must be able to handle multiple cases at the same time. Managing one's cases means managing time; managing time means being able to combine analytical skills with flexibility.

We already know that investigators work the cases assigned, some of which will prove to be more complex and time consuming than others, and that these considerations are not always readily apparent. However, regardless of complexity, to effectively manage their cases and time, investigators, and their supervisors, must employ a screening process. Its purpose is to evaluate the likelihood of the successful disposition of each case assigned.

To be meaningful, investigators and their supervisors must share in these case analyses. Since the former obviously are the ones most familiar with each of their cases, supervisors look to them for status information. By the same token, looking at cases from somewhat of a distance, and being more experienced, supervisors may bring a fresh perspective to what already has been done, and what still needs to be done. The evaluation process also does something more; in reality, it puts each case in one of three categories that might be designated as pending, pending inactive, and closed.

The status of each case helps determine how it is to be handled. For example, two types logically could be considered pending. There are those that in effect have already been solved by existing circumstances. All that remains to be done is the subject's arrest, booking, and questioning. In other words, the investigation itself, including the collection of physical and testimonial evidence, has been completed. Then there are cases that appear solvable with a reasonable amount of effort, but at this time there is insufficient evidence with which to identify, let alone arrest, anyone. There are leads that need to be followed, and once done, they offer hope of a solution.

Pending inactive cases would consist of those on which investigators have not given up hope, but the chances of success at this point are so slim that devoting more time and effort to the investigation cannot be justified. These are matters for which virtually all logical leads have been covered, and there is no evidence of any kind pointing to a particular suspect, but the statute of limitations has not yet run in a criminal matter or no cause has yet been established in an accident. These are investigations that could be reactivated at any time if additional information is received or new evidence is found. Good examples would be the Elizabeth, New Jersey, homicide case cited earlier in the text and reopened after thirty years with the receipt of new information, or the inquiry into what caused the downing of TWA Flight 800.

When all work has been completed, or the statute of limitations has run out without a solution, cases are closed. It is immaterial whether the inquiries are criminal or noncriminal. For instance, the final report would be a closing one whether the subject of a criminal investigation is in custody awaiting trial, the cause of an accident has been established, or all the leads in an applicant investigation have been completed.

To manage their cases and time, investigators must be able to set priorities. In some situations, deadlines for submitting reports or a particularly high-profile case may be a factor, but under no circumstances are any pending matters abandoned. Logic also plays an important role in planning work and pursuing leads. As an example, an investigator with twelve pending cases, four of which require checking motor vehicle records, should examine all of them on one trip to the Department of Motor Vehicles, rather than make four trips. The same would be true if three different cases had leads in the same general part of the city. In other words, proper planning conserves time and effort. This, in turn, allows investigators to work more than one case at a time without detracting from the importance of any.

Not all supervisory roles are the same in case management. The way in which police departments are organized may make it more difficult for their supervisors to manage cases than is true for federal investigative agencies' supervisors.

At the federal level, the relationship between investigators and supervisors is direct. Each investigator is responsible for every case assigned to him or her. This is true even when others help. Regardless of when reports are to be submitted, questions about status and progress can be asked at any time. Then, too, federal investigations are opened differently than police cases. Although supervisors assign cases, for all practical purposes nothing stands between the investigator and the person or incident responsible for the case being opened. These factors permit closer supervision, tighter controls, and better case management on the part of both investigators and their supervisors.

The police department process is different. The first response to an incident, however it may be reported, usually is by uniformed patrol personnel, rarely by detectives; their respective roles have been discussed in earlier chapters. Furthermore, even if the patrol officers and detectives are assigned to the same precinct or district, each group has its own supervisory or managerial hierarchy. There is one set of supervisors for uniformed officers and another for detectives.

This can have an impact on the way in which cases are managed at both the detective and supervisor level. A number of factors can contribute to or detract from effective case management. For instance, critically important is the degree of cooperation that exists between uniformed officers and detectives. If they tend to compete with rather than complement each other, delays can occur, and there can be needless duplication of effort, making cases harder to manage.

In criminal investigations, time is a factor. The more elapsed time between the occurrence and initiation of the investigation, the more difficult the case becomes. Leads become cold, and there is the risk that evidence will be lost. Consequently, if patrol officers are ineffective in locating and identifying witnesses for detectives, and getting information when they first arrive at a crime scene, an additional burden is placed on the investigators. This makes case management more difficult.

We repeatedly have discussed the importance of protecting crime scenes, collecting and preserving evidence, and ensuring its admissibility at time of trial. Making certain that these things are done is an integral part of case management. However, the task is not made easier by having patrol officers as the first responders since they, not the detectives, are the ones who are expected to protect crime scenes. Therefore, unless they fully understand what physical evidence is so that it can be protected, they hinder rather than help the investigation. In addition, patrol personnel frequently will be asked to collect or assist in the collection of evidence for detectives. The evidence may be physical, testimonial, or both. However, if the manner in which they proceed to collect evidence renders it inadmissible at trial, the prospects for a successful conclusion to the case are greatly reduced regardless of the investigator's management skills.

SUMMARY

Good records management systems can contribute significantly to effective case management; in reality, they are intertwined. Executive and managerial personnel are responsible for records management; primary responsibility for case management rests with investigators to whom cases are assigned and their supervisors. However, since department or agency heads are ultimately accountable for their organizations' operations, they cannot completely avoid involvement with the case management aspects.

Supervisory personnel play a critical role in ensuring effective case management on the part of their subordinates. They should be sufficiently familiar with their investigators to know how many cases at a given level of complexity any one of them can handle efficiently and effectively. Supervisors also need to read reports carefully and make certain that all logical avenues of inquiry have been covered.

The primary responsibility for managing cases remains with the investigators to whom they are assigned. Their enjoyment of considerable discretion in doing their jobs does not mean they can allow cases to go unattended. Police officers' transition to detective ranks initially can be difficult from a case management viewpoint given that they then must learn to handle multiple cases instead of focusing on one at a time. All investigators learn that case management is almost synonymous with time management. They have to analyze cases from a solvability viewpoint so that they can set priorities. They should not delude themselves into thinking that all cases can be solved. Pending cases must be diligently pursued, and those that can be closed, closed. It is not just a matter of writing reports; they must be timely in terms of their submission.

Although detectives also have primary responsibility for their cases, unlike federal investigators they necessarily depend on patrol officers for assistance. No matter how limited that help may be, unless there is a high level of cooperation between detectives and patrol personnel, the detectives' ability to manage cases is hampered.

In the final analysis, although investigators are primarily responsible for managing their cases, to be effective, the entire process has to be a team effort. Department and agency executives and managers must make records and access to them available. Supervisors must be realistic in assigning cases; they also have to oversee the work of their units and be ready to consult with and guide their investigators. The latter can neither ignore any of their cases nor assume that the submission of reports is discretionary, something they can do at their leisure.

REVIEW QUESTIONS

1. Why are case and records management important?
2. Is case management a shared responsibility?
3. If so, by whom and in what ways?
4. What factors should supervisors consider in assigning cases?
5. Should an investigator's lack of experience by itself prevent his or her being assigned certain cases?
6. Why is report writing important?
7. Why can it be difficult for a patrol officer to make the transition to detective?
8. Explain the relationship between case and time management.
9. In terms of case management, what purpose is served by analyzing cases for their solvability?
10. Under what conditions should a case be closed?

NOTE

1. Sheriff Duffy's comments are found in the preface to "Solving Crimes: The Investigation of Burglary and Robbery" by John E. Eck (Washington, D.C.: Police Executive Research Forum, 1983), reprinted in 1992.

Chapter 20

❖

Report Writing

Police departments, as distinguished from federal agencies, produce two kinds of reports. One is relatively brief. It is used when taking complaints or when patrol personnel respond to an incident. The other, more detailed and lengthy, is written by detectives and is similar in style to reports written by federal investigators. We discuss investigators' rather than patrol officers' reports in this chapter.

The format used in report writing is within the discretion of the department or agency for which the investigator works. The time limits within which reports are to be submitted and the frequency of their submissions in pending cases also are discretionary on the part of the department or agency. But aside from these factors, how should reports be written and of what should they consist?

In Chapter 19, we said that report writing is an integral part of case management. This is true for both investigators and their supervisors. Reports give them a chance to look at the status of a case in terms of what has been accomplished and what still needs to be done. Furthermore, no matter how good original investigative notes may be, they are only notes. Then, too, since no investigator's memory is infallible, until those notes are fleshed out in report form within a reasonable time, there is a risk that some information of value may be forgotten.

WHAT TO INCLUDE IN A REPORT

As a practical matter, all reports, whether written in connection with criminal or noncriminal investigations, should include certain basic data. Reports obviously must contain the details of the investigation. By the same token, there may be other matters that can be helpful even though they relate to format and are not necessarily essential. This information would be especially helpful to supervisors who have to review reports as part of their case management responsibilities and to other investigators who may be working on the case and therefore need to refer to the reports.

First, what information should be set forth at the very beginning of a report? The author's name should appear. This is the name of the investigator to whom the case is assigned even if that person is being helped by others. The date of the report should be given. It may prove helpful also to set forth the actual dates on which any work on the case was done. The case file number and caption must be included. Captions include both the name of the person (or organization) on whom the investigation has been or is being conducted and the nature of the inquiry. Parenthetically, the nature of federal investigations is such that reports include information about where they are written.

To illustrate possible report captions, let us consider both a criminal and an applicant inquiry. The first is a bank robbery, and the subject has one alias. The caption would be: John Doe, wa Donald Doe; Bank Robbery. *Wa* in criminal cases is an acronym for "with alias" when the subject has but one. If the subject has multiple aliases, the standard acronym is *was*. Thus if the subject has more than one alias, the caption would be: John Doe, was Donald Doe, Richard Roe; Bank Robbery.

An applicant case caption would be similar, but not identical. It might simply be: Mary Smith; Applicant. If the applicant is married but uses her maiden name professionally, it would be: Mary Smith, aka Mary Smith Jones; Applicant. In such noncriminal investigations, when the person may be known by more than one name, captions use the name by which the person is most commonly known, followed by the acronym *aka,* which means "also known as."

Although by no means a universal practice, some organizations find it helpful to have investigators begin reports with a synopsis of facts. As the phrase implies, this is a brief paragraph, using what might be called "teletype language," that sets forth the report's highlights. This gives the reader of the synopsis the gist of the report's contents. An applicant investigation's synopsis might read as follows:

John Doe's birth June 3, 1956, New York, NY, verified. Graduated New York City High School of Science, 1974; B.A. New York University, 1978; J.D. Fordham University, 1981. Associate Jones & Davis,

1982–1992; partner, 1992. No criminal record; no adverse information credit records. Former teachers and personal references favorable; same regarding neighborhood investigation. Active professional and civic organizations.

At some point in the report, the investigation's status should be indicated. Again, this is a matter of format, but it helps those reading the report if the information appears at or near the beginning. Indicating that the report is pending lets the supervisor, or other readers, know that more work has to be done. It also means additional leads will be set forth. A report marked "closed" signifies that, as far as the investigator is concerned, the investigation has been completed. A closing report also requires the supervisor's careful analysis to ensure that no other logical leads are to be pursued. Some agencies indicate status at both the beginning and end.

OBJECTIVITY IN REPORT WRITING

Simply saying the "details" are exactly that does not necessarily convey the importance of a report's contents or how they are written. Throughout the text, reference has been made to the need for investigators to be objective. Objectivity is as important to report writing as it is to the investigation itself.

Although not necessarily part of all investigative reports, a predicate statement at the beginning is the first sign of objectivity; so much so that some agencies require a predicate opening paragraph. Chapter 5 discussed how investigations are initiated. They should be undertaken only in response to either the known or suspected commission of a crime, or because a valid reason for an inquiry exists, as in the case of an accident or an application for employment, and the department or agency has been asked to conduct it. Therefore, unless contrary to policy, it is a good idea to begin writing a report by stating the reason for the investigation.

Objectivity also is shown by prohibiting the inclusion in reports of investigators' personal opinions about any aspect of the case. The only permissible opinions are those of people interviewed in connection with the inquiry. Should someone interviewed express an opinion, this must be made clear; it must not appear as a statement of fact, as in the following:

Mary Johnson, a personal reference, was interviewed at her residence, 10 ABC Lane, Anytown, NY, December 20, 1996, and advised she has known the applicant not only since they were high school classmates, but also as a coworker at the Do-good Company with whom she carpools. Ms. Johnson said the applicant was the vice president's administrative assistant and had been in that job for the last four years. She said she has always found the applicant to be hardworking and honest. She expressed the opinion that the applicant was an ambitious person whose primary concern seemed to be in meeting influential people and making a lot of money.

The example also illustrates what must be included as detail. It does more than name the person who provided the information. First, Mary Johnson is identified as one of the applicant's personal references. Second, the paragraph indicates where and when the interview was conducted. Third, it contains information about her relationship with the applicant. Fourth, it confirms that the applicant has been in her present job for four years. Fifth, it discusses Ms. Johnson's experience regarding the applicant's character (hardworking and honest), and last, Ms. Johnson expressed her opinion about the applicant's ambition and apparent goals.

STATING DETAILS

Stating details is essential in report writing. Persons interviewed must be identified, and their addresses must be included. This applies whether they are victims, witnesses, or people contacted in connection with applicant investigations. When reports contain references to work done at or inquiries made of government offices, the author should not assume or take for granted the reader's understanding of what was done and where. Even if the readers are government employees, pertinent data must be included.

For instance, instead of simply saying the records of the Department of Motor Vehicles were checked, include the address at which they were checked as well. Merely stating that a criminal record was examined is not enough. Is the author referring to criminal court records, local or state police department records, or those maintained by the FBI's Identification Division? If criminal court records, which court were they from? If information was sought about a person's home at a Registry of Deeds office, the county should be indicated. The same is true of inquiries at a probate court about a will or a divorce proceeding. Attention to detail in report writing is every bit as important as it is during the investigation itself. It signals professionalism and thoroughness.

IDENTIFYING CONFIDENTIAL INFORMANTS AND UNDEVELOPED LEADS

There are two aspects to the identification of confidential informants in a report. Both require care. Since they obviously cannot be identified by name or source, many organizations use symbols of some sort for this purpose. The means used for informant identification also is a matter of a department's or agency's choosing. This would be true whether information comes from a person who is an informant or from some form of surveillance, especially if the latter is either electronic or a telephone tap. Thus a report might refer to an informant as Confidential Informant T-1. In any event, regardless of how information included in a report is derived, it must be attributed to a source.

The other and equally important aspect is to indicate an informant's reliability. The investigator's development and use of confidential informants and the importance of reliability were discussed in Chapter 9. Informant reliability is critical in criminal cases. Prosecutors base decisions about whether to go to a grand jury, file an information, and ultimately about proceeding to trial on the apparent strength of a case. For that they rely largely on investigative reports. Consequently, if any information in a report is attributable to a confidential informant, they also have to know if that informant is reliable. The only one who can answer that question is the investigator who has worked with that informant.

Therefore, reports must identify confidential informants by both the symbol of choice and on the basis of their reliability. This does not mean only information from sources that are known to be reliable can be used; it does mean that if investigators have any doubts about their informants they must qualify their characterizations.

For example, information derived from a court-approved electronic surveillance installed by the investigator's agency, an undercover investigator, or a person who has furnished good information to the investigator over time would be reported as coming from a confidential informant of known reliability. Note that reliability refers only to the source, not to the quality of the information provided. A source who has given information of varying quality over time might be characterized as a confidential informant who has on occasion provided reliable information. One whose reliability has not yet been established, would be referred to as of unknown reliability.

Confidentiality notwithstanding, if informants are cited in reports, their actual identities nevertheless must be recorded. This is in the event that at time of trial the court rules on the issue of a criminal defendant's constitutional right to be confronted by his or her accusers and orders the informant's appearance in court. How this process is handled rests with the investigator's organization. One method that has been used successfully lists informants' symbols and actual identities on a separate page at the very end of the report. This page helps the investigator if in the future the informant must be identified and is detached from any copies of the report that may be disseminated outside the organization itself, prosecutors' offices included.

Unless a closing report is being written, or the report's status goes from pending to pending inactive, the last page of the body of the report should set forth undeveloped leads. They indicate the work that still needs to be done. For instance, suppose an organization's case management system requires the submission of reports within certain time limits. A pending report is being written to meet the deadline, but attempts to interview a likely witness have been unsuccessful because the person has been out of town. Arranging for and conducting that interview is an undeveloped lead. New information indicates the subject may have taken an unreported trip abroad; it therefore is questionable. Efforts to confirm such travel by checking credit card records for what they might show, along with airline, hotel, and telephone records, would be undeveloped leads.

Despite the need for detailed information, for investigative reports to be of real value, investigators should remember that their submissions are working documents; they are not destined to win prizes in literature. Although the best reports are those that are clear and concise, details must never be sacrificed for the sake of brevity. In addition, reports will be reviewed by supervisors and possibly disseminated outside the organization; therefore, their authors are responsible for ensuring that they are well written and grammatically correct, that words are spelled correctly, and that proper punctuation and sentence structure are observed.

SUMMARY

Investigative reports are a comprehensive statement of what their authors have uncovered during the investigation. This is true no matter what the format used, the time frames within which they are to be submitted, or the elimination or inclusion of predicate statements—all matters to be decided by individual organizations. However, regardless of departmental or agency choices, all reports should indicate the investigation's status. They also should include the names of the investigators they were written by and when, and captions showing who or what was investigated and the reason. Depending on organizational policy, additional information that might be helpful, such as dates on which work actually was done and a synopsis of facts, might be included.

Objectively written reports are essential if they are to be of any real value, particularly in criminal cases or matters that may result in litigation. They also are a sign of an investigator's professionalism. Objectivity is shown when reports consist of statements of fact, not investigators' personal opinions, and personal opinions given by interviewed persons are clearly identified as such.

It is not unusual for criminal case reports to include information obtained from confidential informants whose identities must be protected. Therefore, the authors of those reports identify informants' information by using a symbol instead of a name. Furthermore, it also is important to indicate how much credibility should be attached to that information by stating the extent to which the source's reliability is known.

The details reported are crucial; much depends on what reports contain. Authors of investigative reports should avoid the mistake of using language or shortcuts on the assumption that readers will know or understand what they mean. In pending cases, this same principle applies in setting forth undeveloped leads. It is the investigator's responsibility to indicate what work has to be done before the case can be closed; it is not for the reader to figure out.

REVIEW QUESTIONS

1. Who decides on the format used for report writing and the times within which reports must be submitted?
2. What is meant by a report's status?
3. What purpose does a synopsis of facts serve?
4. What is meant by a predicate statement?
5. Who decides if predicate statements are to be used?
6. Should investigators include their personal opinions in reports?
7. Should reports include opinions expressed by persons interviewed? If so, should the statement be identified as an opinion?
8. Is it a good idea to use technical language or shortcuts in writing investigative reports?
9. In what two ways should confidential informants be identified in investigative reports?
10. Should pending reports set forth leads that still have to be pursued?

Chapter 21

— ❖ —

The Trial Process

Submitting a closing report does not automatically bring an end to an investigator's role. The nature of the original inquiry determines whether there will be further involvement. Obviously, there is nothing more to be done in applicant investigations. However, in criminal cases, there most likely will be a trial at which the investigator's testimony will be required; it also may be required in noncriminal matters being tried in civil courts. In addition, investigators' testimony may be needed if hearings are held by government-appointed administrative officers, or internally by management representatives in cases involving employees' policy violations. As important as investigators' reports are, they are no substitute for their testimony. It is in these situations that investigators find more is involved than simply making themselves available at the appointed time.

With that thought in mind, we divide this chapter into three parts. The first focuses on the pretrial or prehearing phase and how investigators work with attorneys, the second discusses the trial or hearing itself, and the third deals with the rendering of a decision by the triers of fact.

WORKING WITH ATTORNEYS

With the exception of Chapter 18, we have focused largely on criminal investigations. Consequently, one might well expect this section to be titled working with prosecutors rather than with attorneys, but to do that would be misleading. It would imply that noncriminal cases with which investigators may be involved never go to trial, they never have to deal with opposing counsel, and their initial contact may not come until the time of trial.

Realistically, few investigations are immune from involvement with lawyers. It is immaterial whether a matter is to be tried in a courtroom or before an administrative tribunal. Most initial contact occurs in the pre-trial stages. In civil cases, it can involve lawyers with whom investigators are working as well as opposing counsel. However, the probability of such involvement may be much lower in some cases than it is in others.

Investigators' least likely exposure to lawyers is in connection with applicant investigations. For instance, one ordinarily would not expect any form of litigation to result from these inquiries. Nevertheless, persons denied employment might complain to a state commission against discrimination alleging they were discriminated against for one reason or another. This will require the commission to conduct an investigation. Even if complainants elect to represent themselves before such a commission, one can be certain that organizations against whom complaints have been made will be represented by counsel. The latter may seek permission to question the investigator before any hearing takes place.

Next are civil lawsuits, not all of which call for investigations. In many instances, both plaintiffs' and defendants' lawyers conduct their own inquiries to try to learn as much as possible about the opposition's case before trial. However, there also are times when investigators will do the work in their behalf. Regardless of who conducts the investigation, the attorneys for each of the parties want to find out about the strength of their opponent's case, physical and testimonial evidence included.

For this purpose, both plaintiffs' and defendants' lawyers can use two legal processes; one is called discovery, the other a deposition. Depositions are used as part of trial preparation. They permit attorneys for each side to question under oath those persons who will appear at the trial itself as witnesses for the opposition in an effort to find out what their testimony will be. Thus, it is possible that investigators may be among those deposed. If so, they are accompanied by lawyers who represent the side for which they are to be witnesses, and from whom they will take guidance. The need for care in answering questions at depositions is as great as it is at trials. Conflicts between statements made during a deposition and testimony given at trial can be used to try to discredit the investigator.

Criminal investigators' contact is limited to lawyers whose side they represent. Government investigators work with prosecutors. For example, local and state police officers and sheriffs' deputies work with district attorneys' offices; state police personnel also may work with their state's attorney general's staff. Federal investigators work with the appropriate U.S. Attorney's office. However, public defenders' offices also may use investigators to conduct inquiries in behalf of defendants. If those offices are supported by government funds, their investigators, although government employees, do not work with prosecutors. Furthermore, there is nothing to prevent defendants who can afford them from hiring their own investigators.

In cases lawyers expect to go to trial, part of their preparation consists of meeting with witnesses, including investigators, as often as they believe is necessary. The purpose is to clarify for their own benefit what each witness can testify to, and ensure that what will be said in court can be understood by jurors and judges; it is not to rehearse witnesses or tell them what to say.

They also review with investigators the physical evidence they hope to introduce at trial. In our earlier discussion of evidence, we said that to be admitted, evidence must have been legally obtained, and it must be both relevant and material to the case. To establish relevance and materiality, lawyers must lay a foundation for the introduction of that evidence, often relying on an investigator's testimony as it relates to what is being offered.

Attorneys do not win trials unless they are well prepared for them, and if investigators have played a role, an essential part of that preparation consists of working with them. After all, it is the investigators who have identified, located, and questioned witnesses, and who have collected physical and testimonial evidence on which the lawyers will rely. Therefore, good investigators never underestimate the importance of the lawyers' role regardless of the side for which they may be working.

GOING TO COURT

Principles set forth in this section apply equally to investigators' appearances before administrative tribunals. They deal with preparation, physical appearance, and the way in which testimony is offered. Lawyers present cases in court, but the outcome may well be determined in large part by the credibility of witnesses, especially investigators. This is true for all trials, but it has special significance in criminal cases in which the objective should be justice for victims, but not at the expense of charged but actually innocent defendants when the results can mean a loss of freedom, or possibly even life.

Regardless of the number of meetings investigators may have had with the attorneys in preparing for trial, they still must do their own preparation. Therefore, no matter how good investigators' memories may be, in addition to thoroughly reviewing the case file, it is imperative that they take their original investigative notes on the case with them when they go to court. If investigators, rather than prosecutors or plaintiffs' attorneys, have retained custody of physical evidence, they also are responsible for getting it to court when needed.

No matter how well prepared, even the most experienced investigators have to be cautious when they appear as witnesses. They will be asked questions by both the lawyers with whom they have been working and opposing counsel. Regardless of who does the asking, investigators should never answer any questions that they do not fully understand. If a question is not understood, it is perfectly proper to ask for clarification.

Even when questions are understood, it may be unwise to answer by relying solely on memory. When this situation presents itself, it is quite proper to ask the court's permission to refresh one's memory by referring to the original investigative notes for answers, a request that usually is granted. In this regard, it is important to remember that once notes are referred to, opposing counsel will have a right to examine them. Therefore, investigators must remember this when they first write those notes. They must make certain there will not be anything on that paper that is unrelated to the case at hand. For example, never use the same sheet of paper on which notes are or will be made for notes on other cases, shopping lists, or anything else of a personal nature.

Investigators' personal appearances in court are important. Whether appearing in civilian clothes or uniform, those who are well groomed and tastefully and conservatively dressed give the impression that they are professionals. Clothes should be clean and pressed, shoes shined, and hair, including facial hair where permitted, neatly trimmed. Female investigators' hair should be neatly combed, and too much makeup, jewelry, or heavy perfume should be avoided.

Behavior is equally important. When called to testify, proceed directly to the witness stand to be sworn. Investigators should not stop either before or after testifying to shake hands with the attorneys with whom they have been working. To do so risks raising questions about their objectivity in jurors' minds.

Other factors also play an important role when investigators testify. Among them are such things as the way they sit; their body language before, during, and after testifying; eye contact with lawyers, jurors, judges, and defendants; tone of voice and general presentation; and how they react to cross-examination.

Once testimony begins, the way investigators behave is crucial. The Honorable B. Marc Mogil offers sound advice when he says, "The job of the law enforcement witness on the stand is to answer questions posed by the prosecution and the defense. It is how you react, as much as what you say, that will greatly affect the outcome of the trial."[1]

Listening carefully to all questions, and thinking with equal care before answering, is a must. Answers should be limited to what the question asks, nothing more. For example, if a simple yes or no will suffice, that is all that should be said. A "yes, but" or a "no, but" answer is like the sound of music to an opposing lawyer's ears. In addition, if investigators respond too quickly to prosecutors' questions on direct examination, they give the impression that the answer was memorized; too hasty an answer during cross-examination may prevent the prosecutor from raising a timely objection.

Be honest when testifying, and avoid being specific if uncertain. It is infinitely more professional, and better, to say a defendant was seen driving what *appeared* to be a navy blue car than it is to say it was blue, only to be embarrassed when opposing counsel produces a motor vehicle registration stating the color as black.

Neither should investigators' integrity give way to pressure from prosecutors, as can occasionally happen. As Robert Knightly, a former New York City Police sergeant and now a Legal Aid lawyer, has said, "We [referring to police officers] don't see with the specificity we see in court. . . . There's pressure from the D.A. to make a legal case. They don't want to hear you didn't see something. As long as you give them a prosecutable case, they don't want to know everything that went on out there."[2] This happens notwithstanding remarks made in November 1995 by then New York City Police Commissioner William Bratton and Queens County District Attorney Richard A. Brown, cited earlier in the text, regarding the importance of honesty when testifying, and the risk that cases can be lost when jurors perceive that officers are not being truthful.

The impact of dishonest testimony on the criminal justice system can be great in a number of ways. For example, in early 1997, it was reported that as a result of evidence tainted by the untruthful testimony of officers who had been assigned to New York City's 30th Precinct, 125 criminal cases were dismissed, 98 defendants were cleared, at least 25 civil cases had been filed against the department, $1.3 million had been paid by the city in awards and settlements, and prosecutors had identified another 2,000 cases also affected by this misconduct.[3]

Even greater problems can arise when investigators withhold information, as illustrated by a Connecticut case. In 1981, a 15-year-old boy and 16-year-old girl had been brutally beaten. An arrest was made in 1982, and the defendant was sentenced in 1983. On April 10, 1996, a judge released the defendant on bond ruling that he was "factually innocent" based on the Danbury Police Department's having withheld information, from both prosecutors and defense counsel, that pointed to another suspect.[4]

Being polite to opposing counsel during cross-examination can be difficult. They may attempt to confuse or anger investigators, thus making courtesy all the more necessary. For instance, we already have said it is best to answer questions with a simple yes or no whenever possible. However, there will be times when defendants' lawyers will ask questions to which an unqualified yes or no answer would be misleading, yet they will insist on such an answer. If an investigator, or any witness for that matter, attempts to explain by answering with a "yes, but" or a "no, but," they will demand that the witness limit the answer to a yes or no. Under such circumstances, for investigators to become argumentative, angry, or show signs of frustration detracts from their professionalism and plays into the hands of defense counsel.

Neither can investigators ignore the possibility that some of opposing counsel's questions may be embarrassing. To illustrate we need but refer to the 1996 James Jordan homicide trial discussed in earlier chapters. In that case, the medical examiner testified that a gunshot wound to the chest, puncturing the aorta, caused the victim's death, yet when testifying on cross-examination, an agent of the South Carolina Law Enforcement Division had to admit his failure to see a hole in the victim's shirt when he examined it.[5]

THE VERDICT

Although good investigators must be objective while working, once they have collected all the evidence and written their closing reports, it would be unrealistic to deny that they have formed opinions about a defendant's guilt in a criminal case or liability in a civil matter. It would be equally unrealistic to say they invariably are pleased with the decisions reached by those to whom the facts have been presented. Nevertheless, their opinions are not an issue as long as their testimony is honestly, objectively, and thoughtfully given.

It is true, as we said earlier, that trials of cases in which investigators have been involved can be won or lost depending on the quality of the investigations or presentations by attorneys. At the same time, it would be naive to deny that despite efforts to ensure fairness in all hearings, reading the mind of any juror or other person involved with the decision-making process is impossible.

Historically, there have been more than a few cases where decisions that have been rendered seem to fly in the face of the evidence. When this happens, investigators who have worked those cases understandably are upset and frustrated, yet they cannot publicly show their distaste for the outcome. This is true whether the decisions are made by judges, jurors, government commissions, or hearing officers, or by human resources managers working in a corporate environment.

Any public displays of discontent or disagreement reflect adversely on investigators' professionalism. In addition, and particularly in criminal cases, such displays help undermine the public's confidence in our criminal justice system. Therefore, good investigators are prepared to accept whatever decisions are rendered as the result of a legal or administrative process in matters with which they have been involved.

SUMMARY

It is safe to say that after completing many, if not most, investigations, investigators find themselves working with lawyers. In criminal cases, they work with prosecutors. In civil matters, they work with attorneys by whom they have been retained, but they also may find themselves having pretrial contact with opposing counsel. Pretrial conferences with prosecutors or lawyers who employed them are intended to help the parties prepare for trial; they are not rehearsals to ensure that lines have been memorized correctly.

When investigators are involved, lawyers rely on the physical evidence they have collected, the witnesses they have identified, and their own testimony. Good investigations can help win cases, but in a larger sense, the outcome depends on attorneys' presentations, and even more on the role of those who hear and evaluate the evidence. Consequently, investigators must impress the triers of fact with their professionalism. To do this, they must be mindful of both their personal appearance and conduct when called as witnesses.

There will be times when cases will be decided in ways that investigators believe are against the weight of the evidence. Nevertheless, prudence dictates that they do not publicly express dissatisfaction. That, too, detracts from their professionalism and tends to undermine whatever legal process preceded the final decision.

REVIEW QUESTIONS

1. What are the three main parts of the trial process?
2. Are investigators involved with lawyers only in criminal cases?
3. What is a deposition?
4. What type of investigation is least likely to be followed by lawyer involvement?
5. What purpose do pretrial conferences serve?
6. What three things must investigators do to prepare for trial?
7. Under what circumstances can investigative notes be referred to at trial?
8. Is it all right for investigators to shake hands with the attorneys with whom they have worked either before or after testifying?
9. Why are the personal appearance and conduct of investigators important when called to testify?
10. Discuss why investigators should not publicly express their dissatisfaction with a trial's outcome.

NOTES

1. Honorable B. Marc Mogil, "Maximizing Your Courtroom Testimony," *FBI Law Enforcement Bulletin,* Vol. 58, No. 5 (May 1989), pp. 7–9.
2. "Trading Badge to Seek Justice Before the Bar," *New York Times,* February 24, 1996, p. 23.
3. "New York Pays a High Price for Police Lies," *New York Times,* January 5, 1997, pp. 1, 20.
4. "Man Freed After 13 Years as Judge Says Police Withheld Crucial Facts," *New York Times,* April 11, 1996, pp. B1, B6.
5. "Evidence Handling Assailed in Jordan Father's Death," *The Boston Globe,* January 11, 1996, p. 12.

Glossary

Accelerant: a volatile organic liquid used to start a fire and help it spread more rapidly.

Admission: an express or implied statement that tends to support a suspect's involvement in a crime, but insufficient by itself to prove a person's guilt.

AFIS: Automated Fingerprint Identification System.

Aka: also known as.

Arches: one of the three general patterns used in classifying fingerprints.

Asphyxiation: unconsciousness or death caused by interference with the supply of oxygen to the lungs.

Blunt force wound: a wound produced by an instrument other than one that cuts or penetrates.

Bug: a device such as a hidden microphone or radio transmitter used to eavesdrop.

Bugging: eavesdropping by electronic means.

Burn the surveillance: the behavior of the person conducting the surveillance prompts the subject to know or guess that he or she is under surveillance.

Canvass: to systematically interview everyone in a certain neighborhood or area for the purpose of ascertaining information.

Confession: a subject's oral or written statement in which he or she acknowledges guilt.

Criminalistics: that branch of forensic science that is concerned with the scientific examination and interpretation of the minute details of physical evidence in order to help the criminal investigator or a judge and jury during the course of a trial.

DNA fingerprinting: information gotten through multilocus probe testing of DNA.

Dying declaration: a statement made just before dying by a person who is aware of his or her impending death; such declarations are allowed into evidence in homicide investigations in some jurisdictions even though they are hearsay.

Elements of a crime: the specific acts that, when taken together, compose a crime.

Exemplars: physical evidence specimens of known origin that are used for comparison with similar evidence found at the crime scene.

Fence: to buy and/or sell stolen goods; a person who is in the business of buying stolen goods, usually for their resale.

Fixed surveillance: a surveillance that is conducted from a stationary position.

Forensic: something that pertains to, is connected with, or is used in courts of law or public discussions or debates.

Forensic medicine: the use of medicine in order to determine the cause and/or time of death, or for other legal purposes.

Hearsay: statement(s) made out of court that then are offered in court for the purpose of supporting the truth of facts that have been asserted in the statement(s).

Interrogation: the process of questioning people who are likely to be deceptive or withhold information, most often suspects, their families, or their friends or associates.

Interview: the process used to question victims, eyewitnesses, and persons who reasonably can be expected to disclose what they know.

Latent print: a fingerprint left by a person who touches an object that is invisible unless it is treated or developed in some way.

Lineup: placing a suspect within a group of people who are lined up so that they can be viewed and the perpetrator possibly identified by eyewitnesses.

Mail cover: the copying by postal authorities of printing or writing that appears on the outside of a piece of mail.

Modus operandi (MO): the pattern or method of an offender's operation.

Omerta: the Mafia's code of silence; an oath of secrecy sworn to by new members.

Plant: an ignition device that ignites the first fuel in arson investigations or that helps build the intensity of the initial flame; it may include a timing mechanism; in a surveillance, a technique in which the person conducting the surveillance stays essentially in one location or position.

Points of identification: individual characteristics found in physical evidence that provide the basis for establishing an identification; called ridge characteristics, minutiae, Galton details or Galton minutiae in fingerprints, and striations in firearms.

Profiling: psychologically assessing a crime by recognizing and interpreting visible evidence at the crime scene and forming an opinion of the perpetrator's personality type.

Pyromania: an irresistible compulsion or impulse to start a fire or set something on fire.

Radial loop: a fingerprint pattern with the open end leading in the direction of the thumb.

Rogues Gallery: a photographic file of arrested persons, usually profile and full face, with detailed physical descriptions, dates and places of birth, Social Security numbers, fingerprint classifications, nicknames and aliases, modus operandi, and other pertinent data.

Striations: a series of parallel lines of different width, depth, and separation; scratches due to irregularities or the absence of microfine smoothness on a gun barrel's surface or a jimmy's working edge.

Surveillance: observing an individual, place, or thing, generally, but not necessarily, in an unobtrusive way.

Trace evidence: physical evidence that is so minute in size or its forensic detail that a stereomicroscope, a polarized light microscope, or both are needed for its examination.

Trailer: materials, a device, or a substance used to spread a fire from one point to another.

Trauma: an injury that results from the use of any blunt, sharp, or penetrating force.

Ulnar loop: a fingerprint pattern with the loop's open end going in the direction of the little finger.

VICAP: Violent Crime Apprehension Program.

VIN: vehicle identification number.

Wa: with alias.

Was: with aliases.

Suggested Bibliography

ABADINSKY, HOWARD, *Organized Crime,* 3rd ed. Chicago: Nelson-Hall, 1990.

AULT, R. L., "Hypnosis: The FBI's Team Approach," *FBI Law Enforcement Bulletin,* Vol. 49, No. 1 (January 1980), pp. 5–8.

BEVERIDGE, WILLIAM I., *The Art of Scientific Investigation,* Modern Library rev. ed. New York: Random House, 1957.

BINTLIFF, RUSSELL L., *Complete Manual of White Collar Crime Detection and Prevention.* Englewood Cliffs, NJ: Prentice Hall, 1993.

CORNWALL, HUGO, *Data Theft.* London: Heinemann, 1987.

DI MAIO, DOMINIC J., and VINCENT J. M. DI MAIO, *Forensic Pathology.* New York: Elsevier, 1989.

ELLIFF, JOHN T., *The Reform of the FBI Intelligence Operations.* Princeton, NJ: Princeton University Press, 1979.

FOX, RICHARD H., and CARL CUNNINGHAM, *Crime Scene Search and Physical Evidence Handbook.* Washington, D.C.: Government Printing Office, 1985.

LAQUER, WALTER, *Terrorism.* Boston: Little, Brown, 1977.

MUNSTERBERG, HUGO, *On the Witness Stand.* Littleton, CO: Fred B. Rothman, 1981. (A reproduction of the original 1908 edition.)

MURPHY, HARRY J., *Where's What: Sources of Information for Federal Investigators.* New York: Quadrangle/New York Times, 1976.

MYREN, RICHARD A., and CAROL H. GARCIA, *Investigation for Determination of Fact: A Primer on Proof.* Pacific Grove, CA: Brooks/Cole, 1988.

NATIONAL ADVISORY COMMISSION ON CRIMINAL JUSTICE STANDARDS AND GOALS, TASK FORCE ON DISORDERS AND TERRORISM, *Final Report: Disorders and Terrorism.* Washington, D.C.: Government Printing Office, 1977.

O'CONNOR, JOHN J., *Practical Fire and Arson Investigation.* New York: Elsevier, 1986.

OSTERBURG, JAMES W., *The Crime Lab: Case Studies of Scientific Criminal Investigation,* 2nd ed. New York: Clark Boardman, 1982.

OSTERBURG, JAMES W., and RICHARD H. WARD, *Criminal Investigation, A Method for Reconstructing the Past.* Cincinnati, OH: Anderson Publishing Co., 1992.

POLAND, JAMES M., *Understanding Terrorism: Groups, Strategies and Responses.* Englewood Cliffs, NJ: Prentice Hall, 1988.

RESSLER, ROBERT K., ANN W. BURGESS, and JOHN E. DOUGLAS, *Sexual Homicide: Patterns and Motives.* Lexington, MA: Lexington Books, 1988.

ROBLEE, CHARLES L., and ALLEN J. McKECHNIE, *The Investigation of Fires,* 2nd ed. Englewood Cliffs, NJ: Prentice Hall, 1988.

ROSENBLATT, KENNETH S., *High-Technology Crime.* San Jose, CA: KSK Publications, 1995.

ROYAL, ROBERT F., and STEVEN R. SCHUTT, *The Gentle Art of Interviewing and Interrogation.* Englewood Cliffs, NJ: Prentice Hall, 1976.

SANDERS, W. B., ed., *The Sociologist as Detective.* New York: Praeger, 1974.

SANDERS, WILLIAM B., *Detective Work: A Study of Criminal Investigations.* New York: The Free Press, 1979.

WARDLAW, GRANT, *Political Terrorism: Theory, Tactics and Countermeasures,* 2nd ed. Cambridge, England: Cambridge University Press, 1989.

WESTON, PAUL B., KENNETH M. WELLS, and MARLENE HERTOGHE, *Criminal Evidence for Police,* 4th ed. Englewood Cliffs, NJ: Prentice Hall, 1995.

WIGMORE, JOHN H., *Wigmore on Evidence,* 4th ed., 13 vols. Boston: Little, Brown, 1970–1989.

WINKS, ROBIN W., ed., *The Historian as Detective.* New York: Harper & Row, 1969.

YALLOP, H. S., *Explosion Investigation.* Harrogate, North Yorkshire, UK: Forensic Science Society Press, 1980.

Index